Copper Eskimo

Netsilik
Eskimo

Blackfeet

Kwakiutl

Hopi

Cheyenne

Navajo

Zuni

Tepoztlán

Aztec

Yanomamo

Sertao

Mundurucu

Siriono

Inca

Skolt Lapps

**Inis
Beag**

Abkhasians

Basseri

Kohistani

Israel

Pathan

Yarahmadzai

Tuareg

Rajputs

Gujar

Hanunoo

Nuer

Toda

Dani

Kapauku

**Tchambuli, Arapesh,
Mundugumor**

Tiv

Semai

Kpelle

Ganda

Pokot

Nayar

Yako

Trobrianders

**Mbuti
Pygmies**

Kaguru

Java

Nyakyusa

Tiwi

Tsembaga

Fiji

!Kung

Yir Yoront

Samoa

Mangaia

SECOND EDITION

CULTURAL ANTHROPOLOGY

Serena Nanda
*John Jay College of
Criminal Justice
City University of New York*

Wadsworth Publishing Company
Belmont, California
A Division of Wadsworth, Inc.

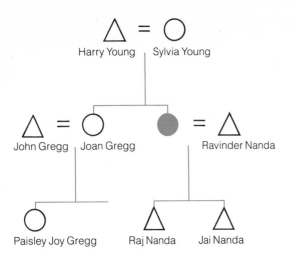

To My Family

Anthropology Editor: Sheryl Fullerton
Production Editor: Sally Schuman
Designer: Cynthia Bassett
Copy Editor: William Waller
Technical Illustrator: Joan Carol
Cover: Cynthia Bassett
Cover Photo: © Galen Rowell
Title Page Photo: © Galen Rowell

Printed in the United States of America

1 2 3 4 5 6 7 8 9 10—
88 87 86 85 84

ISBN 0-534-02749-0

Library of Congress Cataloging in Publication Data

Nanda, Serena.
   Cultural anthropology.

   Bibliography: p.
   Includes index.
   1. Ethnology.   I. Title.
GN316.N36   1984   306   83-10407
ISBN 0-534-02749-0

**Credits for Part and
Chapter Opening Photos**
p. 1, Serena Nanda; p. 2, Marissa Venegas; p. 26, Serena Nanda; p. 50, Raymond Kennedy; p. 66, Serena Nanda; p. 86, United Nations; p. 106, Serena Nanda; p. 126, Serena Nanda; p. 145, United Nations/Sicelloff; p. 146, Simone Larive; p. 174, United Nations/B. P. Wolff; p. 200, Dittman/Foxx; p. 226, United Nations; p. 248, United Nations/Ray Witlin; p. 268, Serena Nanda; p. 294, Dittman/Foxx; p. 324, Joan Gregg; p. 364, John Lenoir.

C O N T E N T S

P R E F A C E

Cultural Anthropology is intended for a one-semester course in introductory cultural anthropology. It has been designed with the idea that, even though the majority of students in the course will not go on to major in anthropology, they will find it a fascinating and useful subject. The core concept of the text is *culture*, and the ethnographic data from our own and other cultures are organized around three major themes: (1) the impact of culture on human behavior, (2) the interrelationships between the different parts of a culture, and (3) the view of cultures as adaptive systems.

Students' understanding of these three themes will lead to an increasing awareness of themselves and the world they live in, of the human past and present, and of the unity and diversity that characterize the human species. With this anthropological perspective, students can begin to "make sense" of the behavior and cultures of peoples unlike themselves as well as gaining insight into their own behavior and society. This awareness is becoming increasingly necessary in order to deal with the plurality of cultures and life styles that characterizes the contemporary United States as well as the world. For both liberal arts and prepro-fessional students, particularly those who enter human service careers, anthropology is an essential intellectual, scientific, humanistic, and practical foundation.

The second edition of *Cultural Anthropology* incorporates some important changes. Primarily, the second edition both adds new material and updates material from the first edition to highlight the usefulness of anthropology in the contemporary world. (These changes and additions are described in more detail in the next section of the preface, "Chapter Overview.") Each chapter now begins with a short, thought-provoking quote that sets the tone for the chapter and may serve as the basis of class discussion after students have read the chapter. A list of questions based on the chapter content follows. These questions will engage the student's interest in the chapter while serving as a guide to the chapter content. The illustrations have been redone to be more relevant and more useful. A continued effort has been made to eliminate sexist and Western bias in terminology. In addition to continuing to use neutral pronouns, the word *human* rather than *man*, *native American* for the indigenous peoples of North America, and the *United States* rather than *America,* we now refer to the Eskimo as Inuit and have replaced the term Bushman with !Kung. The Suggested Reading section at the end of each chapter has also been updated. Many useful suggestions from users of the first edition have helped make the new edition an even more effective teaching and learning tool.

CHAPTER OVERVIEW

Cultural Anthropology introduces the fundamental concepts, theories, methods, data, and references that enable the student to move successfully into more specialized and advanced anthropology courses. The topics included in the text cover the traditional scope of cultural anthropology, while drawing on the most recent anthropological research and presenting a number of different viewpoints and arguments. In **Chapter One,** "Anthropology as a Discipline," the focus is on anthropology as an academic discipline, including an introduction to fieldwork, the major research tool of cultural anthropology. This chapter also introduces the student to some recent research by anthropologists on the society of the United States and describes how the findings of ethnographic research can be usefully applied in our own society. The chapter also suggests the ways in which changes in the contemporary world are affecting both the theory and the practice of anthropology. New material in this chapter includes an expansion of the section on fieldwork, especially fieldwork in North American society, and on applied anthropology.

Chapter Two, "The Biocultural Nature of Human Adaptation," is an important addition in the second edition. Here the findings of biological anthropology are used to illuminate the special nature of human biocultural adaptation, as well as the relation of this adaptation to those of other animals.

Chapter Three, "Theory and Method in Cultural Anthropology," outlines in chronological order, each of the important theoretical perspectives cultural anthropologists have used

in their understanding of culture and human behavior. The chapter begins with the early period of classic evolutionary ecology and cognitive anthropology. New material on the Margaret Mead controversy brings this chapter right up-to-date and will help the student connect this chapter with contemporary issues.

The "culture concept" is the main focus of **Chapter Four.** Various aspects and attributes of culture and cultural change are introduced. This chapter presents the basic definitions and assumptions that are the foundation of later chapters. An ethnography of a deviant subculture has been added to encourage students to think about the limits of cultural variability both within and among cultures.

Chapter Five, "The Cultural Context of Human Behavior," emphasizes the many aspects of human behavior that are patterned by culture. Perceptions of reality, space, and time, body movements and gestures, sex and gender as well as alternative sexual orientations, cognition, and emotions are all discussed in relation to cultural patterning.

Chapter Six, "Language," explores both the special qualities of human language as a means of communication and the structural differences among different human languages. Sociolinguistics, the study of language in its social setting, is illustrated by a new ethnography on the "whiteman stories," which are told by the Apache among themselves as a way of dealing with the conflicts engendered by contact with the larger American culture.

In **Chapter Seven,** "Learning Culture," the ways in which children are brought up to become functioning adults in a culture are examined. In addition to ethnographic cases of personality in adaptation, this chapter also includes material on transitions from adolescence to adulthood, including a new section on female initiation rites. These seven chapters form Part One of the text, "Anthropology and Culture."

Part Two, "Sociocultural Adaptations," examines variation in the major universal dimensions of human socialcultural systems and comprises Chapters Eight to Sixteen. **Chapter Eight,** "Getting Food," brings cultural ecology into focus, describing the major human food-getting strategies and using extended ethnographic examples. The emphasis is on the relationship between cultural diversity and adaptation to different environments with different kinds of technologies. A section on industrialism has been added in this edition.

In **Chapter Nine,** "Economics," systems of production and exchange of goods are discussed, using the ecological perspective on such classic anthropological topics as the kula ring and the potlatch. A new reading in this chapter, comparing leisure time in a European and a preliterate South American tribe, raises provocative questions about our own affluent society.

Chapter Ten, "Marriage, Family, and Domestic Groups," has been moved, along with **Chapter Eleven,** "Kinship and Association," to a new place in this edition. Chapter Ten views both the structures and functions of different kinds of marriage rules and family groups and includes an ethnography of family life on the Israeli kibbutz. **Chapter Eleven** introduces the student to the major kinship ideologies and the kinds of extended groups formed by kinship. The chapter concludes with a section on age villages and other non-kin forms of association.

Chapter Twelve, "Social Ranking and Stratification," examines basic differences between egalitarian and stratified societies and includes new material on sexual stratification. The chapter focuses on ways in which goods and services are distributed in different societies, and its new position in the text connects it more closely with Chapter Thirteen, "Political Systems and Social Control."

The focus of **Chapter Thirteen** is variation in political institutions and the control of behavior in band, tribal, chiefdom, and state societies. Included is a new ethnographic account of the Kpelle moot, which has been so influential in the recent neighborhood justice movement in the United States. Some of the functions of warfare in egalitarian societies are presented, and the chapter concludes with a presentation of a variety of anthropological views on the origins of state societies in different sociocultural contexts.

"Religion," the subject of **Chapter Fourteen,** is viewed in light of its functions in human society. The chapter also focuses on the relation of religious beliefs, practices, and organization to other aspects of the sociocultural system. A new section based on Victor Turner's concept of structure and anti-structure fills in an important gap in the first edition.

Chapter Fifteen, "The Arts," emphasizes the universal functions of these cultural phenomena and the need to understand them in their cultural context.

Chapter Sixteen, "Cultural Change in the Contemporary World," focuses on sociocultural change as a result of urbanization, modernization, and the entry of nonindustrial peoples into the world-wide cash economy. Two new sections, one on peasants and the role of anthropology in community development and one on the effects of tourism on traditional societies, are important additions to this chapter.

FEATURES AND STUDY AIDS

Each chapter is pedagogically constructed to help students identify, learn, and remember key concepts:

▶ **Study questions** at the beginnings of chapters are keyed to major topics and/or concerns.

▶ A **summary of main points** at the end of each chapter helps study and review.

▶ A **glossary** at the end of the book defines major terms and concepts, which are printed in bold type in the text so students can quickly identify them.

Maps, charts, drawings, and photographs have been chosen and placed to illustrate the main points of each chapter.

To aid students' further study, the end of each chapter contains a list of suggested readings that are both interesting and accessible to the introductory student. In addition a list of sources, in the notation system of the AMERICAN ANTHROPOLOGIST, is included at the end of the book.

Although each chapter stands on its own and can be rearranged to fit individual teacher's preferences, the material is also integrated for greater comprehensibility. The substance of each chapter is organized so that the main ideas, secondary ideas, and ethnographic material stand out clearly. Ethnographic examples and extended ethnographic cases are presented with the aim of providing interesting and appropriate illumination of basic concepts, rather than in an attempt to cover the field of anthropological research exhaustively.

An Instructor's Manual includes new multiple-choice, short-answer, and essay questions; updated film suggestions keyed to each chapter; and student-oriented exercises for both class participation and assignments outside of class.

Acknowledgments

It gives me great pleasure to thank the many people who have helped me in many ways in connection with this book. Joan Gregg and Beth Pacheco, who used the material in preparation with their students, made many valuable comments on the readability of the manuscript and the teacher's manual. I am very grateful to the reviewers for their thoughtful and helpful criticisms of the first edition: Angelo Anastasio, Western Washington University; Dean J. Bowman, Bemidji State University; Bradley A. Blake, New Mexico State University; Pat Britz, South Seattle Community College; Dan C. Coker, Abilene Christian University; T. Virginia Cox, Boise State University; Donald Crim, Colorado State University; Morris Freilich, Western Washington University; William Garland, Western Michigan University; Jane Granskog, California State College, Bakersfield; Gerald C. Hedlund, Green River Community College; R. O. Keslin, Texas Technical University; Simon Messing, Southern Connecticut State University; Deborah Pellow, Syracuse University; Sheldon Smith, University of Wisconsin; Max E. White, Clemson University; Marguerite Woodruff, Mercer University; and Franklin A. Young, University of San Diego, Alcala Park. And I am particularly grateful to Joseph C. Berland. For assistance and generous use of their photographs, I would like to thank Joan and John Gregg, Bernhard Krauss, Raymond Kennedy, Jane Hoffer, David Klein, Anne-Marie Cantwell, John Lenoir, Ann Brody, Susan Locke, William E. Grossman, the United Nations Photo Library, the American Museum of Natural History, and the Museum of the American Indian. Sheryl Fullerton of Wadsworth has been consistently helpful and encouraging all along the way, and I thank her for that. The members of my family have been, as always, enthusiastic, and this book is dedicated to them.

Serena Nanda

P A R T   O N E

ANTHROPOLOGY AND CULTURE

C H A P T E R   O N E

ANTHROPOLOGY AS A DISCIPLINE

▶ How do anthropologists look at the world?

▶ What are the difficulties and special challenges of the anthropological method?

▶ What can anthropology teach us about ourselves and other peoples?

▶ What are the practical applications of anthropology in modern society?

The stranger comes for a while and sees for a mile.

Russian Proverb

Anthropology is the comparative study of humankind; its aims are to describe, analyze, and explain both the similarities and differences among human groups. Anthropologists are interested in characteristics that are typical or shared in a particular human population, rather than what is abnormal and individually unique. In their study of human variation, then, anthropologists focus on the differences among human groups, rather than the differences among individuals within those groups. The groups traditionally studied by anthropologists are called **societies.** A society is a group of people who are dependent on one another for survival and/or well-being and who share a way of life. But whether the unit of study is a particular society or a group within a society, anthropologists look at what is typical for that group and how that group differs from others. Only by the study of humanity in its total variety can we understand the origins and development of our species.

PERSPECTIVES IN ANTHROPOLOGY

Anthropologists study our species from its beginnings several million years ago right up

Included in cultural behavior are simple acts, like eating with a fork, with chopsticks, or with one's fingers. The daily rice meal of this Burmese family is one of thousands of patterns of behavior that must be learned by each new generation. (United Nations)

to the present. We study human beings as they live in every corner of the earth, in all kinds of physical environments. Some anthropologists are now trying to project how human beings will live in outer space. It is this interest in humankind throughout time and in all parts of the world that distinguishes anthropology as a scientific and humanistic discipline. In other academic disciplines, human behavior is studied primarily from the point of view of Western society. "Human" nature is thought to be the same as the behavior of people as they exist in the modern industrial nations of Europe and the United States.

Human beings everywhere consider their own behavior not only right, but natural. For example, both "common sense" and Western economic theory see human beings as "naturally" individualistic and competitive. But in some societies, human beings are not competitive, and the group is more important than the individual. Anthropologists see the Western idea of "economic man"—the individual motivated by profit and rational self-interest—as the result of the particular socioeconomic and political system we live in. It is not an explanation of the behavior of the Arapesh hunter in New Guinea, who makes sure he is not always the first to sight and claim the game, so that others will not leave him to hunt alone (Mead 1935:38). In anthropology, more than any other discipline, concepts of "human nature" and theories of human behavior are based on studies of human groups whose goals, values, views of reality, and environmental adaptations are very different from those of modern industrial Western societies.

In their attempts to explain human variation, anthropologists combine the study of both human biology and the learned and shared patterns of human behavior we call culture. Other academic disciplines focus on one factor—biology, psychology, physiology, society—as the explanation of human behavior. Anthropology seeks to understand human beings as total organisms who adapt to their environments through a complex interaction of biology and culture.

Because anthropologists have this "holistic" approach to the study of the human experience, they are interested in the total range of human activity. They study the small dramas of daily living as well as dramatic events. They study the ways in which mothers hold their babies, or sons address their fathers. They want to know not only how a group gets its food but also the rules for eating it. Anthropologists are interested in how human societies think about time and space and in how they see colors and name them. They are interested in health and illness and in the human body and the cultural significance of physical variation. Anthropologists are interested in sex and marriage and in giving birth and dying. They are interested in folklore and fairy tales, political speeches, and everyday conversation. For the anthropologist, great ceremonies and the ordinary rituals of greeting a friend are all worth investigating. When presented out of context, some of the things anthropologists are interested in and write about seem strange or silly, but every aspect of human behavior is significant as part of the attempt to understand human life and society.

SPECIALIZATION IN ANTHROPOLOGY

The broad range of anthropological interest has led to some specialization of research and teaching. The major divisions of anthropology are cultural anthropology, archeology, and physical anthropology.

Cultural Anthropology

Cultural anthropology studies human behavior that is learned, rather than genetically transmitted, and that is typical of a particular human group. These learned and shared kinds of human behavior (including the material results of this behavior) are called **culture.**

Culture is the major way in which human beings adapt to their environments. Cultural anthropologists attempt to understand culture in this general sense: They study its origins, its development, and its diversity as it changes through time and among peoples. They also examine its transmission through teaching and learning and its relation to *Homo sapiens* as a biological species. Cultural anthropologists are also interested in particular cultures; they want to know how different societies adapt to their environments. In its comparative perspective, cultural anthropology attempts to discover what is specific and variable in human behavior and what is general and uniform. Cultural anthropologists ask questions like these: "Is religion universal?" "What kinds of family structures are found in different societies?" They are also interested in the relationships between the different subsystems of a culture—in particular, in their cause-and-effect relationship to cultural change. One goal of cultural anthropology is to understand how culture change works so that we can predict and perhaps direct or control change in productive ways.

Anthropological **linguistics** is a subspecialty of cultural anthropology concerned with language. Anthropological linguists study linguistic variation, the ways in which human languages have developed, the ways in which they are related to one another, how language is learned, and the relationship between language and other aspects of culture. One aim

Dr. Anne-Marie Cantwell carefully uncovers an artifact from a historical site in the heart of a North American city. From bits and pieces of material culture, archeologists add to our knowledge about prehistoric, historic, and contemporary populations. (John P. McCabe)

of anthropological linguistics is ultimately to understand the process of thought and the organization of the human mind as they are expressed in language.

Archeology

Anthropological archeology specializes in studying culture through material remains. Most archeologists study past societies for which there are either no written records or no writing systems that have been deciphered. Archeology thus adds a vital time dimension to our understanding of culture and how cultures change.

The archeologist does not observe human behavior and culture directly but reconstructs them from material remains—pottery, tools, garbage, ruins of houses and public buildings, burials, and whatever else a society has left

behind. Until about 1960, archeologists were mainly concerned with describing the artifacts, or material remains, of prehistoric sites. They would describe the procedures they had followed and the relative frequency and locations of the artifacts, and they would compare those artifacts with similar ones in the same region. The "new archeology" redirects the interests of archeologists to new questions and research. This new archeology is interested not simply in describing prehistoric sites and artifacts but in interpreting and explaining these data in terms of what they say about the culturally patterned behavior that produced them. The new archeology is primarily interested in questions of **culture process,** the rate and direction of culture change.

Physical Anthropology

Physical anthropology is the study of humankind from a biological perspective. A major task of physical anthropology is to study the evolution of the human species over time and the biological processes involved in human adaptation. **Paleontology** is the name given to the study of tracing human evolution in the fossil record. Paleontologists study the remains of the earliest human forms, as well as those nonhuman forms that can suggest something about our own origin and development. Paleontology is a particularly fascinating subject because it tries to answer the question "Where did we come from?"

Physical anthropologists are also interested in the evolution of culture. In the evolution of the human species, physical and cultural evolution interacted in a complex feedback system; neither is independent of the other. The study of the complex interrelationship between physical and cultural evolution is the link between physical anthropology, cultural anthropology, and archeology.

Because early human populations were hunters and gatherers, physical anthropologists study contemporary foraging societies in

The Garbage Project

As we just discussed, archeologists have increasingly come to consider themselves cultural anthropologists, although most of their evidence is the physical remains of past peoples' behavior—the ways in which they altered the environment and left a discoverable record. One of the things that peoples have done for many thousands of generations is discard what they no longer need—what we call garbage. Although Americans can generate mass quantities of garbage, the fact that we discard material things is something we have in common with our ancestors far back in time. For this reason, archeologists have always been interested in looking at garbage. Rather recently, however, it occurred to some archeologists to wonder anew how garbage actually does relate to what people do. Furthermore, they wondered what could be learned about people by examining their garbage. And so archeologists began a project in Tucson, Arizona, that involved looking at contemporary garbage.

Although studying garbage can be amusingly described, the intent is quite serious. Comparing garbage quantity and content with known population characteristics and cultural variables has led to some interesting findings. For example, one might expect large, low-income families to buy large packages of relatively cheap products; small families with larger incomes might be expected to buy more expensive products in smaller packages. Choosing laundry detergent as a case, it was shown that exactly the opposite is true (Rathje and McCarthy 1977:269). The reason is that the poor, having less money at any particular time, spend on immediate needs, using what money is at hand (Gladwin 1967). Although this does not surprise social scientists, "garbology" gives a specific, quantified and long-term demonstration of what is otherwise difficult to measure accurately.

Garbology can also provide an insight into the adequacy of questionnaire data, a form of information favored in a number of social sciences. Although a number of people denied on a questionnaire that anyone in their household ever purchased beer, 82 percent of these households

The study of culture through material remains adds to our knowledge about historical populations. Here, in a dig in New York City, artifacts are found from Native American and Dutch colonial populations. (John McCabe)

discarded garbage that included anywhere from five empty beer cans to three and a half cases of empties. Finally, during the beef shortage of 1973 (when prices rose quickly), the discarded edible beef in Tucson garbage increased. This paradox is apparently resolved by the suggestion that higher prices led consumers to try unfamiliar (especially, cheaper) cuts and to buy in new quantities (larger or smaller than usual), which often apparently led to greater waste of perfectly good food.

Garbology is obviously relevant to a number of questions in social science. There is also a practical application of projects like this. The odd fact is that, considering how much information is collected in American society these days, almost nothing is known about *who* throws *what* away, *how often,* and in *what* form. Thus, Rathje and his associates have become consultants to recyclers and others who can use knowledge about garbage to help improve the quality of American life.

A physical anthropologist, David Klein, observes vervet monkeys in East Africa. Field observations of nonhuman primates have greatly added to our knowledge of the variety of primate behavior patterns, which up until about twenty-five years ago was obtained only from animals in captivity. (David Klein)

order to fill in the fragmentary physical evidence left by early humans. In addition to studying living human groups, physical anthropologists also study living nonhuman **primates** (especially monkeys and apes) for clues that their chemistry, physiology, morphology (physical structure), and behavior can give us in understanding our own species. Although at one time primates were mainly studied in the artificial settings of laboratories and zoos, now much of the work of physical anthropologists involves studying these animals in the wild.

Still another major interest of physical anthropologists is the study of differences among human groups that are transmitted genetically—for example, skin color, blood type, or certain kinds of diseases. In addition to the practical benefits of genetic analysis—for example, in the treatment and prevention of some

harmful hereditary abnormalities—population genetics contributes to our understanding of human evolution and adaptation.

Interdisciplinary Specialties

As anthropologists develop special interests, they begin to work with scholars in other disciplines. The anthropology of law, for example, has led some anthropologists into a closer relationship with those in the legal and criminal-justice fields. Medical anthropology, another new specialization, has led to a greater interest in medicine and public health in modern societies and also to a renewed interest in the healing practices of non-Western cultures. **Sociobiology** is a new interdisciplinary approach to the study of human behavior that brings together anthropologists, ethologists (people who study the behavior of many kinds of animals), geneticists, and biologists. They attempt to apply the perspective of evolutionary biology to human behavior. Cultural ecology (the relationship between culture and the physical environment) has led to interdisciplinary work by anthropologists, geographers, and botanists. Psychology overlaps with many anthropological interests: mental health, cognition (mental processes), learning theory, and cross-cultural studies of personality.

A good example of an interdisciplinary approach to the understanding of human behavior is a research project that was carried out to study a mental illness, called "Arctic hysteria," among the North Alaskan Eskimo (Foulks 1974). This project involved an anthropologist, who had also trained as a psychiatrist, and a biologist, who was specializing in the study of calcium deficiency. The causal factors considered in this study were physical environment, population density, diet, body chemistry, sex roles, social pressures, and cultural change. Such studies draw specialists from many fields and use the theoretical understandings of several disciplines. This is an important trend in scientific research on human populations.

Another fascinating investigation in which anthropologists were involved dealt with Kuru, a degenerative disease of the central nervous system that was found among the Fore linguistic group of the Eastern Highlands of New Guinea and their immediate neighbors. Kuru, which is now known to be a "slow virus" because it can remain in the victim for as long as decades without any apparent symptoms, showed up mainly among adult women and among children of both sexes. Scientists now almost universally accept that it is transmitted through direct contact with diseased nerve tissue. Shirley Lindenbaum (1979), who had done anthropological fieldwork among the Fore, called attention to their alleged practices of cannibalism. She reported that mainly adult women and their children participated in such feasts following the death of a relative or affine

(relative by marriage). Lindenbaum suggested that infection occurred both through preparing of the body for mortuary rites and through partaking of diseased brain tissue. Although the existence of cannibalism among the Fore is now being called into question (Arens 1980), the transmission of the disease mainly to adult women and children may still be explained by their handling of the corpses (Steadman and Merbs 1982). In either case, it was the ethnographic fieldwork of anthropologists that suggested an important cultural role in the transmission of a disease and ultimately, with the repression of indigenous mortuary customs by missionaries and government, of the disease's demise.

In spite of the various kinds of specialized and interdisciplinary interests among anthropologists, the discipline remains united in its interest in human beings as total organisms and in its comparative approach to the understanding of the human species. Although anthropologists as individuals may specialize in physical or cultural anthropology, the aim of the discipline is to discover the nature of both biological and sociocultural processes and the relation between them.

DOING CULTURAL ANTHROPOLOGY: FIELDWORK AND ETHNOGRAPHY

Anthropologists, like professionals in every other academic discipline, have developed a particular way of looking at the world, especially that part of the world that is the subject of their study—the world of humankind. This anthropological perspective has grown out of the particular method of anthropology called **fieldwork.** Fieldwork is the firsthand, systematic exploration of the variety of human cultures by anthropologists. Anthropology uses the naturally existing diversity of human cultures as a substitute for the controlled experimental situation of the laboratory, which for both technical and ethical reasons is of little use in gathering anthropological data and testing anthropological theories. Anthropologists can hardly go out and start a war somewhere to see the effect of warfare on family life. Nor can they control in a laboratory all the factors involved in examining the causes of Arctic hysteria among the Eskimo.

In order to get information and test hypotheses, anthropologists, like natural scientists, go out into the field to observe their subjects in a natural setting. From the results of this method, anthropologists write up an account of the lives of people in a particular society. This written account is called an **ethnography.** Ethnographic data are the evidence around which anthropological theories are built and tested.

In order to have the widest possible range of variation included in the data, anthropologists have been interested in the study of small-scale, technologically simpler societies whose cultures are very different from our own. These societies provide a valuable source of data on the interrelationships of different aspects of culture and the dynamics of culture change, because these interrelationships are easier to untangle in relatively isolated and integrated cultural systems.

Anthropological Fieldwork: Participant Observation

Fieldwork involves participating in and observing the lives of people in the group the anthropologist wishes to study. The writing up of the field data is aimed at presenting as authentic and coherent a picture of the cultural system as possible. The holistic perspective of anthropology developed through doing fieldwork. It is only by living with people, engaging in their activities, and seeing things from their point of view that we can see culture as a system of interrelated patterns. Good ethnography is not based only on the fieldworker's ability to see things from the other person's point of view; it is also based on the ability to see patterns, relationships, and meanings that may not be consciously understood by a person in that culture.

Because an anthropologist is a human being studying other human beings, it is difficult—some say impossible—to make a completely objective study of another culture. An anthropologist's own culture, personality, sex, age, and theoretical approach can all be sources of ethnographic bias. Sex bias, for example, has recently become a methodological issue in anthropology. Much fieldwork has been done by men who have had limited access to women's lives. Furthermore, even women anthropologists have been unconsciously biased by a male-oriented view of social structure and culture. In an attempt to correct this, anthropologists are taking a closer look at the lives of women, the meanings their culture has for them, the ways in which female personality is shaped, and the uses of power in the domestic as well as the public sphere (Rosaldo and Lamphere 1974). Because new data lead to new theory, awareness of ethnographic bias can give us not only a more accurate picture of a particular society but also more useful theories about the interrelationships among different aspects of culture.

Both participation and observation are necessary in good ethnographic fieldwork. The anthropologist observes, listens, asks questions, and attempts to find a way through which she or he can participate in the life of the society over an extended period of time.

Anthropology, like every other scientific discipline, must be concerned with the accuracy of its data. Anthropology is unique among the sciences in that a human being is the major research instrument, and other human beings are supplying most of the data. At least in the initial stages of research—and, most frequently, throughout the fieldwork—anthropologists have to rely to a great extent on informants as well as observation for their data. Informants are people who have a deep knowledge of their own culture and are willing

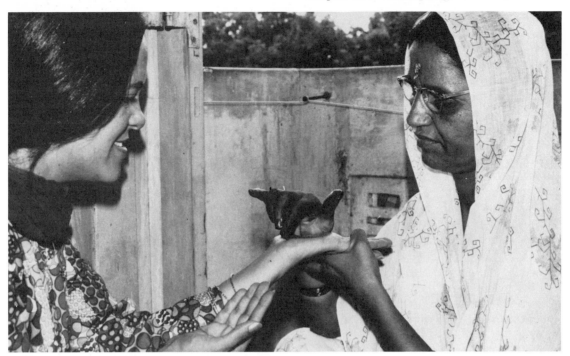

*The author has her hands painted with vegetable dye as part of her
participation in Karva Chowth, a ritual occasion in North India on which
women observe a fast for their husband's welfare. (Ravinder Nanda)*

and able to pass this knowledge on to the
anthropologist. All anthropologists have a few
key informants with whom they work in the
field. These informants are not only essential
for explaining cultural patterns but are also
helpful in introducing the anthropologists to
the community and helping them establish a
wide network of social relationships. It is the
establishment of trust and cooperation in these
relationships that is the basis for sound
fieldwork.

The difficulty of establishing such relationships is humorously described by Napoleon
Chagnon, who worked among the Yanomamo,
the "fierce" people who live in the Amazon
Basin region in Northern Brazil and Southern
Venezuela. Because of the importance of kinship in tribal socities, Chagnon (1977) made
attempts early in his fieldwork to collect
genealogies. What he did not know at that point
was that the Yanomamo had very strong taboos

against mentioning the names of people who
had died and that they did not like to mention
the personal names of living people out of
courtesy, respect, and fear. So the Yanomamo
made up false names for the living and dead
members of their communities and passed
these on to Chagnon as accurate data. The
names, which were collected in public, were
often graphically vulgar and caused great
hilarity among the audience during the
genealogy collection. It was only after months
of painstaking, humiliating effort that Chagnon accidentally found out that he had been
"taken for a ride" and had to start again from
scratch. As his fieldwork progressed, however,
he was very successful in finding some trust-
worthy informants and was eventually able to
build up one of the most detailed ethnographies available in anthropology.

In the early stages of fieldwork, the anthropologist tends just to observe or to perform

Raymond Kennedy, an anthropologist who did fieldwork on the island of Ponape in Micronesia, checks some historical data on that culture with one of his key informants. (Raymond Kennedy)

some seemingly neutral task such as collecting genealogies or taking a census. Within a short time, however, he or she will begin to participate in cultural activities as well. Participation is partly necessary because it is the best way to understand the difference between what people say they do, feel, or think and what kinds of action they take. It is not that people always deliberately lie; but often, when they are asked about some aspect of their culture, they give the cultural ideal, not what actually happens. This is especially true when the outsider has higher social status than the informant. For psychological or pragmatic reasons, the informant wishes to look good in the anthropologist's eyes.

Participation also forces the researcher to think about how to behave in a culturally approved manner and thus sharpens insight into right ways of behavior. Richard Lee (1974), for example, had this experience while working among the !Kung of Africa. The !Kung are a very egalitarian society. Their ecological adaptation requires a high degree of sharing and a minimum of individualism and competition. In order to thank them for the cooperation they had given him in the field, Lee presented the group with a large ox at Christmas. In telling the !Kung about the gift, Lee stressed the large size of the animal and the great amount of meat it would provide. But the !Kung did not thank him for it; they even insulted him by calling the ox skinny and unfit to eat. Only through continued fieldwork and growing friendship was he able to find out what he had done wrong. His gift had been very welcome, but his manner of presentation—boasting and expecting gratitude—had not. !Kung values, in contrast to ours, stress generosity that does not call attention to itself.

If anthropologists are to be allowed to observe and participate in the affairs of the people they are studying, they must gain the trust of the people involved. This requires that they establish themselves in a credible role. One of the easier roles to establish is that of an educator, someone who studies other people's way of life in order to write about it or otherwise report it back to the anthropologist's own society. This role is generally understood—although not always, because the "objective observer" is not present in all cultures. One anthropologist from the United States, Roy Wagner, caused great confusion among members of the Diribi society in New Guinea. The Diribi could not figure out what kind of "work" he was doing. He was "not government, not mission, and not doctor." Finally, they classified him as a *storimasta*, someone interested in other people's ways of life, or "stories." It was hard for them to believe, however, that anyone would pay him for such an activity, as it did not fit any concept of work as they knew it (Wagner 1975).

The professional educator's role is popular, because it lends itself to "objective observation" and the kind of "value-free" study that science is ideally committed to. Some anthropologists are beginning to question, however, whether this role is the only one appropriate in today's world and under the conditions in which fieldwork is carried out.

In the past, anthropology made its strongest contribution to the understanding of humankind by studying small-scale, relatively isolated, nonliterate, technologically simple societies whose cultural patterns were very different from the anthropologist's own. The world is changing, however. Such cultures are being altered, and many are disappearing altogether under the impact of modernization. The societies in which anthropologists have worked are no longer isolated (if they ever really were by the time the anthropologists got to them), and they are being incorporated into larger societies and the emerging nation-states of Asia and Africa. The lives of people all over the world are becoming tied in to large organizations. Oppressed minorities and those who favor new lifestyles are demanding to be heard. They want a share in the power and economic structures of which they are a part. Public pressure is forcing leaders to reconsider goals, values, and methods.

Previously, when anthropologists were working among people who for the most part could not read Western languages and did not have access to published material, there was little political pressure to consider the feelings of informants in writing up ethnographies. This situation has now changed greatly. Many groups being studied have not only been interested in the accuracy of ethnographic accounts but have also been demanding a share of the benefits—financial, professional, or political. This is true for various minority groups in the United States as well as for national governments in the non-Western world. Leaders of new nations want their cultures written up in ways that are politically acceptable and fit newly created cultural images. A discussion of the degree to which ethnographers should or should not be political advocates of the people among whom they are working is motivated both by genuine ethical concern and by the need to gain the trust and knowledge of infor-

mants for whom political activity has become an important part of life. Anthropologists have traditionally tried to stay uncommitted in tribal, village, or social conflicts, but this is becoming more difficult to do. For many peoples being studied, the anthropologist is a resource in the struggle for power, and this changes the nature of the role anthropologists are being asked to play.

In their fieldwork in an urban, largely black community in the United States, Betty Lou Valentine and Charles Valentine (1970) took a more involved role in community affairs than is normally the case in anthropological fieldwork. This involved siding with the people of the community in some of their organized protests against the Establishment in efforts to make centralized bureaucracies more responsive to community needs. Although one of the anthropologists is black, the Valentines found that this did not automatically give them credibility or establish immediate rapport with the community members. They found they had to establish themselves by their actions as neighbors and involved citizens. Although the Valentines did not take leadership roles in community actions, they did go to mass demonstrations and participate in other ways with the community, even when this exposed them to police sanctions and harassment by bureaucrats. They were also confronted with the problem of taking sides *within* the community, because the community itself was not always united about which actions to engage in.

One aim of the Valentines in undertaking their fieldwork was to present an ethnography that would be free from the distortions that have marred descriptions of such communities written by outsiders. As part of this aim the Valentines also wrote about community events from an insider's perspective that they compared point for point with the way such events were covered in the media. The role of advocate in a relatively powerless community vis-à-vis the larger culture not only posed practical problems but also raised challenging

Fieldwork in One's Own Culture

Anthropologists have traditionally worked among peoples whose way of life is different from theirs. In this situation, many difficulties arise in fieldwork. As Chagnon's work among the Yanomamo showed, the people very often do not trust the anthropologist or do not understand his or her work. In distant cultures, the anthropologist must learn a new language or face the possibilities of missed communications when a translator is used. In remote or even not so remote places, anthropologists are faced with often uncomfortable living conditions, new kinds of foods, and customs and behaviors that are not understood or even seem harsh or in opposition to their own values. The culturally based foundations on which people make judgments in everyday life are removed, and the anthropologist may easily experience bewilderment, loneliness, alienation, and vulnerability.

But working as an anthropologist in one's own culture also poses problems—personal, theoretical, and methodological. These problems are illustrated in the work of Barbara Myerhoff, an American anthropologist who worked among Jewish old people in an urban ghetto in California (1978). Professor Myerhoff had previously done research on the religion of the Huichol Indians, who live in the mountains of Northern Mexico. Because of her interest in aging and her previous work in Mexico, she decided to do a study of older Mexican people in Southern California. But as she approached these elderly Chicanos, they kept asking her why she wanted to work with them, and they suggested that she "study her own people." This is something Myerhoff had not thought of doing, and she began to realize that such a project would have both difficulties and benefits. As she points out, working in "other cultures"—whether it involves a male trying to understand females, an American trying to understand Europeans, or a black trying to understand whites—is "an act of imagination, a means for discovering what one is not and will never be." For, as Myerhoff says about her own experiences among the Huichol, however much she learned from them, it was limited by the fact that she would never be a Huichol. But she knew that she would be a "little old Jewish lady someday" and that it would be essential for her, in a very personal way, to understand what that condition is like. This is a particularly significant experience in North American culture, because the young are increasingly cut off from the elderly. Partly because of the North American emphasis on youth and partly because we don't want to recognize the inevitability of decline and dependence that we associate with old age in North America, we shut out the elderly. So the elderly become "invisible" to us, and because we don't know what they are like, we fear old age even more. Our

questions about the value-free stance of social science in general and anthropology in particular. The Valentines' conclusion was that, when anthropologists do fieldwork in communities whose members feel that they are being treated unjustly by the larger society, the anthropologists must participate to some extent in redressing these injustices. This conclusion will not be accepted by all—or, perhaps, even many—other anthropologists. But the Valentines' work does raise questions of method and ethics that have to be considered more seriously by anthropologists today than they have been in the past.

When anthropologists are studying a culture different from their own, their main task is to perceive things from the other people's point of view. Although training in the anthropological perspective is designed to help overcome cultural bias, even well-trained anthropologists slip into projecting their own culturally determined feelings and percep-

fear then leads us to shun the elderly, and the cycle becomes intensified. In working with these elderly Jewish people, who had struggled to overcome and had triumphed in many small ways over the disabilities of being old and poor in North America, Professor Myerhoff considers herself to have had a valuable and rare experience—that of being able to rehearse and contemplate her own future.

In addition to the problems of identification posed by her choice of a research topic, the personal involvement that came from being of the same community as the "natives" also presented both special difficulties and special rewards. The question of guilt frequently raised its head over a number of issues. One of them was the feeling Professor Myerhoff expresses about whether she should just be studying old people or should be helping them. Many of these old people, who began to depend on her as a friend and perhaps to see in her their own children, sometimes tried to make her feel guilty if she missed some time with them at the Senior Citizen Center. They were not intending to hurt her but were expressing one of their few powers—their ability to make others feel guilty. Also, her very lack of knowledge about *yiddishkeit*, the traditional Jewish culture of the *shetl*, or village, in Europe from which her informants came, was a painful reminder to them that they had not passed this culture on to younger American Jews. The ethnography that Professor Myerhoff produced of older Jewish people is not only a valuable look at a part of American life that has been shut out of the public eye but also a

revealing account of the personal and professional pains and pleasures of doing ethnography among one's own people.

Because of the disappearance of "exotic" cultures and because of political sensitivities, it will be more and more difficult for anthropologists to limit themselves to studying "others." The process Barbara Myerhoff went through, first studying the Huichol Indians and then her own people, is justifiable not only out of practical necessity, however. In some sense, it is perhaps the ideal anthropological journey, or what M. N. Srinivas, a distinguished anthropologist from India, calls being "thrice-born." First, we are born into our original, particular culture. Then, our second "birth" is to move away from this familiar place to a far place to do our fieldwork. In this experience, we are eventually able to understand the rules and meanings of other cultures, and the "exotic" becomes familiar. In our third "birth," we again turn toward our native land and find that the familiar has become exotic. We see it with new eyes. In spite of our deep emotional attachment to its ways, we are able to see it also with scientific objectivity. Anthropology originated with this ideal—that of eventually examining our own culture in the same objective way that we can come to understand others, but few anthropologists have been able to do this. In *Number Our Days*, Professor Myerhoff's book, we have an example of what studying one's own people involves as both a personal and a professional quest for meaning.

tions on other peoples, as Lee's experience among the !Kung shows. In studying their own culture, anthropologists must try to maintain the social distance of the outsider, because it is all too easy to take for granted what one knows. Remaining objective may be easier when studying cannibalism, kinship structure, or warfare in other cultures than when being confronted with child neglect, corporate structure, or armed conflict in one's own society.

Goals and Ethics

The changing conditions under which anthropologists are doing fieldwork today have fostered some new directions in anthropology and a reexamination of its goals and ethics. Anthropologists do not agree about these directions. Some feel that anthropology must remain neutral in world affairs—that any kind of political commitment will undermine the scientific objectivity of the discipline. Others believe that, without a commitment to human freedom and social justice, anthropology will become a study of exotica, an ivory tower diversion from the conflicts that are part of social life throughout the world today (Hymes 1972). Some anthropologists believe that the most urgent task is to preserve and record the few remaining relatively isolated non-Western cultures. Others feel that more ethnography is not the answer. Still others believe that in order to be a useful science, anthropology must go back to studying human behavior in the framework of biological evolution. Only then, they say, will we have a basis on which to judge the value of different cultural patterns. Still others believe that the discipline must turn to the study of large-scale organizations and the social changes that are occurring in the contemporary world. Toward this end, more and more anthropologists are studying the culture and society of the United States.

Acting as an anthropologist in a professional capacity, however, means being committed to an ethical position. The professional situation of anthropologists is uniquely varied and complex. Anthropologists are involved with their discipline, the individuals and groups with whom they do fieldwork, governments, and the study of issues affecting human welfare. Such complex involvements require making choices among conflicting values, and they generate ethical dilemmas. In some cases, these dilemmas may be so intense as to lead to a decision to drop a piece of research altogether. The statement of ethics adopted by the Council of the American Anthropological Association in May 1971 holds that the anthropologist's paramount responsibility is to those being studied; the anthropologist must "do everything within his power to protect their physical, social and psychological welfare and to honor their dignity and privacy." This statement includes the obligation to allow informants to remain anonymous when they wish to do so and not to exploit them for personal gain. It also includes the responsibility to communicate the results of the research to the individuals and groups likely to be affected, as well as to the general public. Related to this obligation is the further one to reflect on the possible effects of one's research on the population being studied.

Thus, anthropologists are committed to taking responsibility for the policies that may be formulated by governments on the basis of their research and for how these policies may affect various groups in the society. Their obligations to the public include a positive responsibility to speak out, both as individuals and a collectivity, in order to contribute to an "adequate definition of reality" that can become the basis of public policy and public opinion. These ethical issues have become enormously complicated because of the cultural and social pluralism characteristic of the modern nation-states in which anthropologists carry out research. In almost all societies today, there is a plurality of interests, values, and demands. Although this makes the position of the anthropologist a more difficult one, ignoring the diversity may lead to irresponsible decisions that do not promote the welfare of those among whom anthropologists work and to whom they owe first allegiance in any conflict of interest.

WHAT WE LEARN FROM ANTHROPOLOGY

Understanding Human Differences

Anthropology contributes to our understanding of genetically transmitted differences among human groups, as well as those that result from learning. By increasing our understanding of the importance of culture in human adaptation, anthropology enables us to look more critically at popular ideas about "human nature." Anthropology helps remove the blinders of **ethnocentrism,** the tendency to view the world through the narrow lens of one's own culture or social position. The American tourist who, when presented with a handful of Italian *lira*, asks "How much is this in *real* money?" is ethnocentric. In my own anthropological fieldwork among women in India, I found myself pitied because my informants heard that "in America sons leave their parents' home when they marry." It was difficult to convince anyone that I would be pleased when my own two sons set up homes of their own.

All over the world, people are ethnocentric. They tend to see things from their own culturally patterned point of view, to value what they have been taught to value, and to see the meaning of life in their own culturally defined purposes. But ethnocentrism is more than just the biases of perception and knowledge; it is also the practice of judging other cultures by the standards of one's own. Most peoples in the world regard their own culture as superior, and many consider peoples from other cultures to be less than human. But although all peoples are ethnocentric, the ethnocentricity of Western societies has had greater consequences than that of smaller, less technologically advanced, and geographically isolated peoples. The historical circumstances that led to the spread of Western civilization have given us a very strong belief in its rightness and superiority. We have been in a position to impose our beliefs and practices on other peoples because of our superior military technology and because our industrial technology provides an abundance of consumer goods that other people quickly learn to want. Their acceptance of refrigerators and washing machines has led us to believe that our values and other social institutions are also superior.

The paradox is that, although ethnocentrism gets in the way of understanding, some ethnocentrism seems necessary as a kind of glue to hold a society together. When a people's culture loses value for them, they may experience great emotional stress and even lose interest in living. To the extent that ethnocentrism prevents building bridges between cultures, however, it becomes maladaptive.

Where one culture is motivated by ethnocentrism to trespass on another, the harm done can be enormous. From this kind of ethnocentrism to **racism** is but a short step, and one that has been made in both popular and scientific thought in the West.

The idea that cultural variation, and specifically cultural superiority, resulted from genetic or "racial" variation seemed to make sense: Peoples who looked different from each other also behaved differently. The theory that the peoples of Asia and Africa and those native to North and South America were biologically inferior was comforting to Europeans who exploited their natural resources, took over their lands, and used them as slaves and servants. Up until the late nineteenth century, even some scientists believed in these ideas. This "scientific racism" was used as a justification for building social, political, and economic structures that favored the interests of the "superior" race. Even today, in spite of a century of scientific evidence to the contrary, racism and racial discrimination are still powerful factors in contemporary societies.

One of the most important things we can learn by studying anthropology is that the big differences among human groups are the result of culture, not biological inheritance or "race." The study of **race**—that is, the attempt to classify peoples in terms of shared physical characteristics—was a major concern of the early period of anthropology. A great deal of energy was spent on measuring various kinds of physical attributes: skin color, head shape, height, body build, and hair texture. But many problems arose with the concept of racial classification. Some human populations—for example, the Polynesians, the inhabitants of South India, the African !Kung—were difficult to place in a group because they had the physical attributes of more than one "race." Many of the so-called diagnostic racial traits did not go together; a population might have a characteristic nose shape of one race and the skin color of another. Furthermore, some physical characteristics such as skin color and height

Physical characteristics, language, and culture vary independently of one another. (United Nations)

were found to be affected by the environment. They could not be used as indicators of racial classification or historical connections between different human populations. Even relatively recent attempts to use genetic traits such as blood type to define and classify human "races" met with complications. The more scientists learned about the factors responsible for the relative differences in gene frequencies among human groups, the more "races" they had to add to their classification schemes.

Because the biological similarities among human groups far outweigh the differences, and because racial classifications tell us very little or nothing about other kinds of variation,

some anthropologists want to drop the word *race* altogether. They want to focus instead on studying variation among actual human populations. It is clear that all human beings belong to the same species and that the biological features essential to human life are common to us all. We know that a human being from any part of the world can take on the behavioral and cultural patterns of any group into which he or she is born. The adaptation through culture and the potential for cultural development and creativity are part of a universal human heritage.

Cultural Relativity

Anthropology helps us understand peoples whose ways of life are different from our own but with whom we share a common human destiny. The idea that each culture must be approached on its own terms is called **cultural relativity.** Cultural relativity is a tool for understanding other cultures. With this attitude, we understand cultural patterns in terms of the total culture of which they are a part. Cultural relativity does not mean that all patterns must be judged as equally "good"; every one has a set of values that serve as criteria in judging human behavior. It does mean that other patterns make sense, even if we would not want them for ourselves.

But the value of anthropology is not simply that it teaches us to see cultures from the inside; anthropology demonstrates that cultural patterns have causes and effects that can be understood only from an objective, or outsider's, point of view. The ability to look at a culture objectively is the first step toward a better understanding of one's own society and behavior.

Understanding Ourselves

The critical perspective of anthropology gives us better insight into our own behavior. By introducing the idea that most human behavior is learned, not biologically inherited, anthropology gives us the hope that we can make changes in our culture. By introducing the idea that all parts of a culture are interrelated, anthropology also helps us understand why changes are often very difficult to make in one area only. And the anthropological idea that cultures are designs for living worked out over a long period helps us understand why people resist change, even if it is "for their own good." Anthropology also helps us understand ourselves as individuals influenced by our own cultural pattern and by our society as a whole. The anthropological perspective—that is, the comparative study of whole cultures—contributes to a better understanding of contemporary social problems and conflicts. It can also lead to constructive ways to solve those problems. The anthropological perspective allows us to see that our own culture is only one design for living among many in the history of humankind. Our culture is an adaptation to one kind of environment with a particular level of technology, and it is due to a particular set of historical circumstances. An outsider's view of ourselves and our society is perhaps the most important contribution anthropology can make.

APPLIED ANTHROPOLOGY

Applied anthropology is the organized interaction between professional anthropologists and policy-making bodies, both public and private. I think, however, that the applications of anthropology go beyond the organized involvement of anthropologists, as anthropologists, in policy making and administration. The anthropological perspective can be applied to any situation that involves research or intervention in the lives of people who will be affected by the outcome. Applied anthropology, as it developed in the United States, has always emphasized the distinctive cultural traditions, values, and "felt needs" of the peoples toward whom various government policies were directed, and it has stressed the grassroots participation of people in planning and directing their own lives.

Although few anthropologists have been directly involved in planning and administering policy involving development, their advice and counsel have been used in a number of programs. Examples include U.S. foreign aid projects and the Equal Opportunity Program for native Americans and other minority groups, as well as United Nations technical assistance efforts.

Many recent studies of American society indicate the usefulness of anthropology in our contemporary world. One of these, carried out by James Spradley (1970), concerns the enforcement of laws against being drunk in public and the rehabilitative efforts of the criminal justice system. Although Spradley's study took place in Seattle, its implications are useful throughout the United States.

Society's treatment of men arrested for public drunkenness is based on the perception of these men as alcoholics or public drunks. The view these men have of themselves centers on their nomadic lifestyle; they call themselves "tramps." Using the fieldwork approach of cultural anthropology, Spradley found that these men had a particular experience of time and space and that this shaped their experience in jails and rehabilitation centers. One of the justifications for incarcerating men found guilty of public drunkenness is to "dry them out" and thus rehabilitate them. The period of incarceration therefore increases proportionately with the number of previous convictions for this offense. The men arrested for public drunkenness, however, view the time spent in prison as punishment. Their perspective of time as something "to be done" dominates their prison experience. Whereas in American society we speak of work in the context of time, such as "part-time" or "full-time," for the public drunk, time is transformed from a commodity to a difficult task that must be performed. One is rewarded for working; if "doing time" is hard work, then "you owe yourself a drunk" when the job (time) is done. Spradley's study points out that, not only has the criminal justice system not been successful in carrying out its rehabilitative function, but indeed the drunk's experience with this system actually increases the kind of behavior it is supposed to curb.

Taking into account a whole system includes studying and observing informal as well as formal social relationships. Robert Edgerton (1964), an anthropologist who has undertaken the unusual task of studying the mentally retarded, indicates how useful the anthropological perspective can be. Edgerton studied an institution for the mildly mentally retarded (IQs from 40 to 70) that had changed over the previous fifteen years from primarily custodial care to a therapeutic orientation directed toward preparing at least some of the patients for life outside the institution. The therapy milieu resulted in much supervised activity; this included enjoyable recreation, some of which involved male-female interaction, and vocational training. This institution, like others, however, was understaffed, so that much patient activity could not be supervised. The "problem" of lack of supervision provided an opportunity for Edgerton to do research on how patients managed their unsupervised time.

He found that they used this time mainly for "dating"; male and female patients met in places on the grounds not accessible to staff supervision. Although this dating distracted from the vocational programs, Edgerton concluded that it was very beneficial to the patients. Dating increased the patients' ability to control time and space, to use subtle verbal and nonverbal forms of communication, to understand the rules of behavior among members of the opposite sex, and to control sexual impulses. In most institutions that have a therapeutic orientation, the belief of the staff generally is that unprogrammed time, "if not wasted, [is] at least not so efficient therapeutically as it ought to be." In this study, at least, the data showed that the unsupervised activities of the patients, more than any other, produced improvements in social responsibility and competence that "good supervision had failed to accomplish." This is only one of the many anthropological studies of social services that show that "clients" are often much more capable of rational and complex social interaction than those who plan such systems believe them to be.

The anthropological perspective is also useful in bringing out the fact that the values and traditional behavior patterns of ethnic groups are an important element in understanding how they respond to various programs developed by national governments. One important area of government intervention and planning is health care. Anthropologists know that health and illness are intimately connected with other aspects of culture. Theories of disease, treatment, and cure are all part of the culture of human groups; medical systems are one of the adaptive responses humans make to disease and illness. Almost all the extensive research done on health care in the United States indicates that there is a difference in both the demand and supply of such services according to social class and ethnic background. Not only are different levels of health care facilities supplied to the poor contrasted with the rest of society, but there are also different patterns of use of these facilities.

Among different ethnic groups, cultural values and traditional beliefs account for the inability of many present health care systems to serve their needs. One of many examples is provided by Margaret Clark's study of a Mexican-American community in California (1970). In discussing their own ineffectiveness, Anglo (Western) medical personnel frequently complain that Mexican-American patients are not utilizing the services they provide. Anglo doctors say that the patient waits too long to come to the doctor or hospital and seems uncooperative in refusing to make an immediate decision about a further course of treatment. From a Western perspective, the Mexican-American patient seems irrational and irresponsible. From the point of view of the Mexican-American, however, to give in to sickness is a moral weakness, and thus a culturally valued stoicism inhibits seeking medical attention. Furthermore, for Mexican-American patients it is impossible to make a quick decision about treatment, because such a decision involves family members and friends who will take over their responsibilities if and when they are hospitalized.

Mexican-Americans exhibit a lack of confidence in the Anglo health care system and are reluctant to use it except as a last resort for a number of reasons besides the high cost. One factor is the system of folk beliefs about causes and cures of various illnesses that is not recognized as valid by Anglo doctors. For example, the prevalence of the "evil eye" is "known" in this ethnic group; an Anglo doctor who dismisses this belief as irrelevant is not likely to be respected by people for whom it is a fact. In addition, Mexican-American cultural expectations about how curers should act are in direct contrast to Western conceptions. Within the ethnic community, curers are people who speak the same language as the patient; who are courteous and interested in the patient's personal relationships; who are willing to spend a great deal of time with the patient; and who do not generally charge high fees. Given the "efficiency" orientation of Anglo medical personnel, the difficulty of the language barrier, and the high cost of care, it is not surprising that the Mexican-American population does not utilize the public health system very effectively. This example could be extended to many other groups within the United States and applies even more to disruptions in psychological health and functioning than it does to physical illness.

It is clear that anthropologists do indeed work on problems that have direct implications for policy making in a wide variety of fields. And yet, it is equally clear that anthropological research is often overlooked when policy is made. The role of anthropologists in policy formation has been very uneven and probably hit its high point during World War II, when about 25 percent of anthropologists were employed in research and consultation directly related to the war effort. Margaret Mead, one of the anthropologists deeply involved in this effort, says of that period: " . . . we had, in every government agency, people who were prepared to use what those of us who were outside . . . were producing" (1975, p. 13). This does not seem to be the case today. A good example is in the area of drug use and abuse.

In the United States, cannabis, or marihuana, has been treated in public policy as a lethal, socially dangerous substance, lumped together with heroin, cocaine, and other narcotics and hallucinogens. Recreational use of cannabis first gained popularity in the United States during Prohibition, and it was not made illegal until 1937. At that time, the director of the newly created Federal Bureau of Narcotics waged an intense publicity campaign to convince Congress and the public that cannabis was a lethal drug and that its users were potential murderers and maniacs. Congress was convinced, and the result was the passage of the Marihuana Tax Act of 1937. From that time, federal and state penalties for possession, cultivation, or sale of cannabis have increased in severity. The Federal Bureau of Narcotics has insisted that cannabis users are criminals who support themselves by preying on society and that cannabis use is related to deviancy, parasitism, and marginality (Partridge 1978). Evidence from studies of prison-populations has been used to support this view. In fact, the laboratory and clinical studies of captive populations can contribute little of use to social policy formulation, because very often the social and psychological behavior of such subjects is as much the product of the expectations of the institutions as of the drug use itself.

The few ethnographic studies of cannabis use in natural cultural contexts show that the effects of drugs are not merely chemical but vary dramatically according to their cultural and situational settings. In recognition of this important finding, the National Institute of

Mental Health sponsored anthropological investigations of cannabis use in a variety of cultures: Jamaica, South Africa, Costa Rica, Greece, and Colombia. These studies clearly demonstrated that cannabis use and its effects do vary according to cultural circumstances and that the view of the cannabis user as a parasite on society and a criminally inclined deviant was not accurate in those societies (Rubin 1975). As part of this cross-cultural project, William Partridge studied cannabis use among agricultural workers in Colombia. Here, he found, cannabis use was an integral part of the mutual exchanges that cemented social relations among workers, and cannabis use begins among adolescent males when they begin to adopt adult work patterns. Cannabis is smoked in the context of work and out in the fields and is perceived by its users to make them better workers. Workers' perceptions that cannabis is an energizer were found in Jamaica and other cultures as well. Thus Partridge concludes from his ethnographic study that in this coastal subculture of Colombia, cannabis is used in conditions that promote conformity, social alliance, and productivity and is linked to labor recruitment and achievement of adulthood.

This finding stands in dramatic contrast to the North American perception, which, while perhaps having some truth for our culture, is nothing more than ethnocentric when applied to other cultures. Cross-cultural findings indicate that anthropologists can make a unique contribution to the study of drug abuse by immersing themselves in the traditional ethnographic way, in the field of social relationships where drug users and nonusers carry on their daily life. Through this method, anthropologists can identify the constellation of constraints and incentives that surround the choice either to use or not to use a drug. Certainly this methodology can serve as a basis for distinguishing between the facts and the fictions on which public policy is based and can help formulate a more rational and effective policy than the one now in effect in the United States.

The question remains as to why, when anthropologists know so much, so little use is made of their knowledge? The answer has to do with the fact that the formulation of policy is a political process. Clearly, simply publishing their research findings is not an adequate way for anthropologists to change public policy. Anthropologists recognize that they must become more involved in the political process for their findings to be used. How likely is it that this will happen?

Although the number of applied, or practicing, anthropologists is growing, there are still barriers to their widespread participation in policy formation. One is that the anthropological values of cultural relativity and holism appear to be in conflict with the partisanship required if one is employed by a government agency. Another conflict is that anthropologists, as scientists, see their main responsibility as illuminating the complexity of reality, whereas administrators feel the need to make decisions even when *all* the evidence is not in. Third, anthropologists feel a conflict between the rational ethic of science and the pragmatic concerns central to the politician. The policy maker and politician are subject to political pressures that run counter to the scientist's ethic of basing conclusions on the facts, wherever they may lead, or however politically unpalatable they may be (Hinshaw 1980).

In spite of these difficulties, anthropologists, with their holistic and culturally relative perspectives, can make and are making important contributions in problem solving in the contemporary world. Their perspectives can be applied to any system—a factory, a neighborhood, a city, a region, a nation, even the world. And the usefulness of the anthropological perspective is not limited to those persons working as anthropologists but can also be used by people working in capacities in which they are intervening in the lives of other human beings. There is no end to the kinds of work in which the anthropological perspective can be useful: law and law enforcement, health administration, corporation management, education, politics, urban planning, social work, architecture, and many others.

SUMMARY

1. Anthropology is a comparative study of humankind. It studies human beings in the past and the present and in every corner of the world.

2. Anthropology is holistic. It studies the whole range of human behavior and the interrelationships between the different aspects of human behavior.

3. Anthropology focuses on what is typical within a human group, rather than on individual differences.

4. The aim of anthropology is to discover and explain the similarities and differences among human groups.

5. Physical anthropology focuses on human characteristics that are transmitted genetically.

6. Cultural anthropology focuses on culture, the learned and shared ways of behaving typical of a particular human group. Anthropologists also study culture in general and attempt to discover laws of cultural development that apply to the whole of humankind.

7. Two specialties in cultural anthropology are archeology and linguistics. Archeologists study societies that existed in the past and did not leave written records. Linguists study human speech and linguistic variation.

8. Anthropologists also participate in interdisciplinary research, in which specialists from different disciplines combine their knowledge to investigate a particular kind of behavior.

9. Anthropology uses the methods of the natural sciences rather than the controlled laboratory experiment. Ethnography is the naturalistic observation of human behavior. It is done by participant observation or fieldwork, and the written result of fieldwork is called an ethnography.

10. Various biases can get in the way of an anthropologist's objectivity. Among these are the anthropologist's age, sex, political values, cultural attitudes, and personality.

11. Both participation and observation are involved in good ethnography. Participation means taking part in the ordinary life of the people being studied.

12. Although doing fieldwork in another culture presents different problems from doing it in one's own culture, the ideal of the anthropological fieldworker is to have both the insider's and the outsider's point of view.

13. By showing the importance of culture in human adaptation, anthropology makes us examine biological explanations of differences among human populations more critically.

14. Anthropology reduces ethnocentrism, which is looking at other people through the narrow perspective of one's own culture.

15. Anthropology introduces the concept of cultural relativity, which means understanding a culture from the point of view of its participants. Anthropology can thus present the insider's view of a particular culture.

16. Anthropology can also present an outsider's view of a culture; it can point out causes and consequences of particular patterns of which people in that culture may not be conscious.

17. By taking the outsider view of our own society and culture, we can understand it more objectively and perhaps use this understanding to make more rational changes in our own lives.

18. The complexity of contemporary societies, with their diversity of interests, demands, and values, presents ethical dilemmas for anthropologists. But paramount reponsibility is always to the people being studied; it is their welfare and dignity that must be preserved at all costs.

19. In the contemporary world, anthropological concepts and research have an important place. They have not yet been fully applied, particularly in the United States itself, although anthropologists have begun to work in such problem areas as public drunkenness, health care, and prisons and other institutions.

SUGGESTED READINGS

Agar, Michael H.
  1980   *The Professional Stranger: An Informal Introduction to Ethnography.* New York: Academic Press. The author uses his varied fieldwork in our own and other cultures to discuss the ethnographic enterprise. Particularly useful for students of applied anthropology who are aiming for employment outside of the academic setting.

Farb, Peter
  1978   *Humankind.* Boston: Houghton Mifflin. A book written as a "celebration of our species" by a literate and entertaining author who is a naturalist, linguist, and anthropologist.

Glazer, Myron
  1972   *The Research Adventure: Promise and Problems of Field Work.* New York: Random House. A very readable text using the author's own fieldwork and that of others well known in anthropology—Liebow, Whyte, and Berreman, among others—as a context for discussing the intellectually and emotionally complex experience of participant observation.

Gwaltney, John L.
  1980   *Drylongso.* New York: Random House. A black anthropologist studying black culture in the United States provides us with one of the few examples of native anthropology. This interesting and readable book utilizes the technique of folk seminars, in which the anthropologist serves as a facilitator while members of the community discuss and analyze their lives.

Hymes, Dell, ed.
  1972   *Reinventing Anthropology.* New York: Vintage. Provocative essays on the role of anthropology in the contemporary world.

Powdermaker, Hortense
  1966   *Stranger and Friend: The Way of an Anthropologist.* New York: Norton. An interesting, personal account of fieldwork in four different situations, including the United States.

Rynkiewich, Michael, and Spradley, James P.
  1976   *Ethics and Anthropology: Dilemmas in Fieldwork.* New York: Wiley. Personal accounts of particular problems of ethics that have come up in fieldwork. The articles represent a variety of fieldwork situations and include such topics as secrecy, nationalism, public service, studying elites, conflicting demands of interest groups, and personal values.

THE BIOCULTURAL NATURE OF HUMAN ADAPTATION

▶ How do biological factors play a role in human adaptation?

▶ What is the place of humankind in the natural world?

▶ Baboons and humans: How similar, how different?

▶ Should the term *race* be dropped from the anthropologist's vocabulary?

Nature does not go forward in leaps and bounds.

Leibniz

The notion of what it means to be human is a central concern of anthropology. This notion has been constructed using ideas from physical/biological anthropologists and archeologists as well as from cultural anthropologists and linguists. In fact, anthropology is the only social science to actually incorporate both a biological approach and a cultural history approach in addition to direct behavioral observations.

ADAPTATION: BIOLOGICAL AND CULTURAL

A major contribution to anthropological thought in recent years has been the idea of **adaptation** as a complex process of both biological and cultural adjustment to the environment. Anthropologists, in addition to emphasizing culture as the primary human adaptive strategy, also call attention to the biological aspects of adaptation, because humans are physical organisms as well as culture bearers. This point is well illustrated by the following incident.

Before starting his first fieldwork experience abroad, a young archeologist visited his university's health service and told the physician that he would be doing a field season in rural Central Africa. "Sure thing," the physician said, and he spent 45 minutes putting together an enormous carton of items "you might well need."

The young archeologist was rather shocked. "But doctor, what do the natives do who need these things but don't have them?"

"Well, some have genetic-based resistance, and some have developed an immunity."

"And the others?" asked the neophyte.

"They die."

As this anecdote indicates, different cultural strategies do have different biological consequences. Thus, adaptation is not simply a dry academic concept but a matter of some people's living and reproducing and others' not. We in our society also die and suffer. Between cigarette smoking, inhalation of asbestos, exposure to nuclear fallout, ingestion of sodium nitrates and nitrites, and cases of anorexia nervosa (self-imposed starvation), we do things every day that are harmful to our health. These are added to the threats to survival that are present without our "help."

One of the areas in which cultural preferences have affected human biology is eating. Over the last 80 years, North Americans and other Western, industrial populations have dramatically increased the amount of animal protein and fat in their diets and have significantly reduced their consumption of fruit and vegetable fiber. The National Cancer Institute has suggested that as many as 60 percent of the cancers in women and 41 percent of those in men may be due to such dietary factors (U.S. Department of Health, Education and Welfare, 1975: 775–787). The relevance of this point for westernizing populations can be seen in the following facts:

1. The rate of breast and colon cancer among Polish immigrants to the United States is dramatically greater than that among Polish natives but is similar to that of U.S. natives.

2. The rate of colon cancer steadily and significantly increases among Japanese immigrants to the United States, so that rates reflect U.S. rather than Japanese rates.

3. Similar findings have been made in studies of rural-to-urban migrants in Israel, Hong Kong, and Colombia.

4. The lowest U.S. rates of cancer incidence and mortality are among vegetarian populations such as Seventh-Day Adventists and others (such as Mormons) whose diets depart from the U.S. dietary norm.

Although factors such as genetic constitution and exposure to cancer-causing substances such as tobacco smoke must be considered as well, dietary habits clearly seem to play a significant part in the incidence of cancer. Thus, an aspect of Western culture—diet—is implicated in the biological process of disease. An even more telling example of how culturally conditioned tastes can affect what one eats to the point where some important nutrients are underrepresented in the diet involves flavor preference. When children begin to prefer artificially created substances to natural ones (specifically, Tang to orange juice), then we might suspect that their tastes are wholly in the hands of the mass merchandisers of what is profitable, not what is inherently nutritious. For example, "Wonder Bread is the way kids like bread." Do children inherently like the soft texture, or is that taste the result of ad campaigns? Are manufacturers providing what people want, or are they creating a demand for what they can most profitably supply? Are these dietary changes perhaps best understood as having been brought about by the nature of and changes in the economics of the food production and distribution system of modern industrial societies? For example, what do we make of the fact that a majority of American children is reported to have chosen an artificial over a natural fruit juice? What happens when artificial flavors taste "right" and natural flavors taste "funny"? We know that such preferences are culturally created and can be altered. As people become aware of these findings about the relationships of diet and health, they will surely change their eating habits—or will they?

The relationship of diet to health is seen very clearly in populations whose diet has changed radically over the last decades. One such population is the Inuit (Eskimo). Although the High Arctic environment has few plants, the traditional Inuit subsistence pattern provided a nutritionally adequate diet, most of which consisted of seal, walrus, whale, caribou, and fish. These foods are high in protein and fat and low in carbohydrates, and when prepared in the traditional manner, they furnished all essential nutrients. As a result of this diet, the High Arctic Inuit showed an absence of many of the illnesses characteristic of the population in the United States—high blood pressure, high blood cholesterol and heart disease, and obesity. The Inuit, like other populations in our modern, industrial society, are now deriving more of their caloric intake from foods high in carbohydrates—breads, cereal, and sugar. Because food is now cooked, in contrast to the traditional pattern of eating meat raw, the Inuit are also experiencing a decline in Vitamin C intake, and anemia is a common problem. With the increase in sugar intake and the use of modern utensils and tools instead of teeth, there has also been a dramatic rise in gum problems and tooth decay. As the Inuit become more sedentary, this, along with diet changes, has also caused obesity, especially among women (Moran 1981). The correlations between changing diet and changing health among populations like the Inuit force us to recognize the interaction between biology and culture and to question whether all change is for the good.

Understanding Biological Adaptation

In the eighteenth and nineteenth centuries, when many of our basic biological ideas were being formulated, the giraffe's long neck was used by Jean Baptiste de Lamarck to demonstrate specifically that each generation of giraffes, in reaching for vegetation high up on

In the area of the Sahel, in West Africa, where periodic droughts cause seasonal hunger, human populations may adapt partly through changing rates of growth in muscle and fat mass. (United Nations/Gamma)

the trees, made its neck a little longer. After many generations, the additive effect of this stretching was a long neck indeed. With this example, Lamarck intended to illustrate the idea that evolution involves the inheritance of acquired characteristics. We now know that this idea is incorrect. We are aware that the basic biological process for explaining the giraffe's long neck is **natural selection.** Natural selection means that those ancestors in each generation that possessed the genetically determined characteristic of a longer neck than other giraffes could better reach the food high off the ground. They would thus be favored and pass their genetically determined neck to the next generation more successfully than those that had shorter necks and so were less well nourished. Thus, relative rates of reproduction determine the direction of biological evolution, and reproductive success is the key to understanding natural selection.

The Biological Nature of Humans

Although most of this textbook is concerned with a systematic description of uniquely human cultural characteristics, there are a number of characteristics—some anatomical and physiological, some behavioral—that we share with certain other organisms. It is important to point out the ways in which we are similar to, as well as the ways in which we are different from, other organisms, so that we can see ourselves in our biological context. This will help us understand how our human biology is part of our adaptation to our environment. In order to do this, I will describe those characteristics we share with progressively more restricted categories of animals that are particularly important in human evolution.

First of all, humans are vertebrates, as are fish, birds, amphibians, reptiles, and other mammals. As vertebrates, we possess certain physical characteristics, including a rather large brain, a spine or backbone with a bundle of nerves inside it, paired limbs, and a closed circulatory system. These aspects of human anatomy have all been inherited from ancient forms of life, some of which go back to half a billion years ago. Seeing humans in this perspective helps us appreciate how ancient our evolutionary heritage is.

Humans possess certain traits as mammals, a large category of vertebrates that includes, among others, cats, dogs, whales, and monkeys. Significant mammalian traits are listed below.

1. Mammals have mechanisms that maintain constant body temperature and body heat, as well as hair or fur to retain heat and sweat glands to allow excess heat to be released. This allows them to maintain thermal equilibrium in a wider variety of environments than other vertebrates.

2. Mammals have specialized teeth for specific processing of food (particularly vegeta-bles), whereas other vertebrates tend to have teeth all shaped the same.

3. Mammals (with very few exceptions, such as the spiny anteater) bear their young alive rather than as eggs.

4. The young suckle from the female's milk-producing (mammary) glands.

5. Among mammals, there is more invest-ment of parental and group care for the young. The protracted and close contact between adults and young provides a context for learning.

6. As a whole, mammalian offspring are rela-tively more dependent at birth than those of other vertebrates. Mammals have fewer off-spring but a higher rate of survival among the offspring than other vertebrates.

7. Mammals have a complex brain.

8. Mammals play.

Our mammalian heritage, which is also very ancient (the sweat glands, for example, prob-ably arose in mammals as far back as 200 mil-lion years ago), has been in the direction of such characteristics as adaptation to a wide variety of environments, greater emphasis on learning, and increasing importance of the social group, all of which are critical in the emergence of the primates and, eventually, humans.

Humans are, further, **primates.** Primates are a generally tree-dwelling group of mammals that has in 70 million years of evolution pro-duced the modern prosimians ("primitive" primates—the lemurs, lorises, tarsiers, and perhaps the tree shrews), the monkeys, the apes, and humans. (See Figure 2-1.) Many of our primate characteristics originated as adaptations to a tree-dwelling (arboreal) exis-tence; although we are no longer arboreal, we still possess these traits. As primates we have:

1. prehensility—that is, the ability to grasp with our hands

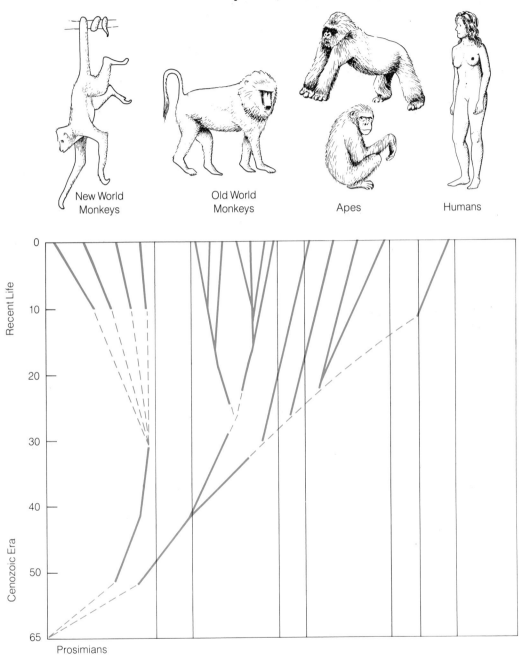

Figure 2-1   *The course of higher primate evolution as seen from the fossil record. It should be kept in mind that different methods, such as the biochemical analysis of albumin, give somewhat different dates, and the dates shown here are only approximate. (Adapted from David Pilbeam,* **The Ascent of Man.** *New York: Macmillan, 1972.)*

2. flattened nails with friction pads on the fingers and toes (a characteristic useful for grasping branches)

3. a thumb that is opposed to the rest of the hand to aid in moving through trees and manipulating objects

4. a large, complex brain specialized for color vision rather than, as with most mammals, for smell

5. overlapping fields of vision, to produce depth awareness of images, and eyes separated by a bony wall from jaws, so that we can look around and remain alert while feeding

6. delayed maturity, or a long period of infant care, allowing play to have a significant part in development

Among primates, humans are most closely related to the apes. The evidence for this affinity is found in a similarity of blood proteins as well as in anatomy and behavior. The modern apes are found in Asia and Africa. The gibbon and siamang, the so-called lesser apes of Asia, are small-bodied and highly specialized for **brachiation** (swinging by the arms from branch to branch), whereas the orangutan, a rather large Asiatic ape, can be described as a careful brachiator. Chimpanzees are African apes that are slightly smaller than orangs and that spend much more time on the ground. Gorillas are enormous African apes that, if they were to brachiate in adulthood, could be scraped off the forest floor with shovels, albeit large ones.

Humans have a common ancestor with the great apes perhaps 15 million years ago. Thus, we did not evolve from an animal exactly or even very much like a modern great ape. Nevertheless we do share certain ape characteristics, especially in our anatomy. For example, as brachiators, apes tend to have broad shoulders (and long arms, a short trunk, short legs, and a fairly slim pelvis). These broad shoulders have long clavicles (see Figure 2-2) to act as struts. Other primates use the clavicle (or collar bone) as a minor strut in brachiation, whereas apes have developed it to broaden

the shoulder. The shoulder also has a shoulder blade (or scapula) that, unlike the monkey's, does not come close to the backbone and a shoulder socket that is open for greater freedom of movement. Add a similar arrangement of muscles, free forearm rotation, and hand deflection at the wrist, and we can see a number of human traits that are similar to an ape's anatomy. We also have other brachiator-like features, such as a short body cavity and a broad chest. But we are not as specialized as apes, in that our arms are shorter than our legs, which makes us poor brachiators.

A summing up of the primate trends makes it clear what their relevance is to human adaptation. Primate locomotion has moved from the four-footed gait of monkeys, to the mainly upright, arm swinging gait of some apes, and finally to the bipedalism (two-leggedness) of humans. This trend was accompanied by increased dexterity of the hands. The importance of vision among primates, including stereoscopic vision and color discrimination, is accompanied by diminished importance of the sense of smell, which in turn correlates with the loss of the mammalian snout. This allows facial features, such as the lips, to become more mobile, making possible a wider range of facial expressions that can be used in communication. The development of eye-hand coordination is related to developments in the primate brain, which increases in both size (relative to body size) and complexity. This trend is already apparent even in the earliest primates, the prosimians. Finally, the trend of the primates is toward a longer life span and, more significantly, toward a greater proportion of life spent in the infant and juvenile stages. This is related to another important primate characteristic—that of being permanently attached to a social group. Group life among primates is essential both for protection and for maintenance of the complex of social learning that is the primate hallmark. All these trends reach their fullest expression in humans and are related to the emergence of culture as the major means of adaptation of our species.

Figure 2-2   *Skeletons above are from a monkey, a gorilla, and a human being. Note the differences in skull shape, form of the vertebral column, pelvis, limbs, hands, and feet. These differences reflect the differences in locomotion. The monkey, walking on four feet, has arms that are somewhat shorter than its legs and walks with its palms down. The monkey's down-turned shoulder sockets prevent true brachiation. Apes are specialized for brachiation; their arms are much longer than their legs and they walk on their knuckles. They cannot walk with their palms down. Humans are less specialized than apes and therefore more adaptable. As infants they crawl with palms down; as youths they can swing (though not very easily or for a long time), and they generally stand and move on two legs.*

We have been concerned here with ways that we, as humans, are anatomically and physiologically like animals to whom we are related in differing degrees of closeness. A natural question arises about the ways in which we are biologically unique. Although this is potentially a very complex question, it can cautiously be answered in the following way:

1. Humans walk on two legs (are bipedal) and stand upright on those legs. That means that we have a nonprehensile foot with short toes, long legs held vertically with firm knees, and well-developed muscles that connect the upper leg bone with the pelvis and lower back. These all work together in the complex task of extending each leg in turn in a controlled way, shifting the balanced body weight from the leg rested on to the one extended, with trunk upright.

2. The human pelvis is not only shorter than that of other primates but also dish-shaped to hold the internal organs. These organs rest on it rather than being suspended from the spinal column as in four-legged animals.

3. Beginning at puberty, the pelvis differs dramatically between males and females. These structural differences allow the female to give birth to large-brained infants.

4. There is an elongation of infancy and childhood, making the human more dependent on the group for a longer period of time than any other primate.

5. The human brain is larger in the frontal area than that of other primates. We have very small facial bones, jaws, and teeth for our overall body size. The connection between the brain and the spinal cord is placed unusually far forward in the skull. This placement and the light facial structure mean that the skull balances easily on the neck and that a rather small amount of neck muscle is needed to hold the head upright.

6. Human teeth are small in comparison with those of other primates and are arranged in a half-oval pattern in the jaws; our canine teeth are exceedingly small, with long roots.

7. Humans do not have functional body hair over most of their body.

8. There is continuous sexual receptivity of the female to the male (compared to sexual relations among primates, which occur only periodically, when the female is in estrus ("heat"). The human pattern intensifies the male/female partnership and is related to the division of labor and emergence of the family among humans.

9. Culture emerges as the major means of human adaptation (culture itself is, of course, not a biological trait, but the emergence of culture is based on the biological changes we have just listed). Although elements of "proto-culture" are found among some primate groups, for no other primate is culture the major means of adaptation to the environment.

These very complex characteristics have evolved at different rates, in a sequence that we only partly understand. For example, canine tooth reduction emerged early in human evolution; upright posture evolved fairly early; brain size increased quite late; and the forehead enlarged very late indeed. These characteristics are all related to the particular adaptations humans have made to their environment. I will have more to say about the complex interaction of these traits later in the chapter where I discuss the early forms of human adaptation.

We have seen how human physical characteristics have emerged out of the primate base and some of the trends characteristic of human evolution that are different from other primates. Some of the social behavior that is characteristic of our species—roles based on sex and age, qualified male dominance, social groups and the bond between the sexes, as well as elements of proto-culture—can be found, in prototype, among other primates. Because there is a great variety of forms of social organization among nonhuman primates, it is difficult to generalize from them to human beings, except to note, as we did earlier, the importance of the social group. Different aspects of adaptation among different primate groups are suggestive of some aspects of human adaptation. Humans are closest anatomically and evolutionarily to apes, and the open, flexible social organization of the chimpanzees, for example, is thought by many to be closer to that of the earliest humans. Other primates, such as baboons, however, are similar to humans in that baboons generally inhabit a savannah environment in Africa, which is thought to be generally like that in which the first humans appeared. Also, different populations of baboons inhabit a wide variety of environments and have different forms of social organization that adapt them to their different environments. This feature of the species is similar to that of humans, where different populations have also developed different forms of social organization to adapt to different environments. Finally, baboons, like humans, are an example of a successful, terrestrial population, unlike apes, who are basically forest dwelling. These features of baboon adaptation explain our interest in them as a species.

Baboons: A Terrestrial Primate Adaptation

The baboons of Africa are a widespread and successful group of terrestrial (ground-dwelling) Old World monkeys. They variously inhabit rain forests ("jungle"), savannahs (grasslands), semideserts, and other areas. Although baboons use trees to escape danger and to sleep in at night when possible, in certain environments there are few or no trees. In such cases, other environmental features may function as substitutes for trees. In some cases, for example, baboons sleep on cliffs. In other cases, they must use anatomical or behavioral features, such as large canine teeth, powerful musculature, close cooperation, and division of labor, which serve to protect the group.

Most members of the order Primates (see Figure 2-1) are arboreal, and, as has been noted, many primate characteristics are adaptations to life in the trees. Thus, we can expect that a number of the distinctive characteristics of baboons will involve the fact that they inhabit different and more varied environmental settings than most other primates. Furthermore, because primates adapt by behavior more than other animals, we can expect that these distinctive baboon characteristics will include significant behavioral as well as anatomical differences from their tree-dwelling cousins.

Because baboons don't have to depend on trees, they are clearly at an advantage over other, completely arboreal primates, which are restricted to forests. Since forests are shrinking

in Africa, largely due to human activities, this advantage will probably become more important in the future. Baboons can travel more easily to various food sources, they can cover more territory with less restriction, and they generally have more options open to them than do other primates. They are found in virtually every corner of Africa south of the Sahara Desert.

Baboons generally have a highly varied diet. In various environments it may include grass stems, seeds and pods, fruits, roots, bulbs, tubers, insects, reptiles, birds, eggs, small antelope, other monkeys, hares, and domestic sheep. Leaf-eating monkeys eat nothing but leaves. Most other primates have more varied diets than that (for example, grasses, fruits, nuts, insects, or combinations of these), but baboons eat an unusually wide variety of foods.

Although, as previously mentioned, ground dwelling is beneficial in some ways, such as ease of travel, it is also dangerous. There are many more predators on the ground than in the trees, and these include hyenas and wild dogs, cheetahs, leopards, and lions. In the trees, moreover, a primate can often avoid an arboreal predator by being small enough to go out on branches that a larger predator (such as a snake) cannot.

On the ground, matters are different. Large size and significant weaponry are valuable to a ground-dwelling primate. Whereas humans have adapted to ground dwelling primarily by culture (technology) and social organization, baboons tend to rely on anatomical features and social organization. Adult male baboons especially exemplify this fact. Male baboons have big, fanglike canine teeth. They also are very large (twice the size of female baboons and the largest of all monkeys) and powerfully built. Although baboons do attempt to escape predators by climbing trees, this is not always possible. It is then that the males' strength becomes a major part of the group's defense. Thus, natural selection seems to have provided for the direct protection of the baboon group (or troop).

Social organization also plays an important

Grooming is an important communication pattern among both male and female nonhuman primates. Here an adult female vervet monkey grooms another female, who is nursing her infant. (David Klein)

part in baboon adaptation. Part of the social organization of baboons consists of a **dominance hierarchy** of adult males. This hierarchy is an organizational structure that each adult male generally accepts and knows his place in. Young males establish their place in the hierarchy by direct encounters practically from infancy. By adulthood, all the baboons know where they fit, and the encounters that were often fights in adolescence are peaceful gestures (called "displays") in adulthood. Displays may include baring their canine teeth, displacing a less dominant animal, or appropriating food, especially meat. The peacefulness of the hierarchy is crucial to the troop's survival, since protection from predators is based primarily on the efforts of the powerful adult males in cooperatively protecting the females and the young while they escape. Among common baboons, those males who are higher in the dominance hierarchy of the troop tend to be larger and more formidable. They also tend to impregnate more females. This greater frequency of mating by the more

dominant males tends to keep young males genetically more like them, which helps ensure the protection of the group.

This pattern of male dominance is not simply a matter of "the strongest rules," however. Numerous examples of two or more less-powerful (often older) males cooperating to dominate a lone, more-powerful male are known, as are complex alliances among males. Secondly, when two troops encounter each other, it is not uncommon for males to change troops, whereas it is almost unknown for females to do so. Females are much more likely to maintain troop membership, presumably because of ties to offspring, perhaps because of their greater vulnerability, but also because males may be seeking improved troop standing by changing. This option can act as a safety valve for less dominant males who otherwise might be "trapped" in a subordinate role. (Of course, such males would have to establish a place in the new troop's male hierarchy, and they might end up further down than they had been.)

Another factor illustrating the fact that simple male dominance is not the only significant feature of baboon troop organization is the importance of grooming. For most primates, mutual grooming is not only a matter of cleanliness (picking dirt and parasites out of one another's fur) but also a peaceful, apparently satisfying daily social activity. Virtually all baboons participate in it. Whether initiated by "presenting" (a gesture of acknowledgment of another's dominance) or "greeting," it is an activity on which baboons spend much time and contradicts the simplistic view that male dominance is the outstanding characteristic of baboon life.

Perhaps the most telling piece of evidence contradicting a view of baboon life based on a simplistic notion of "male dominance" is the fact that the most stable and long-lasting relationship in a troop is the mother-child relationship. The closest baboons can come to a humanlike familial structure is the "matrifocal unit" composed of a mother and her offspring (fatherhood being seldom definitely known to the baboons or a human observer of them) (Lancaster 1975:20–31). Mother-infant bonding is important in virtually all primates and is the first and closest tie a primate can generally have. It is composed of dependence and "socialization" (providing an introduction to the group and a model of and for behavior). Even a fully adult male seems to feel a desire to interact more with his mother and siblings than with others in the group. The baboon mother-infant bond is also intense and emotion-laden (Rowell 1972).

We thus have a picture of large, powerful adult males, in a complex dominance hierarchy, who protect females and young, often at their own peril. At the same time, the mother-child bond and socially integrating activities such as grooming serve to cross-cut and complicate the simple picture of a male-dominated troop. Thus, we have a group of animals whose primate character gave them both anatomical and behavioral/organizational traits that have established them as very flexible and successful.

CULTURE AND COMMUNICATION AMONG NONHUMAN PRIMATES

As might be expected, there are numerous similarities between the behavioral, cultural, or organizational characteristics of humans and those of other primates. We will briefly explore some of these. The first point is a simple but important one: the expression "behavioral, cultural, or organizational" applies to nonhuman primates (at least Old World monkeys and apes) as well as to humans. Specifically, observations of monkeys and apes demonstrate clearly that their lives are composed of numerous behavioral components that are learned by observation, imitation, and—at least occasionally—by "correction" from elders. These include gestures and vocalizations to use with them, food choices, appropriate mothering behavior, and so on. A study of Japanese macaques (Kawamura 1962) resulted in very significant observations of innovations in the basic behavioral area of food treatment, for example, washing sweet potatoes before eating them. The researchers in this study wanted to attract the monkeys nearer the seashore so they could be more easily observed. In order to attract them, sweet potatoes were laid out on the beach. One day a young female began to wash the sand from the sweet potatoes in a small nearby stream. This practice of washing the sweet potatoes spread throughout the group and replaced the earlier practice of rubbing the potatoes clean before eating them. Thus, the research indicates innovation, rather than what otherwise might have been taken to be an "instinctive" behavior; the research also showed that the practice spread on the basis of social relationships between members of the group. These and many other observations suggest that higher primates, at least, tend to share aspects of their behavior that are significantly learned, affect many areas of life, and vary somewhat from group to group within the species. Furthermore, their behavior often indicates the presence of long memories—for example, remembering over many years where permanent water can be located in especially dry years—and complex and variable leadership patterns. These are all characteristics shared with humans, and they suggest some functional commonality with human culture.

Other examples of behavior that are of interest here are the ways in which the great apes have been observed to use tools. Chimpanzees, for example, will break a twig, strip it of leaves, and then insert it into a hole where there are termites. The termites bite the twig, and the chimpanzee pulls the twig out and licks off the termites. Thus, tool use and tool making, previously thought to be uniquely human, appear to be characteristics humans share with nonhuman primates. Chimpanzees have also been observed to hunt small animals and to share the meat, another characteristic once thought to belong to humans alone. Because of the closeness between humans and the great apes, another area of great interest is nonhuman primate communication.

Nonhuman Primate Communication

Studies of nonhuman primate communication, especially of gestures and vocalizations, have been done in field studies (Goodall 1968), among captive groups, and among animals in laboratory settings (Moynihan 1967; Terrace 1979). It has been shown that baboons in the wild, for example, constantly transmit information to one another. Lip smacking, grunts, stares, poses, and screams are parts of the baboon communication system. One long-term study of rhesus monkeys revealed over 120 behavioral patterns that are used in communication.

Because chimpanzees are generally agreed to be humans' closest relations, their communication system is of great interest to social scientists. In the wild, chimpanzees, like other primates, exhibit a wide variety of communication behaviors. They use gestures and physical contact to express feelings. When they meet in the forest, "old friends" kiss and hug, pat each other on the head, or rest a hand on the thigh of the other. Chimpanzees also play a great deal. Some anthropologists believe that play may have been one important way our prehuman ancestors developed the capacity for language. In addition to gestures, chimpanzees use calls to communicate. These calls are quite distinctive—a *waa* bark for danger, a series of soft moans for worry, a hooting to communicate excitement caused by the presence of an abundance of food, and screams and squeals of fear. Each kind of call expresses a feeling within the animal, is "understood" by other animals that hear it, and has effects on the behavior of others (Reynolds 1965). But a primate **call system** is not the same as human language. Although intonation can intensify the meaning of a call—for example, from "danger" to "extreme danger"—a chimp can signal a danger only in its immediate presence. A second important limitation on primate communication is that parts of calls are not combined in new ways to generate new information: each call appears to have just one meaning.

Another research strategy involves teaching languages (sign languages or other human-created systems) to higher primates, especially chimpanzees and gorillas (Terrace 1979). Studies of chimpanzees brought up or trained by humans show that they are capable of a much more complex communiction than they naturally display in the wild. Washoe was a 10-month-old chimpanzee raised in a completely human environment (Gardner and Gardner 1967). She spent all her waking hours in the company of a researcher who "talked" to her in the American sign language for the deaf. Only part of this time was spent in language training. Washoe very quickly learned to respond to her human companion. She also learned to use sign language, and after learning about ten signs, she began spontaneously to produce combinations of signs. For example, she put *water* and *bird* together to make *duck*. Recently, other chimpanzees have been trained in symbolic communication. These chimps have demonstrated an ability to learn many symbols, to combine symbols spontaneously, to conceptualize, to understand spoken English words, and to use signs in correct order. These studies, both the strictly observational ones and those that involve training the animals, clearly show that our nearest relatives have an impressive ability to learn and effectively manipulate complex communicative systems and, apparently, to pass these on to other animals. The animals have variously demonstrated that they can remember past events and emotions, recombine elements of their communication code to form new expressions, purposely lie, joke, and anticipate future events (Patterson and Cohen 1978).

Although all this is fascinating and has clearly altered our notion of higher primate mental life, we have not really answered the more specific question "Are humans different *in kind* from nonhumans in their communicative characteristics?" Our answer may partly depend on our manner of defining human language. If we define human communication very narrowly, we can exclude the communication of other species as part of the definition. There are two important points to consider here.

First, other species have different evolutionary histories from our own. Their communication systems have thus evolved in ways different from ours. Therefore, saying that their communication is not like ours is bound to be true in some ways. The question is, do we know enough about their biobehavioral context to satisfactorily comprehend their communication system in its full richness?

Second, human linguists find that, in order to learn a heretofore unstudied human language, they cannot simply observe what the "natives" do. They must ask questions and interact with native speakers, or they will never achieve a fully accurate or satisfying description of the language. How much more difficult to comprehend communication when we sit as outsiders and watch what we think is going on among members of another species and write about it without the verbal interaction that is essential when doing human linguistics. When we do try to communicate with other species, by assigning a system we ourselves have invented, we are often shocked at the animals' "sophistication."

It has probably become apparent to you that there is a contradiction in the material in this chapter. At one moment, we are looking at human commonality with nonhumans; at another moment, we are examining our separateness. This contradiction relates not only to specific matters of fact—precisely how similar we are and in what ways—but also to the common human desire not to be *just* an animal. This discussion involves complex philosophical issues that, moreover, vary from culture to culture. Different cultures merge or separate the animal and the human world in different ways, and these culturally based ideas affect the way humans see themselves. Whereas at one time, anthropologists emphasized the absolute uniqueness of human culture and communication, they are now seeing more clearly the continuities between humans and higher primates in both these areas.

HOMINID ADAPTATIONS

In order to explain the direction of human evolution, we must first consider the practical situation in which our ancestors found themselves that led them to develop in a different direction from other primates. During the Miocene period (approximately 25 to 5 million years ago), the forests in which virtually all primates lived became smaller. The apes, which had first made their appearance about 35 million years ago, were generally numerous and well adapted to forest life. As the forest shrank, the reduction in habitat put a great strain on the inhabitants. The best-adapted groups tended to survive, whereas the less well adapted left or became extinct. Increasing competition for forest space may have provided the stimulus for some populations then living in the forest to move into the new grassland habitats that were expanding at the expense of forests. As the ancestors of the baboons and humans were outstripped by the better-adapted ancestors of the apes, they were forced to leave, and little by little they began to succeed in the grasslands. This move, which involves selective pressure for flexible, innovative behavior, accounts for many of the biological and, indeed, behavioral/cultural characteristics that became central in human evolution.

Leaving the forest meant that adaptation for brachiation was no longer advantageous, and this adaptation stopped at an early stage of hominid development. When they were threatened, these prehumans probably still escaped to trees when they were available, but other protection was also necessary. Because of a change in diet, canine teeth had become smaller and could not serve as effective weapons. We have little reason to believe that our hominid ancestors were physically very big and powerful, so that primitive tools and weapons held in the hands were probably essential for defense. The value of greater height for vision over longer distances, a trait that was not useful in the forest but would be in the grasslands, encouraged the trend toward upright posture. With modest musculature, our early hominid ancestors could use their simple tools for protection only in groups.

The precise origins of hunting are unclear, though they probably include a scavenging stage. At best, however, even with true hunting, protohumans would not for a long period be able to successfully compete with the big, carnivorous cats for meat. Sounding animals and chasing them long distances requires stamina rather than speed; the ability to concentrate, read tracks, and anticipate behavior; and more cooperation. These are qualities that were selected for in the course of human evolution and that must have been present in rudimentary form in our earliest ancestors to have been at all successful. Furthermore, all this running in the hot sun in an area with few trees requires the ability to get rid of built-up heat effectively. This environmental require-

ment explains humans' lack of functional body hair and also explains why some protection for the head (hair) would be necessary. The probability was that these early humans began to share food and to cooperate on problem solving, such as how to protect the group. This suggests a suppression of competition over food and over females by males (and vice versa). The sexual division of labor—males hunting and females gathering vegetable food— which persists in modern hunter-gatherers, probably relates to the female's pregnancy, childbirth, and extended care of a slow-developing, helpless infant.

The fact, then, that males leave the females and young behind at a home base while they go out and bring back food may account for many of the body differences between males and females. For example, males are 20 percent larger, have less body fat, and have a greater ability to produce bursts of running speed. Peaceful integration of an early human group probably required that the meat acquired in hunting be shared with the male's mate and young—and perhaps more widely. This would serve to help maintain the suppression of sexual competition, which would be necessary if males were to hunt cooperatively. Of course, females, in their turn, shared what they gathered, which probably amounted to a large proportion of the diet in most protohuman groups. Females also no doubt hunted smaller game and had to protect the group in the absence of males as well as cooperatively with them. Males probably also gathered considerable quantities of vegetable foods. The picture that emerges, then, is of cooperation, a sexual division of labor, tool use, and selection for intelligence, manual dexterity, and bipedalism.

The Origins and Development of Human Language

Like all other aspects of cultural and biological evolution, the development of human speech was a long, gradual process. The question for the anthropologist is not exactly when human speech was "invented" but rather what pressures were at work on our remote ancestors that eventually led to the development of human speech (Hockett and Ascher 1964). In his book *The Emergence of Man* (1972), John Pfeiffer suggests that it was our ancestors' use of tools that made language an especially useful adaptation. At that time, several million years ago, the call system of our ancestors was probably not too different from that of modern chimpanzees; that is, it was triggered by immediate events. It was perhaps in play that new activities and new calls related to these activities developed. Evolutionary pressure increased the fitness of individuals who could "reconstruct the past in their minds, and express their images vocally, and conceive new sequences of actions to serve as the basis for future plans" (p. 462). The multiplication of new experiences, especially the coordination between individuals needed for hunting and conveying information to those who remained behind, required more elaborate communication than was possible with a call system. Through a shift of attention from whole calls to parts of calls, a vocal alphabet might develop. With population increases, larger settlements, group cooperation for large-scale hunting, and greater social organization, there was extra pressure for the development of grammatical rules. With each successive phase of human evolution, the world became steadily more complex and required complicated mechanisms to deal with it. It was in this context that human language developed.

In the previous paragraphs, the vocal origin of human speech has been emphasized. It should be pointed out that there are a number of anthropologists and linguists who believe that the original human langage was a silent gesture language. This view holds that the transition to speech occurred less than a 100,000 years ago. Up until that time, hominids would have been using about fifty or so gestures to indicate landmarks, common plant and animal foods, water sources, and directions. As humans advanced technologically, learning how to make sophisticated tools and exploiting their environments in more complex ways, more and more gestures would be required. At this point, gestures were no longer sufficient, and selective forces would have brought about a greater and greater emphasis on spoken language. Both this silent gesture language origin theory and the call system origin theory described above share the view, however, that it was at a stage when overloading of the communication system became severe that something radically different had to evolve, which resulted in the complex speech systems of H. sapiens.

In the preceding pages we have been given a picture of the interaction of various developments as they very gradually led to the development of our species of Homo sapiens. This evolution took place over millions of years; recent discoveries have placed the earliest clearly hominid (human ancestor) form at about 4 million years ago. During these millions of years the hominid line was developing in ways that expanded the human traits just discussed, particularly the size and complexity of the brain and its correlated development, the increasing reliance on culture—learned and shared traditions—as its major means of adaptation. From about 100,000 years ago we have evidence of Homo sapiens, called Neanderthals, that indicates many cultural traits shared with contemporary humans.

Neanderthals: An Early Human Adaptation

If ever we could say that a fossil hominid had received a "bad press," it is the best-known early member of our own species. These creatures are commonly called Neanderthals. They dated from about 125,000 to 40,000 years ago and have been found in Europe and parts of Asia and Africa. Neanderthals are often depicted as hulking brutes with beetling brows, hunched

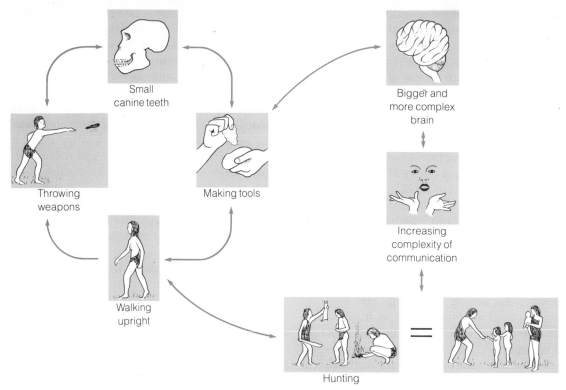

Small
canine teeth

Throwing
weapons

Making tools

Bigger and
more complex
brain

Increasing
complexity of
communication

Walking
upright

Hunting

Figure 2-3 *This figure shows a system of positive feedback that has occurred in the evolution of the human species. Adaptive changes that are part of the evolutionary process are brought about by positive feedback systems. Notice that the positive changes in one component of the system bring about positive changes in other components of the system, which in turn feed back to reinforce the change in the initial component, which in this case is upright walking. Upright posture, which represents the most radical anatomical alteration experienced during human evolution—a major restructuring of the pelvis and the foot—is considered by most anthropologists to be the trigger of human evolution. In human evolution, biological and cultural components have fed into and reinforced each other.*

over with an apish skull position, the males pulling their mates about by the hair—true cave men indeed! Much of this picture is incorrect. Neanderthals did tend to be muscular and have heavy brow ridges and low foreheads, but the rest of the picture resulted from drawings based on an arthritic skull that had been badly restored. Neanderthals had a completely upright posture, a large brain, and many other traits in common with modern humans. They differed from us mainly in the massiveness of their bones, their muscularity, the presence of

a significant brow ridge, the lack of significant forehead development, a long, low, wide brain case, a bulging face, and the lack of much of a chin. Even these traits varied in terms of time, place, and the individual, however.

In terms of culture, Neanderthals had a very efficient technology based on a special method of making stone tools, the use of wooden spears, and the making of decorative objects. What is surprising to many is that these "brutes" actually give evidence of having had a surprisingly complex culture. Their culture included the use of objects that were possibly significant in rituals; burial of the dead (with grave goods, including flowers at one site in Iraq); special arrangements of the skulls of the powerful cave bears, which may signify a religious cult focusing on animals; and the possible survival of handicapped people who had to be supported to some extent, thus suggesting the presence of altruism. All of this evidence is very suggestive of symbolic, even religious, belief and action and suggests strongly the possibility of oral communication, which although it may not have been as flexible as the speech of contemporary humans, was certainly more similar to it than to that of living, nonhuman primates.

HUMAN BIOLOGICAL DIVERSITY

We have examined in this chapter the basic shared character, both biological and cultural, of our species. We will now turn to another aspect of humankind, the biological diversity within our species. The study of human biological diversity is probably most familiar to you as the study of "race." Early studies of race were based on the idea that there were clearly bounded categories of people sharing the same biological traits, into which any individual could be placed. Early efforts in studies of race attempted to construct racial type categories, and many such categories have been constructed over the years. These categories were based on easily visible biological characteristics, such as hair form, skin color, and nose form, and were ascribed to populations inhabiting particular geographical regions, as, for example, African Negroid. As it became clear that there was no exact correlation between continents and so-called racial traits, classifications became more refined and studies talked about composite races, or micro-races, or local races—that is, groups limited to a small, localized area (Garn 1969).

There are a number of criticisms that have been made of the racial typology approach. It is clear, for example, that there are no discreet boundaries between racial groups; rather there is a merging between groups at their peripheries. Also, the racial categories were based on a very small number of traits that were readily visible, such as skin color and head shape, when in fact there are thousands of genetically inherited characteristics, any of which might be used for different purposes of classification. Some of these traits are "invisible," such as blood type, and in any case, we know very little about exactly how most of these characteristics are inherited. Further, racial classifications, even when not so intended by their authors, were frequently used for political purposes, to distinguish so-called superior and inferior peoples, and these classifications became the basis for discriminatory policies, such as restrictive immigration. Because of these political uses and because much of what was done in racial typologizing was of questionable scientific value, many anthropologists suggested the term *race* be dropped altogether. In any case, other approaches in the study of human biological variation have come to largely supplant the racial typologizing approach in recent years.

For the fact is that humans do vary biologically and appear to do so in patterned ways. The question is: "What are the patterns, and what do they mean?"

Some patterned differences are undoubtedly based on natural selection—that is, biological adaptation to environmental conditions, mainly at the local or regional level. This may include adaptation to high altitude, cold climate, crowding, air pollution, and so on. We do not know a great deal about the ways in which selective pressures have been exerted to produce many of the characteristics that we hypothesize are a result of selective pressures, and the processes are very complicated. Skin color, for example, appears to be adaptive to the intensity of ultraviolet light. Since dark skins are found near the Equator, where ultraviolet

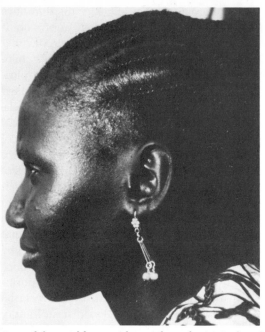 

One of the problems with racial typologies is that there is tremendous variability within so-called races. (Photos by Susan Locke, left, Serena Nanda, right)

intensity is highest, and lighter skins are found as one goes north, where ultraviolet light intensity decreases, it is generally agreed that the more highly pigmented (darker) skin functions to screen out ultraviolet light. One adaptive function of pigmentation is that it protects the underlying tissue from skin cancer, which can be caused by ultraviolet light. Therefore, it is more adaptive to have a dark skin in an equatorial climate. On the other hand, humans need some ultraviolet light in order to manufacture vitamin D, which facilitates the absorption of calcium in the bones and strengthens them. Thus, the problem in northern latitudes is the need to get adequate ultraviolet light. Thus, lightly pigmented skin is more adaptive in these climates. Other characteristics of certain populations, such as the larger lungs and chests of high altitude populations, which were previously thought to be genetic adaptations to the decreased oxygen in the air at high altitudes, have now been found to be characteristics that develop over the lifetime of an indi-

vidual living in such an environment. Still other variations that appear to be genetic may turn out to have a largely nongenetic basis; for example, height is strongly affected by cultural factors such as diet. Other variations, such as the distribution of blood proteins, are more difficult to account for and may in some cases be due to chance factors. Thus the definition of race is complex and varies largely with these few characteristics, such as skin color, that are chosen as the criteria for classification.

A second approach to patterns of biological variation is to study the distribution of well-understood trait complexes—for example, blood types. Using data from field samplings over wide areas, maps are drawn up of the distribution of percentages of blood types A, B, AB, and O in different regions in order to explore gene frequencies. In order to reconcile this rather precise approach to the grand "racial" categorization approach, some anthropologists have tried to study the distribution of a number of genetic trait complexes at a time. The fact that only a few hundred such complexes are well understood, though perhaps hundreds of thousands exist, should give us pause. Nevertheless, a major study using seventeen trait complexes discovered that most genetic variation does not make coherent patterns that are consistent with the racial typologies (Lewontin in Dobzhansky 1972). The distribution of each complex does not coincide with the others, so that racial categorization becomes a hopeless hodgepodge—which is the whole point. Using precise quantitative measures, racial typologizing is of next to no value.

The Cultural Uses of Theories of Biological Determinism

So far, I have treated variation as an essentially objective categorization of distributions of biologically determined traits. Even the most naive reader will anticipate that such classification has commonly been used as a basis not only for classifying on a descriptive level but also for evaluating the differences. The association of certain personality and mental traits with certain races, the evaluation of these traits as inferior or superior, and the characterization of some races as more "evolved" than others are examples of *racist*, rather than racial, categorizations (Klass and Hellman 1971).

As might be expected, those who want a genetic explanation of behavior as a basis for special treatment of another group are most likely to pursue and use it. An excellent example of such use in American culture involves the difference between black and white Americans in intelligence test scores. The difference has been known for a long time; disagreements have centered on how to account for it. The difference is either primarily genetic, primarily acquired (that is, environmentally determined), or some combination of the two. Although no scientist believes that either genetics or environment alone determines IQ

results in individual cases, there is wide disagreement among experts over how to interpret group differences in IQ scores. Many social scientists, especially anthropologists, have argued in recent years for environment as the primary determinant (Mead et al. 1968). But others have voiced opposition, in particular Arthur Jensen (1969). Jensen argues that differences in IQ scores between blacks and whites primarily reflect genetic differences in intellectual capability. He believes, therefore, that compensatory education programs, such as Head Start, and other attempts to boost the scores of blacks and others by "improving" their environment are bound to fail.

Many arguments can be made against Jensen's viewpoint (Montagu, 1975). It has been charged that he is misusing many of his statistical sources—in some cases by not recognizing their meaning; in others by using false data derived from a now discredited authority, Sir Cyril Burt; and in others by making errors in his own comparisons of black and white populations. He also misuses the term *genetic* in taking it to mean unchanging. In fact, many traits with a genetic component, such as IQ test scores, *do* change over the lifespan of a person. Jensen's approach also oversimplifies the concept of intelligence. Intelligence is a very complex process involving learning to adapt to one's environment. How well do IQ tests measure this complex concept of intelligence? We might ask, then, what do IQ tests measure? Could it be academic achievement and potential and not any absolute ability to learn? If this is so, then in blaming the victims for the failure of some compensatory programs, Jensen and his supporters overlook the possibility that we may not know enough about how to accomplish the task involved in compensatory programs, contending instead that the task itself is impossible. Jensen also makes the error of assuming that blacks and whites of the same socioeconomic status ought to have comparable IQ scores, as if socioeconomic status were the sole determinant of environment. This perspective does not take into account teacher

The Concept of Race

The complexity of the concept of race is illustrated in the following statements, which are part of a 1964 UNESCO proposal signed by many leading scientists throughout the world.

1. All humans living today belong to a single species, *Homo sapiens*, and are derived from a common stock. There are differences of opinion regarding how and when different groups diverged from this common stock.

2. Biological differences between human beings are due to differences in heredity, constitution, and to the influence of the environment on this genetic potential. In most cases, those differences are due to the *interaction* of these two sets of factors.

3. There is great genetic diversity within all human populations. Pure races—in the sense of genetically homogeneous populations—do not exist in the human species.

4. Many of the obvious physical differences in average appearance between populations living in different geographic areas of the world have a genetic component. Most often this consists of differences in the *frequency* of the same hereditary characteristics.

5. In humans as well as in other animals, the genetic composition of each population is subject to the modifying influence of such diverse factors as natural selection, tending towards adaptation to the environment, mutations, or random modifications in the frequency of qualitative hereditary characters. Certain physical characters have a universal biological value for the survival of the human species, irrespective of the environment. The differences on which racial classifications are based do not affect these characters and, therefore, it is not possible from the biological point of view to speak in any way whatsoever of a general inferiority or superiority of this or that racial group.

6. The human species, which is now spread over the whole world, has a past rich in migrations, in territorial expansions and contractions. Because of the mobility of human populations and of social factors, mating between members of different human groups has played a much more important role in human history than in that of animals. It has never been proved that interbreeding has biological disadvantages for mankind as a whole. On the contrary, interbreeding contributes to the maintenance of biological ties between human groups and thus to the unity of the species in its diversity.

7. Most racial classifications of mankind do not include mental traits or attributes as a criterion of classification. Heredity may have an influence in the variability shown by *individuals* within a given population in their responses to the psychological tests currently applied. However, no difference has ever been detected convincingly in the hereditary endowments of human groups in regard to what is measured by these tests. On the other hand, ample evidence attests to the influence of physical, cultural and social environment on differences in response to these tests.

8. Neither in the field of hereditary potentialities concerning the overall intelligence and the capacity for cultural development, nor in that of physical traits, is there any justification for the concept of "inferior" and "superior" races. The peoples of the world today appear to possess equal biological potentialities for attaining any civilizational level. Differences in the achievements of different peoples must be attributed solely to their cultural history.*

*Proposals on the Biological Aspects of Race. (Courtesy of UNESCO, 1964.)

attitudes, student expectations of success, and other reflections of a racist cultural context that clearly affect educational experiences and motivation—and, thus, IQ scores.

The persistence of this controversy raises some larger questions about contemporary American culture. The first question is: "Why focus on patterns of *racial* distinctions in IQ?" Other patterns of distinction exist. For example, people in different geographical regions of the United States show mean differences in IQ scores. Should we then assume that, because people in Alabama or North Dakota may do less well on IQ tests than people in New York or California, Alabamians (regardless of race) are genetically inferior? Second, why has the popular press made so much of Jensen's work,* especially when his work has been so roundly criticized by social scientists and geneticists and has such ramifications for funding and decision making in education? Third, could it be that many who are in positions of power in American society prefer a point of view like Jensen's to the alternatives because the alternatives suggest that there are basic problems in the essential structure of the society that is supposed to give equal opportunity and reward "true merit"? This discussion will be continued in Chapter 5 as we pursue the study of the ways in which culture affects the kinds of behaviors—perception and cognition—that are measured by IQ tests.

Various kinds of theories that attempt to account for human behavior and variation in biological terms have been persistently raised in both scientific and popular circles in the United States. One of the more recent such theories is called *sociobiology*. As applied to human behavior, sociobiology attempts to explain not human variation but rather human similarities. It applies various genetic models in an attempt to understand some human behavior patterns that appear to be universal, such as aggression and warfare and male

*See "Return of Arthur Jensen," *Time*, September 24, 1979, p. 49.

dominance, by attributing these traits to an underlying universal human *biogram*. The theories and models of sociobiology grew out of work with insects, and they are questionable on a number of accounts when applied to humans. In the first place, many of the traits that sociobiologists take to be universal, such as warfare or male dominance, are not in fact universal and, even when widespread, can be explained by other, more efficient theories, such as scarcity of resources and cultural adaptation to the environment. In the second place, although sociobiology at best offers explanations of universal human behaviors, it does not account for why cultures vary. It is this cultural variation in different environments that is so characteristic of our species, and it is this question that the remainder of this text addresses.

SUMMARY

1. Humans adapt to their ecological settings (environments) in two significant ways. The first way is through changes in the biological nature of the group by the operation of principles that affect all living things, especially natural selection. Until very recently this aspect of adaptation was hardly at all under our conscious control; now it is potentially somewhat controlled. The second means of adapting to the environment involves potentially extensive alteration of it and creations borne of human ingenuity (for example, technological, social organizational, ideological, and so on). Although this latter means is shared to some extent with certain other animals, humans seem to do this sort of adaptation (cultural) to an extraordinarily high degree.

2. Humans have much in common with other animals as vertebrates, mammals, and primates. However, we also are unique. Both our similarities to and dissimiliarities from other animals help us understand who we are.

3. Questions about the origins of human behavior parallel our ideas about our biophysiological origins. It is likely that major factors in early human behavior development included: close intragroup cooperation, suppression of competition, increasing intelligence and the application of improving manual dexterity to problem solving (for example, making and improving tools), and the development of a well integrated kinship structure including the nuclear family.

4. Another widespread and successful terrestrial primate adaptation is that of the baboons in Africa. Although contemporary baboons in no way duplicate early human adaptation, there are some common points, and they do provide some important insights into the possible social organization of early hominids.

5. Attempts to classify human biological differences have a long history, and—whether they focus on degrees of geographic isolation (race) or on distribution of particular trait complexes (cline)—they are not fully satisfactory as classification devices. Some people also seek biological explanations for very complex patterns of distribution of very complex traits (such as intelligence). Such explanations are very controversial and tend to have political and ideological influences, which there is some reason to believe are at base racist.

SUGGESTED READINGS

Fagan, B. M.
  1980   *People of the Earth: An Introduction to World Prehistory*, Boston: Little, Brown. A detailed introduction to archaeological findings which is quite straight forward.

Frisancho, A. R.
  1979   *Human Adaptation*, St. Louis: Mosby. Takes many examples of human biological adaptation drawn from many sources.

Gould, Stephen Jay
  1982   *The Mismeasure of Man*. New York: Norton. A brilliant and important book, which is an attack on the theories of biological determinism and also contains much that is positive and constructive.

Johanson, D. C. and M. Edey
  1981   *Lucy: The Origins of Humankind*, New York: Simon and Schuster. Entertaining popular account of recent work on early hominid fossils.

Klass, M. and H. Hellman
  1971   *The Kinds of Mankind*, Philadelphia: Lippincott. A good work which still persists among many.

CHAPTER THREE

THEORY AND METHOD IN CULTURAL ANTHROPOLOGY

▶ How can we explain the differences and similarities among different human cultures?

▶ What role does the environment play in shaping culture?

▶ Is culture something people do? Or is it the ideas they have in their minds?

> *I have made*
> *a ceaseless effort*
> *not to ridicule,*
> *not to bewail,*
> *nor to scorn human actions,*
> *but to understand them.*
> Spinoza

People have always been very aware of the differences in ideas, actions, clothing, morals, beliefs, and customs of other people with whom they come into contact. Very often these contacts have produced feelings of shock, awe, fear, hostility, and moral outrage; sometimes they have resulted in interest and admiration. Ethnocentrism has always been the characteristic response of human beings to other human beings who are different from themselves. With few exceptions, contact has not led to the systematic study of the ways of life of other people. In 1877, Edward Tylor, an Englishman, published a book called *Primitive Culture: Researches into the Development of Mythology, Philosophy, Religion, Language, Art, and Customs* in which he introduced the concept of culture as an explanation of variation in human behavior. Tylor defined **culture** as "that complex whole which includes knowledge, belief, art, law, morals, custom, and any other capabilities acquired by man as a member of society." He then defined anthropology as the "science of culture."

Every scientific discipline has a body of theory and a characteristic method by which it tests its theory. A **theory** is a general idea that guides the study of phenomena in any

This contemporary Mexican mural depicts the conversion of indigenous Mexo-American populations to Catholicism. When European peoples came into contact with non-Western peoples very different from themselves, they often regarded them as primitives or savages and destroyed much of their culture in the attempt to bring them into the fold of "civilization." (Serena Nanda)

scientific discipline. A good theory should explain and ultimately predict interrelationships. Scientific objectivity is the willingness to match a theory against new data (evidence) and to accept a new theory that is more consistent with the new facts.

THEORIES OF CULTURE

Cultural anthropology uses several theories in its study of human behavior, culture, and soci-

ety. In the history of anthropology as a discipline, different theories have been popular at different times. Sometimes, old theories have been revived in a modified way and applied to new data or tested by new methods. We will look here at some of the major theories in cultural anthropology.

Classic Evolutionary Theory

The sixteenth century was an age of discovery in which Europeans came in contact with peoples whose cultures were very different from their own and whose level of technology was much simpler. In the three centuries that followed, European philosophers interested in uncovering the origin and laws of development of human society had to deal with the question of these peoples' place in the scheme of human history. It was out of this background that anthropology developed as a science of culture.

The earliest anthropological theory tried to explain cultural development in terms of **cultural evolution,** the process by which new cultural forms emerged out of older ones. Each society in the world was believed to have moved through similar stages of culture, which followed each other in the same order. European civilization was viewed as the "top" of this evolutionary process, and the cultures of "primitive" peoples were treated as earlier stages in the culture of humankind. In the nineteenth century, Lewis Henry Morgan in America and Tylor in England developed this theory.

In 1877, Morgan published a book entitled *Ancient Society.* In it he proposed the idea that human society had passed through three major stages of cultural development. Each stage was marked by a major technological breakthrough and accompanied by changes in other aspects of culture such as the structure of the family and the ownership of property. The first stage, which he called "savagery," was marked by the acquisition of fire and the invention of the bow. Property was collectively owned, and brothers and sisters were allowed to mate with each other. The second stage, "barbarism," saw the beginnings of animal domestication, the use of iron tools in the Old World, and the invention of pottery and the development of agriculture in the New World. In this stage, accumulation of wealth was made possible by new technology and control of property fell into the hands of males. The patriarchal family (control by the father) emerged, and private ownership of property replaced collective ownership. The third stage, "civilization," is marked by the use of the phonetic alphabet and writing. The monogamous family (one man married to one woman) is characteristic of this stage. The state, a form of society based on a politically organized territory, replaces the tribe, a form of society organized by kinship. Morgan's ideas were used by Friedrich Engels and Karl Marx to refine their own evolutionary view of human society. Their theory, like Morgan's, is a materialistic one. All aspects of culture—law, government, family, religion—are affected by the ways in which a society is organized to satisfy its material needs. This organization, in turn, is affected by the level of technology.

The theory that cultural development proceeded by the same steps everywhere was based on the idea of the **psychic unity** of humankind: All human groups have the same mental capacities and the same ability to think logically. When faced with similar problems, they will invent similar solutions. **Independent invention** was the explanation for similarities in culture among societies that were isolated from one another, and the developmental stages explained differences. A society's developmental stage was itself influenced by contacts the society had with other cultures. Tylor recognized that culture contact led to the spread of elements from one society to another, a process which is known as **cultural diffusion.** The classic evolutionists were not interested in history, which is the study of the past through particular events, but rather in discovering the general laws by which cultural development occurred. Thus, although they recognized that diffusion did occur, they did not give it too much attention, believing that independent invention accounted for most cultural similarities. The evolutionary schemes of Morgan and Tylor were based on poor ethnographic data used out of their cultural context. Their interpretations are no longer considered adequate explanations of cultural similarities and differences.

Diffusion Theory

The evolutionary theorists appeared to have overestimated human inventiveness. In reaction, a new group of anthropologists in Europe and the United States turned to the study of cultural diffusion.

German and English ethnologists were still interested in the origins of human culture. They attempted to discover the earliest forms by mapping the distribution of cultural traits in nonliterate societies. The traits most widely distributed were presumed to be the oldest. Some diffusionists were determined to prove that all human culture originated in one place and then spread through culture contact, or diffusion. For example, the similarities among the Egyptian pyramids, Mayan temples, and native American burial mounds led anthropologists like Elliott Smith and W. J. Perry to the conclusion that Egypt was the source of human civilization and culture (Figure 3-1).

The work of the European diffusionists is no longer of much interest to anthropologists. Both diffusion and independent invention are now recognized as contributing to the similarities between cultures. Furthermore, anthropology has largely moved away from the "bits-and-pieces" approach of the diffusionists, who were more interested in parts of culture (culture traits) than in cultures as wholes.

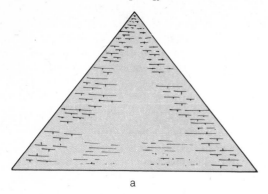

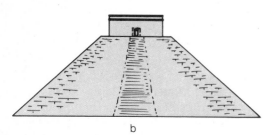

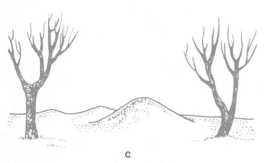

Figure 3.1 Diffusion theorists believed that the Mayan temples (b) and native American burial mounds (c) of the New World were derived from the Egyptian pyramid (a), to which they bear a superficial similarity in shape. Most contemporary anthropologists take the view that these three structures were a result of independent invention rather than diffusion.

The American Historical Tradition

American diffusionists never reached the European extreme; they limited themselves mainly to tracing the origin and spread of spe-cific cultural elements among the Indian tribes of North America. The anthropologists of the ·American historical tradition, among whom are Robert Lowie, Clark Wissler, Alfred Kroeber, and Franz Boas, believed that the laws of cultural process could best be discovered by recon-structing the particular cultural history of each society. Their efforts led to the designation of cultural areas for North America (Wissler 1926; Kroeber 1939) and some outstanding studies of American Indian culture (Lowie 1963).

Boas, the leading American anthropologist of his time, was critical of both the deductive approach of the evolutionists and the piece-meal approach of the European diffusionists. Through intensive fieldwork among various North American Indian societies, Boas came to see that a cultural element—the design of a pot, the detail of a ritual—had to be under-stood in terms of the total culture of which it was a part. He began to insist on the study of cultures as wholes, as systems made up of many interrelated parts (1940). Boas also realized that diffusion was not an automatic result of cul-tural contact. People did not accept every new cultural element to which they were exposed. Even when elements did diffuse from one cul-ture to another, they often changed meaning, ·and even form, when they became part of a preexisting cultural pattern. Boas became interested in the psychological as well as the historical influences that played a part in the similarities and differences in specific cultural patterns.

Boas became increasingly skeptical about the possibility of discovering laws underlying cultural process, and he regarded the search for cultural origins as fruitless. He urged anthropologists to do much more ethno-graphic fieldwork before they attempted to find cultural laws. He himself produced an enor-mous amount of ethnographic data on native American cultures. For Boas, the status of anthropology as a science would depend on the most complete and objective gathering of ethnographic data on specific cultural sys-tems, not on "discoveries" of cause and effect.

Critics accuse Boas of having held back the development of anthropology as a science by his outspoken hostility to the search for general laws of cultural development. But his contributions remain important. He shifted the focus of anthropology from cultural elements taken out of context to the study of culture as an interrelated system. He put anthropology on a sounder basis, not only by his own ethnographic contributions but also by setting high standards in ethnography for future generations. His interest in psychology stimulated work in the field of culture and personality. His insistence on seeing culture in terms of the meaning it has for its participants led to important new work in linguistics and to an emphasis on cultural relativity as a necessary attitude in fieldwork.

Cultural Configurations

Ruth Benedict, a student of Boas, expanded his ideas in her book *Patterns of Culture* (1961). Benedict tried to account for cultural diversity by demonstrating that each culture is a unique **configuration** of interwoven parts, all of which are shaped by the particular theme, or **ethos,** of that culture. Religion, family life, economics, and political institutions all fit together to make up the unique configuration. Because configurations result from particular historical processes, cultures cannot be measured against one another.

Drawing on ethnography from the Kwakiutl, Zuni, and Plains Indians of North America and the Dobu of Melanesia, Benedict described their four cultural configurations in psychological terms. She showed how cultural elements drew their meaning from the cultural ethos and the total configuration of which they were a part.

Though cultural patterns and values remain basic anthropological topics, few anthropologists followed Benedict's theoretical approach, which was criticized as being too impression-

istic. Furthermore, if Boas had stressed cultural relativity as part of the scientific method in anthropology, Benedict carried this concept to the extreme: It seemed that all cultural comparison must be abandoned. Nor did she suggest why a particular culture had developed a particular ethos or what adaptive value an ethos had for a society. In spite of all the criticism, however, *Patterns of Culture* remains an anthropological classic.

Functionalism

In the early years of the twentieth century, American anthropologists were trying to describe traditional native American cultures, using informants who were themselves being affected by the culture of the dominant white society. At the same time, Bronislaw Malinowski was doing fieldwork among the Trobriand Islanders of the New Guinea archipelago, a society whose cultural traditions were still very much alive. As a result of this fieldwork, he developed a theory of culture called **functionalism** (1944).

The central idea of functionalism is that culture serves the needs of individuals. In Malinowski's analysis, culture is the outgrowth of three kinds of human needs: basic, derived, and integrative. Basic needs relate to the survival of human beings as biological organisms—the needs for food, shelter, and physical protection. Derived needs are the problems of social coordination humans must solve in order to satisfy their basic needs—the division of work, the distribution of food, defense, regulation of reproduction, and social control. Integrative needs are the human needs for psychological security, social harmony, and purpose in life that are met by systems of knowledge, law, religion, magic, myth, art. For example, magic functions to reassure people challenged by dangerous undertakings whose outcome is uncertain. Myth provides historical authority for the particular rules and values by which a society lives. Malinowski insisted that every aspect of a culture has a function in terms of one of these three needs.

Malinowski's idea that cultural elements and social institutions have functions that grow out of the needs of individuals in society is basic to much anthropological analysis. But because the human needs he talked about are universal, his theory does not serve as an explanation of cultural variation. For example, if all types of family systems serve the same human need, why do different societies have different systems?

Another aspect of Malinowski's functionalism was that the investigation of one aspect of culture would lead to a description of a whole cultural system. His own ethnography of the Trobriander Islanders (1961) is the best illustration of his theoretical approach. Among the Trobrianders, there was a cultural pattern called the **kula.** From their point of view, the most important aspect of kula was the trading of shell bracelets and necklaces, which took place between trading partners on the different islands that made up the kula ring. Malinowski showed that the kula was not an economic transaction like the impersonal money-goods exchanges in our own society, which are separated from other aspects of culture. Our norms and ethics in economic exchange are not expected to apply to friends and kin, nor are the ethics of personal relations between friends and kin supposed to apply in the marketplace. The kula, however, was related to many aspects of Trobriand life: kinship and political structure, magic, prestige, economy, technology, myth and feasting, and friendship and alliance. Although the kula appeared to be primarily an exchange of goods, it did not fill economic needs only. For the Trobriander, participation in the kula had important psychological functions. Participants derived prestige from generous behavior during the exchanges, and the kula gave them an opportunity to display their wealth. Through the preparations and activities of the kula, ties between participating local groups were rein-

forced, contributing to the integration of Trobriand society. Malinowski pointed out, however, that only the ethnographer, not the native, is able to see the total outline of the vast interconnecting complex of activities that makes up a cultural system. This is true whether the native belongs to the Trobriand Island society or to our own society.

In order to further emphasize the multiplicity of meanings that form the "ethnographic reality" of any particular item of culture, Malinowski talked about the Trobriand canoe. Although a canoe is an item of material culture, unless we see it in its total cultural context and understand its meaning for the native, we have not understood the canoe at all. For example, in the Trobriand Islands a canoe was made for a specific use, with a definite purpose in relation to the kula. We can begin by studying the economics of the canoe, the uses to which it is put, and the way in which it is made. But it is also necessary to investigate who owns the canoe, who rides in it, how this is done, and what the ceremonies and customs of its construction and use are. But even then, says Malinowski, we have not touched the most vital reality of a native canoe. For a canoe, in the Trobriand Islands as well as in our own culture, is surrounded by romance, built up into a tradition. It is an object of cult admiration, a living thing, possessing its own individuality. From a functional perspective, then, we can start with a canoe and wind up knowing about the whole of Trobriand society.

Structural Functionalism

Another kind of functional theory, **structural functionalism,** was developed by A. R. Radcliffe-Brown, who had been influenced by the French sociologist Emile Durkheim. Durkheim had rejected the psychological theories of his day, which attempted to explain social events in terms of individual needs and experiences. According to Durkheim, society, not the individual, must be the focus of study. Social events have an existence that goes beyond the individuals who take part in them. The origin and functions of religion, for example, are to be found in its contribution to social solidarity, not in its psychological functions for the individual. Durkheim's main interest was in social solidarity—the mechanisms by which societies are unified and maintained over time. Influenced by Durkheim's work, Radcliffe-Brown showed that norms, values, sentiments, and rituals have power over individuals and hold society together (1964).

Radcliffe-Brown's particular contribution to anthropology was showing that social systems are made up of structures and activities (1965). Social structures are the relatively persistent patterns by which people relate to one another and to the environment. Structures are inferred from social interaction and **norms,** or rules of behavior for social relationships. Although Radcliffe-Brown was interested in how social structures change, his work was mainly directed toward understanding the ways in which structural continuity and social solidarity are maintained. For him, the function of a structural element was the contribution it made to social solidarity and the continuity of a social system. Much of Radcliffe-Brown's own work, and that of other structural functionalists, centered on kinship, because this is the most important principle of organization in nonliterate societies. An illustration of Radcliffe-Brown's theory is his explanation of "joking relations." Joking relationships are compounded of friendliness and hostility. They resemble what we call "teasing" in our own society. In many societies, joking relationships exist between persons occupying particular social statuses. An example of a joking relationship in our own society is that between a man and his mother-in-law. By presenting ethnographic data from several different societies, Radcliffe-Brown demonstrated that joking relationships exist between people who are tied together socially and yet have conflicting interests in the relationship. By acknowledg-

ing the conflict and dealing with it formally, joking relationships reduce the possibility of open social conflict and contribute to the maintenance of the total social system.

The main criticism of structural functionalism is that, because of its focus on solidarity, integration, function, and stability, it ignores conflict, dysfunction, and change. This limits its usefulness in the study of complex societies; in looking back, it seems also to have imposed a false impression of stability and harmony on nonliterate societies as well. Nevertheless, **social function** is a basic concept in anthropological analysis. Many cultural traits can be examined in terms of what they contribute to the solidarity of a group.

Cognitive Anthropology

Another approach to culture identifies it with rules, meanings, and classifications in language that give clues to the ways in which people perceive and understand their experience. In **cognitive anthropology,** culture is defined as a "blueprint for action" (not action itself); a "grammar," or system of rules, for behavior; and a "code" it is the job of the anthropologist to break. What people learn when they learn "culture" is not just customs but also ways of organizing experience. From this perspective, anthropologists do not observe culture, but rather infer it from the behavior they observe in a particular society. A description of one particular culture is not merely a description of what people do but also a description of the rules or collective ideas behind that behavior. Sometimes, members of a society know and can tell the anthropologist the pattern or rule underlying their behavior; sometimes, they are not aware that an aspect of their behavior is culturally patterned. It is then the task of the anthropologist to find the pattern from observations and inquiries.

But although understanding the person's interpretation of experience is the aim of ethnography, not all anthropologists agree that it is the aim of anthropology. An important objection to the cognitive approach is that the overall results of cultural patterns are not necessarily part of one person's point of view or within her or his ability to grasp as an insider. The understanding of cultural process also depends on the ability of the outsider, the anthropologist, to see causes and effects that are different from, and perhaps even contrary to, the insider's view of experience.

Closely related to cognitive anthropology is **symbolic anthropology,** which treats culture as a system of shared symbols and meanings. An illustration from Clifford Geertz (1973:6) will make this clear:

Consider . . . two boys rapidly contracting the eyelids of the right eyes. In one, this is an involuntary twitch; in the other, a conspiratorial signal to a friend. The two movements are, as movements, identical. . . . One could not tell which was twitch and which was wink. Yet the difference . . . between a twitch and wink is vast; as anyone unfortunate enough to have had the first taken for the second knows.

What Geertz is saying is that the winker is communicating. He is communicating deliberately, to someone in particular, according to a socially established code. A twitch of an eyelid is not culture—it is a physical movement that has no shared meaning. A wink is culture: It is a twitch of the eyelid that has meaning and communicates a special message. These symbolic aspects of human behavior are what are of interest to the anthropologist describing a culture as a system of meaning.

Cultural Ecology

An ecological approach to culture sees cultural patterns as adaptive responses to the basic problems of survival and reproduction. Contemporary **cultural ecology** grows out of the theories of Leslie White (1949) and Julian Steward (1972) and has some links with evolutionary theory. White, like Morgan, was interested

in the general evolution of culture. White's theory was that cultural development proceeds by an increasingly efficient transformation of energy, which leads in turn to population growth, increased productivity, and economic specialization. All other aspects of culture are secondary to this material base. White's theory was a universal one; it applied to human culture in general.

In Steward's multilinear evolutionary theory, cultures are primarily systems that evolved as adaptive responses to specific natural environments. Unlike White, he held that cultural evolution could move along a number of different paths, although societies in similar natural environments and with similar levels of technology would evolve in similar ways. This process of parallel evolution explains some general similarities in developmental stages among societies that are geographically distant from one another. It also explains similarities that cannot be explained by diffusion. According to Steward, the explanation of cultural forms or stages is to be found in the relationship between natural environment, level of technology, and patterns of work in a society.

Not all contemporary cultural ecologists agree with either White's or Steward's evolutionary emphasis on stages of development. They generally agree, however, that the question of how human societies develop particular patterns can best be approached by viewing culture as a system of socially transmitted behavior that serves to connect human communities to their ecological settings. The emphasis here is on culture as a behavior system that includes technology, ways of economic and political organization, settlement patterns, social groupings, religious beliefs and practices, values, and so on. From this perspective, the term **sociocultural system** seems better than *culture*, because the term *sociocultural system* includes the real-life expression of designs for living in particular environments, not just the designs.

In emphasizing the adaptive nature of different aspects of a sociocultural system, cul-

Cultural ecologists help explain how some apparently irrational customs, such as the prohibition on eating beef in India, a country in which some people starve, makes sense as an adaptation to long-run variation in the environment. (Serena Nanda)

tural ecologists and cultural materialists, such as Marvin Harris, have been able to show that beliefs and practices that seem quite irrational may still result in rational utilization of the environment, given a particular level of technology. For example, the Hindu taboo on eating beef despite widespread poverty and periodic famine in India seems ridiculous to Westerners. Yet, according to Marvin Harris (1966), it does make sense as an adaptation. Cows are important in India not because they can be eaten but because they provide bullocks, the draft animals that pull plows and carts and that are essential for agriculture. If a family were to eat its cows during a famine, it would deprive itself of the source of bullocks and could not continue farming. The religious taboo on eating beef strengthens the ability of the society to maintain itself in the long run.

The focus on the adaptive nature of socio-

cultural systems, rather than the ways in which such systems are transformed over time, has led to the criticism that cultural ecology is just another form of functionalism. It explains cultural variation in terms of "what is, is," with no real explanation of how it got that way. This criticism may not be entirely justified and may in fact be based on a misperception of the essence of the ecological approach. Ecological anthropologists do recognize that adaptation is an ongoing process and the primary means by which we adjust to and cope with our environment. Thus, this theoretical approach can in fact be used as a focus for examining how sociocultural systems are transformed. Perhaps a more relevant criticism of ecological anthropology is that it does not give sufficient weight to the symbolic aspects of culture. Nevertheless, cultural ecology does contribute to our understanding of the relationship of

Culture and Personality

Between 1920 and 1950, some anthropologists became interested in the relationship between culture and personality. This interest grew partly out of Freudian psychoanalytical theory and partly out of the interest in the relationship between culture and psychology formulated by Benedict, Boas, and Edward Sapir, a linguist and cultural anthropologist. Some of the early culture-and-personality studies were done to test specific Freudian theories in non-Western cultures. Malinowski (1927), for example, demonstrated that the Oedipus complex (defined by Freud as a sexual attachment of the male child to his mother, accompanied by hatred and jealousy toward his father), which Freud believed to be universal, did not exist in this form in the Trobriand Islands. The Trobriand society was matrilineal (the kinship group was organized around a woman and her descendants), and the mother's brother, rather than the father, was the primary authority in the family. Incest taboos in this society were strongest for brothers and sisters, not mothers and sons, and a boy's major unconscious rivalry was directed toward his maternal uncle, not his father.

Early culture-and-personality studies, having been influenced by Freudian theory, put particular emphasis on child-rearing practices such as feeding, weaning, and toilet training. Margaret Mead, who carried out some of the first studies of child rearing among non-Western peoples, pointed out not only that specific child-rearing practices, such as weaning or toilet training, were responsible for how a child's personality developed but also that such things as the way a child was handled and the unconscious attitudes people communicated to the child played an important role in personality development. It did not matter so much whether a child was weaned early or late; the attitudes communicated in the process of weaning made all the difference. Although most culture-and-personality theorists were interested in the influence culture had on personality, a group led by Abram Kardiner (1945)

wanted to investigate the ways in which personality types might be reflected in patterns of culture. Kardiner and his associates believed that religion, folklore, and political systems might be seen as screens on which the basic personality orientation of a society was projected. They were interested in the relationship between child-rearing practices, the development of basic personality, and other aspects of culture. They saw a basic personality type as an adaptation that grew out of child-rearing practices that were themselves linked to the subsistence patterns of a society.

Later culture-and-personality theorists studied large "modernized" nations. National character studies, as they were called, appeared for Japan (Benedict 1946), the United States (Mead 1942), and the Soviet Union (Gorer 1949), among others. One of the problems with these studies was that it became difficult to generalize about personality in societies composed of several ethnic groups, social classes, and subcultures. Many of these national character studies also made connections between early child-rearing practices and later adult personality traits that were difficult to prove scientifically.

Interest in the cultural patterning of personality also led to an interest in the effect of culture on the so-called abnormal or deviant person. The kind of personality most highly valued in one society might be labeled deviant or mentally abnormal in another (Benedict 1934). Furthermore, different societies had different ways of treating or responding to what we would call abnormal, and even within the history of Western culture, attitudes toward certain kinds of behavior, such as homosexuality or trance, had changed over the centuries.

Because of the difficulty of proving many of the ideas of the early culture-and-personality theorists, this field of anthropology took new directions after 1950. There was a greater attempt to use statistics to prove the connections between child-rearing practices, personality, and other cultural patterns. John Whiting and Irwin Child

(1953), for example, used a large cross-cultural sample in an attempt to demonstrate some of these interrelationships. One hypothesis they tested was that systems of curing illness would reflect techniques that had been sources of gratification in early child rearing. Thus, a culture in which children were indulged in sources of oral gratification, such as feeding, would tend to use oral medicines for curing illness. Whiting and Child also hypothesized about the reverse of this relationship: They attempted to demonstrate that an aspect of child rearing that was frustrating and promoted anxiety would be used to account for illness. If a culture frustrated a child's oral gratification—by withholding food, for example—that culture might be likely to see disease as something that enters the body through the mouth. Both hypotheses were validated statistically, and the work proved to be a major step toward more refined methods of demonstrating the relationships between child-rearing practices, personality development, and other aspects of culture.

Whiting and his associates also tried to relate child-rearing patterns and subsequent personality development to the basic patterns of culture—food getting, division of labor, and residence. This interest in the relation between ecology and personality has gained importance in culture-and-personality studies. In a recent study, for example, Robert Edgerton (1971) investigated four East African tribes that were divided into farmers and herders. He found personality differences not only among the four tribes but also between the farmers and herders within each. Herders were more individualistic compared with farmers, who more often felt the need to consult others in making decisions. Edgerton concluded that, the more an economy depends on herding, the more that soci-

Early culture and personality theorists emphasized the link between child-rearing practices, such as bathing a child, and the kind of personality developed in adulthood. (United Nations)

ety will value independence as a male personality trait.

Although psychologists are now entering the field of cross-cultural personality studies, anthropologists still tend to take a broader view of personality development. For the anthropologist, biological factors, family relations, cultural images, social roles, and specific situational factors all play a part in shaping personality. Contemporary psychological anthropology has also turned its attention in other directions, particularly to the relationships between culture and thought and culture and perception.

human populations to their physical and social environments. It is one of the dominant approaches in contemporary anthropology.

THEORY IN ANTHROPOLOGY AND THE USE OF ETHNOGRAPHIC DATA

The kinds of questions that anthropologists are interested in cannot be answered by the methods used in the physical sciences. Anthropological theories cannot be tested in a laboratory under strictly controlled experimental conditions; the anthropological laboratory is the naturally existing diversity of cultural patterns in different parts of the world, in different natural environments, and at different times in history. The gathering of good ethnographic data through participant observation continues to be the hallmark of anthropology as a discipline and the foundation on which its theories are built and tested.

Although under the influence of Boas the aim of anthropological fieldwork was the collection of detailed information on every aspect of life in a particular sociocultural system, today anthropologists tend to go into the field with some particular theoretical problem in mind, rather than with the idea of presenting the total picture of a culture. They may be interested in the relationship between subsistence and personality, or in symbolism, or in the role of voluntary associations in political participation, or in the relation of family type to economics.

An example is Margaret Mead's study in Samoa. In the 1920s in the United States, psychologists saw the stress experienced by adolescents as a universal and "natural" condition of growing up. Mead believed that the rebellion and emotional distress experienced by American adolescents were related to the particular difficulties of making the transition from childhood to adulthood in our society. She chose to study life in Samoa, where the transition from childhood to adulthood was known to be much easier. Mead found that the adolescent turmoil we know in the United States did not exist among this group of people. Her book, *Coming of Age in Samoa* (1961), is a classic example of the use of ethnographic study for testing a particular anthropological theory—in this case, one involving the relation of specific emotional disturbances to specific cultural patterns.

Forty-two years after this work was published and four years after her death, Mead's ethnography was challenged by sociobiologist Derek Freeman in a book entitled *Margaret Mead—the Making and Unmaking of an Anthropological Myth* (1983). Freeman's attack on Mead takes two forms. He first claims that she misinterpreted Samoan society because of her strong commitment to the theory that culture, not biology, is responsible for the ways in which human beings behave. Based on his own fieldwork over the last 40 years, Freeman holds that Samoa was not the idyllic society Mead describes, but rather one full of tension, aggression, and competition. Contrary to her assertion that Samoan society is one in which there is an absence of guilt and conflict over sex, Freeman, who used evidence from court cases, claims that adolescents and children are under considerable stress, that the culture has a preoccupation with virginity, and that the Samoans are prone to rape, violence, and jealousy. Freeman uses his criticisms of her ethnographic work to put forth his own sociobiological view in which a large component of human behavior, particularly aggression, is seen as biologically determined. Many of Mead's former colleagues and students have defended her work, pointing out that her ethnography was done in 1925, when anthropology was still in its infancy as a science and that she worked well within the tradition of ethnographic methodology as it was known at that time. They point out that although she may have been wrong about some of her facts and emphases, reinterpretation of ethnography is a standard practice in anthropology and is part of the growth and development of the field. Freeman's critics aptly point out that the attention given to his book in the media represents a current sympathy with politically conservative implications of his sociobiological stance (Lessinger 1983). Both Mead's and Freeman's work must be seen in the context of the "nature-nurture" controversy. It was due in great part to Mead's work that the theory that we are products of our environment and that we can reshape that environment if we are willing took hold in American scientific and popular thinking in the decades between 1930 and 1960. In the last ten years, beginning with the publication of E. O. Wilson's *Sociobiology: The New Synthesis* (1975), the stage was set for criticism of the kind of cultural emphases that Mead's work embodies.

The studies about culture and personality carried out by Robert Edgerton and described on p. **198** are another example of the kinds of connections that anthropologists make between theory and ethnographic data.

Another way of using ethnographic data is called the **controlled cross-cultural comparison,** which requires using data from many societies to explore certain cultural relationships. This method was used by Peggy Sanday in exploring the question of whether male dominance is a universal cultural fact and, if it is not, under what conditions it arises. Sanday used data from the Human Relations Area Files, which is a cross-indexed file of hundreds of cultural patterns for hundreds of societies that have been studied by anthropologists, attempting to correlate sexual status with religious belief and ecological conditions. Her use of the cross-cultural data, themselves based on fieldwork done in these different cultures, showed that male dominance should not be considered universal; rather, it tends to occur under specific conditions—namely, ecological stress and war. In situations in which the survival of the group rests more on male actions than female actions, women accept male domination for the sake of social and cultural

Two young Samoan women, taken from a period a few decades before Margaret Mead worked there. Samoa, which was encountered by the Europeans in the 18th century, had already been influenced in important ways by the Europeans, especially the missionaries, by the early 20th century. (Courtesy of American Museum of Natural History)

survival.

From a historical perspective, anthropological approaches to culture are somewhat like the attempt by the seven blind men to describe the elephant. The one who caught the tail described the elephant as a rope, the one who caught the leg described the elephant as a tree, and so on. Anthropologists have approached culture from a number of perspectives and have defined it in terms of what they think is most important to say about it. All the approaches have something to contribute to our understanding of the human experience. Although there is a major division in the field between anthropologists who view culture as a system of ideas or symbols and those who emphasize the material basis of sociocultural systems, there are also attempts to integrate these two points of view. Unlike the seven blind men describing the elephant, anthropologists work with their eyes open: Human culture is a system and it is the understanding of this system in all its aspects that is the aim of anthropology as a discipline.

SUMMARY

1. For the anthropologist, culture is the major explanation of differences between human groups. Cultural anthropology is the systematic investigation of culture in both its general and specific forms.

2. A scientific theory is a general idea that attempts to explain the interrelationships among phenomena. Because theory in cultural anthropology attempts to explain the interrelationships among sociocultural phenomena, cultural anthropology is most often classed with the social sciences.

3. Classic evolutionary theory attempted to uncover the origin and laws of development of culture. It viewed culture in terms of a uniform evolutionary process: the gradual emergence of new forms from previous ones followed the same sequence throughout the world. Cultural similarities were explained by independent invention, which rested on the assumption of psychic unity, the idea that all humankind had the same mental capacities and would invent similar solutions when faced with similar problems.

4. Diffusion theory attempted to account for cultural similarities by the spread of culture traits from one society to another through historical contact.

5. The American historical tradition, led by Franz Boas, was first interested in diffusion and then turned to the study of whole cultures. Boas insisted on the study of particular cultures in their historical and psychological context as the first step toward finding general laws of culture.

6. Ruth Benedict, a student of Boas, tried to characterize whole cultures in terms of unique psychological configurations. She saw each culture as an interwoven pattern of traits, dominated by a particular ethos, or theme.

7. In Europe, functionalist theory was developing from the study of whole societies. Bronislaw Malinowski's functional theory saw culture as functioning to meet the needs of individuals in society.

8. The structural functionalist theory of Radcliffe-Brown stressed the contribution that different parts of a social system make to the maintenance of the total society.

9. Between 1920 and 1950, anthropologists developed culture-and-personality studies. These attempted to understand the influence of culture on both normal and abnormal personality. At first done in small, traditional societies, these studies were expanded by the 1940s to national character studies. After 1950, such studies were more oriented toward an ecological approach to personality. They also used more sophisticated methodology, especially statistical analysis of ethnographic data from many societies.

10. Cognitive anthropology views culture as a blueprint for behavior, rather than behavior itself; symbolic anthropology emphasizes culture as a system of shared symbols and meanings.

11. Cultural ecologists are primarily interested in cultures (or sociocultural systems) as systems of socially transmitted behavior that serve to connect human communities to their ecological settings.

12. Anthropologists may do ethnography either to grasp the entire cultural pattern of a society or to provide data on a more specific theoretical problem.

13. Some anthropologists examine theoretical problems by comparing ethnographic data from a large number of societies, using controlled cross-cultural comparison.

14. Although there is a major difference between anthropologists who view culture as a system of ideas and those who emphasize its material base, each perspective makes a contribution to our understanding of the human experience.

SUGGESTED READINGS

Arens, W.
  1979   *The Man Eating Myth: Anthropology and Anthropophagy.* New York: Oxford University Press. A very readable book that calls into question some of the ethnocentrism and methodology of anthropology as illustrated in the case of cannibalism. A response in the *American Anthropologist* (Brady 1982) is also suggested.

Benedict, Ruth
  1961   *Patterns of Culture.* Boston: Houghton Mifflin (orig. 1934). The presentation of the theory of cultural configuration, with a detailed account of three different cultures. A best seller in its time.

Harris, Marvin
  1974   *Cows, Pigs, Wars and Witches: The Riddle of Culture.* New York: Random House. A witty, fascinating look at such diverse topics as food prohibitions, warfare, messianic cults, and the counterculture in the United States from the standpoint of cultural materialism.

Kardiner, Abram, and Preble, Edward
  1961   *They Studied Man.* New York: New American Library. Essays on the personalities and professional contributions of the most important social scientists of our century.

Netting, Robert McC.
  1977   *Cultural Ecology.* Menlo Park, Calif.: Cummings. An excellent short book that looks at some classic ethnographic data from the standpoint of cultural ecology.

Spradley, James
  1970   *You Owe Yourself a Drunk.* Boston: Little, Brown. A cognitive approach to the study of men arrested for public drunkenness in Seattle.

CHAPTER FOUR

THE CULTURE CONCEPT

▶ Are cultural patterns shared by everyone in a society?

▶ How can the culture concept take individual and subcultural variation into account?

▶ How is culture adaptive? And how and why does it change?

Entire systems of behavior made up of hundreds of thousands of details are passed from generation to generation, and nobody can give the rules for what is happening. Only when the rules are broken do we realize they exist.

Edward Hall

*B*efore discussing the various aspects of culture, we should remind ourselves again of the definition of culture offered by Edward Tylor. He defined culture as "that complex whole which includes knowledge, belief, art, law, morals, custom, and any other capabilities acquired by man as a member of society." Culture, in short, is the patterned way of life shared by a group of people.

CULTURE IS LEARNED

Culture is learned through social interaction with other people in society. Humans, more than any other animal, depend on the social transmission of knowledge for survival. The learning processes through which human cultural traditions are passed on from one generation to another are called **socialization.** The difficulty in seeing the importance of learning in human behavior is that much of what is learned is not consciously taught, nor are we consciously aware of learning it. Culturally distinct ways of thinking, behaving, feeling, and responding become habitual very early in life. That is why much of what humans learn comes to seem "natural."

The importance of learning for humans is related to the prolonged dependency of

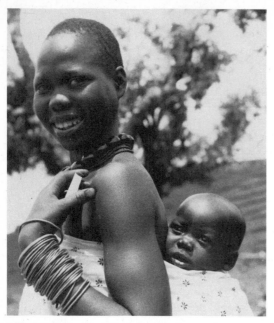

The dependency of the human infant on human social organization provides the basic context in which infants can learn from others while being protected by them. (United Nations)

the human infant and child. Although our complex brain gives us the capacity for learning, it also means that we develop more slowly and need the support of others in order to survive. Human social organization and group living thus provide the basic context in which we can learn from others at the same time that we are being protected by them. Although humans share this interrelated set of characteristics (a high capacity for learning, prolonged dependency, and group living) with other primates, no other species has as great a capacity for learning. And no other animal species depends so much on learned behavior for its adaptation to the environment.

CULTURE IS SHARED

To be considered part of culture, a way of thinking or interacting must be shared among a group of people. Some cultural patterns are shared by all people in a society. Societies in which important beliefs, values, and customs are shared by almost everyone are said to be homogeneous. Although anthropologists are now discovering that even small, traditional societies are less homogeneous than was previously believed, it is in the large, heterogeneous societies that discovering the degree of shared beliefs, values, and practices really becomes a problem. In heterogeneous societies, written law may be a useful guide to the most widely shared cultural traits.

One universally shared cultural pattern in the United States is driving a car on the right side of the road. This custom is not simply the result of law but is built into our response system. Another cultural universal in the United States is our system of weights and measures. Here again, although this pattern is supported by formal teaching and law, it is a way of giving shape to the physical universe that is basic to the way we perceive the world.

Cultural Specialization

Some cultural patterns are shared only by people in certain social positions, or **statuses.** In most societies, for example, there is some cultural specialization between men and women. This specialization derives not only from the sexual division of labor, in which men customarily do different things than women, but also from cultural prohibitions on the kinds of activities women are allowed to engage in. Among the Arapesh of New Guinea, for example, women are not allowed to join the tamberan cult, because the tamberan is the supernatural patron of adult men. Not only are women not permitted to see the tamberan, but they are not even allowed to think about what he might look like or the meaning of the activities that accompany his entry into the village. Margaret Mead, who studied the Arapesh, notes that the intellectual passivity women must accept regarding the tamberan soon becomes a habit. All that is "strange, uncharted and

The celebration of Halloween is a part of children's culture in the United States. Losing its original religious meaning, this holiday has become an opportunity for the promotion of popular, contemporary culture heroes. (Serena Nanda)

unnamed" becomes unfamiliar to them. This not only cuts women off from speculative thinking on many subjects, but also "from art, because among the Arapesh art and the supernatural are part and parcel of each other" (Mead 1963). Thus, intellectual and creative activity becomes a male cultural specialization.

Age is also a universal criterion of cultural specialization, though in most societies age specialization is not nearly as important as it is in the United States. In our own society, the degree to which cultural specialties—in language, music, and behavior—are associated with people between the ages of 12 and 20 has led to the label "youth culture" (Schwartz 1972).

Some occupational specialties exist in most societies. These cultural specialties are most often of a ritual kind. In some societies, they may be learned by anyone who wishes to engage in ritual activity and who seems to be successful at it. In others, ritual specialization may be limited to a few men or women who must first serve a long apprenticeship or join a secret association to learn ritual techniques and handle sacred materials. In India, most occupations are specialties of certain groups called castes, and only people born into a particular caste may practice its traditional occupational specialty.

Subcultures

A **subculture** is a system of perceptions, values, beliefs, and customs that are significantly different from those of the dominant culture. Modern nations may contain many subcultures—based on region, religion, occupation, social class, ethnicity, or life style. One distinct subculture in the United States is the Old Order

E T H N O G R A P H Y

A DEVIANT SUBCULTURE: THE HIJRAS OF INDIA

In 1981 and 1982, I did fieldwork among an extraordinary subculture in India called hijras. Hijras are men who dress and live as women; undergo emasculation, a ritual in which their genitals are surgically removed; and traditionally earn a living by collecting alms and receiving payments for blessing newborn babies. Hijras are devotees of the goddess Bahuchara Mata, and it is in connection with their worship of her that the emasculation operation takes place, traditionally as part of the initiation into the cult. Bahuchara Mata is one of the many mother-goddess figures worshipped all over India. Her picture is found in every hijra house and is worshipped daily, garlanded with flowers, as deities are worshipped in all Hindu homes. Through their dressing as women, and especially through the emasculation ritual, the hijras attempt to completely identify with the goddess. It is through these acts that express their devotion to her that the hijras become conduits of her powers.

The hijras point to a story in the Mahabharata, the great Hindu epic, as their origin myth. In this story, Arjuna, one of the great heroes of the epic, dresses as a woman and lives as a eunuch in the king's court for a year, as a penalty for having lost a bet. In spite of this connection with Hinduism, however, Islam also plays an important role in the hijras' history. The founders of the cult are said to have been Muslim, and all of the contemporary leaders of the nationwide community are Muslims. Hijras maintain that the egalitarianism of Islam has a special appeal for them. In addition, it is likely that today's hijra community grew out of the eunuch class created by the Muslim rulers of India to protect the ladies of the court and teach them singing and dancing.

The word *hijra* is usually translated as "eunuch" or "hermaphrodite," emphasizing sexual impotence. Both in the past and currently, however, men who are not impotent have joined the hijra community, sometimes to earn a living with them. Hijras identify themselves as "in-betweens," using words indicating feminized males, or identify themselves as women. Publicly, they assert that they wish to be treated legally and socially as women, though the degree to which individual hijras actively experience themselves as women varies. They are counted as women in the national census. Not all people with the characteristics of hijras choose to become members of the community and participate in its subculture. It is estimated that there are about 50,000 hijras in India, with about 5,000 of these in Bombay, one of their biggest centers. Most hijras live in the large cities of North India, as it is primarily among North Indians that they do their traditional work.

There is a widespread belief in India that hijras recruit their membership by carrying off infants and small children whom they observe to be intersexed, but my data from hijra life histories contradict this belief, and most hijras vehemently deny it. The hijras I interviewed came mostly from lower-class, middle-caste families. They report having had the desire to dress and act as women from early childhood. In most cases, their parents actively discouraged their cross-dressing and girlish behavior by scolding and beating them until they left home. Members typically join the hijra community as teenagers. While living at home during their early adolescent years, they first "hang around" groups of hijras who come through the cities and dance in public. The next step is to leave the family's house and join a hijra commune in a nearby city. A hijra household accepts new recruits hospitably, but it also asks them to leave if they prove dishonest, disruptive, or unwilling to work and contribute to the household income. If the new recruit stays, an elder hijra will pierce her nose and ears, give her some used clothing and a few pieces of jewelry, and generally look after her. If the new recruit wants to join the community, she will be taken to Bombay to undergo the formal initiation ceremony. After a variable amount of time, many hijras reestablish contact with their families through letters or personal visits.

Hijras are organized into a nationwide set of "houses," or subgroups. There are seven named subgroups, and each one has a guru, or leader. The houses are all ranked equally, except that one subgroup has special functions in mediating disputes between the houses; no hijra conflicts are ever brought to the police or courts. At the formal initiation in Bombay, a ritual takes place at which the initiate is given a new, female name, vows to obey the guru and the rules of the hijra community, and is presented with some gifts and a dhol, or drum, which is sacred to the hijras and is always carried when they perform. The guru writes the initiate's name in a book, and the initiate pays the guru a small sum as an initiation fee. Through this relationship, a lifelong bond of reciprocity is established in which the guru is committed to helping the initiated (called chela, or "disciple"), and the chela is committed to being loyal and obedient to the guru. The guru sends the chela gifts from time to time; in return,

Four hijras who live in the same house and work together. Notice their feminine attire, jewelry, hairdos, and postures. (Serena Nanda)

the chela may send the guru money or gifts as well.

The term *guru* is generally used for all elders in the community, and the only status distinction the hijras maintain is a respect for seniority. There are no religious, caste, or class distinctions that divide their community, though there are individual differences in talent and material wealth. Through other rituals, one hijra may take another as her "daughter," and the daughters of the same "mother" count themselves as "sisters." Through fictive kinship terminology, similar to that used in the larger Indian culture,

female kinship terms are used to relate themselves to other hijras as "grandmother" (on the mother's side), or "aunt" (mother's sister). In institutionalizing these fictive kinship relations, the participants exchange money, clothes, small pieces of jewelry, and sweets and receive similar gifts from others present at the ceremony. This constant reciprocity in social relations, expressed in the exchange of small gifts, cash, and service, is modeled on similar relationships that are so central in the larger Indian society. The widespread network of fictive kin also means (continued on next page)

Two hiras, Kokila and Rehka, tie bells to their ankles in preparation for a dance. Notice that both wear bangles, worn by all women in India who are not widows, and Rehka (right) wears a toe ring, a sign of marriage. (Serena Nanda)

that a hijra can enjoy hospitality in many cities throughout India. Hijras are very mobile, traveling as they wish from city to city and staying weeks or months at a time. Like other Indians, they pride themselves on their hospitality.

In larger cities, a hijra commune may contain forty people, though five to ten members is more typical. One of the most important attractions the community of hijras offers is that an aging hijra can always find security—either a place to stay or a daily chore that can help her earn a little money—among members of the cult.

The primary traditional occupation of hijras is singing and dancing. When a marriage takes place, the hijras find out about it and show up at the wedding or at the home of the groom and sing amusing songs that mock the groom and his family. They are given money for this by the wedding party. When a male child—and, these days, a female child—is born, the hijras sing and dance, imitating the different stages of pregnancy and blessing the baby with the power of the goddess. They collect a fixed amount of money and goods for this performance from the household head, as well as small amounts of cash from the onlookers invited for the occasion. When they hear of a house where a marriage or birth is to take place, they put their special sign on the door, and no other hijra group can perform there. Occasionally, hijras also get parts singing and dancing in films.

Another well-known and public occupation of hijras is asking for alms on the streets, either of passersby or, more commonly, shops. They go in a small group, with one hijra playing the drum, and simply stop in front of a shop, make their traditional and unique handclap as a way of announcing themselves, and wait to receive some money. If a person does not give, they may make insulting or abusive remarks. This is not considered a particularly pleasant way to make a living, as it involves tireless walking, exposing oneself to public ridicule, and possible police harassment. But, since it takes no special talent, one can always do it if money is short and no other means of earning an income is at hand. Prostitution is another important source of income, though it is looked down upon within the community. In Bombay, hijras who are prostitutes cannot live with those who sing and dance. When an initiate joins the community, she is asked how she wishes to earn a living; if she wants to do prostitution, she must find her own quarters, but if she wants to do traditional work and vows not to have relations with a man, she lives with those who do that work. Hijras also do other kinds of jobs, working as cooks and household servants, construction workers, fortune tellers, bathhouse operators. One of the common complaints that the hijra national organization makes to the Indian government is that hijras cannot get decent jobs and are therefore forced to earn their living in illegal or deviant ways.

In spite of the general disapproval of both eunuchism and homosexuality in both ancient and modern India, the hijra role does represent a real institutionalization of an "in-between" gender category. This contrasts with the situation in Western cultures, where only two gender categories are culturally recognized. In India, this role has expanded into a subculture that, though considered deviant, is nevertheless tolerated. Furthermore, hijras, like similar people in other, non-Western cultures, are accorded a measure of respect for their supernatural powers, which are believed to be derived from their combining of male and female qualities. As is the case with all deviant subcultures, many of the aspects of hijra "culture" reflect those of the larger society. Economically, the adaptive strategies of the hijras lead them into work roles that are either menial or despised by others but that nevertheless enable them to survive. As one of their strategies, they live in communes and share income, household chores, and food and other resources. This strategy of sharing and reciprocity has been noted as significant in other poor, marginal communities in complex societies, as well as being characteristic of egalitarian societies. By acting collectively at the national level, hijras have attempted to educate the public about their condition, to win sympathy from the government for houses and jobs, and to be considered and treated as women. Although on the surface the hijras appear to be a bizarre and deviant subculture, they are nevertheless a recognized part of Indian society and are influenced by its culture, which they have molded to suit their own needs.

Amish, who number about 60,000 people and live mainly as farmers in Pennsylvania, Ohio, and Indiana.

Amish religious beliefs require a simple life in a church community away from other influences. Their culture emphasizes learning through doing, a life of "goodness," the welfare of the community rather than individual competition, and separation from contemporary society. The Amish reject television, telephones, automobiles, radios, and other modern conveniences. Their distinctive dress and speech and their habits of manual work are symbolic of their cultural separateness and also contribute to the integration of the community. As an extension of their religious beliefs, the Amish reject formal education beyond elementary schooling. They believe that it would alienate their children from Amish culture and remove them from the community at a time when they should be taking up important responsibilities.

The refusal to send their children for higher education has brought the Amish into conflict with the larger society. In the 1960s a school district administrator for the Wisconsin public schools brought suit against several Amish parents for failing to obey the compulsory school attendance law, which requires children to attend public or private school until the age of 16. This case was later brought up to the Supreme Court of the United States (*Wisconsin* v. *Yoder* 1972). John Hostetler, an anthropologist who is an expert on Amish culture, testified for the defense. He held that formal higher education was not only in conflict with Amish religious beliefs but would also have negative effects on the integration of Amish culture and society. Impressed with Hostetler's argument, the Supreme Court decided that the school attendance law did interfere with the free exercise of religion in this case. Although the Amish were successful in this instance, it is only by constant efforts to isolate themselves from the larger society that they have been able to maintain their distinctive way of life.

The degree to which subcultural variation is allowed to flourish differs from society to society and depends to some degree on the values and behavior patterns of the subculture. The success of the Amish in preserving their culture is due partly to the fact that many of their values—thrift, hard work, honesty, and the importance of family and community life— are also values in the larger culture. They are also a nonviolent people who rarely come into conflict with the law. When subcultural values and customs are in opposition to those of the dominant culture, they may be suppressed, as was the case with polygyny (one man having more than one wife) among the Mormon community in the United States.

Individual Variation and Culture

Anthropology, because of its focus on what is typical of human groups, often leaves us with the impression that there is little or no choice or individual variation from cultural norms. Although it is true that culture affects every aspect of an individual's life, every culture allows some variation in behavior. As you participate in your anthropology class, you may be sitting with your legs crossed, your elbows on the table, your head in your hands, or your chair tilted back. Your eyes may be focused on the teacher or on some of the other students. You may even have your eyes closed occasionally, a permissible alternative to keeping your eyes open because it can give the appearance of deep thought rather than sleep. You may hold a pencil in your hand, take notes, or even doodle. All these behavioral variations are within the culturally acceptable limits for participation in an American college classroom. It is less likely that you will be knitting, taking apart your watch, or reading a newspaper. And it is completely unlikely that you will be standing on your chair, with your back to the teacher, whistling "I'm a Yankee Doodle Dandy."

In every culture, there is some scope for individual variation, creativity, and choice, although there are more options available in some cultures that are technologically complex than in smaller, more homogeneous cultures. Some cultures are also more permissive than others in the amount of variation they allow. But however "loose" the cultural pattern, every culture puts limits on what it considers acceptable in any particular situation. Most people act within these limits without even thinking about it. It is only when the limits are overstepped that we become aware of them. We know limits have been reached when behavior calls forth various expressions of disapproval from others. These sanctions may range from mild ones, such as ridicule, to more serious ones, such as avoidance, physical punishment, banishment, or even death.

Generally, anthropologists have conveyed the mistaken impression that all people, especially in small, non-Western societies, not only share a common culture—that is, act in the same way in the same situation—but also attach the same meanings to their acts. Because of this anthropological emphasis on norms, not enough attention has been given to the different ways in which people perceive the norms and the different subjective meanings the norms have for different individuals. A number of anthropologists have addressed this issue, most significantly those interested in life histories or in what has recently been called "person centered ethnography" (Langness and Frank 1981). The life history is a collaborative effort between the anthropologist and a person who tells his or her life story. Life histories can answer questions about the meaning culture has for individuals, the relationship of personality to cultural norms, deviance or individual differences, and the role of individuals in bringing about and incorporating cultural change.

CULTURE AS REAL AND IDEAL

Anthropologists have most often been concerned with culture as a system of **ideal norms.** Ideal norms are the ideas a society has about what *ought* to be done and the ways in which behavior *ought* to be carried out. A simple example of an ideal norm is the expectation in the United States that, when two adult males are introduced to each other, they will shake hands.

Behavioral norms are what people actually do. These are only sometimes consistent with ideal norms. Thus, most men in the United States probably do shake hands when they are introduced. Other behavioral norms are not consistent with ideal norms. The first Kinsey report (1948) indicated that in such areas as extramarital sex and homosexual experience, there was a considerable gap between what people did and the ideal norms.

Deviance from ideal norms does not happen only in heterogeneous societies. In describing the sexual behavior of the Trobriand Islanders, Malinowski (1929:503) wrote:

From the statements of informants, you will arrive at a conclusion that marriage and sexual intercourse within the clan are neither allowed nor ever practiced and that they do not even constitute a serious temptation to the native. . . . It would be most improper and censured by an indignant public opinion. If discovered [a guilty couple] would commit suicide by jumping from a coconut palm.

Clan incest among the Trobrianders is not punished simply by public censure. There is

The ideal norms of the Cheyenne—bravery, wisdom, and generosity—were represented by their chiefs. Shown here is one Cheyenne chief, Brave Bear. (Courtesy of American Museum of Natural History)

a supernatural punishment as well, a disease in which the belly of the victim begins to swell, the skin becomes white and breaks out in sores, and the person fades away with a wasting sickness. Several people with this disease were pointed out to Malinowski. After questioning his informants, however, Malinowski discovered that cases of clan incest do occur. Furthermore, it was common knowledge that a particular magical ritual performed over a wild ginger root wrapped up in leaves would neutralize the supernatural punishment for this kind of behavior.

Two points emerge from Malinowski's findings. The first is that an understanding of a society cannot be based solely on informants' statements about ideal cultural norms. Malinowski argues that people in all societies are embarrassed to admit that behavior deviates from the ideal. In order to maintain their prestige, they will not easily disclose evidence of nonconformity. Second, this example illustrates that a body of behavioral norms develops as a way of evading the ideal norms. "Everyone knows" about the magic ritual to evade the supernatural sanctions for incest in the Trobriand Islands. Every society is apparently willing to pretend ignorance of certain kinds of deviance. But ideal norms do exert pressure on behavior, even when they are not formally and legally expressed. Culture, as a system of ideal norms, meanings, and expectations, does limit human behavior both by channeling it in culturally approved directions and by punishing known violations.

The Relationship between Ideal and Behavioral Norms

Both ideal and behavioral norms change. Ideal norms may change before behavioral ones do. Among the upper-middle-class Hindus living in large cities in India, for example, the ideal of social equality among all classes of society is widely accepted. This ideal is considerably in advance of actual behavior, which only rarely involves social interaction between individuals of the highest and lowest castes on a basis of equality. In other cases, a change in ideal norms follows a change in behavioral norms. The contemporary American cultural ideal of small families followed the actual limiting of the number of children by parents who wanted to move up the social ladder.

Ideal norms themselves may be contradictory in a particular society, so that people can justify their behavior in terms of more than one norm. In describing the political system among the Soga of Uganda, Lloyd Fallers (1955) shows the conflict of two opposing ideal norms. In traditional Soga society, political institutions emphasized personal rights and obligations. People owed loyalty to their own relatives, patrons, and local rulers. The administrative staff of the state was recruited through kinship and maintained through per-

sonal loyalty. With the coming of the British and the rise of a civil service bureaucracy, an opposing value system came into being. A bureaucracy should ideally treat everyone alike without regard to status or personal relationships. Recruitment to a bureaucracy is based on merit. Fallers emphasizes that both these ideal norms are now institutionalized and have legitimacy in Soga society. This results in many conflicts, particularly for chiefs, who are sometimes pulled in the direction of one of the norms and sometimes in the direction of the other.

Another way of explaining the relationship between ideal norms and real behavior is through the concept of anticipated behavior. Anticipations of deviance from the ideal come to be culturally standardized and help explain behavior patterns that seem contradictory and self-defeating. Elliot Liebow uses this concept to explain the failures in marital relationships among some poor black ghetto dwellers (1967). These men and women, he says, do believe in the ideal of a permanent, monogamous relationship. They get married with the same high hopes as everyone else in our culture. The women, however, based on their knowledge of the difficulty of life in the ghetto and the precariousness of jobs, *anticipate* that their husbands will not in fact be able to take care of them and their children. Therefore, at the first sign of difficulty, they reject their mates in ways that make it difficult for the relationship to continue.

Ideal norms may also be unclear. This allows for a wide range of legitimate behaviors. In the United States, for example, an ideal norm is that a woman should be "a good mother" to her child. But this takes in a wide range of behavior, so patterns of mothering run from almost complete permissiveness to harsh discipline, and all are justified as being "for the good of the child."

Because culture is largely viewed as a limit on action, an individual's manipulation of the culture for personal ends has, until recently, been a neglected topic in cultural anthropology. All the ways in which behavioral norms do not mesh with ideal norms actually give a culture flexibility. They allow people to adjust behavior to changing circumstances. An example of manipulation of cultural norms for personal ends can be seen among upper-middle-class women in India. One important Indian ideal is that women should be in the home and not "moving about" with their friends. Another cultural ideal is that women should spend a lot of time in religious activities. Modern Indian women use the second ideal to get around the first. By forming clubs whose activities are religious, they have an excuse to get out of the house that their elders cannot object to too strongly.

CULTURAL INTEGRATION

A culture is not simply a list of norms, values, activities, and objects. Cultural elements are interrelated to form a system. Although anthropological analysis may require that parts of a culture be studied separately, the idea of culture as "a complex whole," or system, is basic. One way of looking at **cultural integration** is in terms of the consistency of cultural themes or values. Most anthropologists agree that there is a tendency for a culture to be dominated by a particular value system or ideology, although most also agree that no culture achieves complete integration. Cultures may have more than one dominant theme (ethos), and sometimes these themes may be in conflict. According to Ruth Benedict, for example, the culture of the Plains Indians of North America was dominated by the theme of extravagant sensation seeking and individualism. This theme took the form of fasting and self-torture to seek supernatural visions through which a warrior acquired the power necessary to triumph. Other ethnographers have pointed out, however, that there was a second theme in Plains culture, that of the "considerate peace chief" (Hoebel 1960). This theme emphasized gentleness, generosity, reasonableness, and wisdom and called for self-

Fourth of July parades are an attempt to recapture an earlier era of United States history when ideals and dominant values appeared less ambiguous than they do today. (Ravinder Nanda)

restraint and consideration of others. These themes operated in different spheres of Plains life and provided a balance in the culture. It is clear that cultures can and do function with some disharmony and lack of integration, but this may be adaptive. A culture needs flexibility to respond to changes in the physical and social environment. On the other hand, too great a lack of integration in culture may impose intolerable stress on the individual.

The concept of cultural integration raises some interesting questions about American culture. Do we in fact have one theme that characterizes our culture? Or do different activities have different, even contradictory, themes? Some anthropologists have pointed out the contradiction between our economic life, in which the dominant theme is competition and the advance of the individual at the expense of others, and our family life, in which the dominant theme would seem to be cooperation for the good of the *total* group. On the other hand, some anthropologists believe that all of American culture, and especially the family, is characterized by themes of decep-

Cultural Integration and Cultural Change

Because culture is a system, change in one aspect of culture will lead to change in other aspects, whether the initial change was introduced from within the society itself or through borrowing from another culture. Some cultures can handle more change from the outside than others. If a culture is tightly integrated, the introduction of even a seemingly small change can lead to an almost total breakdown. One example of this process involved the Yir Yoront of Australia.*

The Yir Yoront were an aboriginal hunting and fishing people who had not learned the use of metal. They had used stone axes until the introduction of steel axes by Western missionaries. The stone axes had been used in a variety of ways: for gathering firewood, making tools and weapons, gathering wild honey, and fashioning objects for religious purposes. The ax handles were made by men, and all normal men were competent to produce their own, since it was not

*Lauriston Sharp, "Steel Axes for Stone Age Australians," in Edward H. Spicer, ed., *Human Problems in Technological Change.* New York: Russell Sage Foundation, 1952.

a difficult or complex task. The heads were obtained by trade through long-established relations with trading partners in other tribes. Although women and children used axes in a variety of tasks, the ax "belonged" to the man who made it, and a man's wife and children had to ask his permission to use it and had to return it quickly. A man had to ask permission to borrow an ax from an elder kinsman. Thus, the use of the stone ax helped define status relations among various members of the tribe. Women borrowed from men, the young borrowed from their elders. The missionaries, on the other hand, distributed the steel axes to younger men, women, and even children who won their favor. One significant result of this was the undermining of the status hierarchy of Yir Yoront society, as expressed in the subordination of women to men and younger people to older ones. Another result was the loss of interest in trading ax heads. Traditional trading relationships, which were important integrating mechanisms for Australian tribal society, also broke down, and the festivities and communal visiting that accompanied trading lost value. The final result of the introduction of the steel

tion, individual competition, and the desire to control others in our own self-interest (Henry 1963). The opposition of values—equality and inequality, democracy and hierarchy, individualism and conformity—seems to appear as a theme in much of United States social, political, and economic history. Each new generation swings from an emphasis on one of these value opposites to the other.

CULTURE AS AN ADAPTIVE SYSTEM

Adaptation is the way living populations relate to the environment so that they can survive

and reproduce. Culture is the major way in which human populations adapt. The most directly adaptive aspect of culture is the way in which the energy potential of the environment is transformed into food.

Every culture has a basic food-getting strategy and a characteristic pattern of distributing food to members of the society. The extent to which food-getting patterns are correlated with other aspects of the system is not agreed upon by anthropologists, although many would say that there is at least a tendency for such correlation: "Similar technologies applied to similar environments tend to produce similar arrangements of labor in production and dis-

ax was the almost total disintegration of Yir Yoront culture.

This is the shape the Yir Yoront society was in when Sharp wrote about it in the 1930s. But the story is not ended here. A more recent visit, in 1961, by anthropologists Donald and Patricia Crim, showed that the Yir Yoront had not in fact succumbed to the dire predictions outlined above. Instead, some of the Yir Yoront were able to adapt to changed circumstances by a combination of resources made up of some of their own traditional customs and some newly introduced elements of white Australian culture. During World War II, many Yir Yoront moved to mission stations, a seemingly significant departure from their previous nomadic way of life. However, the change was not as drastic as it might appear. Many families settled at the mission for a season, or several years, and then returned again to the bush. This pattern was not totally unlike their traditional pattern of moving about during the dry season and camping in one place during the wet season. The men, who were often employed as stockmen at the mission cattle camp or at nearby cattle stations, traveled away from the mission during the dry season and moved back during the wet season when they took on employment in carpentry, construction, gardening, maintenance of the mission, waste removal, and work in the mission store. A culture emerged which involved new patterns of work, of consumption, and of new authority patterns. Most interesting was the revival of a musical tradition which included traditional elements, previously suppressed by the missionaries, and newer elements, diffused from the West and from other Pacific islands. Hillbilly music, one of the new elements in this emerging pattern, was diffused by the younger Yir Yoront who worked on cattle stations and who saw Western movies and listened to the radio. The hillbilly guitar became a central symbol of Yir Yoront adaptation. The Crims found that the demoralization and personal despair which Sharp had documented thirty years ago had greatly diminished, and that the Yir Yoront had seemed to come to terms with white culture. He sensed a feeling on their part that they had succeeded, despite setbacks, in finding some place, however marginal, in the national culture of Australia. Crim's study suggests that although initial culture contacts may be disastrous for highly integrated societies, such societies may indeed be more flexible than was formerly thought, and can indeed adapt creatively to even drastically changed circumstances. The Yir Yoront are a good example of how adaptive culture is, and how traditional and innovative culture patterns can be used to cope with changing circumstances.

tribution, and ... these in turn call forth similar kinds of social groupings, which justify and coordinate their activities by means of similar systems of values and beliefs" (Harris, 1968:4). For example, the size of the effective social unit responds to the availability of food. Generally, agricultural populations have a higher density of population than hunters and gatherers. Since larger populations require more coordination of labor, agricultural societies tend to have more complex sociopolitical systems than foragers.

The basic assumption of this perspective is that the different food-getting patterns—hunting and gathering (foraging), pastoralism, horticulture, agriculture, and industrialization— make different demands on human beings and lead to the development of different family structures, political structures, religious beliefs and practices, and even patterns of personality (Cohen 1971).

The view that culture is an adaptive system does not necessarily mean that every aspect of the system is adaptive. Some parts of a culture may be neutral; that is, they may contribute little or nothing to survival. Some parts may also be maladaptive, although it would seem that ultimately a maladaptive trait would be modified or die out altogether. Nor does the view of culture as an adaptive system mean that every system is the most efficient design

An innovation is a variation on an established cultural practice. Pictured are storage jars from Morocco, made in the traditional, centuries-old shape but using worn-out rubber tires instead of clay. (Joan Gregg)

for utilizing its environment. Existing sociocultural systems represent one possible solution out of a number of alternatives that might have been equally adaptive in the same environment. Throughout the text, there will be many references to the adaptive value of cultural patterns that seem, upon first observation, to be useless or even maladaptive. An example is the taboo among Hindus against eating beef, which was discussed in Chapter 3.

CULTURE CHANGES

The view of culture as an adaptive system emphasizes stability rather than change. The technologically simpler societies traditionally studied by anthropologists have generally, it is true, been relatively stable. Their designs for living permitted relatively satisfactory adaptations to the sociophysical environment; changes occurred very slowly until the period of contact with the West. Archeologists have been able to document cultural patterns that exhibit stability over thousands of years both in their broad outlines and in some of their details.

And yet we know that all cultures do change in response to the changing requirements of the environment. Some of the changes in a culture are not adaptive, and the archeological record is full of cultures that collapsed and disappeared. Still other kinds of changes lead sociocultural systems into more efficient stages of energy transformation and greater complexity. These major changes the anthropologist calls evolutionary changes. Regardless of whether we look at change with an evolutionary or a historical perspective, we know that, because culture is a system, change in one aspect will lead to change in other aspects. In Chapter 16, we will look at some of the ways in which cultures change as they come into contact with the modern industrialized nations of the West. Here we will focus on the two major processes by which all cultures change, innovation and diffusion.

Innovation

An **innovation** is a variation of an existing cultural pattern that is then accepted or learned by other members of the society. Most innovations are slight modifications of already existing habits of thought and action. Although each individual innovation may be slight, however, the accumulated effects may be great over the long run. An innovation can be the result of deliberate experimentation, or it can come about by accident.

*Useful innovations are accepted by tribal peoples in ways consistent with
their culture. Here Minmara, a member of the Ngatatjara aboriginal group
of Australia, trims a spear using an old Landrover spring. (Courtesy
American Museum of Natural History)*

An innovation means a slight modification of an existing cultural pattern; an **invention** is the combination of existing cultural elements into something altogether new. Although we are likely to think of inventions as primarily technological, invention is not limited to the material aspects of culture. New art forms and new ideas may all be considered inventions. All inventions involve human ingenuity and creativity, but even geniuses are limited in what they can invent by the nature and complexity of the existing cultural pattern. Had Einstein been born into a society that had not developed the complex scientific understandings of Western civilization, he could never have "invented" the theory of relativity. Each genius in a culture builds on what has gone before and moves in the direction of expanding an existing tradition. Even Beethoven, Bach, and Mozart did not compose with the musical scales of India.

Because inventions depend on the recombination of previously existing cultural elements, the more elements are already present in a culture, the more likely it is to produce even more inventions. This partly explains why change occurs much faster in technologically complex societies than in technologically simpler ones. This cumulative effect of change also applies to human culture as a whole. It took several million years for humans to change from hunters and gatherers to agricultural produc-

One Hundred Percent American*

There can be no question about the average American's Americanism or his desire to preserve this precious heritage at all costs. Nevertheless, some insidious foreign ideas have already wormed their way into his civilization without his realizing what was going on. Thus dawn finds the unsuspecting patriot garbed in pajamas, a garment of East Indian origin; and lying in a bed built on a pattern which originated in either Persia or Asia Minor. He is muffled to the ears in un-American materials: cotton, first domesticated in India; linen, domesticated in the Near East; wool from an animal native to Asia Minor; or silk whose uses were first discovered by the Chinese. All these substances have been transformed into cloth by methods invented in Southwestern Asia. If the weather is cold enough he may even be sleeping under an eiderdown quilt invented in Scandinavia.

On awakening he glances at the clock, a medieval European invention, uses one potent Latin word in abbreviated form, rises in haste, and goes to the bathroom. Here, if he stops to think about it, he must feel himself in the presence of a great American institution; he will have heard stories of both the quality and frequency of foreign plumbing and will know that in no other country does the average man perform his ablutions in the

*Ralph Linton, "One Hundred Per-Cent American," *The American Mercury*, vol. 40 (1937), pp. 427–429. Reprinted by permission of *The American Mercury*, Box 1306, Torrance, California.

midst of such splendor. But the insidious foreign influence pursues him even here. Glass was invented by the ancient Egyptians, the use of glazed tiles for floors and walls in the Near East, porcelain in China, and the art of enameling on metal by Mediterranean artisans of the Bronze Age. Even his bathtub and toilet are but slightly modified copies of Roman originals. The only purely American contribution to the ensemble is the steam radiator, against which our patriot very briefly and unintentionally places his posterior.

In this bathroom the American washes with soap invented by the ancient Gauls. Next he cleans his teeth, a subversive European practice which did not invade America until the latter part of the eighteenth century. He then shaves, a masochistic rite first developed by the heathen priests of ancient Egypt and Sumer. The process is made less of a penance by the fact that his razor is of steel, an iron-carbon alloy discovered in either India or Turkestan. Lastly, he dries himself on a Turkish towel.

Returning to the bedroom, the unconscious victim of un-American practices removes his clothes from a chair, invented in the Near East, and proceeds to dress. He puts on close-fitting tailored garments whose form derives from the skin clothing of the ancient nomads of the Asiatic steppes and fastens them with buttons whose prototypes appeared in Europe at the close of the Stone Age. This costume is appropriate enough for outdoor exercise in a cold climate, but is quite

ers. After the first domestication of plants and animals about 10,000 or 12,000 years ago, it took about 5,000 or 6,000 years for writing and cities to be invented. All the other technological knowledge, and the social complexity that came with that knowledge, has been learned in the past few thousand years and involves a rate of change unlike anything known earlier.

Diffusion

As we saw in Chapter 3, anthropologists have always been interested in discovering whether the similarities among different sociocultural systems were due to independent invention or to **diffusion,** the borrowing of cultural elements. Many anthropologists would agree that

unsuited to American summers, steam-heated houses, and Pullmans. Nevertheless, foreign ideas and habits hold the unfortunate man in thrall even when common sense tells him that the authentically American costume of gee string and moccasins would be far more comfortable. He puts on his feet stiff coverings made from hide prepared by a process invented in ancient Egypt and cut to a pattern which can be traced back to ancient Greece, and makes sure that they are properly polished, also a Greek idea. Lastly, he ties about his neck a strip of bright-colored cloth which is a vestigial survival of the shoulder shawls worn by seventeenth-century Croats. He gives himself a final appraisal in the mirror, an old Mediterranean invention, and goes downstairs to breakfast.

Here a whole new series of foreign things confronts him. His food and drink are placed before him in pottery vessels, the proper name of which—china—is sufficient evidence of their origin. His fork is a medieval Italian invention and his spoon a copy of a Roman original. He will usually begin the meal with coffee, an Abyssinian plant first discovered by the Arabs. The American is quite likely to need it to dispel the morning-after effects of overindulgence in fermented drinks, invented in the Near East; or distilled ones, invented by the alchemists of medieval Europe. Whereas the Arabs took their coffee straight, he will probably sweeten it with sugar, discovered in India; and dilute it with cream, both the domestication of cattle and the technique of milking having originated in Asia Minor.

If our patriot is old-fashioned enough to adhere to the so-called American breakfast, his coffee will be accompanied by an orange, domesticated in the Mediterranean region, a cantaloupe domesticated in Persia, or grapes domesticated in Asia Minor. He will follow this with a bowl of cereal made from grain domesticated in the Near East and prepared by methods also invented there. From this he will go on to waffles, a Scandinavian invention, with plenty of butter, originally a Near-Eastern cosmetic. As a side dish he may have the egg of a bird domesticated in Southeastern Asia or strips of the flesh of an animal domesticated in the same region, which has been salted and smoked by a process invented in Northern Europe.

Breakfast over, he places upon his head a molded piece of felt, invented by the nomads of Eastern Asia, and, if it looks like rain, puts on outer shoes of rubber, discovered by the ancient Mexicans, and takes an umbrella, invented in India. He then sprints for his train—the train, not sprinting, being an English invention. At the station he pauses for a moment to buy a newspaper, paying for it with coins invented in ancient Lydia. Once on board he settles back to inhale the fumes of a cigarette invented in Mexico, or a cigar invented in Brazil. Meanwhile, he reads the news of the day, imprinted in characters invented by the ancient Semites by a process invented in Germany upon a material invented in China. As he scans the latest editorial pointing out the dire results to our institutions of accepting foreign ideas, he will not fail to thank a Hebrew God in an Indo-European language that he is a one hundred percent (decimal system invented by the Greeks) American (from Americus Vespucci, Italian ographer).

genuine independent invention accounts for only a small percentage of cultural change. The growth and development of human culture are primarily accounted for by the spread of the most important inventions from one or perhaps two centers of origin. Because diffusion is so important in cultural change, the rate of change is much slower in societies that are geographically isolated. Diffusion, however, does not automatically result from contact. Borrowing takes place only if the borrowed element proves rewarding in some way. Furthermore, once accepted, a borrowed element may undergo many changes as it is worked into the existing cultural pattern.

Cultures change, but some cultures, because of their central location, change faster than others. Twenty-five hundred years of culture change is shown in this view of Athens. (Ravinder Nanda)

Anthropological Approaches to Culture Change

Anthropologists do not always agree on how to approach the study of culture change. In the historical approach, the focus is on the changes that occur in a society as a result of a particular historical event—for example, the coming of the European missionaries to the Yir Yaront territory and the introduction of the steel ax. The evolutionary approach looks for regularities in culture change that may indicate laws underlying the process or processes of cultural development. In Chapter 3, we discussed some evolutionary approaches to culture change.

Nor do anthropologists agree on what is the "prime mover" in cultural change. Does change originate in values and ideology or in the material conditions of life, particularly subsistence economy and technology? Changes in technology, as we have just seen, have a major impact on the transformation of the social and cultural aspects of human life. Values and ideology can also be a source of changes in technology if people are motivated by new ways of thinking to find new ways of relating to the environment. Between the extreme views is a middle ground that holds that no single factor is of overriding importance in determining the organization and content of a given sociocultural system. In this view, cultural change is a result of a cumulative feedback relationship between ecological stimuli, ideology, technology, and social relationships.

SUMMARY

1. Culture is learned; that is, it is transmitted socially, not genetically. The importance of learning in human adaptation is related to the long dependency of the human infant and the group life of our species.

2. Culture is shared behavior, but not all aspects of culture are shared equally within a society. Some are shared by all adults, and others are the specialties of certain groups or social categories. In every culture, a range of individual variation is permitted in any particular situation.

3. A subculture is a cultural pattern significantly different from that of the surrounding culture. The Amish are an example of a subculture in the United States.

4. Culture consists of both ideal and behavioral norms. Ideal norms are what people think they ought to do; behavioral norms are what people actually do. Both ideal and behavioral norms are patterned by culture.

5. The relation between ideal and behavioral norms is complex. In some cases, they correspond; in other cases, the behavioral norms deviate from the ideal. Sometimes behavioral norms change, and this leads to a change in ideal norms. Sometimes ideal norms change first, leading to a change in behavioral norms.

6. Ambiguity, or even conflict, between ideal norms gives a culture flexibility; individuals can manipulate ideal norms for their own personal ends. But conflict between ideal norms can also put stress on the individual.

7. Culture is adaptive. In the general sense, this means that socially transmitted knowledge is the major adaptive mechanism of the human species. In the specific sense, it means that each culture is a design for living that enables a group of people to survive and reproduce in a particular environment.

8. Culture tends to be integrated. The basic social institutions of a society tend to fit together, and the values underlying cultural patterns tend to be consistent. The integration of culture is a tendency; no culture is perfectly integrated.

9. Culture exhibits both stability and change. Because culture is a system, a change in one part of the culture leads to change and adjustment in other parts. The rate of change is dif-ferent in different societies; it depends partly on geographical factors, level of technology, and cultural values regarding change.

10. Two important processes in cultural change are innovation and diffusion.

11. Diffusion is not an automatic process, and borrowed traits are integrated into existing cultural patterns. They are not adopted as is.

12. Anthropologists do not agree on whether ideology or technology is the more important element in change. A middle view holds that culture change is due to a complex interaction among the environment, ideology, and technology, acting so that changes in one area feed back and cause changes in the others.

SUGGESTED READINGS

Freeman, James M.
  1979   *Untouchable: An Indian Life History.* Stanford, Calif.: Stanford University Press. An outstandingly readable and complete life history of an adult male belonging to an untouchable caste in India. An introductory chapter on methodology and a concluding chapter on analysis of life histories are both useful additions to the biographical data that make up the major part of the book.

Langness, L. L. and Frank, Gelya
  1981   *Lives: An Anthropological Approach to Biography.* Novato, Calif.: Chandler and Sharp. A highly useful book for anyone who wants to know about the challenges and problems of doing a life history.

Liebow, Elliot
  1967   *Tally's Corner.* Boston: Little, Brown. An ethnography of Negro street-corner men that highlights the contradictions between ideal and behavioral norms in American society.

Sahlins, Marshall D. and Service, Elman R.
  1973   *Evolution and Culture.* Ann Arbor: University of Michigan Press. A short but important statement of general and specific cultural evolutionary theory.

Spradley, James P. and Rynkiewich, Michael A.
  1975   *The Nacirema.* Boston: Little, Brown. A book of readings on American culture.

THE CULTURAL CONTEXT OF HUMAN BEHAVIOR

▶ Is there an objective reality, or are there only multiple realities?

▶ How does culture pattern the way we "see" the world?

▶ What is the relationship of intelligence to culture?

▶ What kinds of behaviors come "naturally" to humans?

I have on my table a violin string. It is free. I twist one end of it and it responds. It is free. But it is not free to do what a violin string is supposed to do—to produce music. So I take it, fix it in my violin and tighten it until it is taut. Only then is it free to be a violin string.

Sir Rabindranath Tagore

Culture is necessary for the survival and existence of human beings as human beings. Practically everything humans perceive, know, think, value, feel, and do is learned through participation in a socio-cultural system. The few well-documented cases on record of children relatively isolated from society in the early years of life bear out this statement.

One of these cases, that of the "wild boy of Aveyron" (Itard 1962) is of exceptional interest. In 1799, a boy of about twelve was captured in a forest in Aveyron, France. He was brought to Paris, where he attracted huge crowds who expected to see the "noble savage" of the romantic eighteenth-century philosophical vision. Instead, they found a boy whose

eyes were unsteady, expressionless, wandering vaguely from one object to another ... so little trained by the sense of touch, they could never distinguish an object in relief from one in a picture. His ... hearing was insensible to the loudest noises and to ... music. His voice was reduced to a state of complete muteness and only a uniform gutteral sound escaped him ... he was equally indifferent to the odor or perfume and to the fetid exhalation of the dirt with which his bed was filled ... [his] touch was restricted to the *mechanical grasping of an object . . . [he had a] tendency to trot and gallop . . . [and] an obstinate habit of smelling at anything given to him . . . he chewed like a rodent with a sudden action of the incisors . . . [and] showed no sensitivity to cold or heat and could seize hot coals from the fire without flinching or lay half naked upon the wet ground for hours in the wintertime. . . . He was incapable of attention and spent his time apathetically rocking himself backwards and forwards like the animals in the zoo.* *

This description of the "wild boy of Aveyron" is provided by Jean-Marc-Gaspard Itard, a young psychologist who undertook the education of the boy, whom he called Victor. He believed Victor's apparent subnormality was not due to incurable mental disease or idiocy, but to the lack of participation in normal human society. Itard's account of Victor's education makes fascinating reading. Beyond that, it emphasizes that the human potential can be realized only within the structure of human culture and through growing up in close contact with other human beings. Without the constraints imposed by a specific culture, we are not more free, but rather totally unfree, in that none of our human qualities and abilities can develop.

CULTURAL PATTERNING OF "REALITY"

The ways in which human beings perceive both the physical and social environment, what they believe to be true about the environment, and how they organize their responses to it are all patterned by culture. Culture is a "codification of reality," a system of meaning that transforms physical reality, what is *there*, into experienced reality. Dorothy Lee (1959), an anthropologist interested in the different ways peoples

*Jean-Marc-Gaspard Itard, *The Wild Boy of Aveyron.* Translated by George and Muriel Humphrey. © 1962, Prentice-Hall, Inc., Englewood Cliffs, New Jersey. Reprinted by permission of the publisher.

see themselves and their environments, describes her perception of reality as she looks out the window of her house: "I see trees, some of which I like to be there, and some of which I intend to cut down to keep them from encroaching further upon the small clearing I made for my house" (p. 1). She then describes the perception of the Dakota Black Elk Indian, who "saw trees as having rights to the land, equal to his own . . . standing peoples, in whom the winged ones built their lodges and reared their families" (p. 1).

According to Lee, the conceptual frameworks of different cultures provide different ways of perceiving the same physical reality. She believes that all culturally patterned views of reality may contain a different facet of the same truth. These culturally different conceptions of reality also shape our perception of the relationship we have with the natural environment. Thus, continues Lee "the breaking of the soil in the agricultural process may be an act of violence, of personal aggression, of mastery, of exploitation, of self-fulfillment; or it may be an act of tender fostering, of involvement in the processes of the earth, of helping the land to bring forth in its due time; it may be an act of worship, and the field an altar" (p. 1). The individual may be seen as the center, the mover and master of nature, as in Western culture. Or the person may be seen as in harmony with nature, simply actualizing the potential in both animals and inanimate things, as is true among many native American peoples.

Not only the perceptions of reality but also the ways of proving those perceptions to be "real" are culturally patterned. In many cultures, inner experience can be enough. In Western culture, validation consists of "proof," evidence that can hold up under repeated and objective investigations. The contrasts between these two systems are nicely illustrated in an exchange between Carlos Castaneda, a Western-trained anthropologist, and Don Juan, a "sorcerer," or in his own words, a "man of power," among the Yaqui Indians of northern

Among Zen Buddhists, the inner experiencing of reality is achieved through meditation. (Sheldon Brody)

Mexico. Castaneda has been learning Don Juan's "power," which includes the ability to transform himself into various animals. One day Don Juan says that under his commands, Castaneda will be transformed into a crow. These are Castaneda's words about the experience:

I had no difficulty eliciting the corresponding sensation to each one of his commands. I had the perception of growing bird's legs, which were weak and wobbly at first. I felt a tail coming out of the back of my neck and wings out of my cheekbones. The wings were folded deeply. I felt them coming by degrees. The process was hard but not painful. Then I winked my head down to the size of a crow. But the most astonishing effect was accomplished by my bird's eyes. My bird's sight! When Don Juan directed me to grow a beak, I had an annoying sensation of lack of air. Then something bulged out and created a block in front of me.... I remember I extended my wings and flew. I felt alone, cutting through

the air, painfully moving straight ahead ... the last scene I remembered was three silvery birds.... I liked them. We flew together.*

A few days after this experience, Castaneda asks Don Juan "the unavoidable question: did I really become a crow?" And what we mean in Western culture by "really" is explained in Castaneda's next question: "I mean would anyone seeing me have thought I was an ordinary crow?" (pp. 172–73). Modern science, which is the core of the Western validation of reality, teaches us to distrust our inner experience as a source of knowledge. We frequently label people whose inner experiences seem "real" as abnormal if those experiences do not match our own culturally patterned definitions of reality.

*Carlos Castaneda, *The Teachings of Don Juan: A Yaqui Way of Knowledge.* Berkeley: University of California Press, 1968, pp. 122–124. Reprinted by permission.

Cultural Patterning of Time

In his book *The Silent Language* (1959), the anthropologist Edward Hall presented the theory that perceptions of time and space are different in different cultures, and that these perceptions are culturally patterned. Hall called these dimensions of culture "out of awareness," because most people are not conscious of having learned them. In one sense, of course, many aspects of culture are out of awareness. Perceptions of time and space, however, are among the most ingrained of culturally patterned behaviors.

"Time is human; nature knows only change." Telling time is a strictly human invention. Although all cultures have some system of keeping time, in Western industrial societies time is kept track of in what seems to other peoples an almost ridiculous fashion. We calculate not only the seasons, but the years, months, weeks, days, hours, minutes, seconds, and even thousandths of a second. We are very concerned in the United States with being *on time;* we don't like to *waste time* by having to wait for someone who is late, and we like to *spend time* wisely by keeping busy. All this sounds very natural to a North American. In fact, we think, how could it be otherwise? It is difficult for us not to get irritated by the seeming carelessness about time in other cultures, where individuals frequently turn up an hour or more late for an appointment. But "being late" is at least within our cultural framework. How can we begin to enter the cultural world of the Sioux Indians, where there is no word for "late" or for "waiting"? The fact is, of course, we have not had to enter the Sioux culture, but the Sioux have had to enter ours! It is only when we participate in other cultures, on their terms, that we begin to see the cultural patterning of time.

North Americans have a sense of time that is oriented toward the future—not an infinite future, but the foreseeable future. We look back at the past only to measure how far we have come in the present, and look at the present as a stepping stone to future accomplishments. The Navajo, in contrast, look skeptically at the promise of benefits in even the foreseeable future. The future among Hindus is conceived of in terms of more than a lifetime; it extends infinitely through many births and rebirths.

Cultural Patterning of Space

Like time, space is organized somewhat differently according to different cultural patterns. Because North Americans are taught to perceive and react to the arrangement of objects, we think of space as "empty." The Japanese, however, are trained to give meaning to spaces. Their perception of shape and arrangement of what is to us emptiness appears in many aspects of Japanese life. There seems to be a similarity between culturally patterned perceptions of time and space. Just as North Americans think of time as being "wasted" unless one is doing something, so we think of space as wasted if it is not filled up with objects.

The cultural patterning of space can be seen in the arrangements of urban space in different cultures. In the United States, most of our cities are laid out along a grid, with the axes generally north-south and east-west. Streets are numbered in order and buildings are numbered the same way. This arrangement makes perfect sense to us. A city like Paris, which is laid out with the main streets radiating from centers, can be confusing for those who are used to the grid pattern. We tend to "get lost" easily, because walking a relatively short distance in the wrong direction leads us much farther from where we want to go than is true with a grid system. Hall suggests that the layout of space that is characteristic of French cities is only one aspect of the theme of centralization that permeates French culture. Paris is the center of France, French government and educational systems are highly centralized, and in French offices the most

The design of space reflects the culturally patterned need for personal space, which varies in different societies. (United Nations)

important person has the desk in the middle of the office.

Another aspect of cultural patterning of space has to do with the functions of spaces. In middle-class America, we have particular spaces for particular activities. Any intrusion of one activity into a space it was not designed for is immediately felt to be inappropriate. In Japan, this is not the case. Walls are movable, and rooms are used for one purpose during the day and another in the evening and at night. In India, there is yet another culturally patterned use of space. Space in India, both in public and private places, is connected with concepts of superiority and inferiority. In Indian cities and villages, and even within the home, certain spaces are designated as polluted or inferior because of the activities that take place there and the kinds of people who use them.

Spaces are segregated so that high caste and low caste, male and female, sacred and secular activities are kept apart. Archeological evidence uncovered in ancient Indian cities indicates that this pattern may be thousands of years old. It is remarkably persistent even in modern India, where Western influence is strong. Ruth Freed, for example, found this in her study of Chandigarh, a city in North India (1977).

Chandigarh is a modern city designed by the French architect Le Corbusier. Its apartments were built according to European concepts, and the Indians living there found certain aspects of the design inconsistent with their previous use of living space. Freed found that Indian families modified their apartments in a number of ways. Curtains were put up so that men's and women's spaces would be separate. The families also continued to eat in the kitchen, a traditional pattern, and the living room-dining room was used only when Western guests were present. Traditional village living takes place in an area surrounded by a wall. The courtyard gives privacy to each residence group. Chandigarh apartments were built with large windows, reflecting the European desire for light and sun. Many families pasted paper over these windows to re-create the privacy of the traditional courtyard. Freed suggests that the traditional Indian patterns of space use may represent an adaptation to a densely populated environment.

Anthropologists have proposed that culturally patterned perceptions of space may be adaptive in terms of the environment. In different cultures, people seem to need different amounts of what Hall calls "personal space." North Americans, for example, seem to require more distance between themselves and others in order to feel comfortable. People from the Arab countries and Latin America appear to want to stand closer to each other than is true for North Americans and peoples from Northern Europe. It is quite possible that these differences in the need for personal space are adapted to the different levels of population density in North America and Europe, on the one hand, and in the Middle East and Latin America, on the other. Whatever the reasons for the different experiences peoples have with space and time, these "out of awareness" cultural patterns are often a source of personal conflict and mutually negative stereotyping.

CULTURAL PATTERNING OF PERCEPTION AND COGNITION

Cognition refers to the ways in which human beings perceive, understand, and organize their responses to the environment. Interest in the relationships among culture, perception, and cognition has a long history in anthropology.

Because they relied on the reports of travelers and missionaries, early scholars were mainly concerned with the *differences* in perception and thought between Europeans and the non-Western peoples they encountered. Some of these scholars attributed the differences to innate differences in mental processes. They characterized non-Western peoples as mentally deficient, childlike, incapable of abstract thinking, lacking ideas of causality, and unable to differentiate between reality and fantasy. By the turn of the twentieth century, however, anthropologists were arguing that there was a basic similarity in both cognitive and perceptual processes among all human groups.

It is generally taken for granted in modern cross-cultural research on perception, for example, that the uniformities outweigh whatever differences may be found. Given the common experiences with the physical world shared by all peoples, a strong case can be made that physically normal adults in every human society have the same fundamental perceptual abilities: they can recognize familiar objects under varied conditions (object constancy), have depth perception, and have an ability to coordinate information from several sensory sources (intersensory integration) (Munroe and Munroe 1977:64). The most influential contemporary anthropologists and cross-cultural psychologists also hold that there is no evidence that different reasoning processes are characteristic of different cultures. That is, there is no evidence for a "primitive" mentality or logic.

As Michael Cole points out in his excellent survey of cross-cultural psychology, the thinking of Don Juan, the Yaqui sorcerer, seems quite different from our own style of thought. Yet in his interpersonal relations, Don Juan demonstrates problem-solving techniques "compelling enough" to greatly influence Castaneda (the anthropologist trained in Western scientific thinking) (Cole and Scribner 1974:169). Cole and the other contemporary anthropologists who believe that basic thinking processes are the same among all humankind emphasize that all peoples employ logic and are concerned with the relationship of cause and effect; furthermore, all classification systems are arrived at by the same processes of abstraction and generalization. It is the content of culture—values, beliefs, and the ways of classifying the world—that differs among different human groups.

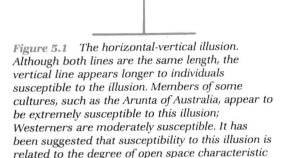

Figure 5.1   The horizontal-vertical illusion. Although both lines are the same length, the vertical line appears longer to individuals susceptible to the illusion. Members of some cultures, such as the Arunta of Australia, appear to be extremely susceptible to this illusion; Westerners are moderately susceptible. It has been suggested that susceptibility to this illusion is related to the degree of open space characteristic of particular environments, such as the Australian desert in which the Arunta live.

Culture and Perception

Research in anthropology and the new field of cross-cultural psychology has shown interesting *differences* in specific perceptual and cognitive abilities, as well as the basic similarities. One area of research has been on visual perception. Differences among cultures have been found for color differentiation, susceptibility to optical illusions, and pictorial depth perception. It is possible that ability to differentiate color and susceptibility to an optical illusion have some physiological component. For example, the color-naming systems of cultures in tropical zones characteristically contain fewer names for different colors than those in nontropical cultures. It may be that tropical cultures, which tend to be technologically simple, have no need for complex color-naming systems. Peoples of the tropics are also somewhat insensitive to blue color, however, and this may be the reason that names for these colors are not contained in their languages. A physiological component has also been suggested for the response to optical illusions (such as the one shown in Figure 5-1). The degree of pigmentation on the retina may affect one's ability to detect contours and, thus, one's susceptibility to illusions.

A cultural-ecological explanation of differences in susceptibility has also been developed. The Arunta of Australia, for example, are extremely susceptible to the illusion in Figure 5-1. The Arunta live in flat, open desert, and they see great stretches of desert that, on the retina, would be projected as foreshortened planes but that they would learn to interpret

as lengthier planes extending away into space. Shown Figure 5-1, a person from this environment would tend to perceive the vertical line as representing a plane extending along the line of vision and would therefore perceive it as longer than the horizontal line (Munroe and Munroe 1977). Peoples who do not live in environments with a great deal of vast, open space are less susceptible to this illusion.

Performance on tests of spatial ability (see Figure 5-2) also show great variation among cultures. Spatial ability means an ability to sort out the different components in an environment, to separate an element from its context, and to locate oneself accurately in relation to environmental features. A number of studies confirm the hypothesis that cultural patterning, particularly ecology and child-rearing practices, have an important impact on the development of spatial-perceptual abilities (Berry 1974). (See the accompanying box.)

Figure 5-3 illustrates the relationship between ecology, culture, socialization, and individual perceptual and cognitive skills. The figure suggests that the environment is the basic factor in human existence. Culture and child-rearing practices (socialization) are ways in which humans adapt to their environment.

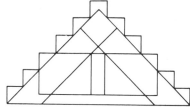 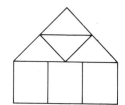

Figure 5.2   Items from the Embedded Figures Test. The simple figure on the left is located in each of the other two figures. This test is one measure of spatial perception, and the results appear to differ among different cultures. From H. A. Witkin, "Individual Differences in Ease of Embedded Figures," Journal of Personality, Volume 19, September 1950–June 1951, pp. 1–15. Copyright 1951 by Duke University Press. Reprinted by permission.

Nutrition and disease are also affected by ecology; in these two areas there is an overlap of cultural and biological factors. There are also different gene frequencies for human populations in different environments. All these factors—culture patterns, including child rearing, what people eat and what diseases they are subject to, and the specific gene pool characteristics of their population—influence the perceptual, personality, and adaptive characteristics of the individual. This schematic diagram only begins to suggest the complicated nature of the interaction of culture and biology, group and individual history, in the mental and behavioral outcomes characteristic of any particular individual.

In addition to increasing our understanding of the relationship between the ecological demands placed on a society, various aspects of culture, and the development of specific perceptual and cognitive abilities, Berry's study has a more general relevance. When we see the tiny differences in test scores between the Scottish and Inuit sample populations, as well as the significant differences between the scores of the traditional and more urbanized populations *within* each culture, racial factors cannot explain perceptual and cognitive variations. Furthermore, the differences in performance between the Inuit and the African Temne, as well as among other non-Western peoples who have been tested, would seem

to finish once and for all any notion of a "primitive mentality."

Culture and Cognition

Cognitive competence, or intelligence, consists of many capacities, skills, and adaptive responses to the environment. In our own society, we see "intelligence" as a particular way of solving problems that involves the ability to abstract, analyze, and reintegrate data into new patterns. This analytic cognitive style is at one end of a continuum; a global cognitive style is at the other. On tests, an individual with the global cognitive style has more trouble separating the different elements in a pattern, taking them from their context, and recombining them in novel ways. Although the analytic cognitive style appears to develop with age, there is some empirical research that shows the important ways in which culture patterns cognitive skills and style (Witkin 1974). As the material on the Temne and the Inuit indicates, different perceptual-cognitive skills appear to be adaptive in different ecological situations. One style is not superior to another but rather is more suitable in different environments and life situations. The value of the *analytic* style in our own society has an obvious relationship to formal education, the specialized nature of industrial technology, and the rise of scientific thought as a way of understanding the world.

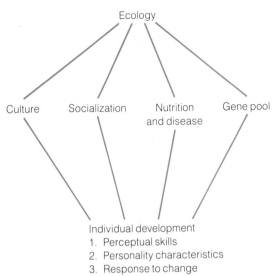

Ecology

Culture   Socialization   Nutrition   Gene pool
and disease

Individual development
1. Perceptual skills
2. Personality characteristics
3. Response to change

Figure 5.3   Individual development in its relationship to ecological and other factors, both biological and cultural. (Berry 1974)

The relatively undifferentiated landscape of the snow-covered arctic is an important factor in the high degree of visual discrimination found among some Inuit populations. (United Nations/Canadian Government Travel Bureau)

Cross-cultural research is only now beginning to shed some light on the relationship between many different cognitive skills and the cultural patterns and ecological settings in which they exist. It appears, for example, that child-care patterns that encourage freedom and separation of the child from the family tend to be correlated with and are assumed in some way to produce a more analytic style. The high scores on Western intelligence tests for the Tiv, a people of Africa, emphasize the importance of a cultural explanation of intelligence as this applies to human populations. The Tiv, a non-literate people, stand out in sub-Saharan Africa for their child-rearing patterns. Most other African peoples (like the Temne) teach respect for authority and obedience to elders. The Tiv put less pressure for obedience (vis-à-vis assertiveness) on children. Tiv children also stand out for the extent to which they have spontaneously and enthusiastically participated in intelligence testing experiences.

The mainstream of anthropology and cross-cultural psychology tries to show that understandings of the universe and of relationships within the universe are learned and do not reflect any innate or biologically inherited differences in intelligence among human groups. No matter what the differences in the ways in which different peoples perform on "intelligence" tests, all human groups studied demonstrate the capacity to remember, generalize, operate with abstractions, form concepts, and reason logically.

Intelligence tests do *not* provide valid information on innate differences in mental capacities among human groups. They *do* predict well the academic success of different groups, which is what they are designed to do. Intelligence tests measure the specific ability to perceive relationships using abstract symbolic material: numbers, forms, spatial relationships, and word meanings. This is just one culturally patterned way of understanding the world. It is because the culture on which intelligence tests are based is the same as the cultural understandings required in the middle-class American school that the tests can predict academic success (Alland 1973:177).

Not only do standard intelligence tests

Ecology, Culture, and Perception

A comparison of two groups—the Temne, a horticultural tribe of Sierra Leone in Africa, and a group of Inuit from Baffin Island who depend on hunting for their food supply—shows the influence of culture on perception. The Temne score relatively low on tests of spatial ability and differentiation. The Inuit score extremely high, coming very close to a sample of Scottish subjects, which provided a Western population for comparison with these two non-Western groups. The explanation of these test scores is provided by comparing the cultural ecology of the Temne with that of the Inuit.

The physical environment of the Temne is highly differentiated; it is full of colorful vegetation and is naturally structured. The Temne, as farmers, are not very mobile; they tend to "stay put" on their land. Given this particular ecological relationship, it is not necessary to develop spatial discrimination skills. The Inuit are in a completely different position. Their physical environment consists of "endless, uniform, snowfields"; theirs is a highly undifferentiated environment. Furthermore, hunting requires the Inuit to travel widely. In this situation, the Inuit need spatial perceptual skills to find their way. They must be aware of minute details in the physical environment and be able to locate themselves in relation to objects around them. These perceptual skills are obviously related to survival among the Inuit.

The Temne and the Inuit have very different child-rearing patterns. Temne parents try to enforce strict discipline through physical punishment, and there is an emphasis on conformity to adult authority. The Temne mother plays an extremely dominant role in raising the children, and a child is not encouraged to take on adult roles or responsibility. This kind of child rearing is associated with a *field dependent* perceptual-cognitive style, one aspect of which is a less well-developed ability in spatial awareness and visual discrimination. Among the Inuit, on the other hand, punishment of children is generally avoided, and the child is given a lot of freedom. Self-reliance, individualism, individual skill development, and curiosity and ingenuity are encouraged. This child-rearing pattern is correlated with a generally high degree of differentiation and leads to a *field independent* perceptual-cognitive style, which in turn is correlated with a high degree of spatial awareness and visual discrimination.

The differences between the two groups in their arts and crafts are also related to their different perceptual skills. The arts and crafts of the Inuit are known for skill in design and execution. Those of the Temne are considered to be of relatively poor quality and tend to be produced by a few specialists in the society. A high quality of arts and crafts engaged in by the general population promotes the early learning of spatial manipulation and discrimination of detail and is positively related to spatial perceptual competence. In language, too, the contrast between the Temne and Inuit shows the influence of culture on perception. The Temne language contains relatively few terms that express geometrical-spatial concepts, while the Inuit language contains many (Berry 1974).

measure just one "codification of reality"; they measure it in a context that is not equally meaningful for different groups in our society. For middle-class children, who have some reason to believe that their performance on tests is related to success in later life, the motivation for taking them is obviously higher than for children who believe that their fate is sealed by race or ethnicity, no matter how well they may do on a test. The effect of motivation, sophistication in taking tests, and culturally different attitudes toward testing must all be taken into account in interpreting the intelligence test scores of different groups of people.

DOING WHAT COMES NATURALLY?

The importance of cultural patterning is not easy to understand, particularly in areas of action and emotional response that we assume to be "natural"—sex, eating, feeling, and expressing certain emotions and attitudes. Natural, in the case of every society, is natural according to its own beliefs and customs. In this next section, we examine some of the ways in which basic human behavior patterns and responses are influenced and shaped by culture.

Sexual Practices

If the cultural component in food habits is easily understood, that in sexual habits is not. Of all the kinds of human behavior, sexual activity is most likely to be viewed as "doing what comes naturally." But a cross-cultural perspective on sexual practices tells us that every aspect of human sexual activity is patterned by culture and influenced by learning.

Culture patterns the habitual responses of different peoples to different parts of the body. What is considered erotic in some cultures evokes indifference or disgust in others. Kissing, for example, is not practiced in many societies. The Tahitians have learned to kiss from the Europeans, but before this culture contact they began sexual intimacy by sniffing. The patterns of social and sexual preliminaries leading to sexual intercourse also differ among cultures. The Trobriand Islanders, as described by Malinowski, "inspect each other's hair for lice and eat them . . . to the natives a natural and pleasant occupation between two who are fond of each other" (1929:335). This may seem disgusting to us. To the Trobrianders, the European habit of boys and girls going out on a picnic with a knapsack of food was equally disgusting, although it is a perfectly acceptable custom for a Trobriand boy and girl to gather

wild foods together as a preliminary to sexual activity.

Who is considered an appropriate sexual partner also differs in different cultures. The common feeling in the United States that homosexual activity is somewhat shameful or abnormal is not shared universally. In some societies, such as that of the Sambia of New Guinea, a period of obligatory homosexual relationships is part of the initiation for every adolescent male, who as an adult is expected to enter a heterosexual marriage (Herdt 1981). In this culture, and in others in the New Guinea Highlands, it is believed that only men can create men, and this process involves a long period during which boys live away from their parents in a men's cult house and engage in homosexual activity as part of their training to be vigorous, strong warriors. In other cultures, such as those in parts of Samoa, homosexual practices almost never occurred until they were introduced by Europeans. In these cultures, homosexuality is seen as an activity that just does not make much sense if members of the opposite sex are around, but there is no concept that it is a sin, a sickness, or a crime, as has been true in much of European history. In Europe and the United States, the attitude toward homosexuality is changing; in 1974, the American Psychiatric Association dropped homosexuality from its list of mental illnesses, and several states have decriminalized homosexual activity between consenting adults. Homosexuality has also been decriminalized in many European countries, and there has been a movement by activist homosexual groups in the United States to ban discrimination on the basis of sexual preference. For many people in the United States, the aim is to have homosexual relationships considered as just another form of sexual activity that should not be labeled deviant and should not be stigmatized by either social, political, or economic sanctions.

Unlike the United States and other Western cultures, many non-Western cultures have had

The Indians of the North American Plains allowed more variation in gender identity than is true in the United States. The role of the berdache allowed men who felt that they could not live up to the Plains warrior ideal to wear women's clothing and perform women's tasks. This male Crow Indian, "Finds-Them-and-Kills-Them," takes on the female role. (Courtesy of Museum of the American Indian, Heye Foundation)

culturally institutionalized roles for people who do not conform to either the male or female gender role. Among the Indians of North America, for example, there were often three or even more gender roles: women, men, and those who were born of one sex but who wished to live as members of the other sex. Among the Plains Indians, the berdache was a man who dressed in women's clothing, took on women's tasks, and was often considered to have special supernatural powers and privileges in society (Whitehead 1981). As we have seen in Chapter Four, a similar role exists in India around which has been built a subculture that,

although considered deviant, nevertheless shares many of the norms and values of the larger society.

In addition to these variations in attitudes toward sex in different cultures, there are also many other variations. The ages at which sexual response is believed to begin and end, the ways in which people make themselves attractive to the opposite sex, the importance of sexual activity in human life—all these are patterned and regulated by culture and affect sexual response and behavior. Partly because anthropology grew up in an age in which sexuality was a forbidden topic and partly because of the difficulty of observing sexual activity, ethnographic descriptions often ignore this topic. What information we do have is enough to show the great contrasts in different societies. A comparison of just two cultures, the Irish of the island of Inis Beag and the Polynesians of the island of Mangaia, who are at opposite ends of a continuum regarding sexual behavior, makes clear the role of culture in this area of life.

John Messenger describes Inis Beag as "one of the most sexually naive of the world's societies" (1971). Sex is never discussed at home when children are near, and practically no sexual instruction is given by parents to children. Adults express the belief that "after marriage nature takes its course." (As we shall see, "nature" takes a very different course in Inis Beag than it does in Polynesia!) Women are not expected to enjoy sexual relations; they are a "duty" to be endured, for to refuse to have intercourse is considered a mortal sin. There appears to be widespread ignorance in Inis Beag of the ability of females to reach a climax, which in any case is considered deviant behavior. Nudity is abhorred by the islanders, and there is no tradition of "dirty jokes." The main style of dancing allows little bodily contact among the participants, but even then, some girls refuse to dance because it means touching a boy. The separation of the sexes begins very early in Inis Beag and lasts into adulthood. Other cultural patterns related to

As economic opportunities for women change, so do conceptions of female sexuality. (Jane Hoffer)

sexual repression here are the virtual absence of sexual foreplay, the belief that sexual activity weakens a man, the absence of premarital sex, the high percentage of celibate males, and the extraordinarily late age of marriage. The differences in sexuality between men and women are expressed by a female informant as "Men can wait a long time before wanting 'it' but we [women] can wait a lot longer" (p. 68).

Although the belief that total sexual freedom exists in the South Sea islands is a Western myth, the island of Mangaia, as described by Donald Marshall (1971), presents a strong contrast to that of Inis Beag. In this Polynesian culture, sexual intercourse is one of the major interests of life. Although sex is not discussed

at home, sexual information is transmitted to boys and girls at puberty by the elders of the group. For adolescent boys, a two-week period of formal instruction about the techniques of intercourse is followed by a culturally approved experience with a mature woman in the village. After this, the boy is considered a man, by himself and by others. This is an interesting point of comparison with Inis Beag, where a man is considered a "lad" until he is about 40.

Sexual relations in Mangaia are carried out privately, but there is continual public reference to sexual activity. Sexual jokes, expressions, and references are not only common but also expected as part of the preliminaries to public meetings. This pattern of public verbal references to sex contrasts with the public separation of the sexes. Boys and girls should not be seen together in public, but practically every girl and boy has had intercourse before marriage. The act of sexual intercourse itself is the focus of sexual activity. What Westerners call sexual foreplay is generally engaged in by Mangaians after, not before, intercourse. In Mangaia both men and women are expected to take pleasure in the sexual act and to reach a climax. Female frigidity, male celibacy, and homosexuality are practically unknown. So it is not simply that different societies hold different attitudes about sex but also that these attitudes pattern the sexual responsiveness of males and females in that society.

Like any other aspect of culture, beliefs about human sexuality and sexual practices are integrated into a pattern and functionally related to other aspects of the total sociocultural system. In the absence of artificial birth control, for example, beliefs and practices that limit heterosexual intercourse may be adaptive in contributing to population control.

Sex and Gender

Sex refers to the *biological* differences between male and female, particularly the visible differences in external genitalia and the related difference in the role each sex plays in the reproductive process. Gender refers to the *social* classification of masculine and feminine. Every society gives cultural recognition to the sexual division of the species into male and female, but cultures differ in what they consider masculine and feminine. Some male-female differences in behavior appear to be very widespread, however (D'Andrade 1974). Males, for example, have been observed to be more likely to initiate activity than females in various cultures. Females have also been observed to be more altruistic than males.

An important study on the question of whether the characteristics defined as "feminine" in Western culture were universal was carried out by Margaret Mead in New Guinea (1963). Mead studied three different cultures and found that male and female roles and masculine and feminine temperament were patterned differently in each culture. Among the Arapesh, both men and women were expected to act in ways we in the United States consider "naturally" feminine. Both sexes were concerned with taking care of children and with nurturing generally. Neither sex was expected to be aggressive. In the second culture, the Mundugamor, both sexes were what we would call "masculine"—aggressive, violent, and with little interest in children. In the third society, the Tchambuli, the personalities of males and females were different from each other but opposite to our own conceptions of masculine and feminine. Women had the major economic role, showed "common sense" and business shrewdness, and carried out the mundane tasks. Men were interested in esthetics. They spent much time decorating themselves and gossiping. They also had their feelings easily hurt and sulked a lot.

Mead's study showed that the whole repertoire of behavior, emotions, and interests which go into being masculine and feminine are patterned by culture. In the process of growing up, each child learns hundreds of culturally patterned details of behavior that become incorporated into its gender identity. In addition to all the direct instructions about being masculine or feminine that every culture imparts, culture unconsciously affects masculinity and femininity by providing different images, aspirations, and adult models for girls and boys. In assessing the idea that biology determines gender, anthropologists have pointed to the great variability in human societies regarding the behavior, temperaments, and roles of women and men. As always, the anthropologist attempts to deal with the question of the relation of biology to culture by looking outside our own Western traditions, for it is only in this way that we can grasp the variety in human life. What we see is that whatever biological dispositions may be characteristic of one sex or the other, these are responsive to a tremendously wide range of cultural patterning.

Cultural Patterning and Emotions

The range and quality of human emotions are potentially the same for all human groups. It is in the course of growing up in a particular culture that the range narrows and becomes shaped to a pattern. Fear, love, anger, hostility, shame, guilt, grief, joy, and indifference become channeled by culture so that they appear in different situations, are directed toward different objects and persons, or hardly appear at all. Each culture selects, elaborates, and emphasizes certain emotional possibilities and defines certain feelings about oneself, others, and the world as appropriate or not. This is communicated in direct and indirect ways. A boy who learns not to cry may have been told that "crying is only for girls." He is also surrounded by males who do not cry. Both experiences help pattern his inner responses to situations.

Because human emotions have an "inner" reality, they are felt to be "natural." Drawing on our own experience, we consider it natural for a mother to love her child, for an individual to be jealous of another's success, or for people to be sad when someone dies. The seeming naturalness of human emotions leads us to see them as causes for certain kinds of behavior. War is then explained by humankind's natural aggression, marriage is viewed as the result of love, motherhood is seen as an expression of the maternal instinct, and free-enterprise capitalism is considered the inevitable expression of a natural desire to get ahead in the world. In all this, we have lost sight of the role of culture and its tremendous impact on the human psyche. We project emotions that we have been trained to feel onto peoples in other cultures. We consider our own emo-

The flexibility of certain features of the human face, particularly the mouth, means that humans can express a wide variety of emotions in facial expression. Although some of these expressions, such as the smile, which expresses happiness, are considered to be pan-human, culture also has a powerful influence on just when and how such emotions are expressed. (Serena Nanda)

tional responses "natural" and responses that differ from ours "unnatural."

It becomes hard for us to understand cultures in which several women married to the same man are not jealous of one another or cultures in which mothers neglect their children's health, permit them to die, or even kill them. Every culture sets up expectations not only about how people are supposed to behave but also about how they should feel in different situations. In our own culture, we are taught that it is not good to "carry a grudge," to store up anger or hatred against a person who has hurt us. In cultures where the blood feud exists, not only are people allowed to feel the desire for revenge, but their very honor will depend on it. A man who does not avenge a hurt loses face for himself and his whole group of kin.

The expression of emotions in body or facial movement is also of interest to anthropologists, particularly because such expressions are important ways of communicating. A basic issue here is whether there are universal ways of communicating. Evidence that there is a cross-cultural universality in the facial expressions used to convey happiness, surprise, fear, anger, disgust, and sadness raises the issue of whether these expressions may have a biological basis (Ekman 1977). At the same time, it is equally clear that culture and experience have a strong effect on the shaping of facial expression, just as they do on bodily movement. Some emotions, like contempt, seem to have culturally specific facial movements. In other cases, the importance of masking emotions will affect all facial movement in the presence of other people. Where people are taught to be polite and sensitive to the feelings of others, as in Japan, this will affect the facial movements used in the presence of others. In the same situation, Japanese smile more, for example, than Americans do.

The Cultural Patterning of Selfishness and Aggression

One of the characteristic responses of individuals in North American society is to "look out for number one." John and Beatrice Whiting (1973) studied this "egoistic" attitude in a number of different cultures. They contrasted egoistic behavior, in which the self was the primary beneficiary of interaction, with altruistic behavior, in which another person benefited more. Through carefully controlled observations and comparisons of children, they found that in those cultures where women contributed importantly to the economy and younger children were therefore depended on to help with domestic chores, particularly taking care of a younger sibling, altruistic behavior was more frequent than egoistic behavior. It should not surprise us to discover that the culture rated highest on egoistic behavior was Orchard Town, U.S.A. In a later chapter, we will study more specifically the ways in which

early socialization is related to the development of group-oriented versus individualistic kinds of behavior.

Related to the view in the United States that selfishness is part of "human nature" is the tendency to see aggression as an innate and "natural" human predisposition. The idea that the human species has an aggressive "instinct" most often comes up in connection with warfare. Given the frequency of war throughout human history, it would seem to make sense to believe that humankind has an aggressive, warlike nature. If we examine the matter carefully, however, it can be shown that this theory does not hold up. War is between societies, not between individuals. Many (perhaps most) of the individuals who fight in wars are not there because they are aggressive, but because their society insists that they participate. Furthermore, the degree to which propaganda is used in modern warfare indicates that aggression must be evoked by culturally appropriate means against a culturally approved enemy.

It is true that human beings are among the very few animal groups not provided with a biological mechanism that inhibits killing a member of the same species. Humans thus have the potential for intraspecific lethal aggression, and there is no denying that it has frequently been used. Biological interpretations of human aggression are attractive to us because they seem to explain in a simple manner much of the behavior found in Western society. But this kind of explanation fails to take into account the importance of cultural patterning, which can be observed only by looking at the total variety of human cultures.

There are some cultures in which there is little or no organized aggression and in which aggressive behavior by individuals is severely condemned and may almost be nonexistent. One such culture is that of the Semai of the Malay Peninsula (Dentan 1968). The Semai are slash-and-burn agriculturalists who have only recently given up a dependence on a hunting and gathering existence. Under the pressure of the dominant Malays, the Semai have

The influence of genes on sex roles is a question being intensely discussed in contemporary anthropology. Is the self-sacrificing behavior human beings often show toward their close kin genetically determined or learned through participation in a sociocultural system? (United Nations)

retreated to the hills and mountains of central Malaya. They consider themselves, and are considered by others, as a nonviolent people. They believe that anger is a bad thing, and the ethnographer observed that they rarely do get angry. Semai life is not without conflict, however, usually over the sexual favors of women. When an individual is offended by another, the Semai believe, the offended person will become prone to an accident if he or she stays angry. Thus, one reason that Semai do not want to become angry is that in their culture it is the angry man who gets hurt. If a man feels himself offended by another, he can ask for compensation for his distress. If the offender admits the offense, he will pay the compensation. If not, hostility simmers, leading at the very most to insults and the spreading of rumors. No murder has ever been recorded in Semai society.

The Semai are very gentle, even with animals. A man will not kill an animal he has raised himself, but exchanges it with someone in another village, knowing that it will be killed but not wanting to do it himself. Yet when the Semai joined the military during the 1950s in response to the Malayan government's attempt to put down guerrilla activity, they were not only able to kill but also seemed to enjoy it. How can this be explained? The answer cannot be found in a human instinct for aggression. The Semai culture was built on nonaggression, and the same Semai who served in the army went back to their nonaggressive way of life. If aggression were an instinct, it could not be modified by changes in situations so rapidly.

The variability in the amount, expression, and direction of aggression within human societies testifies to the importance of cultural patterning. In societies in which warfare is a highly valued cultural pattern, males will be taught to be more aggressive than those in cultures in which warfare is absent. Warfare itself does not exist in all societies, and its presence and the form it takes are best explained in terms of ecology. Only under specific circumstances does the human potential for aggression become mobilized in the service of warfare. Human behavior is based on customs and values that develop only in the context of specific social and environmental conditions. Although culture is rooted in human biology, it frees humans from strictly biological controls over behavior to a degree far beyond that of any other animal. An understanding of the cultural context of human behavior—the ways in which specific patterns specify and provide the necessary context for the development of biologically based capacities—is critical to an understanding of what it means to be human.

SUMMARY

1. Human capacities and human behavior develop only within a human sociocultural system. Dramatic evidence of this is demonstrated by the nonhuman behavior of children brought up in relative isolation from other human beings.

2. Culture patterns the ways in which human beings perceive physical reality. Culture also patterns what people believe to be true about their universe.

3. Keeping track of time is a human invention. The passing of time, the sense of past and present, and the way time is used are different in different cultures.

4. Cultural patterning affects the way humans perceive and see relationships in space, the way in which spaces are used, and how much space people feel they need to be comfortable.

5. One of the basic principles of anthropology is that all human groups have the same capacity for intelligent behavior. Intelligence tests do not measure innate mental capacities of different human groups. Standardized intelligence tests given in the American school are constructed in terms of only one cultural system: that of the middle-class American.

6. Because of the tremendous variability in culture, it is difficult to say what human nature consists of. Every society tends to look at its own ways of behaving as not only right but also "natural." The difficulty in isolating the genetic bases of human behavior is that everything human beings do is patterned by the specific culture in which they live.

7. The great variety in human sexual behavior indicates that culture plays an important role in patterning and regulating sexual drives and responsiveness. In this sense, we may say that human sexual behavior is learned.

8. *Male* and *female* are biological categories. *Masculine* and *feminine* are cultural creations. By looking at cultures outside Western civilization, anthropologists try to understand the relationship between sex (male and female) and gender (masculine and feminine).

9. Body and facial movements are patterned by culture, although evidence from recent research also indicates that some facial expressions may be universal.

10. Culture patterns not only the forms of outward behavior but also the inner life of the individual. How people feel and what motivates them to act are part of a conscious and unconscious teaching process that is culturally variable.

11. In the United States, we are taught to "look out for number one." The equation of individual self-preservation with "human nature" is contradicted by the ethnographic evidence from many non-Western societies.

12. Intraspecies aggression is a potential in the human species. Societies vary greatly, however, in the degree to which individuals act aggressively, and some societies have practically no physical aggression. Aggression is not a human instinct but rather a possibility that is patterned differently in different cultures.

SUGGESTED READINGS

Alland, Alexander, Jr.
1972   *The Human Imperative.* New York: Columbia University Press. A book that can easily be understood by the beginning anthropology student, it persuasively demolishes the case for aggression as a human instinct.

Barash, David P.
1977   *Sociobiology and Behavior.* New York: Elsevier. An introduction to sociobiological theory and research. The last chapter is devoted to the usefulness of sociobiology in understanding human behavior.

Bates, Marston
1971   *Gluttons and Libertines: Human Problems of Being Natural.* New York: Random House. An entertaining and informative book by a natural scientist on such topics as food, sex, rebellion, and the pursuit of happiness.

Cole, M., and Scribner, S.
1974   *Culture and Thought.* New York: Wiley. A summary of the important research in cross-cultural psychology, including a historical perspective on scientific interest in this issue.

Lane, Harlan
1977   *The Wild Boy of Aveyron.* New York: Bantam. Based on original documents, this book about a "wild" child raises provocative questions about human nature.

Money, John, and Tucker, Patricia
1975   *Sexual Signatures.* Boston: Little, Brown. A distinguished researcher in human sexuality discusses the biological and cultural components involved in being a man or a woman.

CHAPTER SIX

LANGUAGE

▶ What are the special characteristics of human language?

▶ How are human languages similar to and different from one another?

▶ How does language shape the ways we perceive the world?

▶ Do we communicate by how we speak as well as what we say?

▶ Can you explain how language changes?

> *"When I use a word," Humpty Dumpty said, in a rather scornful tone, "it means just what I choose it to mean—neither more nor less."*
> *"The question is," said Alice, "whether you can make words mean so many different things."*
> *"The question is," said Humpty Dumpty, "which is to be master—that's all."*
>
> Lewis Carroll

All animals communicate. **Communication** is the act of transmitting information that influences the behavior of another organism. Interaction in all animal species depends on a consistent set of signals by which individuals convey information. These signals are channeled through visual, olfactory (smell), auditory (sound), and tactile (touch) senses, which are just a few of the many senses humans and animals have. Among animals such as honeybees, the type of information communicated can be quite complex. Through stereotyped and patterned movements, a scout bee conveys the direction and distance of a field of pollen-bearing flowers to the others. But although bees can "say" a lot about where flowers are, they cannot "say" much about anything else. Animals use sounds as well as movements to communicate, or share, information. Crows caw as a signal of danger, and crickets chirp when they are ready to mate. Among higher animals, especially primates, as we saw in Chapter Two, far greater amounts of information can be transmitted about many more subjects. Although all animal species exchange information related to the basic requirements of survival, only human language, whether spoken, signed, or written, is capable of recreating complex thought patterns and experiences in words. Without human language, human culture could not exist.

COMMUNICATION AND LANGUAGE

Human Language

Human language is a unique system of communication, distinct from any other animal communication system in three ways. In human language, a limited number of sounds (hardly any language uses over fifty) are combined to refer to thousands of different things and experiences. The association between a meaningful sequence of sounds and what it "stands for" is purely conventional in human language. The animal is no more a *dog* than it is a *chien* (French), a *perro* (Spanish) or a *kutta* (Hindi). Words "stand for" things, and the symbol (the word) is not tied to the thing it stands for. It is this capacity to separate the vocal symbol from its referent that is absent in the call systems of nonhuman primates. It is this capacity to recombine sounds to create new meanings that makes human language such an efficient and effective communication system. If we had to use a different sound for every item of meaning, we would wind up with either a very small vocabulary or an impossibly large number of sounds.

Not only is human language efficient, it is also immensely *productive:* humans can combine words and sounds into new meaningful utterances they have never heard before. The English sentence below uses words in a combination none of us has probably ever heard before, and yet can be easily made and understood by any English-speaking person: "I don't know the man who took the spoon that Horace left on the table that was lying upside down in the upstairs hallway of the building that burned down last night" (Southworth and Daswani 1974). Speakers of any human language can generate an almost infinite number of such sentences. This productive capacity of human languages makes them extremely flexible instruments for communication, capable of conveying all kinds of new information.

The third distinguishing characteristic of human language is its ability to convey information about something not in the immediate environment. We can describe things that happened in the past, will or may happen in the future, exist only in the mind, and are hypothetical (may not happen at all). This "displacement" characteristic of human languages allows us to think abstractly. Among other animals, communication is always about the present and the particular: a particular threatening object is in a particular place at this particular time. Human language generalizes; it categorizes some objects and events as similar and other objects and events as dissimilar. Humans can talk about a particular tree ("this tree I see in front of my house") and also about trees in general ("trees are standing people with rights to the land"). Language allows trees to be differentiated from bushes and bushes from flowers and flowers from grass. Hundreds of thousands of natural and manufactured objects have significance for human beings. Taking command of this incredibly complex world means classifying objects and events in an orderly way. Human language is the most effective means for doing exactly that. These qualities of human language—conventionality, productivity, and displacement—allow humans to make plans, to understand and correct mistakes, and to coordinate their activities. They also give our species a distinct advantage over other animals.

By translating experience into language, humans build up a storehouse of knowledge that can be transmitted to new members of the group. Although some of the things humans teach one another could be learned without language, teaching through language is more efficient and adaptive than relying on the slower and often clumsy process of imitation used by

Where the population of a nation speaks two mutually unintelligible dialects, as in the People's Republic of China, a common written language is an important means of communication and an instrument of forging national unity. (Bernhard Krauss)

other animals. Furthermore, some human behavior patterns such as religion, law, and science, would not be possible without the symbolizing capacity of human language. It is through this capacity for accumulating experience and passing it on by teaching others in the social group that human culture has developed.

Although at one time even many anthropologists and linguists believed that contemporary human languages could be classified into "primitive" and "civilized," less complex and more complex, inferior and superior, we know today that this is not so. Although some linguists are coming to believe that the vocabularies of literate urban peoples are richer and more complex than those of preliterate peoples, all human languages are similar in that they possess a well-defined system of sounds, finite in number and combined to form words, phrases, and sentences according to definite rules. Although the vocabulary of each lan-

guage reflects what is important in terms of a particular physical and sociocultural environment, every language has a vocabulary adequate to deal with that environment. Vocabulary can be expanded in any language, with new words added as cultural change requires. All human languages have the capacity to categorize phenomena in the natural environment; the capacity for abstract thought is a property of all human languages. No language limits its references to concrete or individual phenomena, and thus no language as a system of communication can be considered less developed than any other. Nor does any human language reflect a limited mental capacity on the part of its speakers. Languages *do* differ in the specific ways in which they categorize the environment, and these differences affect perception and thinking, as we saw in Chapter Five. We will examine this aspect of language and its relationship to culture later in the chapter.

Acquiring Language

The fact that linguistic symbols are nearly all arbitrary—that is, conventions by which certain sounds are attached to certain objects and events—emphasizes the social aspect of language. In this sense, language is a part of culture. An individual learns a language only by interaction with other human beings who speak that language. An individual from any human population, if taken at birth and brought up in a different society than that to which the parents belong, will grow up speaking the language of the group in which he or she is raised. The normal physical and mental apparatus of human beings everywhere allows them to learn any language with equal ease.

If you are wondering what language a human being would speak if he or she were not taught any particular language, the answer is *none.* In one attempt to determine this, the Egyptian pharoah Psammetichus ordered two infants reared where they could hear no human voices. He assumed that they would "naturally" talk in the language of their ancestors. To his ears, their babbling sounded like Phrygian, which he concluded was the original human language. King James IV of Scotland tried a similar experiment, and he claimed that the two infants spoke Hebrew. This, not surprisingly, coincided with the theory of biblical scholars at that time, who asserted that Adam and Eve had spoken in Hebrew. Because experiments involving isolating human beings at birth are morally unacceptable today, cases of children brought up in isolation, such as Victor, the "wild child" of Aveyron, are always of great interest to the scientific community. In Victor's case, Dr. Itard's training did result in showing that Victor could hear and understand much of what he heard. But although Victor lived in human society until he was 40, he never learned to speak. His case suggests that there may be a critical period of language development in the human animal. It seems that, if speech is not learned at a certain age, the capacity to learn it at all is seriously impaired.

Recent studies of how children learn language indicate that human beings may have an innate (inborn) predisposition or mechanism for learning language patterns or rules. Children actually take the initiative in learning language. By six months, the babbling of the infant gives way to consonant and vowel sequences and repetitive patterns. It is apparent that children "discover" language on their own, though this can be done only in the context of a particular social group speaking a particular language. Most adults do not know the rules of the languages they speak, certainly not well enough to teach them to children. What happens is that children are surrounded by a flow of sounds, words, and intonations. They not only imitate these but also take the initiative in forming combinations of words they may have never heard before but that are consistent with the rules of the language. Even when they do not understand the meaning of what they are saying, they can speak grammatically, using the different parts of speech in correct relation to one another. This understanding of how children learn language has led to an increased interest in the biological basis of human language.

The human brain appears to be uniquely constructed for the development of language. Not only are the visual and auditory areas directly connected to each other, but both areas are directly connected to the area concerned with touch. Thus, human children are able to make the association between the visible image, the feel of an object, and the sound pattern, or word, used to designate it, even though the word itself is an arbitrary symbol.

STRUCTURAL VARIATION IN LANGUAGE

Every language has a structure—an internal logic and a particular relationship between its parts. The structure of any language consists of three subsystems: **phonology** (a system of sounds), **syntax** (the relationship between forms and the rules for combining forms), and **semantics** (a sytem that relates forms to meaning). Descriptive linguistics, a subfield of linguistics that studies the structure of a given language at a particular time, is the basis of historical linguistics, which studies the change in the structure of a language over time, and of comparative linguistics, which seeks to understand the relationship between different languages based on a comparison of their structures. One of the interests of descriptive anthropological linguistics is to record the structure of as many different human languages as possible. The first thing a descriptive linguist does in studying a language is to record the sounds and regular combinations of sounds in that language. These sounds are usually written in the International Phonetic Alphabet. The IPA was developed to represent all the sounds used in the different languages of the world and allows the linguist to record in writing sounds that are not used in his or her own language. When the linguist figures out how a particular sound is made, that sound can be represented phonetically with an IPA symbol. Let us look now in more detail at these subsystems of language structure.

Phonology

A phone is a sound. All languages use only a limited number of sounds out of the vast range of sounds that can be made by the human vocal apparatus. Sounds used in one language may be absent in other languages. English, for example, does not make use of the "click" sound of the language of the !Kung of southern Africa or many of the tonal sounds of Chinese. Furthermore, combinations of sounds are used in different ways in different languages. For example, an English speaker can easily pronounce the "ng" sound in *thing* at the end of an utterance, but not at the beginning; yet this sound is used in the initial position in Swazi, a language of Africa.

The anthropological linguist is greatly aided by the tape recorder in recording the many sounds of human speech that are part of the phonemic structure of a language. (Raymond Kennedy)

Not every sound used in a language conveys meaning. The smallest sound unit in a language that distinguishes meaning is called a **phoneme.** An example will make clear what is meant by a phoneme. The sound [d] in the English word *day* and [ð] in the English word *they* are phonemes. Their significance is shown by the fact that the words *day* and *they* have different meanings, and this meaning is carried by the initial consonant: [d] as contrasted to [ð]. Spanish also uses these sounds. But in Spanish the sounds [d] and [ð] are not phonemes—that is, they do not serve to distinguish words from one another. These sounds are used in different contexts: [d] at the beginning of words and [ð] when the sound appears in the middle of a word. Thus, they do not create a difference in meaning between utterances. A person who says *nada* using the sound in *dia* will still be understood to be saying "nothing," although people may think the accent is "wrong" or "foreign."

Most languages utilize only about thirty phonemes in their structure. By an unconscious process, the native speaker of a language not only learns to make the sounds used in the language but also to differentiate between those sounds that are significant (phonemes) and those sounds that are not. The ordinary person does not consciously think about the phonemic pattern of his or her language. It is only when trying to learn another language or hearing a foreigner speak our own language that we become aware of the variation in sounds and phonemes.

Grammar: Morphology and Syntax

A **morpheme** is the smallest unit of a language that has a meaning. In English, -s, as in *dogs*, means plural; un- means negative, as in *undo*; -er means "one who does," as in *teacher*. Because -s, -un, and -er do not occur by themselves, but only in association with another unit of meaning, they are called *bound* morphemes. A morpheme such as the word *giraffe* is called a *free* morpheme, because it can stand alone. A word is the smallest part of a sentence that can be said alone and still retain its meaning. Some words consist of only one morpheme. *Giraffe* is an example of a single-morpheme word. *Teacher* has two morphemes, teach and -er. *Undoes* has three morphemes: un-, do, and -s.

Languages differ in the extent to which their words tend to contain only one, several, or many morphemes. In Chinese, most words have only one morpheme. English, like Chinese, has many single-morpheme words—*dog, house, car*—but also many words that contain more than one morpheme—plural words such as *dogs, houses, cars*; and words for one who does—*worker, teacher, gambler*. English also has words with three morphemes: *Teachers*

consists of the morphemes teach, -er, and -s. English also has words with four morphemes: *undesirables*. The four are un-, desire, -able (a suffix turning a stem word into an adjective), and -s. English might then fall midway on a continuum between Chinese, with its mainly single-morpheme words, and languages like Navajo or Eskimo, which have many words with eight or ten morphemes.

Morphemes combine with other morphemes to make up complex words, phrases, and sentences. The combination of morphemes in any language is fixed by rules. One part of descriptive grammar has to do with formulating the particular rules in a language by which morphemes are arranged to make words. One of the rules of English grammar is that the morpheme for plural, -s, follows the element it is pluralizing. In other languages, the pluralizing morpheme may come before the element it pluralizes. Things are not quite that easy, however. The plural of "dog" is made by adding -s, but the plural of "child" is not made by adding -s. A grammar therefore specifies not only the general rules of morpheme combination but also exceptions to the rules and the rules for different classes of exceptions.

Syntax is the part of grammar that has to do with the arrangement of words to form phrases and sentences. Languages differ in their syntactic structures. In English, word order is important to convey meaning. The syntax of the English language gives a different meaning to these two sentences: "The dog bit the man" and "The man bit the dog." In German, the subject and object of a sentence are indicated by word endings rather than word order. In attempting to understand the syntactic structure of a language, the descriptive linguist establishes the different form classes, or parts of speech, for that language. All languages have a word class of nouns, but different languages have different subclasses of nouns. In the Romance languages (Spanish, French, and Italian), as well as in many others, nouns are divided into masculine, feminine, and neuter subclasses. This gender classification applies to verbs, indefinite and definite articles, and adjectives, all of which must agree with the gender classification of the noun. Other languages make class distinctions that we do not use in English; for example, Papago, a native American language, classifies the features of the world into "living things" and "growing things." Living things includes all animated objects, such as people and animals, while growing things refers to all inanimate objects, such as plants and rocks.

All linguists agree that the grammatical categories of one language cannot be used to describe another language. Languages differ in the numbers and kinds of grammatical categories they have and how these categories are indicated. Thus, the information which in English would be expressed as "The dog bit the man" would be "Dog bite man" in Chinese. In China, the tense of the verb need not be indicated, as it must be in English, although it can be brought in by using a time word such as *now* or *yesterday*. In Chinook, an Indian language spoken in the American Northwest, conveying the same information would require the speaker to use morphemes indicating the following: "singular-feminine-subject-dog singular-masculine-object-man singular-feminine-subject-singular-masculine-object directive-bite instantaneous-past." The rules of grammar in different languages not only require different information to be included in a sentence but also differ in the ways they do this.

Although grammatical rules carry meaning, the grammar of a sentence can be understood independently of its meaning. To use a now classic example (Chomsky 1965), consider the following sentences:

"Colorless green ideas sleep furiously."
"Furiously sleep ideas green colorless."

Both sentences are meaningless in English. But the first is easily recognized as grammatical by an English speaker, whereas the second is both meaningless and ungrammatical. The first

sentence has the parts of speech in English in their proper relation to each other; the second sentence does not.

Transformational Grammar

Traditional descriptive grammars formulate the rules of a language by breaking down sentences into constituents (parts of speech) and analyzing the relationships these parts of speech have to one another and to the sentence as a whole. But this kind of descriptive grammar cannot account for all the features of a language. Traditional descriptive grammars cannot, for example, account for the ambiguity of certain sentences. The sentence "They are flying planes" (Allen and van Buren 1971) can be understood to have two meanings: " . . . those specks on the horizon are planes flying in the air," and " . . . my friends are flying planes."

A traditional descriptive grammar that understands sentences by breaking them up into their elements and stops there will not be able to show that the sentence "They are flying planes" has two different meanings. Nor can traditional descriptive grammars account for the differences we feel between the following two sentences: (1) "The picture was painted by a new technique," and (2) "The picture was painted by a real artist." A traditional grammar would have to represent the structure of these sentences in the same way.

Because of these and other limitations in traditional descriptive grammars, a new approach to understanding language called **transformational generative grammar** was developed by Noam Chomsky in the 1950s. Instead of focusing on the parts of speech in a sentence and their relationship to one another, transformational grammar focuses on the relationship between levels of language structure. According to transformational grammar, languages have two levels, deep

The "Wizard of Id" Brings You This Message

A palace guard rushes up to his king in a state of anxiety. In the background, one can see a mob approaching the palace. It is a mob of angry peasants, armed for warfare with clubs and other improvised tools of aggression. The palace guard shouts, "Your majesty, your majesty, the peasants are revolting!" The king is facing away from the window and remains unaware of the tumult among the populace. In a state of regal grace and superiority he answers, matter of factly, "Yes, they certainly are."

The confusion of communication that results from this problem of syntactic ambiguity can be handled by transformational grammar. At the level of deep structure, there are two sentences, each with its own meaning and its own set of rules that transform these different deep structures into the same surface structure.

Guard's communication
Deep structure: The peasants are revolting against you.
Surface structure: The peasants are revolting.

King's communication
Deep structure: The peasants are revolting to me.
Surface structure: The peasants are revolting.

structure and surface structure. The deep structure of a language is revealed in basic, or kernel, sentences. These kernels are simple, declarative, affirmative, active sentences: "John loves Mary." They can be transformed by a set of rules into a variety of surface structures. For example, the rule for transforming the positive into the negative would lead to this surface structure: "John does not love Mary." The rule for transforming the declarative into the interrogative would lead to "Does John love Mary?" and so forth. Not all sentences that seem similar—that is, have similar surface structures—have the same deep structure. The two sentences "The picture was painted by a new technique" and "The picture was painted by a real artist" can be shown to have different deep structures and different transformational histories. The first is derived by a double transformation from "John painted the picture by a new technique." The second is the passive of "A real artist painted the picture." Transformational grammar can also account for the surface ambiguity in the sentence "They are flying planes" by showing that the two meanings are generated by different deep structures and can be represented differently at this level.

The excitement created by transformational grammar can be better understood in the context of the goals of linguistic theory. A grammar is an account of the competence, or implicit knowledge, of a speaker of a language. It describes and attempts to account for the ability of a speaker to understand a sentence in the native language and to produce an appropriate sentence on a given occasion. Ideally, the competence of a speaker-hearer can be expressed as a system of rules that relates signals to their meanings. The problem for the grammarian is to discover and make explicit the system of rules the speaker-hearer knows only implicitly. For the linguist, however, the correct statement of the grammatical principles of a language is of interest primarily for what it tells about the more general question of the nature of universal grammar. A universal grammar, in turn, is of interest primarily for the information it provides concerning innate intellectual structure. The aim of linguistic theory is to understand the nature of mental processes, the ways in which sentences are produced and understood, and the ways in which linguistic competence is acquired. The success with which transformational grammar accounts for linguistic competence has opened up new vistas in the science of linguistics and in our understanding of the workings of the human mind.

Vocabulary

A **vocabulary** is the total stock of words in a language. The relation between culture and language is perhaps most clearly seen in vocabulary. In industrial society, the vocabulary will contain many words reflecting technological complexity and specialization. In a technologically simpler society, the vocabulary will be different. The vocabulary of all cultures is elaborated in the direction of what is most important in that culture. The Subanum of the Philippines, a relatively simple agricultural society, have 132 separate words for the diagnosis of disease (Conklin 1969). This same society possesses over a thousand words for the plants in that environment. The Inuit have many different words for snow: snow on the ground (*aput*), falling snow (*gana*), drifting snow (*piqsirpog*), and so on. This elaboration of Inuit vocabulary has an obvious relationship to the importance of weather conditions for survival.

Because vocabulary reflects the way people with a certain culture perceive their environment, anthropologists use vocabulary as a clue to understanding experience and reality in different cultures. Through vocabulary, anthropologists attempt to get a "native's" view of the world not influenced by the anthropologist's own classification system. This perspective has long been used in studying the vocabulary for kinship. In English, for example, the word *brother-in-law* lumps together my sister's husband, my husband's brother, and the husbands of all my husband's sisters. In Hindi, a language of northern India, there are separate terms for my sister's husband (*behnoi*), my husband's elder brother (*jait*), my husband's younger brother (*deva*), and my husband's sisters' husbands (*nandoya*). Kinship vocabulary is a good clue to the nature of the most significant family relations in a culture. The sin-

gle term *brother-in-law* in English reflects the similarity of a woman's behavior toward all the men in those different kinship statuses. The variety of words in Hindi reflects the fact that each of these categories of people is treated differently.

Anthropologists also attempt to discover the criteria for applying a particular label to an aspect of the physical or social environment in order to understand how a culturally specific area of meaning is divided into parts and how these parts are related to one another. One kind of relationship is that of exclusion, or contrast. Thus, going back to our example of kinship, English terminology contrasts *brother-in-law* with *sister-in-law* by the criterion of sex. *Brother* is contrasted with *brother-in-law* by the criterion of blood versus affinal relationship (relation through marriage). But both *brother* and *brother-in-law* are included in *relative*, a more general category that contains people related both by blood and marriage. The category of relatives contrasts with the category of close nonrelatives—friends—and this category contrasts with unknown people, or strangers.

LANGUAGE AND CULTURE

We have just seen how language, especially in its vocabulary, reflects cultural emphases, and the ways in which cultures divide up their physical and social environment. But language does more than just reflect culture; it is the way in which the individual is introduced to the order of the physical and social environment. Language, therefore, would seem to have a major impact on the way an individual perceives and conceptualizes the world. This importance and special role of language were made clear by Edward Sapir (1949), who wrote:

Human beings do not live in the objective world alone . . . but are very much at the mercy of the particular language which has become the medium of expression for their society . . . the fact . . . is that the "real world" is to a large extent unconsciously built up on the language habits of the group. No two languages are ever sufficiently similar to be considered as representing the same social reality. The worlds in which different societies live are distinct worlds, not merely the same world with different labels attached.

If my language has only one term—*brother-in-law*—that is applied to my sister's husband, my husband's brothers, and my husband's sisters' husbands, I am led by my language to perceive all these relatives in a similar way. Vocabulary, through what it groups together under one label and what it differentiates with different labels, is one way in which language shapes our perception of the world.

Anthropologists have long been interested in the ways in which grammatical categories influence the perception of reality. Both Sapir and a student of his, Benjamin Whorf, investigated the ways in which different peoples "see" the universe through the medium of their languages. The **Whorf-Sapir hypothesis,** as it has come to be called, asks these two questions: Are concepts of time, space, and matter given in substantially the same form by experience to all people, or are they in part conditioned by the structure of particular languages? Are there correspondences between linguistic patterns and cultural and behavioral norms? Most anthropologists would probably give a qualified yes to both questions, although we have little actual research to document these answers.

Harry Hoijer (1964) applied the Whorf-Sapir hypothesis to the Navajo, an Indian tribe in Arizona and New Mexico. He demonstrated that many aspects of Navajo grammar (for example, the conjugation of active verbs, the reporting of actions and events, and the framing of substantive concepts) emphasize movement and specify the nature, direction, and status of such movement in considerable detail. Where English would say, "One dresses," "One is young," and "He is carrying a round object," Navajo would say, "One moves into clothing," "One moves about newly," and "He moves along

handling a round object." The Navajo language conceives of the universe as being in motion; position is defined as a withdrawal from motion. Where English would say "on," Navajo would say "at rest." Parallels to this linguistic conception of the universe in motion are found in many aspects of Navajo culture. In Navajo mythology, for example, gods and culture heroes restlessly move from one place to another, seeking by their motion to perfect the universe.

Although some correspondences between grammatical categories and cultural themes or world views have been demonstrated, linguistic determinism is not an absolute or established fact. For example, the necessity to distinguish gender in the Romance languages does not correspond to the relative importance of gender in these cultures when compared, for example, to its importance in Chinese and Polynesian cultures, neither of which has gender classes in its language. And the lack of gender classes for nouns and adjectives in English does not correspond to any fact of culturally perceived equality between male and female. This illustrates one of the many difficulties in accepting the Whorf-Sapir hypothesis and illustrates why it is not totally accepted by anthropologists.

THE ETHNOGRAPHY OF COMMUNICATION

Anthropological linguistics has mainly been interested in languages as systems of knowledge independent of the ways in which people actually speak. The relatively new field of **sociolinguistics** focuses on speech performance: the actual encounters that involve verbal (and also accompanying nonverbal) communication between human beings. Whereas traditional anthropological linguistics assumes a homogeneous speech community, sociolinguistics is interested in variations in language use as these can be observed by the ethnographer. Finally, whereas the anthropological

Sociolinguists are interested in the study of speech performance: how people actually speak and what choices they make in different social situations. (Serena Nanda)

linguist usually works with one informant and attempts to elicit the ideal pattern of a language, the sociolinguist observes verbal behavior among different individuals and groups in society.

The sociolinguist attempts to identify, describe, and understand the cultural patterning of different speech events within a speech community (society or subsociety). For example, a political speech has different purposes and is limited by different norms from those for a political discussion among friends. The norms regarding political speeches will be different in different cultures: who can participate as speaker and audience, the appropriate topics for such a speech, what kinds of cultural themes can be used, where such speeches can take place, the relation between the speaker and hearer in this context, the language used for political speeches in a multilingual community, and so forth. Sociolinguists are interested in the ways in which speech varies depending on an individual's position in a social structure or social relationship. In some cultures, different speech forms are used depending on whether the speaker and hearer are intimate friends, acquaintances on equal footing with each other, or of distinctly different social statuses. In French, German, and Spanish, among other languages, there are formal and informal terms of address that are lacking in English. Parents in these cultures use the informal term to address their children, but children use the formal term to their parents. In Hindi, the status of a husband is much higher than that of a wife. A wife will

E T H N O G R A P H Y

THE INDIAN AND THE "WHITEMAN"

Scene: It is a clear, hot evening in July. J and K have finished their meal. The children are sitting nearby. There is a knock at the door. J rises, answers the knock and finds L standing outside.

1. **J:** Hello, my friend! How're you doing? How you feeling, L? You feeling good?
(J now turns in the direction of K and addresses her.)

2. **J:** Look who here, everybody! Look who just come in. Sure, it's my Indian friend, L. Pretty good, all right. (J slaps L on the shoulder and, looking him directly in the eyes, seizes his hand and pumps it wildly up and down.)

3. **J:** Come right in, my friend! Don't stay outside in the rain. Better you come in right now. (J now drapes his arm around L's shoulder and moves him in the direction of a chair.)

4. **J:** Sit down! Sit right down! Take your loads off you ass. You hungry? You want crackers?

Maybe you want some beer? You want some wine? Bread? You want some sandwich? How about it? You hungry? I don't know. Maybe you sick. Maybe you don't eat again long time. (K has now stopped what she is doing and is looking on with amusement. L has seated himself and has a look of bemused resignation on his face.)

5. **J:** You sure looking good to me, L. You looking pretty fat! Pretty good all right! You got new boots? Where you buy them? Sure pretty good boots! I glad . . . (At this point, J breaks into laughter. K joins in. L shakes his head and smiles. The joke is over.)*

This joke is one of an inventive repertoire that the anthropologist Keith Basso heard among the Western Apache, with whom

*Keith Basso, *Portraits of "The Whiteman."* New York: Cambridge University Press, 1979. Reprinted by permission of the publisher.

he had been doing fieldwork for years. It is one of the "Whiteman" jokes, or rather elaborate satirical routines, that the Apache do for one another as a way of expressing their sense of difference from Anglo-Americans. These jokes form part of a process of social criticism and self-definition. In them, the Apache try to "make sense" of the Anglo-Americans with whom they have had to deal for a long time and to confer order on Apache experiences with Anglo-Americans. In these jokes, Apaches play at being "Whitemen," imitating them in speech and nonverbal gestures and behavior.

When Western Apaches stage joking imitations of Anglo-Americans, they portray them as gross incompetents in the conduct of social relations. Judged according to Apache standards for what is right and normal, the joke-teller's actions are intended to seem extremely peculiar and

never address her husband by his name (certainly not in public), but will use a roundabout expression that would translate into English as something like "I am speaking to you, sir."

It is also clear that in socially stratified societies, speech norms are different in different social classes. Elites and working class people not only have a different vocabulary but also pronounce words differently. Where variation in pronunciation exists, one form will be considered proper, or the "prestige" form, and another will be associated with lower socio-economic status. Individuals may be aware of these two forms and vary their pronunciation in different contexts. Some people who use the "lower" form in casual speech will switch to the prestige form in more careful speech. For example, William Labov (1972) studied the pronunciation of certain vowels used in ordinary speech in New York City. He found that

"wrong." This joke shows the different ways in which Anglo-Americans appear to the Apache to be ignorant of how to comport themselves appropriately in public situations. In line 1, the use of "my friend" indicates the Apache view that Anglo-Americans use this word much too loosely, even for people whom it is clear they hold in low esteem. Among the Apache, a friend is a person one has known for many years and with whom one has strong feelings of mutual confidence and respect. "How you feeling?" as a question to a mere acquaintance indicates a breach of personal privacy for the Apache and indicates an unnatural curiosity about the inner feelings of other people. In Line 2, the joke is criticizing what the Apache view as the unnecessary and embarrassing attention given to the individual in social situations by Anglo-Americans. Among the Apache, both entering and leaving a group should be done unobtrusively to avoid causing anyone to feel socially isolated and uncomfortable. In the use of the personal name L, in lines 1, 2, and 5, the joke teller contrasts the Apache view of a name as

an item of individually owned and valued property with the Anglo-American behavior, which uses such names loosely and without propriety. Also, the repetition of the name indicates the Apache view that "Whitemen" must have very bad memories and thus must continually remind themselves whom they are talking to. When J slaps L on the back (line 2) and looks him in the eye, the Apache view such behavior as aggressive and insolent. Among the Apache, adult men are careful to avoid touching each other in public, as this is viewed as an unwarranted encroachment on the private territory of the self. In Line 4, the Anglo-American is viewed as being bossy, for to insist that a visitor engage in this kind of behavior implies that he is a person of little account whose wishes may be safely ignored. The rapid-fire questions and repetitions about food in this line are viewed by the Apache as a form of coercion, and the line "Maybe you sick" contrasts with the Apache understanding that talking about trouble can increase its chances of happening. In line 5, the attention to L's physical appearance and new boots is

another example to the Apache of how Anglo-Americans force others into self-consciousness and embarrassment. Since this kind of remark appears to be well-received among Anglo-Americans, however, the Apache conclude that "Whitemen" are deeply absorbed with the surfaces of themselves, an absorption that is related to their need to be regarded as separate and distinct from other people.

Joking is an important means of communication in all cultures. To the Apache, "Whitemen" are frequently neglectful and insensitive in how they conduct themselves in the presence of Indian people. These imitations of Anglo-Americans are statements about what can happen to dignity and self-respect when two systems of cultural norms collide in social encounters. Anglo-Americans may not often get an opportunity to see how they are regarded by others, and the "Whitemen" stories collected by Basso, which are normally performed only among Apache, are a rare opportunity to be on the receiving end of a "native" view of their world.

pronunciation of these vowels (characteristic of a "New York accent") varied with socioeconomic class, ethnicity, and age of the speaker. The degree of speech variation also correlated with social class. The lowest class of people did not vary their speech much from casual talk to careful speech. Upper-middle-class people, whose pronunciation normally falls midway between the extreme correct form and the extreme stigmatized form, also showed little variation. The most extreme variations were exhibited by members of the lower middle class, who used the stigmatized forms in casual speech but the correct form in careful speech.

This study might be interpreted as demonstrating that those on the bottom do not vary their pronunciation because they have little hope of moving up socially, those at the top do not vary their pronunciation because they are relatively secure in their social position,

In societies where men wear veils, the height of the veil and the degree to which it exposes the face is an important means of nonverbal communication. (United Nations/AID/Purcell)

and those in the middle (lower middle class) vary their pronunciation most because they are "social climbers" and therefore are the most sensitive to behaving in "correct" ways. But in any case, Labov's study makes clear what many of us know but do not like to admit: we do judge a person's social status by the way he or she speaks. The function of speech is not limited to communicating information. What we say and how we say it are also a way of telling people where we are socially—or, perhaps, where we want to be.

In many new nations or speech communities, more than one language is known and used by the ordinary person. Sociolinguists are interested in the different contexts in which one or the other language would be used. In India, for example, where many upper-mid-

dle-class people are fluent in English, the native language is used at home among family even if all the people present speak excellent English. The language a person chooses to use can be a way of solidifying ethnic or familial identity or of distancing oneself from another person or group.

Nonverbal Communication

Ethnographers are also interested in nonverbal communication. In Chapter Five, we noted the work of Edward Hall on space and time. Think of some of the ways in which, to quote Hall, "time talks" and "space speaks." In our culture, what are we saying to a person when we show up for an appointment forty minutes late? Are we saying something different if we show up ten minutes early? Is a Latin American who shows up late for an appointment saying the same thing?

Part of a nonverbal communication pattern is how close we stand to another person, whether we face him or her directly or stand at an angle, and whether our arms are folded in front of us or hanging down at our sides. All cultures use nonverbal gestures to communicate. Some of these gestures are conscious; some are unconscious. What people say with their facial expressions is a powerful form of communication. Among the Tuareg, a tribal people of North Africa, whose men are veiled, the position of the veil is an important part of nonverbal communication (Murphy 1964). A Tuareg man will only lower his veil among intimates and persons of lower social status. When he is engaged in an encounter in which he does not wish to commit himself to a particular course of action, he will wear the veil very high on the bridge of his nose, so that the other party can read as little as possible from his facial expression. In our culture, as in many cultures, the eyes are considered an important clue to what a person is feeling and thinking. This explains why some people wear dark glasses in the shade. By hiding the eyes, an individual attempts to control the flow of communication and, through this, the entire encounter. Because nonverbal communication is more ambiguous than verbal communication, it leaves the "speaker" with more options. To "say it with flowers" does not involve the same degree of commitment as "saying it with words."

LANGUAGE CHANGE

Language, like other parts of culture, shows both stability and change. The first step in studying language change is to identify it. Historical linguists study different stages of a language in order to identify the kinds of changes that have taken place. The fact that language does change can easily be seen in the differences between the Old English and Modern English versions of the Lord's Prayer:

Fæder ūre þū þe eart on heofonum, sī þīn nama ȝehālȝod. Tōbecume þīn rīce. Geweorþe þīn willa on eorþan swā swā on heofonum. Ūrne ȝedæȝhwāmlī-can hlāf syle ūs tō dæȝ. And forȝyf ūs ūre ȝyltas, swā swā wē forȝyfaþ ūrum ȝyltendum. And ne ȝelæd þū ūs on costnunȝe, ac ālȳs ūs of yfele.

Our Father, which art in heaven, hallowed be Thy name. Thy kingdom come, Thy will be done, in earth as it is in heaven. Give us this day our daily bread. And forgive us our trespasses, as we forgive them that trespass against us. And lead us not into temptation, but deliver us from evil (Lehnert 1960).

Historical linguistics can be applied to phonology, morphology, or vocabulary. With regard to phonology, linguists have been able to discover certain regularities in the ways in which sounds change. These regularities are called **phonetic laws.** An example of a phonetic law is the change from the accented vowel *ā* in Old English to the vowel [ow] in Modern English. This phonetic law is illustrated in the following examples (Sturtevant 1947:65):

Old English	Modern English
bān	bone
bāt	boat
fām	foam
mān	moan
stān	stone
rād	road

This is an example of internal change. Language change can also come about through borrowing. When the Apache borrowed certain words—*loca, rico*—from the Spanish, a new phonemic occurrence was introduced, that of "l" and "r" in initial position, which was not part of the Apache phonemic pattern.

The vocabulary of a language also undergoes both internal and external changes. Words change their meanings, and new words are added. Sometimes, as cultures come into contact, cultural items are borrowed and the original name for the item is kept. Pajama is an item of clothing borrowed from India, and we have kept the original Indian word, incorporating it into the English vocabulary. In other cases, words or combinations of words already present in the language are applied to new cultural items. Some native American groups, upon seeing their first horses (introduced by the Spanish), called them "ten dogs," and North Americans refer to their automobiles in terms of "horsepower." The Apache, who had a particular way of classifying parts of the human body, applied this classification to the automobile, which was introduced to their reservations in the 1930s. This practice resulted in the extended meanings for parts of the automobile that are listed in Table 6.1.

Historical linguists use the data on internal linguistic change to discover the relationships between different languages. If two languages appear related, what is the nature of the relationship? Are the similarities due to historical contact between cultures and resultant borrowing? Or are similarities between certain languages a result of their being derived from the same ancestral language? In other words,

Table 6.1 *Apache Words for Parts of the Human Body and the Automobile*

Human Anatomical Terms		Extended Auto Meanings
External Anatomy		
daw	"chin and jaw"	"front bumper"
wos	"shoulder"	"front fender"
gun	"hand and arm"	"front wheel"
kai	"thigh and buttocks"	"rear fender"
ze	"mouth"	"gas-pipe opening"
ke	"foot"	"rear wheel"
chun	"back"	"chassis"
inda	"eye"	"headlight"
Face		
chee	"nose"	"hood"
ta	"forehead"	"auto top"
Entrails		
tsaws	"vein"	"electrical wiring"
zik	"liver"	"battery"
pit	"stomach"	"gas tank"
chih	"intestine"	"radiator hose"
jih	"heart"	"distributor"
jisoleh	"lung"	"radiator"

From *Word play: What happens when people talk*, by Peter Farb. Copyright © 1973 by Peter Farb. Reprinted by permission of Alfred A. Knopf, Inc.

do similar languages have a historical or a generic relationship?

When the similarities appear too numerous, too regular, and too basic to be accounted for by borrowing, a generic relationship is assumed. Comparative linguists attempt to work out the relationships between generically related languages. By comparing the basic vocabularies (the words most resistant to change) of the descendant languages, comparative linguists attempt to reconstruct certain features of the ancestral language, or protolanguage. Table 6-2 shows the words in Sanskrit, Greek, Latin, and Gothic on which is based the reconstruction of the numbers one to ten in the original proto-Indo-European language (Sturtevant 1947):

The rate at which basic vocabulary is retained from an original language is assumed to be 80 percent per 1,000 years. Thus, by computing the percentage of shared basic vocabulary words between two languages, an estimate can be made of how long ago the two separated out from an original ancestral language.

Comparative linguistics has been successful in documenting the relationships between many languages and grouping them into language families. Although this has been done in greatest detail for Indo-European languages, the technique has also been applied to non-European languages. Thus, comparative linguistics is an important way of tracing cultural and historical processes. Through reconstruction of a protolanguage, comparative linguistics can also tell us something about the culture of the people who spoke that language. For example, because the basic vocabulary of proto-Indo-European contains words for trees and animals that existed in northern Europe, this may have been the home of the original Indo-Europeans.

Traditional linguists have mainly been concerned with internal language change. Sociolinguists are interested in language history, or the study of historical events that affect language change. Some of the contemporary problems here have to do with the impact of industrialization, acculturation, social stratification, and national politics, as these relate to changes in language structure and language use. Sociolinguists are also interested in the social factors within a society that affect changes in both structure and language use. As Labov showed in his study in New York, sound change not only follows phonetic laws; it is also affected by the pattern of social stratification in a society, since different social classes adopt a sound change at different times.

SUMMARY

1. All animals communicate. Although nonhuman primates have a complex communication system, they lack the features of true human language: conventionality, productivity, and displacement.

Table 6.2   *The Comparative Method*

Sanskrit	Greek	Latin	Gothic	Proto-Indo-European
	oinē 'ace'	ūnus	ains	oinos
duă, dvā	dyō, dōdeca	duo	twa	duō, dwō
trayas	treis	trēs	þreis	treyes
catvāras	tettares	quattuor	fidwor	kwetwŏres
panca	pente	quīnque	fimf	penkwe
sat	hex	sex	saihs	sêks
sapta	hepta	septem	sibun	septm̂
aśtāu	octō	octō	ahtau	oktōu
nava	ennea	novem	niun	newn̂
daśa	deca	decem	taihun	dekm̂

From Edgar H. Sturtevant, *An Introduction to Linguistic Science*, 1947. Reprinted with permission of Yale University Press.

2. Conventionality means that human languages use a limited number of sounds in combination to make an infinite number of meaningful utterances.

3. Productivity means that humans can produce and understand an infinite number of utterances they have never said or heard before.

4. Displacement refers to the ability of human languages to describe things and experiences not immediately present in the environment.

5. Human speech is adaptive: it is efficient and flexible. It allows humans to think, to plan, to coordinate activities, to store up knowledge, and to teach others. The complexity of culture depends on the human ability to communicate through speech.

6. All human languages display the same capabilities of conventionality, productivity, and displacement. There are no primitive languages.

7. A child takes the initiative in learning language and learns to speak grammatically without being taught grammatical rules. This suggests that human beings have a precultural, or innate, language-learning capacity. This potential for speech will only be realized, however, through interaction with other human beings speaking a human language.

8. All languages have structure. The three subsystems of a language are a sound system, a grammar, and a vocabulary. Phonemes are minimal sound units that carry meaning; syntax is the combination of morphemes used to produce meaningful utterances; vocabulary links words to their meanings.

9. The grammatical categories of a language are the vehicles by which people think. Grammar and vocabulary structure perception of the environment. The ways in which different cultures perceive reality through the grammatical categories of their language may show relationships to other aspects of that culture.

10. A language is not the same as speech. A language is a system of knowledge independent of the way it is used; speech is what people actually do when they communicate with one another. Sociolinguists are interested in speech behavior as it is culturally patterned and varies according to social factors.

11. Language changes. Historical linguists are interested in internal linguistic change. Comparative linguists attempt to discover which languages are generically related. Sociolinguists are interested in the historical and social factors in language change.

SUGGESTED READINGS

Burling, Robbins
1970   *Man's Many Voices.* New York: Holt, Rinehart and Winston. An excellent introduction to all aspects of language, including topics not usually covered in introductory texts, such as Black English and word games.

Farb, Peter
1974   *Word Play: What Happens When People Talk.* New York: Knopf. As is usual with this author, this book is comprehensive, entertaining, and interesting for the nonspecialist.

Gumperz, John J., and Hymes, Dell, eds.
1972   *Directions in Sociolinguistics.* New York: Holt, Rinehart and Winston. A compilation of interesting articles from a number of different cultures on a variety of kinds of speech performances.

Southworth, F. C., and Daswani, C. J.
1974   *Foundations of Linguistics.* New York: Free Press. This is a good complete introduction to the study of language written in a straightforward, clear manner.

Stross, Brian
1976   *The Origin and Evolution of Language.* Dubuque, Iowa: William C. Brown. A highly readable book that includes a discussion of what the fossil record suggests about the evolution of human speech.

CHAPTER SEVEN

LEARNING CULTURE

▶ What are the biocultural bases of human culture learning?

▶ How does culture influence personality?

▶ In what ways is child rearing different in India and in the United States?

▶ What do we learn in school besides the "Three R's"?

Human infants become adults only by growing up in a human society. More than any other species, human beings are dependent on others for survival and growth. Human infants cannot survive without the care of other people. They cannot get food, cannot move around, cannot cling, and cannot force adults to respond to their needs. The human's period of helplessness and dependency on others is the longest in the animal world. It is the price *Homo sapiens* pays for its big brain and its enormous potential for learning. And it is during the long period of infancy that cultural pattern-ing has its strongest effect. The infant simply has no choice about learning to respond in culturally patterned ways. Thus, the infant grows up into a child and later into an adult not simply as a human, but as a particular kind of human: a Kwakiutl, Trobriand Islander, Briton, or Tahitian. **Encultura-tion** is the term anthropologists use to refer to the ways in which human infants and children learn to be adult members of their society, while **socialization** refers to the learning processes through which human cultural traditions are passed on from one generation to the next.

BIOLOGY, SOCIALIZATION, AND CULTURE

The human infant, in spite of its helplessness, is not simply an "empty slate" on which culture writes its pattern or a lump of clay on which culture impresses its own shape. As we have seen in the previous chapter, human beings have a biologically based disposition to learn human behavior. The human child actively participates in culture. Human brains and nervous systems are organized to promote social interaction with others, learning, and adaptation to the requirements of a particular sociocultural system. In addition to the biological characteristics of the species, each human being brings a unique genetic inheritance to the socialization process. Becoming a human being, therefore, is the result of a complex interaction between universal human capacities and culturally variable child-rearing practices, individual heredity, and the common experiences patterned by culture.

Anthropologists are not in complete agreement about what exactly these innate human capacities and potentialities are. We know that infants have not only physical needs but emotional ones as well. Studies of infants in a variety of situations have demonstrated that "tender loving care" is a prerequisite for healthy emotional development (Spitz 1975). This need also exists among nonhuman primates. Experimental studies demonstrate that infant monkeys who are deprived of the company of their mothers do not develop in the same way as other monkeys. They play less; they are less curious, more hostile, and sexually clumsy. Male monkeys raised apart from their mothers show little interest in female monkeys as adults. Female monkeys raised apart from their mothers show little interest in their own babies (Harlow 1962).

All human beings also pass through a similar sequence of developmental stages, each characterized by an increase in the capacity to deal with the physical and social environment. At each stage, physical, mental, and psychological potentialities unfold if they are given at least a minimum of encouragement. Physically, the infant increases in muscular coordination; from an immobile creature barely able to focus the movement of eyes and limbs, it begins to be able to lift its head, focus its eyes, sit up, creep on all fours, stand, and then walk by itself. Mentally, it increases its capacity to differentiate and classify objects and people in the environment. Its curiosity increases. Human infants will, if given a chance, take an active role in trying new ways of behaving and exploring the world around them. Psychologically, the infant increasingly develops a sense of itself and others. As the infant grows, it learns to modify its demands so that it will meet with success in its social environment. The infant becomes increasingly able to distinguish what actions will bring gratification and what actions will be met with no response or negative response from others. Cultural variability in child rearing must be seen against the background of universals that grow out of the biological characteristics of the human organism: the needs for physical gratification and for emotional contact with others, and stages of developmental capacities. Thus, socialization must be seen against the different stages of the life cycle.

Every system of cultural transmission takes into account these different stages of life, although the definition of the stages may vary from culture to culture. Infants are treated differently from children; children reach puberty and eventually become adults; adults are distinguished as middle-aged and old. With each of these status changes, different roles are assumed and different kinds of cultural transmission take place. Although in anthropology we have traditionally emphasized early socialization rather than the transmission of culture in later life, we are now paying greater attention to learning in adulthood and among the old.

Not only do societies transmit culture in

terms of life stages, but not all people in a society are given the same social conditioning. Status differences and the roles, or behavior patterns, associated with them must be considered in investigating the way culture is transmitted. In societies where social ranking and differentiation are important, what one learns may be largely a function of one's position in the social hierarchy. At the very least, every society treats males and females differently.

SEX ROLE SOCIALIZATION

This process of sex role socialization frequently begins at infancy or shortly thereafter. The ways in which this is done and its effects on behavior and personality are always of interest to anthropologists. Two important processes associated with sex role learning are imitation and internalization through identification with a same-sex role model. In play, for example, girls most frequently imitate the domestic activities of their mothers or elder females who stand in this relation to them; boys imitate their fathers or other males. This imitation is subtly encouraged along the lines of sex even when it is not a consequence of direct teaching. Girls and boys are both discouraged from imitating activities culturally considered appropriate for the opposite sex and rewarded for imitating activities considered culturally appropriate for their own sex. The internalization of gender identification—that is, the inner conceptualization of self as being masculine or feminine—is tied up with the playing out of these sex-related activities.

Part of the controversy in the study of sex role socialization is the extent to which the differences that have been found to be related to sex are based on biology (Draper 1974). Since learning begins at birth, untangling the complex interaction between biology and culture becomes extremely difficult. When adult expectations of children become stereotyped according to sex role, it may be this expectation, even more than possible biological differences, that explains the differentiation in male and female behavior and personality.

The complex way in which biology and culture may interact to produce differences in male and female behavior is illustrated by the findings that girls seem to have greater verbal ability and boys greater spatial ability. It is generally agreed that girls have a better and earlier ability to acquire language than do boys and that they are more sensitive to social cues than boys. Boys, on the other hand, are almost universally shown to have superior spatial ability. If we assume that these abilities have some biological basis, we can also assume that they would be incorporated into parents' expectations of children. They would expect little girls to talk more and respond to others and might talk more with them. They would allow, reward, or even initiate activities in which boys can explore their environment. Subtle but persistent interactions with others based on the initial biological differences may play a large role in explaining some sex-role-related patterns in adults—for example, the greater success girls have in school (which rewards verbal ability and social sensitivity) and the superior performance of males on tests of spatial ability.

But the evidence is not clear. In practically all societies, small boys are allowed to roam farther from their home than small girls. This is both consistent with, and may be a cause of, the superior spatial abilities of males. Yet studies of exceptional girls in one East African society who were allowed to roam farther from home than was typically the case showed they matched their male counterparts on tests of spatial ability. Such findings put us back to a position in which sex role socialization appears to be best understood in terms of both biological and cultural components interacting in complex ways. One useful model for understanding this process may be that socialization practices act back upon and intensify possible biological predispositions that are different in males and females.

Sex role socialization often involves the informal participation of children in the appropriate economic roles of their sex. Here, small boys in Fez, Morocco, hold the golden threads that their tailor fathers are using to make embroidered djellabahs, the local garment. (United Nations)

EARLY SOCIALIZATION AND PERSONALITY

Child-rearing practices in all cultures are designed to produce adults who will be able to function effectively in that culture. In order to be able to do this, adults must learn certain skills, norms, and values; they must learn the cultural *content*. But the transmission of culture involves more than content; in the socialization process, children learn more than just skills and knowledge. The transmission of culture involves patterning children's attitudes and values as well as their outward behavior. The shaping of values and personality, or the inner life of the child, often does not take place consciously. Through unconscious, although culturally patterned, interaction with others, the growing child learns to respond to the world in culturally selected ways. From the vast potential of emotional responses, cultures select out some that are considered appropriate. Through the details of their experience with others, children learn to pattern their emotional responses in culturally approved ways.

Culture as Communication

The covert aspect of socialization calls attention to culture as a communication process. From this point of view, what is important in cultural transmission is not so much what children are taught or not taught but the ways in which things happen to them and the attitudes of the people around them with whom they are interacting (Schwartz 1976).

The subtle ways in which personality is shaped through unconscious cultural patterning is illustrated in a study of Japanese and American mothers and infants carried out by William Caudill and his associates (1973). In an earlier study, Caudill noted that Japanese adults were much more accepting of one another's dependency needs than were Americans, for whom the emphasis was on independence. Caudill hoped to throw some light on this difference in adult personality by studying the relationships between mothers and infants in Japan as compared with those in the United States.

He found that the actual time infants spent in various activities, such as sleeping and feeding, were the same in both cultures. Japanese and American mothers also spent almost the same amounts of time feeding, diapering, and dressing their infants. American infants, however, spent more of their waking time in an active manner—playing with toys and with their hands. Japanese infants were more passive when awake. In order to check whether this difference might have a genetic basis, Caudill tested matched samples of Japanese-American infants, those who genetically were Japanese but whose parents and grandparents had been born and lived in the United States. The Japanese-American infants turned out to be significantly like the American infants and unlike the Japanese sample.

Caudill then turned his attention to the "style" of caretaking in an attempt to account for the difference between the Japanese and American infant behavior. American mothers encouraged their infants to be active and vocally responsive, whereas the Japanese mother acted to soothe and quiet the baby. The American mother, for example, spent more of the baby's waking time looking at, positioning the body of, and chatting with her infant. The Japanese mother did more carrying, rocking, and lulling. Caudill relates these and other differences in caretaking style to a basic difference in psychological attitude between Japanese and American mothers. American mothers see the baby as a separate person who should learn to think and do for itself. Encouraging vocalization is one way in which the American mother "teaches" her infant to express its needs. Jap-

The ritual of the birthday party teaches children in the United States to place importance on the self and encourages individualism. (Serena Nanda)

anese mothers, on the other hand, have a much closer attachment to their infants. A Japanese mother feels she knows what her infant needs; there is no need for it to "express" itself. This is consistent not only with the lesser vocalization of the Japanese baby but also with the greater physical contact between the Japanese baby and its mother. Thus, the dependency of Japanese and the independence of Americans, differences that show up in the adult personality, seem to come under cultural direction as early as three to four months of age.

Personality as an Adaptation

The idea that personality develops as an adaptation to the basic food-getting pattern of a society is not new in anthropology but has recently attracted increasing attention. One important anthropological project examining the interrelation between food getting, social

E T H N O G R A P H Y

CHILD REARING AND PERSONALITY IN VILLAGE INDIA*

One of the cultures studied in the six-culture project was that of the Rajput caste in the village of Khalapur in Northern India. Two basic principles that organize Indian village society are caste and family. The castes, which are groups traditionally associated with particular occupations, are ranked as superior or inferior. Although castes change their position in the hierarchy, an individual cannot move from one caste to another. An individual's social mobility or social status is dependent on the caste into which he or she is born. A person is also a member of a family group. In Northern India, the family is generally patriarchal, patrilineal, and patrilocal. This means that the males have the power, inheritance is through the male line, and the wife goes to live in her husband's home after marriage. Family and caste are the most important arenas of social, religious, and economic activity. The group, not the individual, is the center of culture and society, and people who set themselves against the group risk being left without the sup-

port of the social networks on which success in India depends.

Child-rearing practices in Khalapur are directed, both consciously and unconsciously, toward training the child to function effectively within the social framework of family, caste, and village. Three aspects of child-rearing practices related to this are training in emotional unresponsiveness, training in controlling aggression and assertiveness, and the lack of training in self-reliance.

The Rajput caste claims descent from the ancient warrior kings of India. Today, however, they are mostly farmers. Rajput dwellings in the village of Khalapur include separate quarters for males and females, which is a typical Indian spatial configuration. The women's quarters are within an enclosed courtyard. Rajput women practice purdah: they wear a veil in front of all male strangers and any men in their husband's family who are older than their husband. The life of Rajput women and small children is largely lived within the confines of the courtyard. The men have their own quarters, where they spend most of their time; they socialize, eat, and frequently sleep apart from the women.

Training in emotional unre-

sponsiveness begins at birth. Although Rajput infants will be picked up and attended to when they are hungry or fussing, for the most part they are left in their cots, wrapped up in blankets both to keep off insects and to avoid the evil eye. Except for anxieties about a baby's health, it is not the center of attention. A baby receives attention mainly when it cries. At that time someone will try to distract it, but when it becomes quiet the interaction will stop. Adult interaction with babies is generally aimed at producing a cessation of response, rather than stimulation of it. Infants and children of all ages are not shown off to others for fear, parents say, that they will attract the evil eye. Children are also not praised by their parents, who fear that this will "spoil" them and make them disobedient.

Rajput children spend their first two years as passive observers of courtyard life. They are never left alone, yet neither are they the center of interest. Rajput mothers do not tease or frustrate their children, but neither are they very emotionally responsive toward them. Unresponsiveness is itself a message; the child learns that moodiness will not be tolerated. Few demands are put on Rajput

*Based on John T. Hitchcock and Leigh Minturn, "The Rajputs of Khalapur," in Beatrice Whiting, ed., *Six Cultures: Studies of Child Rearing.* © 1963 by John Wiley & Sons. Reprinted by permission of the publisher.

children; they are not pressured or even encouraged to become self-reliant. Weaning, which generally occurs without trouble, takes place at two to three years; but if the mother does not become pregnant, a child may be nursed into its sixth year. Elimination is also no problem. Babies are not diapered, and when the baby is being held by someone it is simply held away from the body when it urinates. The mother will try to anticipate bowel movements and hold the baby over a trash pile outside the courtyard at the appropriate time. When a child can walk, he or she is led outside the courtyard to urinate or defecate; since this is done in public by adults, the child can easily imitate the proper behavior.

In many ways, Rajput children are discouraged from doing things on their own and encouraged to seek aid from others. Babies, for example, are not encouraged to crawl. They learn to walk when they are ready, and mothers say they see no reason to rush this. When a baby can walk alone, it wanders about the courtyard or may be taken by an older child to the men's house. Village women do little to guide children's behavior by explaining or reasoning with them. There is also little direct instruction to small children. Children are not considered trainable until they can talk; no demands are made on them to modify their behavior until they can walk and say a few words. Small children learn the skills, customs, and values of the group through observation and imitation. In the first five years of life, the child moves very gradu-

ally from observer to participant in village and family life.

The preschool child plays most of the time. Although some of this play involves imitating adult activities, such as farming and cooking, children are not encouraged in any way to participate in adult activities. The chores a child is given are mainly directed to helping the mother, who is confined to the courtyard. Thus, children may go to the store, carry water, or deliver messages to the men's house. There is little feeling that children should be given chores on principle in order to train them in responsibility. Rajput children take little initiative in solving problems by themselves. Instead, they are taught whom they can depend on for help in the web of social relations of kin group, caste, and village. Children follow the adult pattern of giving aid only when asked and often only if it is insistently demanded. Although chores increase somewhat as the child gets older, it is not a Rajput custom to require children to work if adults can do it. Children are not praised for their work, and a child's inept attempt to do an adult job is belittled. Thus, children are reluctant to undertake what they cannot do well.

This lack of responsibility is consistent with the pattern of values in a caste society. In the Indian caste system, menial and manual work is considered not only degrading socially but ritually polluting. Many Rajputs are quite wealthy and employ servants to do the menial tasks that in other cultures might be assigned to children. Finally, as a caste of warriors, Rajputs have

India

• **Rajputs**

contempt for farming, although that is how they earn their livelihood. A Rajput family that can afford it will hire laborers to do the farm work. Even if a Rajput man does his own farming, he passes on a negative attitude about this work to his sons.

The third aspect of child rearing in Khalapur related to the requirements of Indian social organization is the inhibition of aggression and assertiveness in small children. There is some ambivalence here. The caste system and the family system require an individual to be submissive to those above but dominant with those below. Also, as a warrior caste, Rajput males feel they ought to maintain an aggressive image. The lack of consistency in training children to control aggression reflects this. On the one hand, mothers *say* a child ought to be passive, submissive, and restrained in the presence of others. Fighting among children is discouraged. (continued on next page)

Most of the mothers never give the child advice to "fight" or even to "fight back," and several were shocked that the anthropologist would even consider giving such advice to a child. On the other hand, the mothers allow a certain aggression against themselves, especially on the part of sons. Males learn pretty early that women have a low status in the village and family and can thus be abused, at least verbally. Men are more willing than women to teach a child to be aggressive. Although they believe a child should not start a fight, fathers in Khalapur do admit telling their children to fight back. This aggressiveness is reinforced by the traditional storytelling and drama of Hindu mythology, in which the bravery of the Rajput warriors is an important feature.

Rajput child rearing thus emphasizes emotional unresponsiveness, represses individuality, and teaches children to know whom to ask for aid, rather than to solve their problems themselves. They are not encouraged to be outwardly aggressive, but they do learn to be dominant with their social inferiors. Child-rearing practices in Khalapur make sense in terms of the social structure of a caste hierarchy, limited geographical and social mobility, and living in an extended family in which group harmony rather than individual assertiveness is a basic requirement.

structure, child rearing, and personality is the study of six cultures carried out by Beatrice Whiting and her associates (1963). The basis for this project was the thesis that maintenance systems—which include the basic economy and aspects of the social structure, such as residence—set the parameters for child-rearing practices. These, in turn, shape adult personality, which in turn is reflected in other cultural elements such as religious beliefs and folklore (see Figure 7-1).

SOCIALIZATION IN LATER LIFE

Learning one's culture is a process that continues after infancy and early childhood, although most social scientists agree that the earliest years are crucial. In looking at later socialization, anthropologists have been interested in a number of aspects of the transmission of culture. One is the relationship between early enculturation and later enculturation. As children grow up and move into new and adult roles, is what they have learned in childhood useful for those roles? Is there, in other words, cultural continuity in socialization?

Cultural Continuity and Discontinuity

Ruth Benedict (1938) characterized American culture as containing major discontinuities between what is expected of children and what is expected of adults. Children in our culture are not expected to be responsible; they are supposed to play, not work. Few children in America have the opportunity to contribute in any meaningful way to the basic tasks of society. Children take on responsibility only when they become adults. A second major discontinuity is that children are required to be submissive, but adults are expected to be dominant. This is especially true for males. Sons must obey their fathers, but as fathers they must dominate their sons. A third major discontinuity has to do with sex. As children, Americans are not allowed to engage in sexual behavior, and for many people just the thought of childhood sexuality is repellent. As adults, however, especially as men and women marry, sex is considered to be a normal, even valued, activity.

In great contrast to the discontinuities experienced by the individual learning to participate in American culture is the continuity

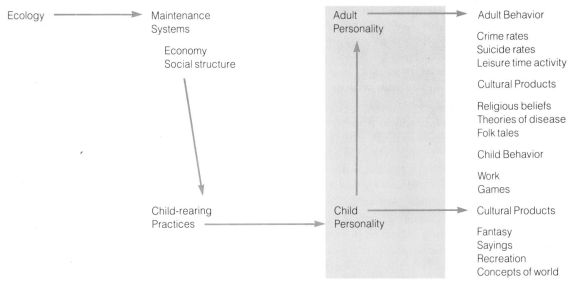

Figure 7.1   *A theory of the relationship of personality to culture based on the following process:* Ecology *determines the* maintenance system, *which includes the basic economy and elements of social structure. For example, climate and soil determine the nature of crops grown in an agricultural society and whether herding is present. The way in which people get food determines in part the arrangement of people in space and household composition. This in turn sets the parameters for* child-rearing practices. *Different child-rearing practices lead to differences in the* personality of children *and also differences in* adult personality. *These personality dimensions will in turn be reflected in* cultural products *such as religion and folklore. From Beatrice Whiting, ed.,* Six Cultures: Studies of Child Rearing. *© 1963 by John Wiley & Sons. Reprinted by permission of the publisher.*

of socialization among many native American societies. The Cheyenne, a Plains Indian tribe, exhibit a great degree of continuity in their culture. Cheyenne children are not treated as a different order of people from adults. They are regarded as smaller and not yet fully competent adults, although by American standards the competence of Cheyenne children is quite astounding. The play of small children centers on imitation of and real participation in adult tasks. Both boys and girls learn to ride horses almost as soon as they can walk. This skill is related to the importance of the horse in traditional Cheyenne culture, in which buffalo were hunted on horseback. By the time they are six, little boys are riding bareback and using the lasso. By eight, boys are helping to herd the horses in the camp. As soon as they

can use them, boys get small but good-quality bows and arrows. Little girls who are just toddlers help their mothers carry wood and water. Boys and girls learn these activities in play, in which the routine of family life is imitated. Girls play "mother" to the smallest children; boys imitate the male roles of hunter and warrior and even the rituals of self-torture that are part of Cheyenne religious ceremonies.

Control of aggression is an important value among the Cheyenne, and aggression rarely occurs within the group of adults. A chief rules not by force and dominance but by intelligence, justice, and consideration for others. The needs of the group are more important than the need of the individual. The Cheyenne learn this lesson at an early age. Infants who cry are not physically punished, but they will be removed from the camp and their baskets hung in the bushes until they stop. This is an early lesson in learning that one cannot force one's will on others by self-display. Aggression and lack of control of one's emotions do not bring rewards for either children or adults; rather, they result in social isolation.

The repression of sexuality is another lesson traditionally learned early in childhood and carried through adult life. A Cheyenne girl is considered unchaste if a boy even touches her genitals or breasts, and she cannot enter into a respectable marriage. From the time of her first menses, a girl puts on a "chastity belt" of rope and rawhide that she takes off only at marriage, and in fact she may continue to wear it even during marriage when her husband is away fighting or hunting. Males are also taught to control their sexual impulses. They cannot even think of courtship or marriage until they have been in a war party. Sexual control continues to be an ideal even in marriage. The Cheyenne ideal is to space children ten to twelve years apart. A couple that takes a vow to refrain from sexual relations for this period after the birth of a child is highly respected in the camp.

Although Cheyenne childhood seems to require a great deal of discipline, responsibility, and competence, these demands are consistent with the demands on adults. There is no discontinuity between Cheyenne childhood, adolescence, and adulthood. The transition to adult status is very easy, being a continuum of what was learned in childhood. For a boy, the public recognition of this status comes with his first participation as hunter and warrior, which occurs at about the age of twelve. This is a real and important event, and his achievement is publicly rewarded by his parents' praise and a feast given in his honor. As Hoebel (1960), the ethnographer of the Cheyenne, says: "Cheyenne youths have little reason to be rebels without a cause. They slip easily into manhood, knowing their contributions are immediately wanted, valued and ostentatiously rewarded."

Initiation Rites

It has been suggested by a number of anthropologists that there is more discontinuity in socialization for males than for females (Chodorow 1974). For boys to become men frequently requires an assertion of independence that involves a rejection of feminine qualities and identifications. For girls, the transition to adult status is more of a continuation of their early life, which is organized around and involved with the family, primary and personal relationships, and caring for others. The need for boys to break away from female identifications and female dependency may be one explanation of the frequency of male **initiation rites** in many societies around the world. From this perspective, male initiation rites can be seen as bridging the gap where discontinuities exist between early childhood socialization and the requirements of an adult masculine role. Thus, John Whiting and his associates (1967) have shown that male initiation rites are more likely to occur in cultures where there is a strong identification of the boy with his mother and hostility toward the father. This may grow out of sleeping arrangements in which children sleep with the mother apart from the father. In these cases, says Whiting, male initiation rites are necessary to ensure the development of an adequate male role.

In many societies, a boy between the ages of five and twelve must undergo an initiation, after which he is publicly recognized as a man. This "rite of passage" is frequently lengthy, dramatic, and painful, and it often involves circumcision. During this initiation, a boy may also be taught tribal lore as well as more practical elements of culture. From this perspective, some anthropologists have seen initiation rites primarily in terms of their educational functions. They are the equivalent of the formal schooling received by children in our own society. Still another explanation offered for male initiation rites is that of dramatizing the values of society in a context outside the inti-

Male initiation rites are a common feature in the world's cultures and mark the transition from childhood to adulthood. On the eve of his circumcision ceremony, a boy rides a horse accompanied by dancers and musicians in a village in Indonesia. (United Nations)

macy of the home (Hart 1967). By taking the child out of the home, the initiation rite emphasizes the importance of citizenship—the fact that an individual must be responsible to the whole society and that society as well as the family has an interest in him. A fourth function suggested for male initiation rites is that of explicitly affirming and maintaining the solidarity of the male bond in society and the importance of male organization to social life. Still other interpretations have focused on the symbolism of the rites themselves. Bruno Bettelheim (1962), a psychoanalyst who studied rites that involve circumcision, suggests that they are symbolic of the male envy of the female power of bearing children. The bloodletting associated with the rites is an attempt to imi-

tate and thus participate in these life-creating powers at a symbolic level.

Female initiation rites also exist in many societies, although they are not found as frequently as initiation rites for males. Such rites are different from society to society; sometimes the initiate is isolated; sometimes she is the center of attention. Some of the rituals are elaborate and take years to perform, others are performed with little ceremony. Given the great variety, a female initiation rite may be defined as consisting of prescribed ceremonial events, given to all girls in a particular society, celebrated between their eighth and twentieth years. The rite is often a cultural elaboration of menarche but does not include betrothal or marriage customs (Brown 1965). There are a number of possible interpretations of such rites. Brown found that such rites are more likely to occur in societies in which the young girl continues to reside in the home of her mother after marriage. This suggests the rites are a way of announcing a girl's status change, which is made necessary by the fact that she spends her adult life in the same place as she spent her childhood. Though the girl may continue to do the same kind of tasks she did as a child growing up, she now has to do them as a responsible adult. The rites are thus the means by which the girl publicly accepts her new legal role. Where a girl moves to her husband's home after marriage, this move itself signals the change from childhood to adult status.

Another reason, often made explicit in those societies that perform such rites, is that the rites are a way of teaching the girls what they will have to know as adults. Bemba women explain their elaborate girls' initiation rite called *Chisungu* (Richards 1956:125) by saying that they "make the girls clever," using a word that means "to be intelligent and socially competent and to have a knowledge of etiquette."

Although such rites do indeed seem to have a teaching component, this cannot be a full explanation of them, because such rites do not exist in all societies where females perform domestic and subsistence tasks. It is suggested, therefore, that only in societies where women have a central role in subsistence will such rites be performed, in order to assure both the girl and others of her competence and to impress upon her the importance of her adult role.

Finally, Brown also offers an explanation of female rites that inflict a great deal of pain, such as extensive tattooing or a genital operation. These rites are often found in societies with male initiation rites where both a genital operation and seclusion are part of the ritual. Thus, these female rites may be interpreted both as an imitation of male rites and as a way of resolving a conflict of sexual identity, which grows out of the same conditions of infancy that explain the male rites.

In the United States, where there are no formal male initiation ceremonies, the informal male peer group is an important institution for socialization into the male role. (Serena Nanda)

The Marginal Status of Adolescents

Anthropologists have looked at later socialization in terms of the ways in which adolescents, who are in a marginal status, become fully incorporated into their culture. Where cultural continuity is present, as among the Cheyenne, youth are not marginal. There is a gradually increasing social participation from childhood through adulthood. In many societies where there is discontinuity, where a youth must change in order to become an adult, dramatic rituals of initiation ensure that this change is made. In other societies, like our own, there is a discontinuity but no ritual. Young men, particularly, are left on their own to "initiate themselves." This may lead to the formation of youth gangs or to various other informal peer-group activities in which peers socialize one another into the male role. This behavior is frequently rebellious and contrary to society's values, but not always. Among the Xhosa of South Africa, youth groups engage in activities that dramatize the male role, provide an arena for physical and sexual activity, and yet are in full accord with the adult values and roles of the culture (Mayer and Mayer 1970).

Here again we are back to the two-faced coin of enculturation: On the one hand, each child must grow up and in doing so achieve the competence and psychological growth necessary for healthy human functioning. On the other hand, each culture must find a way of transmitting its values and knowledge to the growing child and youth so that the basic culture will be continued. As we have seen, and will continue to see in later chapters, there is great variability in the ways in which this is done. Many cultures seem far more successful than our own in providing cultural continuity and yet allowing the needs of different stages of development to be met within the cultural structure.

SOCIALIZATION AND FORMAL EDUCATION

A child who was asked to recite the multiplication tables for his teacher began "la-di-da-di-da, la-di-da-di-da," at which point the teacher interrupted to ask him what he was saying. He responded that he knew the tune but he did not yet know the words (Cole et al. 1971).

Although few anthropologists have devoted their attention to the school as an agent of socialization, Jules Henry has been particularly concerned with the kind of learning that goes on in American schools. Henry points out that the school not only formally instructs children in the skills they will need to participate in a highly industrialized society but also transmits some basic cultural values without the students' or the teachers' being aware of what is going on. In the following incident, "At the Blackboard," Henry observes that competition as a social value is covertly learned along with the overt content of mathematics:*

Boris had trouble reducing "¹²/₁₆" to the lowest terms and could only get as far as "⁶/₈." The teacher asked him quietly if that was as far as he could reduce it. She suggested that "he think." Much heaving up and down and waving of hands by the other children, all frantic to correct him. Boris pretty unhappy, probably mentally paralyzed. The teacher, quiet, patient, ignores the others and concentrates with look and voice on Boris. She says, "Is there a bigger number than two you can divide into the two parts of the fraction?" After a minute or two, she becomes more urgent, but there is no response from Boris. She then turns to the class and says, "Well, who can tell Boris what the number is?" A forest of hands appears, and the teacher calls Peggy. Peggy says four may be divided into the numerator and denominator.

Henry goes on to say: "Boris' failure has made it possible for Peggy to succeed, his depression is the price of her exhilaration; his misery the occasion for her rejoicing." Whether Boris has learned math is questionable. Perhaps Boris's "nightmare at the blackboard" was a lesson for him in controlling himself so that "he would not fly shrieking from the room under the enormous public pressure." Boris has learned the fear of failure, which, according to Henry, is one of the things a child must learn in order to get along in the competitive society of the United States.

As formal schooling has been introduced into many cultures through contact with the West, more anthropologists are turning to the role of the school in socialization. Many of these studies address the problems that occur when Western-style middle-class schools and education are imposed on traditional kin-based, non-Western communities. The education in typical Western schools is based on a particular kind of cognitive style: the ability to see abstract relationships that are mediated largely through language. The school atmosphere encourages an active mode of learning, solving problems on one's own, and a situation in which the teacher is involved in an impersonal and impartial role of instructing. Teaching style, educational context, and cognitive skills appear to conflict with traditional informal socializa-

*Jules Henry, *Culture Against Man.* New York: Random House, Inc., 1963, p. 295. Reprinted by permission.

Formal education is an important means of inculcating values consistent with the goals of modern nation states. Political education of young people has been extremely important in contributing to the remaking of Chinese society since 1948. (Bernhard Krauss)

tion in non-Western cultures. There, learning takes place in the context of life, teaching is largely by example, verbal instruction plays a minimum role, and many of the problems are posed in terms that require a single solution to a particular case, rather than the ability to generalize. Although numerous studies have shown that with special training children from such traditional learning contexts can develop other cognitive skills and perform well on Western "intelligence" tests, as a rule there is conflict between the two systems, and many children from traditional cultures do not do well in school.

Cross-cultural studies of schoolchildren demonstrate the relationship between culture, cognition, and school performance. A recent long-term study that compares personality traits and school performance between children in Mexico and the United States (Holtzman et al. 1975) obtained significant cross-cultural differences for all the cognitive measures, nearly all the cognitive-perceptual style variables, and most of the personality and attitudinal measures. The authors see these dif-

ferences as hinging on the active coping style of American children versus the passive coping style of the Mexican children, and on the emphasis in American culture on intellectual curiosity and independent thinking, in contrast to the Mexican emphasis on interpersonal relationships. These two important cultural differences correspond to differences in the home life of Mexican and American children. Mexican families were less likely to have intellectually stimulating reading material in the home. Only rarely did Mexican parents read regularly to the preschool child, whereas American parents read on a regular basis to their children. Most Mexican children were unable to read, count, or write before entering school. American children could, a point in which their parents took great pride.

The mother's education in the Mexican families was significantly lower than in the matched American sample. The typical number of children in the Mexican family was almost twice that in the American family. So the Mexican mother has to devote more time and energy to managing the house and has less time to stimulate the child's intellectual interests. The presence of other relatives in the Mexican household also discourages the pursuit of solitary intellectual activities.

The different modes of formal education in the two cultures intensify the differences in Mexican and American culture. The Mexican emphasis on rote learning and lots of homework encourages a passive learning style that does not lead to independent thinking. This contrasts with the more active learning style characteristic of American schools. The passive coping style characteristic of Mexican culture affects children's attitudes toward testing. A Mexican child is willing to cooperate on a test but will seldom take the initiative in the testing situation. The American middle-class child, on the other hand, sees testing as a challenge to be mastered, an opportunity to show how much he or she can do.

These cultural differences are modified by social class. A study using tests similar to those

Culture Conflict and Formal Education

In a monograph called *The New Mathematics and an Old Culture* (1967), John Gay and Michael Cole present this "culture conflict" as it exists for the Kpelle of Liberia, in West Africa. Traditionally, Kpelle learning is based on the unquestioned acceptance of authority and rote learning. For the Kpelle, the "world remains a mystery to be accepted on authority, not a complex pattern of comprehensible regularities." Kpelle children do not look for patterns in visual stimuli or in words, nor do they think of numbers, measurements, and time in terms of laws and regularities. Among the Kpelle, for example, objects are counted and can be put into sets, but there are no words for independent abstract numerals in their language. Numerals must always be used to modify a noun or pronoun, as in "two of this and two of this make four of them." The abstraction "two and two make four" is not a normal part of Kpelle thinking, and this presents an obvious source of difficulty when multiplication is taught to Kpelle children through rote memorization of the multiplication table.

Although Kpelle learning is functional for tra-

ditional Kpelle culture and consistent with the highest Kpelle values of conserving the past and learning to conform to traditional norms, it inhibits learning the scientific culture of the West, which is transmitted through the school. The Kpelle schools try to teach new concepts through old methods. Children are taught Western mathematics, which requires a problem-solving approach, through the old methods of rote learning and imitation. Gay and Cole suggest that teachers must try to break through this authority structure, using material and analogies from the child's daily life and putting them in a framework that will make Western education comprehensible and meaningful. Western culture is impinging on Kpelle life at a very fast pace, and the school is one of the most important agents of Western culture. It is the teacher's task to help the Kpelle child cross the bridge from the old to the new. The teacher must make the classroom a living example of the scientific method, drawing from the child and from the strengths and concepts in Kpelle culture.

used above but carried out among upper-class Mexican families with children enrolled in an American school in Mexico City shows that most of the cognitive differences between the Mexican and American children disappear. Social class and type of schooling are clearly interrelated, and together they account for differences in group scores on intelligence tests, success in school, and chances for higher-status professional and managerial positions in the society.

Some anthropologists who have studied public schools among lower-class and minority-group populations in the United States have found in them the same conflict of cultures that occurs when formal schooling is introduced into traditional contexts—and the same failures. In describing a school in Harlem, Gerry

Rosenfeld (1971) calls attention to the cultural differences between the black, lower-class students and the white, middle-class teachers, to the different conceptual frameworks that organize life in the school and outside it, to the low expectations teachers have for students, and to the subsequent failure of the children in school. Rosenfeld sees the teacher in the ghetto school as a transmitter of a different culture. He or she is an agent of socialization similar to the "outsider" who teaches in a "native" school: largely alienated, even hostile, and ignorant of the culture of the students being taught. Until the teacher learns to understand the cultural context and the life of the student and to get involved with the student as an individual, student performance in such schools will continue to be poor. A common result of the imposition of an alien and irrelevant system of education is that children do not learn what they are supposed to learn; rather, they learn a set of evasive strategies that subvert the intended goals of the teacher and become in themselves the child's primary adaptation to the schoolroom.

It is problems like these in the United States that are directing more anthropological attention to the socialization process as it occurs in both traditional contexts and in the formal context of the school. It is an interest consistent with the anthropological focus on cognitive styles and the ways in which such styles are related to larger cultural patterns and to social-class differences in stratified societies.

SUMMARY

1. Developing into a normal functioning adult is the result of the complex interaction between universal human capacities and culturally variable child-rearing practices. Enculturation is the culturally specific ways in which human infants are reared to become functioning members of a particular sociocultural system.

2. Adequate mother-child interaction is necessary for adequate human development, both physical and emotional, and it also appears to be of great importance among nonhuman primates.

3. Enculturation proceeds differently for males and females almost from birth. Overt teaching and covert communication patterns and role modeling are the most important factors leading to sex role differentiation among adult males and females in a particular culture.

4. The enculturation process not only transmits the skills and knowledge of a culture but also shapes the values, attitudes, and personality of the growing child. The expectation is that people who have grown up with culturally patterned experiences will have similar personality tendencies.

5. An important theory confirmed by much recent research is that personality develops as an adaptation to the requirements of the basic subsistence pattern of a culture. This point is illustrated by the example from Khalapur, India.

6. The major factor that shapes the conforming and dependent personality of the Indian village child is the pattern of joint family living and the need for familial harmony.

7. Enculturation continues past childhood; even adolescents and adults learn new roles and activities. In some traditional cultures, there appears to be greater continuity of enculturation than in our own; adults do not have to unlearn attitudes or skills they have learned as children. The Cheyenne are an example of a culture with major continuities in enculturation.

8. Anthropologists have suggested that males may experience more discontinuities in enculturation than females, as the dependent male child must make the transition to an independent and assertive male role. In many cultures, male initiation rites help the individual make this transition from boy to man.

9. Where cultural community is lacking and there are no male initiation rites, young men may "initiate themselves," as exemplified in the American youth gang and informal adolescent peer group.

10. Although in traditional societies enculturation is largely an informal process, in complex, highly technical societies formal education (school) plays an increasingly important role. Schools not only teach the formal problem-solving thought processes necessary for competence as an adult but also indirectly communicate the American values of competitiveness and individualism.

11. Western education has not always been successful in traditional cultural contexts, where other values and learning contexts conflict with those presented in school. Children from lower-class homes, where cultural values and content may not support or reinforce the school culture, may also not achieve success in school and are likely to score less well on various tests of ability than children from middle-class homes. This is demonstrated by a cross-cultural study comparing the United States and Mexico and by studies of ghetto schools in the United States.

SUGGESTED READINGS

Barnouw, V.
   1973   *Culture and Personality.* Homewood,
           Ill.: Dorsey. A survey, suitable for the
           beginning student, on the relationship
           between culture and personality.

Edgerton, Robert B.
   1971   *The Individual in Adaptation: A Study of
           Four East African Peoples.* Berkeley: University of California Press. Compares the
           personalities of four different cultures
           and the farmer and herder divisions
           within each group.

Mead, Margaret
   1961   *Coming of Age in Samoa.* New York: Dell
           (first publ. 1928). The classic study of
           adolescence in a society where the transition from childhood to adulthood is
           much less turbulent than in our own.

Munroe, R. L., and Munroe, R. H.
   1977   *Cross-Cultural Human Development.*
           New York: Aronson. A survey of cross-
           cultural research on such aspects of
           human development as physical growth,
           cognition, sex roles, and aggression,
           including a more intensive look at three
           cultures—the Gusii of Africa, the Trobriand Islanders, and the Ainu of Japan.

Whiting, Beatrice, and Whiting, J. W.
   1974   *Children of Six Cultures: A Psycho-Cultural Analysis.* Cambridge, Mass.: Harvard University Press. The most recent
           analysis of the comparative data on
           child rearing gathered as part of the six-
           culture study referred to in the text.

PART TWO

SOCIOCULTURAL ADAPTATIONS

CHAPTER EIGHT

GETTING FOOD

▶ What is the relationship between environmental and cultural variation?

▶ Why are anthropologists so interested in contemporary hunters and gatherers?

▶ Can you explain why horticultural tribes and agricultural peasants have different lifestyles?

▶ What are the major economic features of industrial society?

Considering the great importance of the mongongo and the long distances walked by the !Kung to reach the groves, one would imagine that some attempt would have been made to grow the mongongo trees in the sandy soils near the permanent water holes, making possible a more sedentary life. I asked Xashe, "Why don't you try growing the mongongo tree?"

He answered, "Why should we plant when there are so many mongongos in the world?"

Adapted from *The !Kung San: Men, Women and Work in a Foraging Society.**

Anthropologists view a human population and its environment as an interacting ecosystem. The environment, or surroundings, of a human population includes both a physical and a social aspect. In its physical aspect, the environment is climate, soil quality, existing plant and animal life, and the presence of vital resources such as water, vitamins, and proteins. In considering the capacity of various environments to support human life, both the quantity and the quality of natural resources must be taken into account. Most environmental zones permit a diversity of food-getting strategies. Some environmental zones are harsher than others and more limiting in the types of cultural adaptations they support. The productivity of any particular zone, however, must be considered in connection with the type of technology used to exploit it.

THE ENVIRONMENT AND CULTURAL DIVERSITY

In considering the effect of environment on culture, including subsistence patterns (food

*The !Kung San: Men, Women and Work in a Foraging Society. by Richard Lee. Cambridge, England: Cambridge University Press, 1979, p. 204.

getting), we can say that the environment places limits and provides possibilities but does not determine culture. Each environment always offers some alternatives, and even within culture areas, variation always exists.

The level of technology is the deciding factor in the utilization of a particular environment. In the Midwest of the United States, for example, the complex technology of the industrial age has allowed an adaptive pattern of intensive mechanized agriculture. This area today supports millions of people. In aboriginal America, it supported a much smaller population of hunters and gatherers. In the same way, a desert area that can support very little human life without irrigation can be made to bloom and support much larger populations through an intensive agricultural pattern of adaptation. In explaining the particular subsistence pattern of a society, many factors must be taken into account: the nature of the broad environmental zone; variation within the zone, both short-term and long-term; social groups in the environment; and the level of technology and other cultural factors.

Environmental Zones and Food-Getting Systems

The earth contains six major environmental zones, each of which has a particular climate, soil composition, and plant and animal life (Figure 8.1). The major area of the earth's surface (26 percent) is covered by grasslands, sometimes called steppes, prairies, or savannas. These areas, which can support hunters and gatherers and also populations dependent on herding animals, are inhabited by 10 percent of the world's population. Where complex machine technologies exist, these areas can be made enormously productive for agriculture. Desert regions or dry areas make up 18 percent of the earth's land but contain only 6 percent of its population. Desert areas do not all conform to the popular image of sand dunes and the complete absence of water. Many deserts are covered by brush, and in some areas oases, or fertile concentrations of soil, exist and support small agricultural settlements. With a simple technology, deserts can support hunters and gatherers. With extensive irrigation, some areas can support intensive agriculture and relatively dense populations. The arctic and subarctic zones cover 16 percent of the earth, but as we would expect, they support only a tiny fraction of the earth's population—less than half of 1 percent—who live mainly by hunting, herding, and trapping.

Almost three-fourths of the world's population lives in the two remaining major environmental zones. The tropical forest zone, with abundant rainfall and luxuriant vegetation, takes up 10 percent of the earth's land mass but supports 28 percent of its population. The typical pattern of subsistence in these areas is extensive agriculture (sometimes called horticulture). The most hospitable environmental zone for contemporary human populations is the temperate forests. Today, 43 percent of the world's population lives in these zones. Again, we can see how technology must be taken into account in understanding population distribution. It is only with iron tools that the hardwood trees in these temperate forests could be cut down and the fertile soil used for agriculture. Without iron tools, the trees presented an insurmountable difficulty. Mountains, which vary in climate and other characteristics according to their elevation, occupy 12 percent of earth's land surface and are inhabited by 7 percent of its population, engaged primarily in pastoralism and extensive agriculture.

Sometimes a number of societies make similar adaptations to a particular ecological zone and through diffusion come to develop similar cultural patterns. Where this happens, anthro-

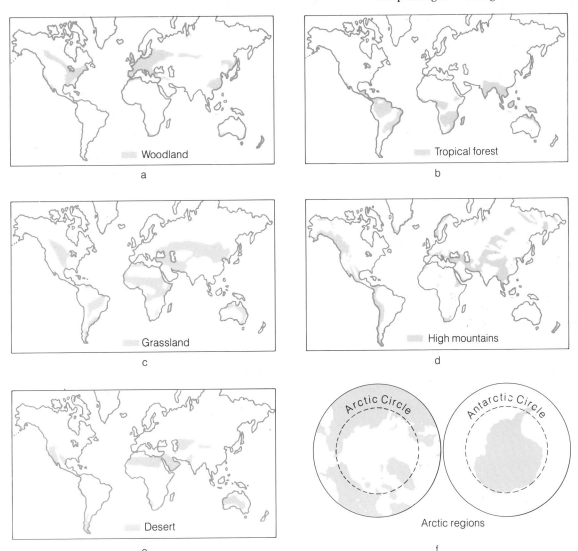

Figure 8.1   *Six major environmental zones of the world, shown in order of decreasing population.*

pologists speak of a **culture area.** Although the concept of a culture area has its uses in explaining certain developments, culture areas also contain cultural variation. Among the American Plains Indians, for example, there were important differences in values and con-figurations among the different tribes in spite of the basic similarity in the subsistence pattern. Similar cultural variation exists among the Eskimo, who have in general made similar adaptive responses to their relatively limiting natural environment.

Seasonal Variation and Cultural Response

Due to climatic variation, food resources vary in availability and abundance at different times of the year in any particular local environment. Many aspects of a food-production system will reflect this seasonal variation. Among the Hanunoo of the Philippines, who are horticulturalists, there is an impressive system of intercropping, or planting of different crops at different times of the year when the weather is most favorable for each. Rice, the main crop, is planted in June and harvested in October; in between, a short-season maize crop is planted and harvested. Between October and May, several dry-season crops such as beans, sugar cane, and potatoes are also grown (Conklin 1969). Hunters and gatherers are, of course, also sensitive to seasonal change, because it affects the availability and abundance of game and wild food. Game migrates with the changing seasons, and the hunting groups adjust in size and social organization, as we will see for the Copper Eskimo later in this chapter.

Long-Run Variations in the Environment

Sociocultural systems also develop in response to variations that are unpredictable over the short run—such as drought, floods, or diseases that affect animals—but that are a persistent part of the environment over the long run. Subsistence patterns most directly reflect adaptation to long-run environmental uncertainty. Food habits and preferences, for example, can be adapted to a wide variety of resources, rather than being limited to those that are not so readily available. Australian aboriginal peoples, like the Tiwi, have a very simple technology, but they utilize an enormous variety of plant and animal foods in their environment—kangaroos, opossums, mice,

wild dogs, whales, frogs, turkeys, smaller birds, lizards, snakes, bird and lizard eggs, fish, roots, fruits, nuts, seeds, flowers—and are thus unlikely to be severely affected if some of these foods become unavailable.

A group can also structure its diet so that, although it uses a wide variety of resources, it also has one that is dependable—that is, in constant abundant supply. The !Kung of the Kalahari, for example, although they know the plants and animals in their seemingly hostile environment well and do use this knowledge to give their diet variety when possible, can always fall back on the protein-rich nuts of the mongongo tree. These nuts are abundant, easily stored, and little affected by environmental variation (Lee 1968).

In addition to using various subsistence strategies to increase survival in a particular environment, a group adapts to the environment by regulation of population. In cultures where the level of technology affords only a limited exploitation of the environment, and where safe and reliable methods of artificial contraception are unknown, abortion and infanticide are used to limit population growth. Other culturally determined practices and beliefs also result in limiting population. Late weaning and postpartum taboos on sexual intercourse, for example, regulate population by spacing births. Sometimes methods of increasing a group's survival seem harsh to us, but they are necessary because of extreme food shortages. Among some Inuit groups, for example, old people were left on the ice to be exposed to a sure death in particularly hard years when food was scarce. Sometimes it was an old person who suggested this course of action. These suicides or "mercy killings" indicate not a lack of concern for human life but rather a commitment to the survival of the group.

In addition to these more obvious ways of adapting to environmental uncertainty, a society can establish trade relations with other groups and thus expand its resource base. This, for example, is always necessary for pastoral groups who do not also do a little farming themselves. Furthermore, some of the ways in which sociocultural systems adapt to long-run environmental uncertainty may not be a part of the cultural consciousness, as we saw earlier in Marvin Harris's explanation of the Hindu taboo on beef. Frequently, the role such beliefs and practices play in regulating population or increasing the rational utilization of the environment may only be understood through anthropological analysis.

Although increasing technological efficiency is an obvious way of increasing control over the environment, the enormous diversity of sociocultural systems is evidence that technologically simpler societies have been able to make satisfactory adaptations even without modern science. Although nonliterate peoples may not express it in the technical terminology of modern science, they have a much wider knowledge of their environment than they have generally been given credit for. Harold Conklin, who studied the horticulturalist Yagaw Hanunoo of the Philippines, found, for example, that they had forty linguistic categories referring to soil quality and mineral content. They understood what causes soil erosion and had developed techniques to conserve the soil. The Hanunoo distinguish over 1,500 types of plants in their environment and cultivate over 400 in fields and gardens, frequently experimenting with new types. In this sense, their knowledge exceeds that of modern scientific botany, in which plants are grouped into species by grosser criteria than those used by the Hanunoo. The Hanunoo also recognize over 450 animal types in their environment. These people clearly understand the connection between human food-getting activities and their impact on the environment, and they utilize this knowledge in an efficient way to exploit various food resources. Similarly, even where the technology for hunting and agriculture among nonliterate peoples seems primitive compared with our own machine technology, these groups have in fact developed quite adequate strategies for fulfilling their needs. They

With the introduction of the horse by the Spanish, hunting bison on the American Plains became a more productive strategy than agriculture. This drawing, by Bear's Heart, was made in 1875. A hundred years later, the American bison are virtually extinct. (Courtesy of Museum of the American Indian, Heye Foundation)

make up for the lack of sophisticated technology by human skill, such as in observing the habits of various animals and in stalking them.

The Social Environment and Food-Getting Strategies

Cultural patterns, including how people get their food, are adjusted to the presence of different groups in the environment. Some peoples who originally inhabited a larger area, like the Semai of Malaysia, have recently been pushed back by other groups into marginal areas and have had to change their subsistence patterns. The Mbuti of the Ituri Forest in northeastern Zaire have adapted to the tropical forest as hunters and gatherers, but almost all the Mbuti bands are closely associated with their non-Mbuti neighbors, who are agriculturalists. These other people fear the forest and will not enter it. This has allowed the Mbuti to exploit the forest while at the same time making use of their more culturally sophisticated agricultural neighbors, with whom they trade and sometimes live for parts of the year (Turnbull 1961). Human groups (like other animal communities) tend to engage in specialized adaptations to the environment that, over time, become integrated in their cultural systems and are an important part of their identity. A specialized adaptation to a local environment by a particular group is called its **niche.** Frederik Barth (1956) describes a pattern of social interaction in Pakistan in which three ethnic groups, the Kohistanis, the Pathans, and the Gujars, have a different niche within the same mountainous area. They are able to live peacefully because each group exploits a different aspect of the environment. The Pathans are farmers, utilizing the valley regions for raising wheat, corn, and rice. The Kohistanis live in the colder mountainous regions, herding sheep, goats, cattle, and water buffalo and raising millet and corn. The Gujars are full-time herders and utilize marginal areas not used by the Kohistanis. The Gujars provide milk and meat products to the Pathan farmers and also work as agricultural laborers during the busy seasons. Such patterns of specialized and noncompetitive interactions among cultures in a local environment are found in many parts of the world and seem especially characteristic of the pastoral peoples.

The Influence of Culture on Environment

The relationship between the environment and culture is not one-way. Although, as we have just suggested, the environment affects culture, culture also affects the environment. The ways in which people get food and the ways in which they live all have an impact on nature. On the one hand, technology and knowledge can transform deserts into gardens. On the other hand, as we know all too well today, the presence of human populations can have a devastating impact on nature. In industrial societies, factories and automobiles have contributed to polluting the air we breathe. Different methods of getting a living, whether hunting, trapping animals, cultivation, or keeping herds of livestock, all affect animal and plant life, quantity of natural resources, the soil cover, and the soil itself. The management of resources is clearly a pressing problem in the world today. One of the contributions of ecologically oriented anthropologists is to show that a wide variety of food-procurement strategies make good ecological sense and that what may at first appear to be a more efficient exploitation of a particular environment may turn out to raise as many problems as it solves.

MAJOR FOOD-GETTING PATTERNS

There are five basic patterns of utilizing the environment to support human populations (Cohen 1971): hunting and gathering, pastoralism, extensive agriculture, intensive agriculture, and industrialization. Although it is useful to describe basic types, there is a great deal of diversity within each type. Furthermore, any particular society will normally have one dominant way of utilizing the environment, but most actually use a combination of patterns in filling their needs. Each type of adaptation has a characteristic level of productivity (yield per person per unit of land) and efficiency (yield per person per hour of labor invested), though situations vary depending on the particular ecological interaction. Each type of food-getting pattern also seems to have some social correlates (accompanying forms of social organization) and dominant values, though again, many anthropologists are more interested in examining specific cultural adaptations to a particular local environment than in formulating cultural typologies.

Hunting and Gathering

Hunting and gathering, or **foraging,** relies on food that is naturally available in the environment. Included in this strategy are the hunting of large and small game animals, fishing, and the collecting of various plant foods. Hunting and gathering does not involve the production of food, either directly, by planting, or indirectly, by controlling the reproduction of animals or keeping domestic animals for consumption of their meat or milk.

In the past, hunting and gathering occurred in more diverse environments than is true today. For 99 percent of humankind's existence, life was supported by a hunting and gathering existence. Today, only about 30,000 of the world's people live by this strategy. Most contemporary hunters and gatherers occupy marginal areas, having been pushed back by culturally dominant or militarily superior agricultural peoples (see Figure 8.2).

Anthropologists are particularly interested in contemporary hunters and gatherers, because this pattern was such an important part of early human history. The sexual division of labor (males hunting, females collecting food), the sharing of food in the group, and the development of language all came into existence as correlates of the hunting and gathering way of life. But although contemporary hunters and gatherers can give us important clues to understanding the early life of humans, these groups do not in any way represent a way of life unchanged from the past. Hunting and gathering, too, has changed and is in fact rapidly disappearing as a way of human life.

Hunting and gathering strategies vary in their productivity. Although it is true that some hunters and gatherers have faced starvation, the marginal existence of contemporary hunters and gatherers may be due to recent effects of culture contact. But even here, some foraging groups make out rather well, thanks to their ingenious technology and their wide knowledge of the environment. Lee points out that the !Kung actually have a more secure existence than their Herero neighbors, who are agriculturalists and cattle herders. Because the Herero rely completely on water and pasturage for their cattle, they leave themselves open to starvation in years of drought. The Plains Indians also did well with a hunting strategy, especially after the introduction of the horse by the Spaniards in the sixteenth century. Some Plains groups, such as the Cheyenne, gave up an agricultural life for the more productive hunting of bison. But in general, hunting and gathering supports fewer people per unit of land than other food-getting strategies. Among the !Kung, forty-four people are supported per one hundred square miles of land, but this figure is somewhat higher than is generally true for hunting peoples today.

Hunting technology is simple but not crude, and ingenious methods are used to hunt a wide range of different animals. Because hunting is a prestige activity, it is only recently that much attention has been given to the collecting of vegetable foods. For many foraging groups, vegetable foods make up a substantial part of the diet (up to 80 percent), and it is this rather than hunting that makes foraging a relatively secure way of life. Foraging thus tends to be a generalized pattern of adaptation that utilizes many different aspects of the natural environment for subsistence. The Copper Eskimo described in the accompanying Ethnography represent a specialized hunting adaptation to a relatively harsh and limiting environment. Their traditional adaptation, which depends mainly on the hunting activities of the men, is not typical of hunter and gatherer societies, most of which rely much more heavily for their caloric intake on the gathering of vegetable foods, which is done by women, as among the !Kung, or even on the hunting of small game by the women, as among the Tiwi of Australia.

Contrary to stereotypes, hunting and gathering is not a particularly difficult and ineffi-

Figure 8.2   This map shows the location of the major human groups discussed in this chapter.

cient way of life in terms of the number of hours required to maintain an adequate food supply. Marshall Sahlins (1972) has called hunters and gatherers "the original affluent society." James Woodburn (1968), who studied the Hadza of Tanzania, estimated that they spend less time and energy obtaining their subsistence and appear to be better off nutritionally than neighboring agricultural tribes. Lee estimated that an adult !Kung spends an average of two and a half six-hour days per week in subsistence activities, and a woman can gather enough in one day to feed her family for three days.

There appear to be some typical social correlates of the hunting way of life. Hunters are generally **nomadic,** with their movements following the availability of game and wild plants. A typical form of social organization among hunters is the small camp made up of kinsmen, coming together when seasonal conditions permit. Recent investigation has shown that the typical hunting band is much more flexible in its membership than was previously believed. Among the Blackfeet bison hunters of the North American Plains, even strangers would be included in the camp. With the notable exception of the Kwakiutl and other fishing and foraging societies of the Northwest Coast of North America, there tends to be little occupational specialization in foraging societies and few differences in power and authority. There is ordinarily a division of labor by age and sex; women collect plant foods, and men hunt. Women in these societies also make clothing and contribute in other important ways to the economy, such as by carrying and processing food. There tends to be a higher degree of sexual equality in such societies than in other ways of life—for example, pastoralism or horticulture.

Pastoralism

Pastoralism primarily involves the care of domesticated herd animals. It is a specialized adaptation to an environment that, because of

The Kurds of Iraq, pictured here, engage in nomadic pastoralism, in which all the members of the group—men, women, and children—move with their herds throughout the year and there is no permanent settlement. Women are responsible for the water supply and take care of the feeding of the fowl that accompany them in their moves. Men herd the animals. (United Nations)

hilly terrain, dry climate, or unsuitable soil, is not sufficiently productive to support a large human population through agriculture. It can support native vegetation sufficient for animals if they are allowed to range over a large area. The main animals herded by pastoralists are cattle, sheep, goats, yaks, or camels, all of which produce both meat and milk. Because the herd animals found in the New World were not of a variety that could be domesticated (with the exception of the llama in Peru), pastoralism did not develop as a New World way of life. The major areas of pastoralism are thus found in East Africa (cattle), North Africa (camels), Southwest Asia (sheep and goats), and the sub-arctic (caribou and reindeer).

Two characteristic patterns of pastoralism are **transhumance** and **nomadism.** In transhumance, herd animals are moved regularly throughout the year to different areas as pastures become available at different altitudes or in different climatic zones. Generally, the males take the animals to the different pastures, while the women and children and some men remain

E T H N O G R A P H Y

THE COPPER ESKIMO OF THE CANADIAN ARCTIC: A SPECIALIZED HUNTING ADAPTATION

The extreme arctic environment poses many problems that the human populations there must successfully cope with in order to survive. Because the land is unsuitable for agriculture, the Eskimo, or Inuit, must utilize both the rich animal resources of the ocean and land animals such as the caribou. The material culture and technology of the Inuit are admirably designed to cope with their harsh physical environment. One of their major problems, for example, is keeping warm in cold weather yet not getting overheated during periods of strenuous work. The Inuit design of clothing admirably meets this test. Fur provides warmth, yet there are also many air vents regulated by drawstrings. Further, the Inuit dress in layers, which trap the warm air and act as insulators; in warmer weather, the outer layer can be removed. Boots, gloves, and parkas have an impermeable outer layer, keeping out dampness and wind. Boots and gloves are lined with grass for further insulation. Inuit shelters are also ingeniously designed to hold heat and keep out wind. The snow shelter (igloo), by its shape and composition, provides excellent, warm

shelter and can be effectively heated by a seal-oil lamp, which also provides light. The Inuit summer tents, made of two attached layers of sealskin, can also provide warmth during cold snaps by trapping heated air between the layers.

The Inuit also adapt to their environment through a variety of social and cultural practices. Through a bilateral kinship system (which formally recognizes relations on both the male and female side of the family), a taboo on the marriage of cousins, adoption, exchange of spouses, and meat-sharing partnerships, they extend the social network beyond individual households. The result is a flexible social organization that ensures cooperation, mutual aid, and responsibility for others, thus allowing local populations to expand and contract in response to the fluctuating availability of resources. The socialization of the Inuit, which involves both playing and training in skills such as observing, stalking, and killing game, is very successful in providing the group with hunters who have both the knowledge and the experience to provide enough food to feed their

families. Their religious rituals and ceremonies are effective in providing outlets for the isolation of the long, dark winters, and they serve as safety valves for the release of anxiety and tension. The various Inuit groups of the arctic actually exploit a number of micro-environments, and this accounts for the cultural differences among them. One of the basic differences is between the coastal Inuit of what is now Alaska, who depended on whaling and sea resources generally, and the inland Inuit, who although doing some seal hunting also depended on hunting caribou as an important part of their subsistence strategy (Moran 1979).

The Copper Eskimo, so called by Europeans because of their use of native copper tools, live in the Canadian Arctic.* They have lived as hunters in this extreme climate for over a thousand years (see Figure 8.3). The tundra habitat in which they live contains some trees,

*Based on David Damas, "The Copper Eskimo," in M. G. Bicchieri, ed., *Hunters and Gatherers Today.* New York: Holt, Rinehart and Winston, Inc., 1972, pp. 3–50.

moss, grass, and flowers, but many areas are virtual wasteland. The climate is variable, with a long, cold winter and a short, cool summer. From around September to June, the water areas become sheets of ice. The main land animal hunted was the caribou, which provided both meat and skin used in clothing. Fish, hare, and fowl were important supplements to the diet. Plant life was scarce, and berries were eaten only during a brief season. When a caribou was killed, the first thing eaten was the half-digested reindeer moss that remained in its stomach. The seal was the most important sea animal hunted, providing a major source of food for people and dogs, fat for fuel, and skins for summer clothing.

The Copper Eskimo culture was adapted to a seasonal cycle in response to the availability of different animals at different times of the year. From late May to November, the Eskimo fished and hunted caribou, often driving them into lakes and harpooning them from kayaks. The caribou migrate in the winter to the richer forest areas to the south. During November and early December, the Eskimo lived on stores of dried and frozen caribou meat and fish, while the women sewed winter clothing. In December they moved to the sea ice for the winter seal hunting season. Snow houses were built in from the coast, and a radius of about five miles (considered a convenient walking distance from camp!) was exploited for sealing.

In the winter, seals live in the water under the ice. They make breathing holes by scratching

Figure 8.3 *The location of the Copper Eskimo*

with their flippers on the new ice, and have the ability to breathe up through quite a lot of snow. Each seal makes many holes during a winter and may use any one of these. The hunter finds the holes with the aid of specially trained dogs. The method of winter sealing is called "he waits," for that is what a hunter must do. He settles down on a block of ice and waits for an indicator to move, showing the presence of a seal. He may wait for hours or even days. Many men are needed for successful breathing-hole sealing, so the Copper Eskimo winter populations ranged from about 50 to 200 people, with the average group about 100. In spring, the group dispersed into smaller units in response to the lesser requirements of caribou hunting. Caribou are usually scattered into small herds, easily hunted by a few men. Fish were the most important source of food in

the spring. They were widely available over the area in numerous lakes, and so did not require communal effort to catch.

Although most ethnographies of the Eskimo concentrate on the activities of the men in providing food through hunting and furs for sale through trapping, women also play an important role in the economy, contributing through their complementary activities to the survival of the group. In addition to caring for children, Eskimo women prepare hides for sale or use, prepare meat for storage, and sew and repair the clothing that is essential for the hunters. In the case of sealskins, the blubber must be scraped off and the skin washed, stretched on a frame to dry, and then, when dry, scrubbed again. Similarly, caribou hides must also be

(Continued on next page)

scraped in order to make them flexible enough for use. Meat and fish must be cut up and gutted for storage. Although most of the cloth clothing worn by the Eskimo is bought, women still make fur clothes and boots, which are conceded by all to be much more effective than anything that can be bought in a store. In addition, the women cook, wash, clean the igloo, and may also contribute more directly to the food supply in some Eskimo groups by fishing and hunting small birds (Briggs 1974).

The routine just described was altered somewhat by the introduction of new technology by the whites. By 1925, rifles, traps, and fishnets substantially influenced the Eskimo food-getting pattern. Using rifles to hunt caribou led to a lengthened caribou season and a correspondingly shorter sealing season. More Eskimo stayed inland, not only hunting caribou but also trapping and setting nets in lakes and streams to catch fish. Other aspects of the economy also changed. With the rifle, the kayak hunting of caribou ended, and the kayak fell into disuse. Large caribou drives also became less frequent. With a rifle, one man could succeed at long-range caribou hunting, which then became a much more individual pursuit.

The market for fox furs among whites led to the trapping of foxes. Trapping drew the Eskimo into the marketing system of the outside world, providing them not only with goods that increased the exploitation of the environment but also with food, tobacco, tea, canvas tents, and clothing. With the establishment of fox traps, dog team travel became more important, since mobility was needed to set and watch traps. Where previously a typical family had owned two dogs, many might now own five or six, and the dogs might actually consume more meat than a man's family.

By the mid-1950s, the decline in caribou due to hunting with rifles led to further changes in Eskimo life. Some Copper Eskimo populations shifted to areas where seals could be hunted year-round, and fishing also became more important. In other areas, the decline of the caribou led to an increased amount of time spent in breathing-hole sealing, a reversion to the aboriginal pattern. Still other Copper Eskimo populations moved to areas where they could be employed by the gov-

The ways in which human populations adapt to their environments through different food-getting strategies is an important factor in cultural variation. The Eskimo are an example of a specialized hunting adaptation. Here two Eskimo women from Coppermine set fishnets under the ice. (Courtesy of The American Museum of Natural History)

ernment, which had established Distant Early Warning radar installations in the arctic. Trading posts were established and also attracted permanent settlement. Handicrafts and tourism contribute to the present Eskimo economy, and when necessary, the Canadian government provides welfare payments and airlifts of food.

at a village site. In a nomadic form of pastoralism, the whole population—men, women, and children—moves with the herds throughout the year. There is no permanent village.

Pastoralism by itself cannot support a human population; food grains are needed as a supplement to the diet. Therefore, either pastoralism is practiced along with cultivation, or trading relations are maintained with cultivators from whom food grains are obtained. In terms of social organization, in most pastoral groups a woman joins her husband after marriage, and herds are transmitted from fathers to sons. Recent studies have shown a great diversity in pastoral adaptations, and the very flexibility that has allowed pastoral groups to

These Masaia herdsmen of East Africa engage in transhuman pastoralism, in which men take the cattle to different areas as pasture becomes available. The women and children remain in the village. (United Nations/ Ida Pickerelli)

survive in marginal environments makes this strategy difficult to categorize. Because pastoralism always includes either cultivation or trade, this also leads to rather important variability among pastoralists. Many pastoralists have also been drawn into a market economy, and this too is an important part of contemporary pastoralist adaptations. Pastoralism, like hunting, depends on an extensive knowledge of the natural environment. Like hunting, it is also a nomadic adaptation, and the movement patterns of pastoralist groups are of central importance in understanding their culture.

Extensive Agriculture

Extensive agriculture, sometimes called **horticulture,** involves the production of plants using a simple, nonmechanized technology.

An important defining characteristic of extensive agriculture is that cultivated fields will not be used permanently, year after year, but will remain fallow for some time after being cultivated. This is one of the important contrasts between an extensive and an intensive agricultural strategy. Horticulturalists plant and harvest with simple tools, such as hoes or digging sticks, and do not use draft animals, irrigation techniques, or plows. Extensive agriculture has a relatively lower yield per acre than intensive agriculture and does not use so much human labor as other forms of farming. Extensive agriculturalists grow enough food in their fields or gardens to support the local group, but they do not produce surpluses that could involve the group in a wider market system with nonagricultural populations. Population densities among horticultural peoples are generally low, usually not exceeding 150

E T H N O G R A P H Y

THE YARAHMADZAI OF BALUCHISTAN: A PASTORAL ADAPTATION*

The chief problems presented by human groups adapting to grassland environments revolve around the exploitation of water and pasture. Because of the patchy characteristics of the environment, nomadism is the most common means of securing an adequate supply of these resources. As part of their adaptive strategies, pastoralists have to make important decisions about the size and composition of their herds. These decisions, in turn, reflect both their evaluation of the diet needed to sustain the group and their need to maintain social exchanges with their neighboring cultivators,

*Adapted from Philip C. Salzman, "Multi-Resource Nomadism in Iranian Baluchistan," in William Irons and Neville Dyson-Hudson, eds., *Perspectives on Nomadism*. Leiden, the Netherlands: E. J. Brill, 1972, pp. 61–69. Reprinted by permission.

since some agricultural contribution to the pastoral diet is always required.

The Yarahmadzai are a patrilineal tribe of some several thousand people, living in the area of southeastern Iran known as Baluchistan (see map). The total tribal territory is about 3,600 square miles. The plateau on which the Yarahmadzai live is at 5,000 feet and is cut by high mountains. The winters are cold

and the summers hot. Some years there is no rain at all, and the maximum tends to be about six inches a year, most of which falls in the winter. The main natural vegetation is grass, although some areas are completely barren. The area is bounded to the east by a vast desert that contains almost no vegetation.

In winter (December, January, February), each local community of the tribe has a traditional

people per square mile (McNetting 1977). There is great variation in horticultural productivity, however. In the highlands of New Guinea, cultivation of the sweet potato supports populations of up to 500 per square mile.

Although extensive agriculture may be practiced in dry lands, such as among the Hopi Indians, who live in northeastern Arizona and cultivate maize, beans, and squash, it is typi-

cally a tropical forest adaptation. As such it is found mainly in Southeast Asia, sub-Saharan Africa, some Pacific Islands, and the Amazon Basin in South America. In these environments, a form of cultivation called **swidden,** or **slash and burn,** is practiced. In slash and burn agriculture, a field is cleared by felling the trees and burning the brush. The burned vegetation is allowed to remain on the soil, which

camping area on the plateau consisting of about five to twenty tents. The herds of goats and sheep are taken out together by shepherds, and camels are herded separately by camel boys. At this time, there is practically no vegetation for the animals to eat, and they exist primarily on the accumulated fat of the previous spring. During the winter months, the entire Yarahmadzai area is barren, so there is no point in moving. Their strategy is to "sit tight," protect the animals as best they can, and compensate for the lack of pasturage by feeding the camels with roots, the goats and sheep with grain, and the lambs and kids with dates, processed date pits, and grain. As this is the rainy season, water is normally available. Since no food is produced, the community depends on stores from the previous year.

In spring (March, April, May), grass begins to appear, and plants to bud. Because of the variability of the rain and winter runoff water from the mountains, the availability of pasture varies from year to year within the territory. Thus, the community does not know beforehand where it will go. After spending quite a bit of time gathering information about where the pasture is

good, the camp packs up and migrates. In the period observed by Philip Salzman, his camp moved seven times, covering distances of five to twenty-five miles. As even pasturage in a good area is quickly exhausted, all the camps are rather constantly moving from place to place.

In the first part of summer (June and July), the pasturage begins to dry up. Recently, the Iranian government has introduced some irrigation technology into the area, and many of the tribesmen migrate to these areas to harvest grain. The livestock grazes on stubble and fertilizes the ground with droppings. From March to July, the animals give enough milk both for their young and for heavy consumption by the people. Milk is consumed in many different forms and preserved as dried milk solids and butter. The butter is sold or exchanged for other products, mostly grain.

In late summer and early autumn (August, September, October), the Yarahmadzai migrate to the lowland desert, leaving their winter tents, goats, and sheep on the plateau in the care of young boys. The group makes an eight-day migration to the groves of date palms. During

this time, they live in mud huts, harvesting and eating dates and preparing a number of food products for the return journey. Dates, date preserves, and date pits are all needed for consumption in the winter; salt, which is gathered from salt wastes, is consumed year-round; and palm leaves are woven into ropes for tying and packing tents and baggage. The date palms are easily cultivated; a river drains into the desert basin, creating a sandy soil with a five-foot water table into which the date palms sink their roots. Because of the heat, wind, and lack of rain, however, it is not possible for sheep and goats to live there, even for a short time.

In November, the group migrates back to the plateau. Those tribesmen who are also cultivators plant grain at this time, and women go off to work for cash in nearby towns. This labor is a substitute source of subsistence for the extensive livestock raiding of an earlier era, which has since been stamped out by the government. Pastoralism, date cultivation, and additional sources of subsistence are all necessary to an economy that exists in such a marginal and unproductive environment.

prevents its drying out from the sun. The resulting bed of ash acts as a fertilizer, returning nutrients to the soil. Fields are used only for several years (one to five) and then allowed to lie fallow for a number of years (up to twenty), so that the forest cover can be rebuilt and fertility restored. Swidden cultivators require five to six times as much fallow land as that under cultivation. Swidden agriculture can have a

deteriorating effect on the environment if fields are cultivated before they have lain fallow long enough to recover their forest growth. Eventually, the forest will not grow back, and the tree cover will be replaced by grasslands. It is this irreversible ecological deterioration that has caused swidden agriculture to be considered both inefficient and destructive by Western observers.

E T H N O G R A P H Y

THE DANI: NEW GUINEA HORTI-CULTURALISTS*

The Dani live in the central mountains of West Irian (Western New Guinea), above the tropical jungles of the coast (see map). Because of the altitude, rainfall is evenly distributed throughout the year, and temperature variation is slight. In the tropical forest, there are a few wild animals. Although a few wild foods are collected from the forests and fields, these do not play an important role in the Dani diet. Basically, the Dani rely on the products from their gardens and on their domesticated pigs for subsistence. Like many other highland New Guinea peoples, the Dani make the sweet potato the main item of their diet. Other cultivated plants that are eaten

*Adapted from Karl Heider, *The Dugum Dani*. Chicago: Aldine, 1970.

are taro, banana, ginger, sugar cane, and greens. For ordinary meals, sweet potatoes are merely cooked and eaten; ceremonial meals consist of steamed vegetables and pork.

The Dani cultivate three kinds of gardens: great ditched fields on the floor of the Grand Valley, hill slope gardens, and small garden plots behind the houses in their compounds. The bulk of the sweet potato crop is grown on the valley floor. In these gardens, a typical swidden round of activities takes place: The fields are cleared of brush and trees that have grown since the last planting, and the cleared vegetation is burned. The sod is then turned with digging sticks, which are the only agricultural implements among the Dani. Sweet potatoes are planted with vine cuttings from other gardens and

spread with the fertile mud that comes from the cleared ditches. A few months later, the gardens are weeded, and about seven months later, the harvesting begins. When the plot is exhausted, pigs are allowed to root over the field. Fields lie fallow anywhere from one to twenty years. Since there is no seasonal growing period in the valley, sweet potatoes are harvested year-round. Each household maintains several garden plots that are kept at different stages of growth. During the harvesting time for any one plot, enough potatoes are harvested to feed the family for the following day. The valley fields, in contrast to those on the slopes, are cultivated intensively, normally not allowing a chance for heavy vegetation to grow up. The ditching and use of the mud as

Recent anthropological investigation has shown, however, that swidden cultivation is not an uninformed, casual, and careless food-getting strategy. Swidden cultivators often have well-developed techniques of clearing, firing, fertilizing the soil, and crop rotation. The Kofyar, a people of the Jos plateau in Africa, for example, have an impressive system of stepped terraces that are constructed to deepen the soil, stabilize sloping ground, and prevent runoff and erosion. Among the Tsembaga of New

Guinea, planting of several crops is carefully ordered; sweet potato leaves cover the soil at ground level, taro leaves project over this mat, hibiscus and sugarcane stand still higher, and banana trees spread out above the rest. This ordering results in a garden that has maximum leaf exposure to sunlight, protects the soil, discourages insects, and provides a variety of foods as insurance if one crop fails (Rappaport 1971).

Although some swidden cultivators depend

cover supplies the necessary refertilization of valley gardens.

A more extensive slash and burn cultivation is practiced on the slopes. Here sugar cane, taro, cucumber, and yam are more common than sweet potato. In the village gardens, the Dani plant tobacco, banana, and a few vegetables. Banana plants grown in the compound are used for food but also have other uses; the trees shade houses, the leaves are used as wrappers for food, and the outer stem is softened to use for binding. Pigs provide an essential source of protein. Most men have from one to twenty pigs. Every day, the pigs are taken from their stalls to root in the nearby forest or in fallow gardens. Herding is tedious and means a lot of responsibility. Pigs also play an important role in Dani culture; they are used for exchange and eaten on ceremonial occasions.

The basic division of labor among the Dani is according to sex. Usually, men do the heavy work, women the light work. Men fight, build houses, and clear fields and gardens; women plant, weed, harvest, cook, and make salt. Children frequently herd the pigs. In their basic economy, the Dani are pretty self-sufficient. They provide their own food, shelter, and clothing from materials found or grown in the area. Except for ax and adze blades, needed for felling trees and butchering pigs, the subsistence economy of the Dani is self-contained, and small residential groups are economically independent. The ceremonial economy requires that each Dani group is dependent on a broad trade network.

primarily on one crop, many more cultivate several. Because plants grown by swidden cultivators do not provide all the necessary proteins for human health, however, horticulturalists may also hunt and fish or raise some domestic animals. In New Guinea, for example, domestic pigs are an important source of protein; the Hopi raise sheep; and the Kofyar keep goats, chickens, sheep, and cows.

Because swidden cultivation requires shifting of fields, it has been assumed that horticulturalists shift residences as well. This is not necessarily the case; some swidden cultivators do occupy villages permanently or at least on a long-term basis. In horticultural populations, there is a typical division of labor by sex. The men do the clearing, burning, planting, weeding, and fencing; women harvest, carry plant foods back to the village, and transform raw food into cooked or processed edibles. Where hunting is practiced, it is a male task, although either men or women may fish.

Horticultural peoples supplement their diets by a number of different means. Fishing with a bow and arrow is practiced in Papua New Guinea. (Courtesy of Office of Information, Port Moresby, Papua New Guinea)

Females may help plant, weed, and harvest. They also care for pigs, where these are raised.

There is great variety in social systems among horticulturalists. The basic unit is most frequently a group of people who believe that they are descended from a common ancestor. This descent group most frequently reckons descent through males, but societies in which descent is reckoned through females occur in greater proportion among horticultural peoples than in any other type of society. This may be related to the important role of women in the cultivation of plants and cooperative domestic activities.

In spite of the generally low population densities, the size of horticultural villages may be quite large, ranging from 100 people up to 1,000. It appears that small, low-density village societies are more egalitarian than those with larger populations and higher density, although generally it can be said that horticulturalists have more formalized group leadership than hunters and gatherers. These societies also frequently engage in warfare, which may be a way of regulating population size and density.

Intensive Agriculture

Intensive agriculture is characterized by the use of the plow and draft animals, and by more effective techniques of water and soil control than are used by horticulturalists. The same piece of land is cultivated permanently and needs no fallow period. Plows are more efficient in loosening the soil than are digging sticks or hoes. In turning of the soil, nutrients are lifted to the surface. Plowing requires a much more thorough clearing of land, but it also allows land to be used year after year. Irrigation is another important pattern in intensive agriculture. Although some horticulturalists do practice some simple methods of water conservation and control, intensive agriculture in dry areas can only be carried out with sophisticated irrigation techniques. In hilly areas, intensive agriculture requires some form of terracing in order to prevent crops and good soil from being washed down the hillside. Pre-industrial intensive agriculture also utilizes techniques of natural fertilization, selective breeding of livestock and crops, and crop rotation, all of which increase productivity. Whereas horticulturalists have to increase the land under cultivation in order to support a larger population, intensive agriculture can support population increases by more intensified use of the same piece of land.

Many more people can be supported per acre of land with intensive agriculture. A comparison of extensive and intensive agriculture in Mexico demonstrated, for example, that with irrigation, which permits two crops a year, a given amount of land can support almost fourteen times as many families as the same area exploited by slash and burn techniques. A dramatic example of the differences in productivity of slash and burn versus intensive agriculture is offered by the island nation of Indonesia. Java, which makes up only 9 percent of the Indonesian land area, supports over two-thirds of the Indonesian population. The "outer islands," which make up almost 90 percent of the land area and support about a third of its population, are mainly exploited by swidden

E T H N O G R A P H Y

TEPOZTLÁN: A PEASANT VILLAGE IN MEXICO*

Tepoztlán is a village of 4,500 people located 60 miles south of Mexico City (see Figure 8.4). The peasants of Tepoztlán basically grow corn, which, when ground and made into flat, thin cakes called *tortillas,* is the mainstay of the traditional diet. The land around the village is rocky, steep, and forested; little is available for agriculture. Although 90 percent of the villagers engage in agriculture, this by itself cannot support the population. Most Tepoztlecans seek out other sources of income, many of them working at a variety of jobs during the year.

There are two methods of cultivation in Tepoztlán, slash and burn hoe culture, and plow culture. Although the ideal in Tepoztlán is to own land privately, 64 percent of the families own no land at all. Those that do generally own very small plots. Around Tepoztlán, only 15 percent of the land area is cultivable by plow and oxen and about 10 percent by hoe culture.

*Adapted from Oscar Lewis, *Tepoztlán, Village in Mexico.* New York: Holt, Rinehart and Winston, 1960.

Figure 8.4   *The location of the village of Tepoztlán.*

Hoe culture is practiced on communally owned land, and plow culture on privately owned land. Plow culture requires relatively little time and labor, but considerable capital. Hoe culture is carried out by families; plow culture depends to a greater extent on hired labor.

The basic tools of production in plow culture are the plow, the machete, the hoe, and the ax. Both steel and wooden plows are used. The work cycle of plow culture consists of preparing the land, planting, cultivating, and harvesting. In August, during the rainy season, new land is broken in preparation for planting the following year. This is done with the steel plow. One man with a single team of oxen can plow on the average about two-fifths of an acre a day. If time permits, the new fields are plowed up twice. Planting usually begins in early June, after the beginning of the rains. The finest ears of corn, which have been set aside after the January harvest, are saved

(Continued on next page)

agriculture. In Java, intensive wet rice cultivation using elaborate irrigation terraces supports an average of about 480 people per square kilometer. Some of the more crowded parts of the island have population densities of up to 1,000 per square mile. This contrasts sharply with the maximum population density of swidden areas, which has been estimated at about 50 persons per kilometer (Geertz 1963).

The greater productivity of intensive agriculture results not only from more sophisticated technology but also from greater use of

for seed. The corn is then placed in the fields to rot, and the fields are cultivated two or three times at twenty-day intervals. After the third cultivation, about mid-August, planting is finished. The corn ripens in September. Between late September and November, when there is little work in the fields, the villagers look after their animals, cut wood, and do various home maintenance tasks. In early November, the harvest begins. The leaves are stripped at this time, and the corn is picked in early December. Each family, sometimes with the aid of hired laborers, harvests its own field. By early January, most fields are harvested and the corn is placed, unshelled, in storage bins. The women may shell what they need for daily consumption or small-scale trade. Around April or May, the men do the large-scale shelling, using a native volcanic rock or dry corncobs tied together over which the corn is rubbed. The shelled corn is stored in sacks.

In this particular area, hoe cultivation has a greater yield than plow cultivation. It is much more exhausting work, however, and also has less status than plow cultivation. Because of the capital investment required by intensive agriculture, many Tepoztlecans have engaged in hoe culture. As a short-run adaptation this makes sense, but the amount of land needed makes it a poor long-run strategy for the village, whose population is increasing.

Tepoztlán has relatively little livestock, and most of it is of poor quality. Climate and topography are not conducive to raising high-quality cattle or sheep. The main care given to animals by those families who have them is to guard against their being stolen. Horses, donkeys, and mules are owned for work, and riding a horse is considered a luxury. About 40 percent of the village families own hogs. Most of the animals used for food are slaughtered in the village itself. · Milk is sold locally by about a dozen families. Most is converted into cheese, which is also sold in the village market. One of the most important sources of income for poor families is the production of charcoal, a part-time activity carried out in conjunction with farming. Another important home industry is rope making, and fibers are obtained from the local maguey plants. Many women raise chickens, turkeys, and pigs; others grow fruit, vegetables, and flowers to supplement the family income. In order to earn extra cash, Tepoztlecans also engage in such nonagricultural occupations as teaching, baking, masonry, storekeeping, butchering, barbering, and carpentry. This trend toward nonagricultural work has accelerated in the last thirty-five years. Although the economy of Tepoztlán is essentially a household economy, in which the primary motive for production is subsistence of the family, the village depends on trade with nearby regions for many necessities, such as salt, sugar, rice, and chili. From urban centers it obtains cloth, agricultural implements, sewing machines, lamps, kerosene, guns, medicines, and other goods.

Like most peasant villages, Tepoztlán has undergone some important changes in the last thirty years. One of the most interesting ones is the result of the *bracero* movement. *Braceros* are temporary agricultural workers in the United States. In 1948 there were fewer than thirty in Tepoztlán. By 1957, over 600 men in a village population of some 4,500 had worked as *braceros*. Before the *bracero* movement, there was a shortage of agricultural land; but with so many young men going to the United States, many fields in Tepoztlán now lie idle. The *braceros* can earn more in a few months of labor in the United States than they could in almost two years in the village. This is just one of the important ways in which the economy of Tepoztlán is tied to the outside world, a pattern increasingly significant for peasant economies everywhere.

labor. Intensive agriculturalists must work long and hard to make the land productive. In terraced agriculture, for example, ditches must be dug and kept clean, sluices constructed and repaired, and all terraces leveled and diked. It has been estimated that growing rice under a swidden system requires 241 worker days per yearly crop, whereas wet rice cultivation requires 292 worker days a year. Intensive agriculture also requires more capital investment than horticulture. In horticultural societies, the only necessary tool may be a simple digging

Intensive rice farming can be enormously productive but is back-breaking work. The greater productivity of intensive agriculture results from more sophisticated technology, such as irrigation, and from intensification of labor. Here women plant rice outside Jogjakarta, Indonesia. (United Nations)

stick. In intensive agriculture, apart from the cost of human labor, plows have to be bought, and draft animals raised and cared for. Although intensive agriculturalists may have more control over food production, they are also more vulnerable to the environment. By depending on the intensive cultivation of one or two crops, they can face disaster in case of a crop failure. Draft animals may be struck by disease, again affecting the cultivator's ability to produce.

Intensive cultivation is generally associated with stable village life and other complex forms of social organization. With the development of intensive agriculture and population increase, we see the rise of cities, an increase in occupational specialization, social stratification arising from great differences in wealth, political centralization, and the development of the state. Cultivators who form part of complex state organizations are called **peasants.**

Although peasants produce mainly for subsistence of the household, they are distinguished from other kinds of cultivators by their participation in larger social and political entities, such as the state. Whereas horticulturalists produce for the subsistence of the local group and own the land they use for cultivation, peasants have little control over their land and produce to support nonproducing populations. The characteristic of a peasant economy is that part of its agricultural production is commandeered by a politically dominant and non-food-producing class. The peasant must pay for access to land either in cash, a percentage of the harvest, the donation of agricultural labor to the landowner, or tribute to the state. Because modern peasants are required to maintain their own seeds, tools, and animals, they must participate in market economies over which they have no control. In this way also, they are distinguished from horticulturalists and from farmers in industrial societies. Farmers in the United States, for example, have more control over their land and other means of production and produce for a market in order to maximize personal profit.

In industrial societies, where labor is a commodity, children's labor may be a valuable asset. These migrant children are working in a field in North Carolina. (United Nations)

As Eric Wolf says (1966:), "The American farmer runs a business; the peasant runs a household." This distinction should not be taken too literally, however; the small farmer in the United States is faced with many of the same decision-making issues as his counterpart in less industrialized countries. Furthermore, although contemporary peasants do engage in economic practices that seem to limit productivity, most are involved in world markets, and certainly in growing cash crops, they do attempt to maximize their profits.

Industrialism

The basis of industrial society is the use of machines and chemical processes for the production of goods. Although we call the transition from agricultural to industrial society the "Industrial Revolution," the change did not come about overnight, as the word *revolution* might lead us to believe. Industrialism began

in England in the early 1700s, and within 100 years it came into its own as a dominant force with the establishment of mass-production techniques in processing steel and with the invention of the steam locomotive. Compared to the amount of time it took humans to move from hunting and gathering to agriculture, however, a period of many thousands of years, the speed with which industrialism established itself may indeed be called revolutionary. Furthermore, industrialism is a revolution because of the enormous changes it brought about in society, not only in the economic sphere but in all other spheres as well. John Bodley (1982), writing about some of the excesses of industrialism as a way of life, emphasizes that compared with earlier forms of economic organization and production, industrialism was "explosive" in its effect on population growth, its consumption of goods and resources, and its need to expand beyond its own boundaries. Prior to industrialism, for example, the doubling of the world's population is estimated to have taken about 250 years. After industrialism, however, the population of Europe in the year 1850 doubled in just over 80 years, and the European populations of the United States, Canada, Australia, and Argentina tripled between 1851 and 1900. A little over 100 years later, in 1970, the doubling time of the world's population was only 33 years. This population growth is in contrast with growth among tribal populations, which, constrained by a variety of social and religious controls, tend to maintain themselves in equilibrium with their resources.

In addition to population growth, industrialism has also brought about a tremendous growth in per capita consumption of goods, and industrial economies are based on the principle that consumption must be constantly expanded and that material standards of living must always go up. This pattern contrasts with tribal economies, which put various limits on consumption and thus are able to make lighter demands on their environments. Industrialism, on the other hand, promotes resource consumption at so great a pace that it quickly outgrows its own boundaries and results in both export of population and import of resources. In this way, the whole world has been gradually drawn into the market system that has its source in industrialism.

Industrial societies require very large, mobile, skilled, educated, and specialized labor forces, whose activities are well coordinated. They also require the creation of complex systems of exchange between those who supply raw materials and those who use them in manufacturing, as well as between manufacturers and consumers. A central feature of industrial societies is that they are socially stratified. In capitalist industrial societies, there is private ownership of capital and the means of production, whereas in socialist societies, capital and the means of production are controlled by the state. But in both cases, there are at least two social classes, a large labor force that produces goods and services and a much smaller class that controls what is produced and how it is distributed.

Industrialism brought about (and continues to bring about) many changes in society. Some of the most important are the movement of people from rural to urban areas, a decrease in the organizing roles of kinship and religion, and the rise of a special kind of formal organization called a bureaucracy. The effects of some of these changes on more traditional societies will be discussed in Chapter Sixteen.

THE EMERGENCE OF VARIOUS FOOD-GETTING STRATEGIES

For most of human life on earth, people have exploited the environment through hunting and gathering. With the increasing improvement of tools during the last several hundred thousand years, hunters and gatherers were able to spread out into many parts of the world, exploit many kinds of environments, and develop many cultural systems. About 25,000 years ago, humans arrived in Australia and the New World. Population increased in both the Old and New Worlds, even with relatively simple foraging technologies, but this strategy set certain limits on population densities and, consequently, on the complexity of social organization.

About 10,000 years ago, human groups began to domesticate plants and animals in the Old World. About 4,000 years later, similar developments took place in the New World. At one time, anthropologists talked about the transition from a foraging to a food-producing strategy as a "revolution." Increasingly, archeological evidence is demonstrating that this transition was not revolutionary but gradual, although it was revolutionary in the new possibilities it opened up for cultural development. The earliest evidence of plant cultivation and the domestication of animals comes from Southwest Asia. It has been suggested that food production developed gradually out of a broad-spectrum foraging economy and resulted from experimentation with different forms of wild plants in new habitats. The domestication of animals, similarly, involved a gradual change in the relationship between humans and the wild sheep, goat, ox, and pig that they hunted (Flannery 1973).

Although archeologists have been able to show that village life is not synonymous with the domestication of plants and animals, increased populations could be supported, and sedentary village life became widespread with the advent of food production. With the increased population pressure, more intensive means of agriculture were developed, and human labor had to be more closely coordinated and controlled. In conjunction with these developments, state societies developed in the Near East, in Southwest Asia, in China, and also in Mexico and Peru.

Why intensive agriculture did not arise elsewhere—and why, in fact, some populations, such as the Australians, never made the transition from foraging to food production—has to be discussed in terms of the specific relationship between human populations and their environments. In some cases, such as the arctic, intensive agriculture could not develop. In other cases, such as in the fertile valleys of California, aboriginal foraging was so productive that there was little pressure to make the transition to food production. Even in contemporary horticultural or pastoral societies, where methods of intensive agriculture are known, the transition to this adaptation is by no means inevitable. In some cases, other strategies may involve less risk and therefore may be more adaptive over the long run. Ideology may also play a role, as different strategies become closely tied up with group identity. This seems to be true for many pastoral peoples, who despise their cultivating neighbors. For many hunting peoples, such as the Mbuti Pygmies, their whole culture and ideology are intimately associated with exploitation of the forest in which they live. In some cases, the transition to intensive cultivation is not made because it appears to require too much effort.

The history of humankind as a whole has moved in the direction of developing ways of exploiting the environment that are more efficient, can support greater population densities, and require more complex systems of sociocultural integration. With industrialization, which involves the use of machines rather than human or animal energy, we have seen incredible increases in productivity and efficiency. From a typical preindustrial system, in which 80 to 100 percent of the population must be actively involved in food production, we have moved to a situation in industrialized nations in which 10 percent or less of the population can produce food for the other 90 percent. But industrialization, like other systems of adaptation, also raises problems. Industrialization has enormous potential for production and enormous potential for destruction as well. Only time will tell if new cultural forms and values will emerge to allow us to control technology to the advantage of the entire human race.

SUMMARY

1. Basic to the success and survival of every culture is the development of knowledge and technology for getting food in a particular environment.

2. Social organization, beliefs and values, religious ritual, and regulation of population growth also contribute to adaptation to the physical environment.

3. Different physical environments present different problems, opportunities, and limitations to human populations. Therefore, the physical environment influences, although it does not determine, culture. There are always at least a few cultural alternatives possible in any environment. The level of technology is the determining factor in the utilization of the physical environment.

4. The subsistence (food-getting) pattern of a society develops in response to seasonal variation in the environment and environmental variations over the long run, such as drought, flood, or animal diseases.

5. Subsistence patterns are adjusted to the presence of different groups in the environment, as well as to physical factors such as climate, soil quality, and availability of water.

6. The environment influences culture, but culture also affects the environment. Through different patterns of exploitation, human societies affect the environmental zones in which they live.

7. The five major patterns of exploiting the environment to support human populations are hunting and gathering, pastoralism, extensive agriculture (horticulture), intensive agriculture, and industrialism.

8. Hunting and gathering, which relies on food naturally available in the environment, was the major food-getting pattern for 99 percent of the time humans have been on earth. This way of life is rapidly disappearing, although even today it provides a more than adequate living for those groups that practice it.

9. The Copper Eskimo of the Canadian Arctic represent a specialized hunting-gathering adaptation: unlike other foraging societies, they do not have a large component of vegetable food in their diet.

10. Pastoralism involves the care of domesticated herd animals, which alone cannot provide the necessary ingredients for an adequate human diet. Supplementary food grains are required, and therefore pastoralism either is found along with cultivation or involves trading relations with food cultivators.

11. The Yarahmadzai of Baluchistan are an example of a group that is predominantly pastoralist but also utilizes a variety of other means of obtaining food: wage labor, date cultivation, and trade.

12. Extensive agriculture (horticulture) uses a simple, nonmechanized technology. Fields are not used permanently but are allowed to lie fallow after several years of productivity. Horticulture is typically a tropical forest adaptation and requires the cutting and burning of jungle to clear fields for cultivation.

13. The Dani of New Guinea are horticulturalists, and like others in New Guinea they also have domesticated pigs that provide needed animal protein. Other horticultural groups do some hunting or fishing to provide the protein supplement necessary for human survival.

14. Intensive agriculture uses both land and labor intensively, and a more complex technology involves plows, irrigation techniques, or mechanization. This food-getting pattern supports the largest population densities, and it is thus associated with sedentary village life and the rise of the state.

15. Peasants are cultivators who produce mainly for the subsistence of their households but who participate in the larger political entity called the state. Tepoztlán, a village in Mexico, has the typical characteristics of a peasant village: although agriculture is the main source of subsistence, there is also a well-developed market, participation in the larger cash economy of the state, wage labor, and some occupational specialization. Unlike farmers in the United States, peasant cultivators have little control over the land they work.

16. Industrialism is a system in which machines and chemical processes are used for the production of goods. It requires a large, mobile labor force and involves a complex system of exchange between all elements of the economy.

17. As a whole, humankind has moved in the direction of using more complex technology, increasing its numbers, and developing more complex sociocultural systems. With the rise of industrialization, many old problems have been solved and many new ones created.

SUGGESTED READINGS

Bicchieri, M. G., ed.
1972   *Hunters and Gatherers Today: A Socioeconomic Study of Eleven Such Cultures in the Twentieth Century.* New York: Holt, Rinehart and Winston. A good book for the introductory student. The articles cover a variety of geographical areas and include the ways in which such societies have changed through contact.

Forde, Daryll
1952   *Habitat, Economy and Society.* New York: Dutton. An introduction to the ethnography and human geography of sixteen non-European peoples. The important aspects of economy and society are highlighted for each group.

Lee, Richard
1979   *The !Kung San: Men, Women and Work in a Foraging Society.* Cambridge, England: Cambridge University Press. An extremely detailed yet thoroughly readable book about one of the last human groups that still relies heavily on hunting and gathering.

Turnbull, Colin
  1972   *The Mountain People.* New York: Simon
             and Schuster. A fascinating, shocking,
             and controversial ethnography about
             what happens to human relations in an
             African culture in which people are
             starving.

Vayda, Andrew P.
  1969   *Environment and Cultural Behavior.* Gar-
             den City, N.Y.: Natural History Press. An
             excellent reader edited by a leading cul-
             tural ecologist. Includes ecological
             perspectives on the traditional anthro-
             pological topics of religion, the potlatch,
             agriculture, and family systems.

CHAPTER NINE

ECONOMICS

▶ Why are hunters called "the original affluent society"?

▶ Who has more free time, a French housewife or a tribeswoman from the Amazon?

▶ How do different societies organize work?

▶ Why is reciprocity so important in non-state societies?

Egypt . . . possesses so many wonders. . . . In most of their manners and customs they exactly reverse the common practice of mankind. The women attend the markets and trade, while the men sit at home at the loom; the women likewise carry burdens upon their shoulders, while the men carry them upon their heads. A woman cannot serve the priestly office . . . but men are priests; sons need not support their parents unless they choose, but daughters must, whether they choose or no.

From *The History of Herodotus*

*E*very society produces, distributes, and consumes (uses) goods and services. Every society therefore has an economy, a system for managing these processes. Its people also display certain economic behaviors—certain motivations and choices in the production, distribution, and consumption of those goods and services. We will look first at the study of economic behavior and then at economic systems before looking in detail at various patterns of production and distribution.

ANTHROPOLOGISTS STUDY ECONOMICS

Economic Behavior

Formal economics, which is a way of looking at human behavior, developed in the context of the Western industrial market economy. The basic assumption of formal economics is that human material wants are unlimited, but the means for achieving these wants are not. All people must therefore make choices about how to use time, energy, and capital in order to achieve desired ends. A further assumption of formal economics is that people **economize**—that is, make choices among alternative courses of action in a rational manner. Here, *rational* means choosing a course of action that will maximize the individual's well-being and profit.

Economizing is seen as the key to understanding both the production and consumption of goods. Will a business firm cut down or expand its production? Will it purchase a new machine or hire more laborers? Where will it locate its plant? Will it manufacture shoes or gloves? How much will be spent on advertising its product? All these decisions are assumed to be rational—that is, based on the desire to maximize profit. Individuals are also assumed to act rationally, to allocate scarce resources in ways that increase their individual material well-being. How does one allocate one's income, which is limited, among an unlimited number of desires? Will an individual save to buy a new car, send the children to college, fix the roof on the house, take a vacation, or buy a spouse a gift? Or will he/she save it all? Will leisure time be spent playing with the children, getting a second job, or going back to school to get a degree in order to improve one's economic chances in the future?

The definition of economics as the study of economizing made sense in the kind of society in which formal economics developed. Is formal economic theory equally useful in the study of primitive and peasant societies? How much of the behavior in these societies can be understood in terms of maximizing one's individual material well-being? The data from anthropology show that, although in every society people make choices in terms of means and ends, these choices are governed by values different from those in our own society.

Marshall Sahlins (1972) has questioned the whole idea of using the concept of scarcity in relation to hunting and gathering societies. He calls them the "original affluent societies" not because they are rich, but because what they desire is limited, and their technology is more than enough to meet their needs. According to Sahlins, the assumption that human needs are unlimited and resources are scarce is fundamental to capitalism, under which production units are motivated by profit. It is by no means a condition of all human societies; economizing is not a universal human value. Sahlins says: "We should entertain the . . . possiblity that hunters are in business for their health, a finite objective, and that the bow and arrow are adequate to that end" (p. 5). This point of view helps explain some behavior that appears puzzling—for example, "the inclination of hunters to consume at once all stocks on hand, as if they had it made" (p. 5). It also helps explain the economically nonproductive use of leisure time characteristic of many hunting societies.

Among the Hadza of Tanzania, for example, food is obtained without great effort. The Hadza live in an area with an abundance of animals and vegetable food. The Hadza man spends much of his time gambling, and there is no attempt to use leisure time to increase wealth. Surrounded by cultivators, the Hadza have, until recently, refused to give up their hunting way of life, because it "would require too much work." Such behavior seems irrational or "lazy" only if we assume that people have unlimited desires for more than they already possess (Woodburn 1968).

Enjoyable use of leisure time is only one of the ends toward which human effort may be expended. Increasing social status or respect is another value toward which individuals may direct their energies. In our own society, prestige is primarily tied up with increased consumption and display of goods and services by the individual. Within the value systems of other societies, individuals also make choices based on the desire to be respected by others. But prestige is associated not with individual display, but rather with generosity and the giving away of goods to others. Those who have

!Kung women filling eggshells with water. Among the !Kung, women play an
important role in the economy, but both men and women spend much of
their time socializing. (Courtesy of the American Museum of Natural
History)

much more than others may be considered
stingy, and they may lose rather than gain
prestige. "Conspicuous consumers" and stingy
individuals become objects of envy and even
subject to accusations of witchcraft. In our own
society, although we expect to help relatives
or close friends who are "down on their luck,"
we frequently do this only reluctantly, and we
often break off social relations with others who
continually borrow. In other societies, social
relations have priority over economic ones.
Friends, relatives, and neighbors are expected
to and do help one another out in times of
need with little conscious thought of being paid
back.

One allocation of resources in traditional
societies that often seems excessive to Westerners is the investment in expensive ceremonial or ritual occasions that appear to have
no direct material benefit to the individual, and
may even cause a family to go into debt.

Although we in the United States also engage
in this kind of "uneconomic" behavior, such
as spending far more on a wedding than we
can "rationally" afford, it is difficult for us to
understand such behavior in societies where
the material standard of living is below what
we consider minimal.

In nonindustrial societies, few aspects of
behavior are strictly economic. Most economic activity in such societies is viewed by
the people themselves as having social, ceremonial, or moral ends. The anthropological
study of economics, called **substantive economics,** must therefore encompass an understanding of the relation of means to ends that
goes beyond the maximization of individual
material interest. Individuals everywhere make
rational choices on the basis of self-interest.
But although individuals do the "economizing," culture and society, values and social
structures, provide the framework within which

Work Time and Free Time: A Comparison of Two Societies

For many people in Europe and the United States, modern life offers an unparalleled abundance of material goods. Have these goods made people happy? Have these goods made people happier than people in societies with much less material wealth than ours? The industrial technology and urban living that have made these material goods available also bring a price in the "quality of life." Although some people say that the gains far outweigh the costs, others say the opposite.

Edward Sapir, a creative and philosophical anthropologist, examines this question in an article called "Culture, Genuine and Spurious" (1949a). He defines a "genuine" culture as one that is balanced and harmonious and is directed toward fulfilling spiritual as well as practical human needs. In this kind of culture, the individual is never a mere cog in a wheel, whose activities are but a means to an end. Rather, in a genuine culture, the major activities of the individual "directly satisfy his/her own creative and emotional impulses" and are thus ends in themselves. According to Sapir, the main difficulty of our modern culture is that "in harnessing machines to our uses," we have not been able to avoid "harnessing most of mankind to the machines." For Sapir, the millions of individuals who grind away their working hours in routine, mechanized, unsatisfying work are "appalling sacrifices to civilization."

More recently, the question of how much progress modern civilization represents has been studied by two anthropologists, Allen and Orna Johnson,* who compared the working time and nonworking time of people in France and the Machiguenga of the Peruvian Amazon. The Machiguenga have a horticultural and hunting subsistence strategy. They are self-sufficient in that almost everything they consume is produced

*Adapted from "In Search of the Afflluent Society," by Allen Johnson, *Human Nature*, September, 1978. Used by permission of the publisher, Harcourt Brace Jovanovich, Inc.

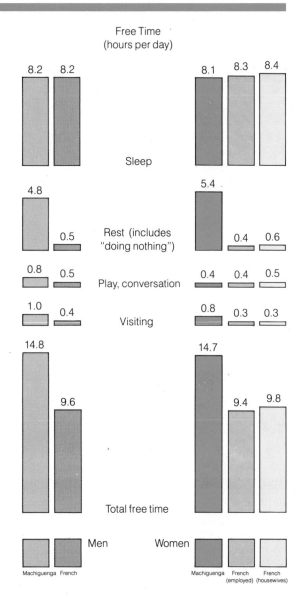

Free Time
(hours per day)

by their own labor with local resources, the main exception being the simple metal axes used in horticulture, which they get from the Peruvians.

The Johnsons' research indicates that both French men and French women spend more time working than do Machiguenga men and women, the men by one and a half hours, the women by

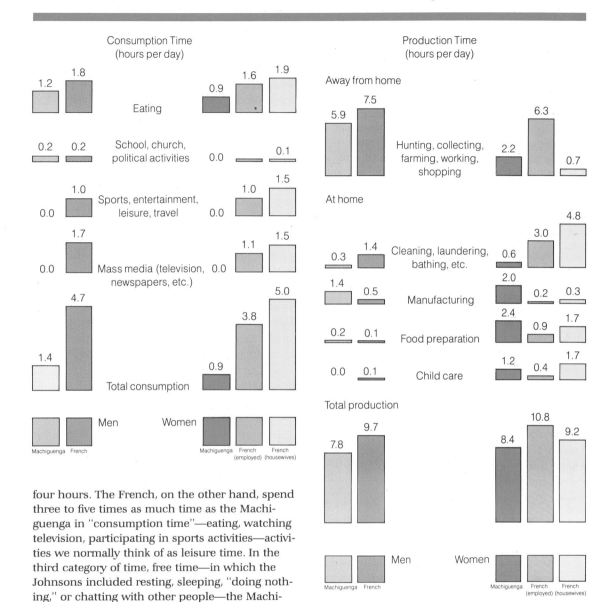

four hours. The French, on the other hand, spend three to five times as much time as the Machiguenga in "consumption time"—eating, watching television, participating in sports activities—activities we normally think of as leisure time. In the third category of time, free time—in which the Johnsons included resting, sleeping, "doing nothing," or chatting with other people—the Machiguenga were found to surpass the French by several hours a day (see graphs).

It appears, therefore, that free time has not increased as a result of technological progress, nor has time spent in working decreased. There *has* been an increase of leisure time at the expense of free time, and we may look at this in two ways. On the one hand, increased consumption of goods seems exciting and a source of plea-

sure in what would otherwise be boring time. On the other hand, the pressure to spend time in consumption increases the sense that "time is short" and may be a source of anxiety or guilt that detracts from our pleasure. People in modern societies increasingly feel that "free time" is "wasted time" (see Chapter Five).

Except that they lack the clearly superior Western medicines for certain sicknesses, such as parasitic diseases or eye infections, the Machiguenga do not suffer from their relatively low level of material affluence, according to the Johnsons. They easily produce more food than they use daily, saving the surplus for periods of crisis or for feeding guests and relatives. They are healthy, and the high quality of their lives is manifest in their warm family ties, integrity, peacefulness, and intimacy with nature.

In the past, anthropologists and others have tended either to romanticize primitive life, ignoring its difficulties, or else to view it as incontest- ably inferior to their own. The Johnson research suggests that, although people used to life in the affluent West will probably not want to live in a materially simple society, we should begin to question the costs of industrial technology and society: its harmful effects on the environment, the pressure to consume and the speeding up of time, the alienation of human relations, the mechanization and boredom of work, and the deprivation of unemployment. Studies of people like the Machiguenga can help us question our own goals and address questions about the quality of life in a more balanced way.

these choices are made. Anthropology makes an important contribution to the study of human behavior by demonstrating that rationality has different meanings for different societies. This understanding is of real practical value as nonindustrial societies begin programs of modernization and economic development. People who have never participated in a market economy will not necessarily see its value. Sudden changes in the economy can have unexpected consequences unless planners and administrators are aware of differences in values.

Economic Systems

An economic system is the part of a sociocultural system that deals with the production, distribution, and consumption of goods and services within a particular society. Economics deals partly with things, with the tools used to produce goods and the goods themselves. More important, it deals with the relationship of things to people and with people to one another in the process of producing, distributing, and consuming goods. Anthropologists are interested in understanding the relationship between the economy and the rest of a culture. One aspect of this interrelationship is that culture defines or shapes the ends sought by individuals and the means of achieving those ends. Society and economy are interdependent in other ways. The ways in which production is organized have consequences for the institution of the family and for the political system. Conversely, different types of political organization also have consequences for the modes of production and distribution of goods. How does a particular level of technological complexity affect the organization of work? How do the processes of production, distribution, and consumption relate to the formation of social classes or the absence of social differentiation? What is the consequence of different economic systems for economic growth and social change?

In primitive and peasant societies, it is often difficult to separate the economic system from the rest of culture. Economics is embedded in the total social process and cultural pattern. Few groups are organized solely for the purpose of production. Rather, production is carried out by groups such as families, larger kinship groups, or local communities. Productive units in traditional societies have many purposes; their economic activities are only one aspect of what they do. The distribution or exchange of goods is also embedded in relationships that have primarily social and political purposes, as is consumption. Under these conditions, in order to study the economics of a society, the anthropologist must build a model of a particular system from many activities that are not just economic in that culture.

PRODUCTION

In order to produce, people must have access to basic resources—land, water, and the materials from which tools are made. Every society has norms or rules that regulate access to and control over these resources as well as labor. After looking at the allocation of land, the basic resource of survival, we will turn to the organization of production—the composition of work groups and the division of labor in society. We will then look at capital—goods that are not directly consumed but are used to produce other goods.

Allocation of Natural Resources: Land

Access to and control over land is basic to every productive system. In our own society, most land is privately owned. It belongs to an individual by right of sale, and the individual who owns it has the right to keep others off and dispose of it as he or she wishes. This system of private ownership is not generally found among hunters and gatherers, horticulturalists, and pastoralists. In these societies, rights to use the land are vested in groups rather than in individuals. An individual acquires the right to use a piece of land by virtue of belonging by birth to the group in whom the right to use the land is vested. But even the group that has rights to use the land may not dispose of it at will; land is "inalienable" and may not be sold. With this type of land "ownership," no individual is deprived of access to basic resources, since every person belongs to a group within the society. Control over land, therefore, is not a means by which one group can exploit another or develop permanent control

In peasant societies, economics is embedded in the total social structure, and production is often carried out by families. (Serena Nanda)

over other groups. Where rights to land do not include the right to keep others out, we cannot really speak of land "ownership" at all. Let us look at what this means in four types of societies: hunters and gatherers, pastoralists, horticulturalists, and intensive agriculturalists.

Hunters and Gatherers The requirements of a hunting and gathering way of life mean that a group of people must spread out over extensive areas of land. The division of land into exclusively defended and privately owned areas would make little sense, since animals roam freely. The adaptive value of flexible boundaries is directly related to foraging strategies, because ranges can be adjusted to a change in the availability of resources in a particular area. Since everyone knows where food is located, there is little concern that one or another group will gain exclusive access to basic resources. Thus, although certain areas are customarily used by particular groups within the society, these areas by no means *belong* to that group.

Among the !Kung of the Kalahari, for example, camps are located near water holes. The traditional area exploited by a local group is measured by one day's round-trip walk (about

In horticultural societies, such as Ponape, land is communally owned, but fruit trees may be privately owned. Here a man carries breadfruit, a staple of this Pacific horticultural society. (Raymond Kennedy)

twelve miles from the camp) in all directions. Thus, each camp has a core area of about six miles surrounding each water hole. By fanning out from the water hole, camp members gain access to food resources within about one hundred square miles. Points beyond this are rarely utilized. Although camps may be moved five or six times a year, they are not moved far. Sometimes the move is only a few hundred yards; the farthest move is about ten or twelve miles (Lee, R., 1968).

Hunters and gatherers require freedom of movement not only as a condition of success in their search for food but also as a way of dealing with social conflict. Hunting bands are kept small in order to exploit the environment successfully. In such small groups, conflict must be kept to a minimum. When arguments break out, individuals can move to other groups without fear that they are cutting themselves off from access to vital resources. If land were individually or even communally "owned" and defended against outsiders, the freedom of movement in hunting societies would be severely limited.

The adaptiveness of flexible relations to the land for hunting groups seems to be demonstrated by recent studies of nonhuman primates in the wild. Gorilla groups, for example, appear to inhabit and use ranges that overlap considerably and do not have exclusive territories that they defend. Chimpanzees also appear to constantly change group membership, and even different baboon groups have been observed to come into close daily contact without fighting over territories. Contrary to such popular theories as Robert Ardrey's "territorial imperative," anthropological research on both nonhuman primates and contemporary hunters and gatherers shows no evidence of a human instinct to occupy and defend a geographical area (Alland 1972).

Pastoralists   Among pastoralists, access to grassland and water is gained through membership in corporate kin groups, but livestock is owned and managed by individual heads of households. Pastoral tribes have traditionally defined access to pasture and migration routes by arrangements with local authorities who have control over these areas. Within pastoralist camps, all members share equal access to pastures. It is this access rather than ownership that is important. Among contemporary pastoralists, access to land for grazing livestock is frequently established by contracts with the landowners of villages through which the pastoralists move in their migrations. These contracts, which must be renewed every year, specify the rent for the pasture, the borders of the area, and the date by which the area must be vacated.

Horticulturalists   In horticultural societies, land tends to be communally owned by an

Witn the rise of intensive agriculture and later with industrial capitalism, the notion of private land ownership and denying outsiders access to basic resources becomes central to the economic system. (Serena Nanda)

extended kin group, although rights to *use* a piece of land may be given to households or even individuals. The users of the land may not sell it or otherwise transfer it, however, because ultimately the land belongs to the larger community. Individual ownership of land does not make sense with a slash and burn horticultural strategy. Usually, plenty of good land is available, and an individual has little use for land that was once farmed but now lies fallow. Once the land goes out of production, the claims to it gradually fade away, although fruit trees that have been planted may remain in private possession (McNetting 1977).

Among horticulturalists, the designated elders or officials of the group usually allocate plots to the members of the group or the heads of households. What is important in horticultural societies, therefore, is not exclusive title

to land, but rather the work involved in clearing and cultivating. The rights to cleared and productive land and to the products of that land are vested in those who work it, most often the domestic group or household. Because it is possible that the user of the land may die while the land is still productive, some system of inheritance of use rights is usually provided for. Cultivated plots in horticultural societies may be exclusively used and even defended against trespassers, but this system does not deprive anyone of the land necessary for subsistence.

Where population densities are low or great areas of land are available for cultivation, land use and group ownership are not a problem in horticultural societies. But when specific geographical conditions limit the amount of available land, or when population pressure increases, land shortages do occur. Sometimes this is dealt with by the development of warfare, which serves to redistribute populations. Sometimes it is taken care of by the development of more efficient technology. As technology advances and the material base of a society expands, notions of private property develop. It is therefore in systems of intensive agriculture that private ownership of land becomes important.

Intensive Agriculturalists   Under intensive agriculture, the material and labor investment in land becomes substantial. As land remains continually and indefinitely in production, it can feed more people than those who work it. It can support nonagricultural specialists and a class of landowners. Private or family ownership of rigidly defined fields becomes an economic asset of great value in a society that permits the landowner, not the cultivator, to claim the surplus. That person can then enjoy leisure and command the services of craftsmen. Intensive agriculture therefore tends to be associated with individual land ownership, with the leasing or renting of property, with a political organization characterized by a ruling landowning class, and with occupational specialization. Under such conditions, a peasantry emerges. Peasants, as you may remember from Chapter Eight, are agriculturalists who must pay rent on the land they work. Part of what they produce is thus taken by a ruling class.

Individual ownership of land may grow out of population pressures that produce land scarcity and lead to intensified methods of agriculture. Under these conditions, communal control of land creates conflict as people begin to grumble about their share. Those who have improved the land are unwilling to see the investment of their labor revert to a family pool. This may be particularly true when cash crops such as coffee are concerned, since these require long-term care and yield harvests over many years. Individuals thus become tied to particular plots of land. In a study (Brown and Podolefsky 1976) of land use and rights in the New Guinea highlands, it was found that individual ownership of land was correlated with high population density and intensive agriculture. Individual rights to land (though within the framework of "group territory") occurred where plots of land were in permanent use or had a short fallow period (less than six years) and where trees and shrubs had been planted by the owner.

The Organization of Labor

In primitive and peasant economies, the basic unit of production is not a group organized solely around economic functions. Most often, the household or some extended kin group carries out production as part of its many activities. These groups produce goods mainly for their own use. Their goals are often social or religious, rather than strictly economic. Labor is not a commodity bought and sold in the market, but rather one aspect of a role that derives its primary meaning and reward from membership in a social group such as the family. Work, therefore, is not a "job"; it is an aspect of social participation (Lee, D., 1959). This pattern is very different from that in industrial societies, where the basic unit of production is the business firm, which is organized only for economic purposes. A firm does not produce goods for the use of its members; the items it produces are sold for profit. Under this system, labor becomes a commodity, bought and sold on the market just like milk and shoes. Work is carried out in an impersonal setting, and the rewards of work are primarily economic.

But the important difference between the business firm and the household is not the motivations of the actors: Households as well as firms are guided by the desire to maximize, and households also look for profit when they are involved in cash transactions. The point is that the structure of the household as a producing unit limits economic growth, because households have other functions, such as social and ritual functions. Households are also restricted because they can draw labor from only a small group. Nor can a household liquidate if it makes poor choices in the allocation of its resources. Furthermore, it may use resources in economically unproductive ways for ceremonial or social goals (Nash 1967). The business firm, in contrast, is geared toward economic growth and can make its decisions solely on an economic basis. Even when they are not geared solely to the profit of the individual owner (as is true, for example, in the socialist nations), firms are always looking for technological innovation and expansion of productivity. In economies where households are the producing units, then, there can be little expansion, and innovation is not a by-product of economic activity. What this means is that large-scale production and the mass distribution systems with which we are familiar tend not to develop where economic systems are made up of households.

Division of Labor by Sex   The sexual division of labor is a universal characteristic of human society. In every society, some tasks are considered appropriate only for women and others only for men. The most obvious basis for the division of labor between men and women is that only women can bear and nurse children. Child care is thus a universal female role, with a biological foundation in the physical differences between men and women. Since it is women who get pregnant and nurse, this tends to make them less mobile than men, which may account for the fact that hunting large animals and warfare (in nonindustrial societies) is an almost exclusively male occupation.

The extent to which biological sex differences are an explanation for sex role differentiation is a matter of dispute among anthropologists. Ernestine Friedl (1975), among others, points out that the care of small children can be shared by others—older children, neighbors, relatives, old men and women not engaged

The major characteristic of production in industrial society is that labor is a commodity, work is a job, and the production unit is a business firm, or factory, organized solely for profit. (ILGWU–Justice Photo)

in food production, and even fathers. Friedl suggests that the division of labor in society is not an inevitable result of the fact that women bear and care for children, but rather that the number of children a woman has is adapted to the division of labor in society and the role women play in getting food. Cultural norms with respect to family size and systems of child care may be arranged to conform with women's productive work, rather than the norms of work being an adaptation to pregnancy and child care. Most anthropologists emphasize the tremendous variation in the sex-related division of labor, and they look for explanations in the environment, food-getting strategy, and level of sociopolitical complexity of the particular society.

In foraging societies where hunting is done by one or a few individuals, it is always the men who hunt large animals. In most foraging societies, women collect plant foods near the base camp, although among the Hadza and also among the Paliyans of India (Gardner, P., 1966), each man collects most of his plant food himself, and women do the same for themselves and their children. Where hunting is a communal activity, as among the Mbuti Pygmies, women and men from several families collectively drive the animals into some central area, although men do the actual killing. In some societies, men and women also work together gathering nuts or fishing in streams.

In horticultural societies, there is a greater variety in the sexual division of labor, although here too there appears to be a male monopoly—that of clearing the land. Friedl (1975) suggests that men are assigned this task for several reasons. Not only is felling trees and cutting underbrush heavy work, but new land is often on the frontiers of other groups and may require warfare (a male activity) in order to gain access to it. Furthermore, game is more available in uncleared land, and among horticulturalists hunting is a male activity. Planting, weeding, harvesting, and carrying produce may be assigned to men or women. The most common pattern among horticulturalists is for men to clear the land and both men and women to cultivate. In some cases, women are responsible for cultivating the basic staples, and men raise only the prestige crops used in exchange. In highland New Guinea, for example, women raise sweet potatoes, which are the main food for humans as well as pigs, and men raise sugar, taro, and bananas, which are used only in exchange. A common pattern in West Africa is that both men and women cultivate staples and prestige crops and women raise additional staples that they use for trade.

A relatively rare pattern of sex specialization in food production exists among the Yanomamo of the Amazon basin in South America. Here the men clear and cultivate, with the women giving only minor assistance. Men also hunt and gather honey. Women gather wild plants, and both sexes fish, but most of the food supply comes from the gardens cultivated by the men. One explanation of this pattern is that the Yanomamo are constantly engaged in warfare and raiding other villages for their women. This makes it quite dangerous for women to work unprotected in the forest. Among the Hopi Indians of Arizona also, men cultivate the staple crops—corn, beans,

and squash—with simple irrigation techniques, while the women raise a few vegetables in small gardens near the village.

Wherever hunting and deep sea fishing occur among horticulturalists, these activities are done by men, although women may collect small fish from streams and kill small animals. Where domesticated animals are raised, whether the work falls to men or women seems to depend on the kinds of animals. If pigs are domesticated, as in New Guinea, women usually feed and care for them (though men exchange them); this may be because pigs root in the vicinity of the home and can more easily be taken care of by women with small children. Sheep, goats, and cattle, which graze at some distance from the home, are usually herded by men or boys.

Carrying food home from the fields is practically always part of a woman's role; a man may or may not also do this. The major daily work of cooking and processing food, which is a difficult task when it involves grinding grains and pounding root crops, is women's work everywhere, although the preparation of food for ceremonies is often the task of men.

Sex role specialization in craft activities varies except for metalworking, which is always a male task and perhaps developed out of the making of metal weapons for hunting and war. Weaving is done by women in the American Southwest, but by men in Africa. In Europe, India, and Central Africa, men are the potters, but in West Africa and the Americas, women are the potters. Making bark cloth is a male task in Africa but a female task in Southeast Asia. Baskets are usually made by women if they are for domestic use but by men when they are sold.

Division by Age   The division of labor by age is also universal. In our own society, childhood is prolonged, and young people do not generally engage in productive activities. In other societies, even very small children actually contribute to community life. At the other end of the spectrum, the elderly in our society are

In addition to the processing of daily food, young Kurdish women take care of the water supply and cattle and look after the chickens and turkeys. (United Nations)

often forcibly retired from the work force when they are still in good health. In the United States, where an honest day's work is an important part of people's self-image and their most important connection to the larger social whole, this forced disengagement of the aged from productive tasks can lead to isolation, loneliness, and diminished feelings of self-worth (Clark 1973). In many traditional societies, by contrast, the older person continues to make an important contribution to economic life. An outstanding example of this kind of society is the Abkhasians, a people famous for their longevity, who live in an area between the Black Sea and the Caucausus mountains in the Soviet Union. The Abkhasians were once herders but now live and work on collective farms. Almost everyone in the community works regularly. "Retirement" is unknown. After the age of eighty, and more so after the age of ninety, the workload decreases, but work does not stop. Men who have been shepherds no longer follow the herds up the mountains but instead may tend farm animals. Old men cease plowing and lifting heavy loads but continue weeding. Women of advanced age no longer work in the fields, but they continue to do housework, feed chickens, and knit. One study of 28 people over the age of 100 showed that they worked an average of 4 hours a day (Benet 1976).

The Abkhasians are an exceptional people. But even in traditional societies where such health and vitality do not exist, older people often contribute to society by taking on the roles of ritual specialists, guardians of cultural traditions, and agents of enculturation. In societies without writing, older people who know and remember are valuable members of society, respected and socially involved even past the time of strictly economic productivity.

Specialization in Complex Societies   Nonindustrial societies have relatively simple technologies. Although many of their tools and techniques are ingenious and fit the requirements of the environment, toolmaking does not require skills beyond those that can be learned as part of an informal socialization process. The work involved in making the tools of production can be done by every normal adult and requires no machines or scarce materials. Because there are no specialized operations, there is little need for specialization of labor. Almost everyone can do every job.

In nonindustrial societies, all adult men and women are actively engaged in the quest for food. The few specialists—for example, religious practitioners—are usually part-time specialists and also engage in food production. The characteristic division of labor is not by job but by age and sex. This contrasts with our own society, in which production is highly specialized.

In addition to the division of labor by sex and age that is found in all societies, complex societies are characterized by a great variety of occupational roles and productive specializations. In the caste system in India, for example, only people belonging to certain hereditary kinship groups are allowed to perform certain services or produce certain kinds of goods. Literally thousands of specialized activities—washing clothes, drumming at festivals, presiding over religious ceremonies, making pots, painting pictures—are traditionally performed by various castes within a village, or even by villages as a whole.

The division of labor in society becomes more specialized and complex as population increases and agricultural production intensifies. Industrialization as an adaptive strategy requires the most specialized and complex division of labor, and only a small proportion of the population is directly involved in producing food. We all know how complicated our mass production techniques and service delivery systems are, and we are familiar with how specialized jobs have become. Although specialization of production undoubtedly has advantages in terms of efficiency and the ability to produce large quantities of goods, we must also consider what price may have to be paid in terms of other, nonmaterial human values.

Capital

Capital is goods used to produce other goods. Where money exists, capital includes the money used to purchase these goods. In the small-scale economies we have been describing, capital goods are limited. Among hunting peoples, weapons used in the hunt are capital goods. Among fishing societies, they include water craft and elaborate trapping and netting devices that require great investment of time and labor. In agricultural societies, the tools of cultivation and storage facilities are part of capital. In pastoral societies, the main form of capital is livestock. Animals produce goods that are directly consumed, such as milk, and they are also kept to produce other animals and are used in exchange. Capital goods in primitive and peasant societies are normally owned individually, except for those that are too costly for one individual to buy. In peasant societies, for example, cooperatives may be set up for the purchase of such things as tractors. In every society, some time and energy must be invested in the maintenance of capital goods. Storage facilities must be built and maintained; tools must be made, replaced and repaired; and animals must be fed and taken care of.

An important point of contrast in economic systems is the extent to which the members of a society have access to capital goods. Differential access to important capital goods develops with more complex political forms, as well as with more complex and specialized technology. In hunting and horticultural societies, where technology is simple and tools are made by hand, every normal adult has access to capital. No one is deprived of the means of producing food or manufactured items. In politically and technologically more complex societies such as some chiefdoms or states, access to the means of production falls into the hands of a ruling class. Ownership of the means of production may be limited to a small group, whose members thereby gain power over others and control their labor. Capitalist societies are those in which, among other things, capital is invested for profit, rather than used simply for the subsistence needs of the group. Because capitalism is associated with market economies and money, we will discuss it in the next section on distribution.

DISTRIBUTION: SYSTEMS OF EXCHANGE

In all societies, goods and services are exchanged. There are three main ways in which this exchange occurs: reciprocity, redistribution, and the market. Each system appears to be predominantly associated with a particular kind of political and social organization, although more than one kind of exchange system frequently exists in any particular society (Polyani 1944). Where there is more than one system, each will normally be used for the exchange of different kinds of goods and services. Let us look first at reciprocity.

Reciprocity

The mutual give and take among people of equal status, which is actually a continuum of forms of exchange, is called **reciprocity.** Three types of reciprocity are distinguished from one another by the degree of social distance between the exchanging partners. Generalized reciprocity, which is usually carried out among close kin, has the highest degree of moral obligation. Balanced reciprocity is characteristic of the relationship between friends, or members of different tribes in a peaceable relationship with one another. Negative reciprocity refers to exchanges between strangers or peoples hostile to one another (Sahlins 1972).

Dugout canoes are an important form of capital among the horticultural Paramacca Maroons of Surinam, who also fish in lakes. A man gets his matrilineal kinsmen to help him, and he helps them in turn. (John Lenoir)

Generalized Reciprocity **Generalized reciprocity** involves a distribution of goods in which no account is kept of what is given and no immediate or specific return is expected. Such transactions are ideally altruistic—that is, without any thought of economic or other self-interest. Assistance is given and, if possible and necessary, returned. In our own society, we are familiar with generalized reciprocity as it exists between parents and children. Parents are constantly giving things and providing services to their children "out of love," or at least out of a sense of responsibility. What would we think of a parent who kept an account of what a child "cost" and then expected the child to repay this amount? What parents do expect is perhaps some gratitude, love, respect, and the child's happiness.

Generalized reciprocity involving food is an important social mechanism among hunting and gathering peoples. In these societies, a hunter or group of hunters distributes meat among the kin group or camp. Each person or family gets either an equal share or a share dependent on its kinship relationship to the hunter. Dentan (1968) describes this system among the Semai of Malaya:

After several days of fruitless hunting, a Semai man kills a large pig. He lugs it back to the settlement. Everyone gathers around. Two other men meticulously divide the pig into portions sufficient to feed two adults each (children are not supposed to eat pork). As nearly as possible each portion contains exactly the same amount of meat, fat, liver, and innards as every other portion. The adult men take the leaf wrapped portions home to redistribute them among the members of the house group.

Similar systems are used by the !Kung of the Kalahari and the Inuit.

A North American might wonder: "What does the hunter get out of it? Aren't some people always in the position of providing and others always receiving?" It is true that the hunter does not gain more from his kill than anyone else in terms of the amount of food he consumes. Still, he is bound by culturally prescribed rules of "generosity" to share. In these small societies, where the good opinion of others is really necessary for survival, the desire not to be thought stingy is a strong motivation to share and to do one's share. Since all men in the society are bound by the same rules, in the long run the system will provide everyone with an opportunity to give and receive. Generalized reciprocity also has important adaptive functions. One hunter and his family probably could not consume the meat from a large animal at one sitting. Without techniques for storing and preserving food, the meat would go to waste if it were not distributed among groups larger than the family.

Balanced Reciprocity   **Balanced reciprocity** involves a clear obligation to return, within a specified time limit, goods of nearly equal value. The fact that balanced reciprocity is most often called "gift giving" obscures its economic importance in societies where it is the dominant form of exchange. We are familiar with balanced reciprocity when we give gifts at weddings or birthdays or exchange invitations or buy a round of drinks for friends. In these exchanges, it is always the "spirit" of the gift and the social relationship between the givers that is verbalized as important. The economic aspect of the exchange is repressed. We also know, however, that an unreciprocated gift or a return gift of very different value will evoke negative comment. Similarly, accepting an invitation involves the obligation to offer a similar invitation in the future.

The social obligation to give, to accept, and to return is at the heart of balanced reciprocity. A refusal to receive or a failure to return the gift is taken as a withdrawal from a social relationship. Because a gift that is accepted puts the receiver under an obligation to the giver, most people like to "pay off" the debt by making a return gift. In balanced reciprocity, however, the payoff does not have to be immediate. In fact, an attempt to return the gift immediately is an indication of unwillingness to be obligated, and therefore also an indication that a trusting social relationship is neither present nor desired (Mauss 1954).

Balanced reciprocity is often characteristic of trading relations among non-Western peoples without market economies. Such trade, which is frequently carried out over long distances and between different tribes or villages, is often in the hands of trading partners, men who have a long-standing social relationship with each other. Social rules between trading partners permit trade with others not related by kinship where no authority, such as the state, exists for protection.

The most famous anthropological study of this type of trading is that of the kula ring, described by Malinowski in his ethnography of the Trobriand Islands off New Guinea (1961). The kula is an extensive, intertribal trade among a ring of islands (Figure 9-1). Two kinds of articles are prominent in this trade, each type

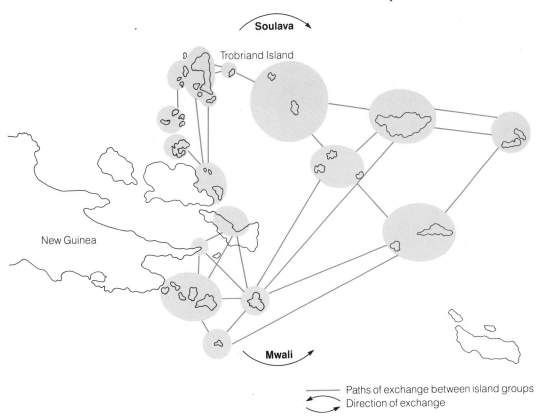

Figure 9.1   *The kula ring. This map shows the islands participating in the trade and the movement of the ritual exchange of necklaces* (soulava) *and armshells* (mwali).

moving in a different direction. *Soulava*, long necklaces of red shell, move clockwise. *Mwali*, bracelets of white shell, move counterclockwise. As each of these articles travels around the islands, it meets, and is exchanged for, an article of the other type. Every detail of the transaction is fixed by tradition. In every village on the participating islands, some of the men take part in the kula. These men receive the necklaces or bracelets from their trading partners, hold them for a while, and then pass them on. No man keeps any article in his possession permanently. These trading partnerships are permanent, lifelong affairs.

For the Trobriander, as Malinowski describes it, the satisfactions of the kula trade were tied up with the prestige and sentiment associated with holding the kula valuables. But the kula exchange can also be viewed as a mechanism of social integration. Through the trading partnerships, the groups that participate are socially bound to one another. Malinowski also noted that associated with the trade of kula valuables are a great number of secondary activities and features. Thus, side by side with the ritual exchange of armbands and necklaces, the natives also carry on ordinary trade, bartering from one island to another a great number of utilities, often unprocurable in the district to which they are imported. This suggests that the kula trade has important economic functions that have been obscured by the people's emphasis on the trading of kula valuables. It is clear that the functions of such exchanges are not necessarily recognized by the people participating in them, who are motivated by more personal considerations.

The importance of trade and balanced reciprocity in establishing alliances is clearly demonstrated among the Yanomamo. Yanomamo society is characterized by hostile relations between different villages. Villages are always looking for alliances, yet at the same time their pride forbids them from openly seeking ties with others. Trading is a good way to begin building up friendly relationships between villages. Each Yanomamo village has one or more products in which it specializes. These include dogs, hallucinogenic drugs, arrows, cotton yarn, baskets, pots, and, lately, steel tools. Napolean Chagnon, the Yanomamo ethnographer, says this specialization cannot be explained by the distribution of natural resources; each village is capable of producing all these things itself. Chagnon explains economic specialization and the "need" to trade among Yanomamo villages as an adaptation to the need for forming alliances. In other words, trade is an adaptation to the sociopolitical environment rather than to the physical one. Trade here functions as a "social catalyst," the "starting mechanism" through which mutually suspicious villages can be brought together over time. These contacts eventually lead to feasting, the exchange of women in marriage, and somewhat stable military alliances (1977).

Negative Reciprocity   **Negative reciprocity** is the "unsociable extreme" in exchange between equals. It is conducted for the purpose of material advantage, and it is based on the desire to get something for nothing (gambling, theft, cheating) or to get the better of a bargain (barter or haggling). Negative reciprocity is either an impersonal or an unfriendly transaction. As such, it is generally carried out by those who stand in the position of "outsiders" to each other. Both in our own society and in tribal and peasant society, outsiders, however they may be defined, are considered "fair game." In a large, complex society, where

economic dealings are mainly carried out among strangers, abstract principles of morality develop that should apply to everyone. Tribal and peasant societies are more likely to distinguish between the insider, whom it is morally wrong to cheat, and the outsider, from whom every advantage may be gained. Among the aboriginal Navajo, for example, the rules vary with the situation; to deceive when trading with foreign tribes is a morally accepted practice. Even witchcraft techniques are considered acceptable in trading with members of foreign tribes. Among pastoralists, negative reciprocity in the form of theft of livestock was an important way in which animals changed hands. For the Plains Indians, who hunted buffalo on horseback, horse raids were an important aspect of the economy.

Redistribution

In **redistribution,** goods are collected or contributed from members of a group and then given out to the group in a new pattern. Redistribution thus involves a "social center," to which goods are brought and from which they are distributed. There are many contexts in which redistribution is the mode of exchange. In household food sharing, pooled resources are reallocated among family members. In state societies, redistribution is achieved through taxation, an obligatory payment on the part of the people in return for which various services are provided by a government.

Redistribution is especially important as a mechanism of exchange in societies where political organization includes chiefs or "big men." These act as "social centers" to which goods and food are contributed by the population and from which these are redistributed back to the people through communal feasting. These feasts, which are sponsored by a chief or "big man," sustain his political power and raise his prestige. At the same time, they reaffirm the values and solidarity of the society.

A speaker for the Chief Who Gives Away Blankets, at Fort Rupert on the Northwest Coast of North America. "Potlatches" were an important feature of the social organization among Northwest Coast peoples. (Courtesy of the American Museum of Natural History)

The Kwakiutl Potlatch

The **potlatch** of the Kwakiutl Indians of the Northwest Coast of North America is one example of redistribution in action. In Kwakiutl society, social ranking was a primary interest. Every time a chief wanted to demonstrate his prestige in relation to other chiefs, he had to give a potlatch. Potlatches were feasts in which many kinds of wealth were distributed by the chief to the people and to chiefs from other villages who were his guests. They might be held to celebrate births, deaths, marriages, or a youth's coming of age. The number of guests present and the amount of goods given away, or even destroyed, revealed the wealth and prestige of the host chief. The host publicly traced his line of descent and claimed the right to certain symbolic privileges, such as the ownership of a particular song or dance.

Each of these claims was accompanied by feasting and the display and giving away of large quantities of food and manufactured goods, such as blankets, carved wooden boxes, boats, fish oil, and flour.

When there was a competitive potlatch—that is, when two men competed for the same symbolic privilege—one of the rivals might ostentatiously destroy great quantities of property—canoes, blankets, and, in former times, even slaves—in order to show how great he was and how little his possessions meant to him (Rohner and Rohner 1970). During these feasts, the host boasted about himself:

I am the great chief who vanquishes,
I am the great chief who vanquishes.
Oh, go on as you have done!
Only at those who continue to turn around in
* this world,*

Pig feasts, at which great quantities of meat and other goods are distributed by a host to his guests, are an important mechanism of redistribution among horticultural peoples of New Guinea. (Courtesy of Office of Information, Port Moresby, Papua New Guinea)

Working hard, losing their tails (like salmon), I
*   sneer,*
At the Chiefs under the true great chief.
Ha! have mercy on them! put oil on their dry
*   brittle-haired heads,*
The heads of those who do not comb their hair.
I sneer at the chiefs under the true great chief,
I am the great chief who makes people ashamed
(Benedict 1961:192).

The potlatches were thus an expression of the Kwakiutl ethos of social competition and individual rivalry.

Competitive feasts are not always characterized by the boasting and extremes of the Kwakiutl. This feature of potlatching is now believed by anthropologists to have been in-tensified when the Kwakiutl began to participate in the cash economy of the Canadians. The outside source of income resulted in the "inflation" of potlatching and the "wastefulness" of the destruction of goods described by informants to anthropologists in the late nineteenth and early twentieth centuries. Apparently, traditional potlatches were similar to the feasts that still exist in various parts of New Guinea and the islands of the Pacific.

In Ponape, a Micronesian island, for example, the competitive production and display of food at community feasts is not done with boasting, but with modesty. The prestige foods in Ponapean feasts are yams and breadfruit, contributed by the guests, and pigs and *kava* (an intoxicating beverage), contributed by the hosts. Those who bring yams and breadfruit are very modest about their display. A man who is considered "number one" in terms of the size and quality of the foods he brings will always protest that someone else's products are better than his own (Bascom 1970).

The earlier attention anthropologists gave to boasting and rivalry and to the motivations of the individual actors in these competitive giveaways obscures some of their ecologically adaptive functions and their economic importance as means of redistribution. Prestige economies, such as those described for the Kwakiutl and the Ponapeans, serve as a way of pushing people to produce more than they can immediately consume. It is a way of providing reserves that can be used in times of shortage and is particularly necessary where food preservation techniques are not well developed. Systems of feasting also provide a way for food surpluses to be distributed among villages that are not in equally good environments. In lean years, such communities could accept the invitations of chiefs from other villages and receive food in return for the diminished status involved in receiving rather than giving. When things got better, the recipients could become hosts, distributing food and goods to others who needed it and thus regaining some of their lost prestige.

Market Exchange

The predominant feature of **market exchange** is that goods and services are bought and sold at a money price determined by the impersonal forces of supply and demand. Unlike reciprocity and redistribution, in which the social and political roles of those who exchange are important, a market exchange is impersonal and occurs no matter what the social position of the participants. Market exchange is thus the most purely "economic" mode of exchange, the one in which participants are interested only in maximizing material gain. In a society integrated by the market, social or political goals are less important than economic goals. Organization around strictly economic purposes and activities is a dominant feature of social life.

Market exchange is based on the existence of **all-purpose money**—that is, a medium of exchange that is used to purchase a wide range of goods and services and that is a standard of value for stating prices. This feature distinguishes true market systems from societies in which money exists but only certain kinds of goods and services are exchanged for money. Societies with market economies must also be distinguished from those in which reciprocity or redistribution is the primary integrating mechanism, but where marketplaces also exist for the exchange of certain kinds of goods. These societies, which are found in New Guinea and West Africa, may be said to have "peripheral" markets; the important means of production, land, and labor are not exchanged through the mechanism of the market (Dalton 1967).

In systems of market exchange, labor is a commodity; people work for wages that are regulated, like other commodities, by supply and demand. Where, in addition to this feature, we find the private ownership of land and capital goods, and the investment of capital for profit (either in production or through interest on loans), we may talk of a **capitalist society.** A true capitalist society can exist only in connection with the state as a political system, because a powerful central authority is necessary to enforce the contracts on which market exchanges are based. Because the private ownership of basic resources results in denying some people access to these resources, permanently differentiated economic and social classes are also an important feature of a capitalist society. True capitalism is a late development in the history of humankind and in its purest form is best illustrated by the industrial nations of nineteenth-century Europe and the United States.

Leveling Mechanisms

Leveling mechanisms are practices, values, or forms of social organization that result in evening out the distribution of wealth. Leveling mechanisms force accumulated resources or capital to be used in ways that do not result in significant or permanent economic differences. They ensure that social goals take precedence over economic ones and thus result in socially stable, though economically static, social systems.

Leveling mechanisms have many different forms. Obligatory generosity as a basis of prestige and political power prevents the formation of social classes. Another leveling device is redistribution through feasting. Manning Nash describes a number of leveling mechanisms that operate in the village of Amatenango, in the Chiapas district of Mexico (1967). One is the organization of production by households. As mentioned earlier, economic expansion and accumulation of wealth are limited where households, rather than business firms, are the productive units. Another factor in Amatenango is that inheritance is bilateral; all a man's children share equally in his estate. This makes it difficult for large estates to persist over generations. Furthermore, a number of different village offices must be assumed by men in the village. This prevents

E T H N O G R A P H Y

PRIMITIVE CAPITALISTS: THE KAPAUKU

Some technologically primitive societies seem to contain many of the features of capitalist society. The Kapauku of western New Guinea (Figure 9-2), described by Leopold Pospisil (1963),* are a good example. The Kapauku are basically horticulturalists. The sweet potato, their main staple, is grown to feed both people and pigs. The breeding and trading of pigs is the major source of prestige and political leadership. Kapauku technology is quite simple, but the economy has many features of capitalism. The economy rests on the use of money. Both cowrie shell and two types of necklaces function as common media of exchange and the common measure of value. The exchange of all kinds of goods— food, domesticated animals, crops, land, and artifacts—is made through purchase. Money is also used for payment for labor in cultivation, for medical and ritual services, and for fines for misconduct. Cowrie shell money comes in various "denominations," and like modern money is easily portable. Cowrie shell is obtained through trade with coastal communities, which is sometimes a difficult

*Leopold Pospisil, *The Kapauku Papuans of West New Guinea.* New York: Holt, Rinehart and Winston, 1963.

Figure 9.2   *The location of the Kapauku.*

enterprise. The value of cowrie shell is fixed by its scarcity and is relatively stable. Market prices for different commodities are thus also relatively stable, and an "ideal" or "fair" price is established by tradition for different goods and services. However, supply and demand can alter the price in any particular situation. Prices may also be affected by the relationship between the trading partners or the social status of the buyer. Prices are usually lower between close relatives, for example. Prices may also be lowered if the buyer is a rich man or a political leader, either in the hope of future favors or as gratitude for past ones. In this respect, the Kapauku market system differs from a true market

economy, where—theoretically at least—the price is the same for everyone.

Although buying and selling occurs among the Kapauku on a daily basis, most business is transacted on ceremonial occasions, particularly that of the pig feast. Hundreds of animals are killed, and the meat is distributed through sales, loans, and repayment of debts. In addition, the trading of other products, such as native tobacco, bowstrings, salt, bows and arrows, chickens, net bags, and axes also takes place. The pig feasts are an important institution of interregional trade as well as ceremonial and social functions.

Although practically everything is exchanged among the

Kapauku through buying and selling, most of these exchanges take place within local kin groups. This is another difference between the Kapauku economy and a true market system. In their buying and selling, however, the Kapauku are strictly profit motivated. Domesticated animals are bought for money and raised for breeding and profit, rather than for domestic consumption. Artifacts are also produced for sale. The extension of credit is an important way in which money is redistributed, although no interest is usually charged on loans. The borrower may promise to pay a few extra cowrie shells for the favor of being lent money, but if he chooses not to do this later, there is no cause for legal complaint. Such a person, will, however, lose prestige and be regarded as untrustworthy.

Individualism, which is a major characteristic of capitalist societies, also has a prominent place in Kapauku life and culture. Every item in the society is individually owned; common ownership is unknown. The Kapauku maintain that two men cannot own a plot of land together because they would steal from each other's crops, and each would avoid as much work as he could get away with. Money, movable property, houses, canoes, and land thus have only one owner. Even tracts of virgin forest belong to an individual. There is no family, lineage, or village property. When cooperative efforts are needed to build large structures for the benefit of the whole community, such as a drainage ditch, specific individuals own segments of the property and take care of the upkeep of their segment only. If a structure collapses or has to be taken apart, the individuals who built it come to claim the logs that went into the building. Wives and husbands also possess property individually, as do male children who are old enough to work a piece of land. Nor do people like to work cooperatively. A garden plot is divided into individual sections, and even co-wives do not work together.

Also unlike many horticultural peoples, the Kapauku do not share their food on a communal basis. Individuals own the food they produce and act as hosts to the rest of the household. If a man has been treated to a meal in his own house by one of his co-residents, he must reciprocate by acting as host in turn. Even husbands and wives commonly exchange food rather than share it. Husbands provide pork, game, sugar cane, and bananas; wives return these "gifts" by supplying sweet potatoes, which they cultivate.

Although the Kapauku sound like capitalists in many ways, there are two important differences between their economy and society and our own. The first is that, although land is individually owned, in practice it is a kinship unit that controls a "territory." Since there is "mutual affection and a strong sense of unity" within a territory, no one appears to be denied access to the means of subsistence. Furthermore, although "grown men are expected to have gardens of their own" and the ethnographer found only two exceptions, the men without gardens helped their brothers and received part of the garden produce. Furthermore, an old man cannot validly sell his land without the consent of his sons. If he tries to, his heirs can repossess the land by giving the purchase price back to the buyer. Although property can be disposed of by the will of a dying man, no sons, brothers, fathers, or nephews can be deprived of their share of the land under any circumstances. Because of the importance of land in providing basic subsistence, this hedging of "individual ownership" is an important difference between Kapauku capitalism and our own economic system.

A second important difference is that Kapauku capitalism does not result in the establishment of permanently differentiated social classes. Kapauku wealth is displayed by generosity; a man who has much may lavishly distribute food or be generous in extending credit in order to keep up his reputation as a leader. Because pig breeding and trading is an activity many different people can engage in, the status system is constantly in flux. New men are constantly "coming up," and a rich headman may lose his position to a younger, more successful man. Wealth is therefore tied up with power only temporarily. The culturally prescribed obligation of a "big man" to be generous if he wishes to retain his influence acts to keep wealth fairly evenly distributed among the Kapauku.

their holders from working all the time, and the responsibilities of the offices take up some of a family's extra resources. A man must serve in twelve such offices before he can "retire" from public life, so the cost continues throughout adulthood. In addition to these twelve offices, there is the *alferez*, a ritual position filled by a younger man. Part of the requirement of this office is the sponsoring of a community feast, which involves paying for the food and liquor and also renting the costumes. Men are selected for this prestigious office by their ability to pay, and it is an enormous drain on the economic resources of a household. Should a family in Amatenango manage to accumulate more than its neighbors, village sanctions of gossip and accusations of witchcraft come into play. A man who is thought to be a witch is likely to be killed. Such accusations are most often leveled at those who are rich but not generous and who refuse to accept the communal obligations of taking office. Thus, through the interplay of social and economic forces, through the value system of the community, and through informal but powerful systems of control, economic differences are minimized, and the stability of the society as a whole is ensured.

SUMMARY

1. Formal economics, which focuses on action that maximizes the individual's well-being and profit (economizing) has limited application to economic systems in which the production, distribution, and consumption of goods are part of other aspects of culture and society. A major task of the anthropologist studying non-Western and traditional societies is to build a model of the economic system extracted from activities and norms that are not solely economic from the people's point of view.

2. Although technological development has resulted in a dramatic increase of material productivity and consumption in the West, it also results in changes in the "quality of life," as is suggested by the comparison in the use of time between the modern French and the Machiguenga of Peru.

3. Access to and control over land is basic to every productive system. Among hunters and gatherers, there are few exclusive rights to land; among horticulturalists, land is controlled by the kin group. It is mainly with the rise of intensive agriculture that land becomes subject to private ownership by individuals. Generally speaking, the more the investment of labor and technology and the less land available, the more likely private ownership will be.

4. In tribal and peasant economies, the basic unit of production is a kin group. Resources are produced and used mainly by this group, and production often has social and religious rather than strictly economic ends. This provides an important contrast with Western societies, where the basic unit of production is the business firm, whose interests are almost solely economic.

5. There is little specialization of labor in tribal and peasant societies, compared with the high degree of occupational specialization in industrial societies. Two universal bases of occupational specialization are sex and age.

6. The sexual division of labor has some universal aspects: hunting, fighting, and clearing the land are done among horticulturalists by men. Women are predominantly responsible for children, and they gather crops and do the daily processing of food for domestic use. Beyond this, the sexual division of labor is highly variable; a man's job in one society may easily be a woman's job in another.

7. Capital, goods used to produce other goods, is limited in small-scale economies. In noncapitalist societies, most members have equal access to capital goods, and no one group is deprived of the ability to produce.

8. In all societies, goods and services are exchanged in some way. Three systems of exchange are reciprocity, redistribution, and the market. Reciprocity exists in all societies but is the characteristic system of exchange in band and tribal societies. Redistribution is the characteristic mechanism of integration and exchange in chiefdoms, and the market system predominates in industrial societies. Systems of exchange function to integrate various elements of a society; they have a social as well as an economic function.

9. Leveling mechanisms are norms and activities that result in an evening out of wealth among a population. The many different kinds of leveling mechanisms—obligatory generosity, witchcraft accusations, gossip, religious obligations to give—all work to force accumulated resources to be used in ways that do not result in significant or permanent economic differences among individuals and groups within a society.

including much information on the ceremonial behavior of the potlatch, showing its many social and economic functions.

Toffler, Alvin
1981   *The Third Wave.* New York: Bantam. A readable analysis and best-seller about the sociopolitical consequences of the major economic revolutions in human history: domestication of plants and animals, industrialization, and the computer revolution.

SUGGESTED READINGS

Dalton, George, ed.
1967   *Tribal and Peasant Economies.* Garden City, N.Y.: Natural History Press. A reader suitable for an introduction to economic systems. Contains many of the most important articles in the field of economic anthropology.

LeClair, E. J., Jr., and Schneider, H. D., eds.
1968   *Economic Anthropology: Readings in Theory and Analysis.* New York: Holt, Rinehart and Winston. A collection of readings organized around substantive economic theory. Shows the ways in which economics is embedded in society and culture.

Malinowski, Bronislaw
1961   *Argonauts of the Western Pacific.* New York: E. P. Dutton (first publ. 1922). The classic on the kula exchange by an outstanding anthropological fieldworker.

Mauss, Marcel
1954   *The Gift.* New York: Macmillan. The classic on reciprocity in tribal societies.

Rohner, Ronald P., and Rohner, Evelyn C.
1970   *The Kwakiutl: Indians of British Columbia.* New York: Holt, Rinehart and Winston. An ethnographic monograph

MARRIAGE, FAMILY, AND DOMESTIC GROUPS

► What are some of the universal functions of marriage and the family?

► Why do some societies prefer that people marry their first cousins?

► Why do most societies have parents arrange their children's marriages?

► How does economics influence the shape of the family and the household?

One of the most respected patriarchs explained to me his doubts about the superiority of men: "Here they say that a man is worth more than a woman, but I don't know if this is true. A man can carry heavier burdens and can walk longer distances, but a man can't sleep with a man. He needs a woman. And he cannot have children. What do they say in your country?"

from "Guatemalan Women: Life under Two Types of Patriarchy"*

Every human society must solve three basic problems: the regulation of sexual access between males and females, the division of labor between males and females, and the need to assign responsibility for child care. This chapter takes up humankind's solutions.

MARRIAGE AND THE FAMILY: FUNCTIONS

The need to regulate sexual access stems from the continuous receptivity of the human female to sexual activity. The human male also has the potential to be sexually aroused continually, rather than just at certain times of the year. Sexual competition could therefore be a source of serious conflict in society if it were not regulated and channeled into relatively stable relationships that are given social approval. These relationships need not be permanent, and theoretically some system other than marriage could have developed. But with the absence of effective contraception and the

*"Guatemalan Women: Life under Two Types of Patriarchy," by Eileen Maynard, in *Many Sisters*, Carolyn J. Matthiasson, ed. New York: Free Press, 1974.

Marriage in Bolivia. Among the functions of marriage is the regulation of sexual access between males and females, setting up an exchange of goods and services between males and females, and assigning responsibility for the care of infant children. (United Nations/Rothstein)

of human infants and the prolonged care of children. A relatively permanent relationship between an adult male and an adult female provides a structure (the family) in which the male can provide food and protection and the female can nurse and provide the intense interaction needed for the healthy development of the human child. Marriage is a way of assigning responsibility for this care. Still another function of marriage that is important in accounting for its near universality in human societies is its linking of different families and kin groups. Thus, marriage leads to cooperation among groups of people larger than the primary husband-wife pair, which would appear to be of great advantage for the survival of the species.

Marriage refers to the customs, rules, and obligations that establish a special relationship between a sexually cohabiting adult male and female, between them and any children they produce, and between the kin groups of husband and wife. Although marriage and the formation of families rest on the biological complementarity of male and female and on the biological process of reproduction, both marriage and family are cultural patterns. As such, they differ in form and functions among human societies. In our own society, the marriage tie is the most important in the formation of the family, but this is not true everywhere. In many societies, the most important family bond is between blood relations rather than husband and wife. In some, it is the blood tie between generations (father and children or mother and children) that is the most important. In matrilineal societies, the tie between brother and sister is the most important. We must be careful, therefore, not to think of the family only in terms of the form it takes in our own society.

From a cross-cultural perspective, it appears that the most basic tie in society is between mother and child. The provisioning and protective male role *may* be played by the husband of the mother, but it may also be played by her brother. Even where marriage is an

near certainty that children would be born from such relationships, a relatively permanent union between a male and female that involves responsibility for children as well as economic exchange would seem to be more adaptive than other alternatives. In any case, the near universality of marriage indicates that it is the most adaptive solution to these human problems.

Earlier, we pointed out that differences in strength and mobility between males and females lead to some universal differences in economic roles in hunting and horticultural societies. Marriage is the way most societies arrange for the products and services of men and women to be exchanged. We have also mentioned the necessity for the intense care

important emotional relationship, as on the Israeli *kibbutz*, the division of labor and the care of children may not be in the hands of the married couple but in the hands of the community as a whole. Anthropologists are coming to the conclusion that the most useful way to approach the study of marriage and the family is not to establish definitions that will apply to every known group, but rather to look at the different ways in which the basic needs of sexual regulation, infant care, the division of labor, and the establishment of rights and obligations are legitimized in different societies.

MARRIAGE RULES

Incest Taboos

Every society has rules about mating. In all societies, there are some prohibitions on mating between persons in certain relationships or from certain social groups. The most universal prohibition is that on mating among certain kinds of kin: mother-son, father-daughter, and sister-brother. The taboos on mating between kin always extend beyond this immediate family group, however. In our own society, the taboo extends to the children of our parents' siblings (in our kinship terminology called first cousins); in other societies, individuals are not permitted to mate with others who may be related up to the fifth generation. These prohibitions on mating (that is, sexual relations) between relatives or people classified as relatives are called **incest taboos.**

Since sexual access is one of the most important rights conferred by marriage, incest taboos effectively prohibit marriage as well as mating among certain kin. The outstanding exception to the almost universal taboo on mating and marriage among members of the nuclear family are those cases of brother-sister marriage among royalty in ancient Egypt and in traditional Hawaiian society. Incest taboos have always been of interest to anthropologists, who have attempted to explain their origin and persistence in human society, partic-

Among the royal families of ancient Egypt, brother-sister marriage was preferred. This represents a rare exception to the almost universal presence of such taboos in human societies. (United Nations)

ularly as they apply to primary (or nuclear) family relationships. Many theories have been advanced, and we will look here at four major ones.

Inbreeding Avoidance   The inbreeding avoidance theory holds that mating between close kin produces deficient, weak children and is genetically harmful to the species. The incest taboo is therefore adaptive because it limits inbreeding. This theory, proposed in the late nineteenth century, was later rejected for a number of decades on the ground that inbreeding could produce advantages as well as disadvantages for the group, by bringing out recessive genes of both a superior and an inferior character. Recent work in population genetics has given more weight to the older view that inbreeding *is* usually harmful to a human population. The proportion of negative recessive traits to adaptive recessive ones is very high, and in the human animal inbreeding has definite disadvantages. Furthermore, these disadvantages are far more likely to appear as a result of the mating of primary relatives (mother-son, father-daughter, sister-brother) than of other relatives, even first cousins. It would seem, then, that the biological adaptiveness of the incest taboo as it applies to the nuclear family must be considered in explaining both its origins and its persistence.

The question raised here, of course, is how prescientific peoples could understand the connection between close inbreeding and the biological disadvantages that result. But the adaptive results of the incest taboo need not have been consciously recognized in order to persist; rather, groups that had such a taboo would have had more surviving children than groups without the taboo. This reproductive advantage would eventually account for its universality as groups without the taboo died out.

Familiarity Breeds Avoidance   The theory that familiarity breeds avoidance holds that the incest taboo is just a formal prohibition for a natural aversion to sexual relations between people who have grown up together. There are two sources of evidence that such an aversion may develop. Some studies of the Israeli *kibbutz* show that children "who sit on the potty together" have little sexual interest in one another. Studies of *kibbutz* marriages tend to show that mates are almost never chosen from the peer group. Most frequently they are chosen from another *kibbutz* altogether, in spite of the fact that the *kibbutz* does not discourage marriage between members. *Kibbutz* members themselves attribute this lack of sexual interest in their peers to the fact of their having grown up together (Talmon 1964)

A study of marriage in Taiwan by Arthur Wolf (1968) makes a similar point. Some Taiwanese practice a form of marriage in which a girl from a poor family may be given away or sold as an infant to a family with a son, with the expectation that she will be his wife. She is brought up with the son as his playmate, and at the proper time they marry. Wolf found that these "daughter-in-law-raised-from-childhood" marriages are much less successful than other marriages. There are more sexual difficulties, fewer children, and a higher rate of extramarital affairs.

Although the evidence from Israel and Taiwan may show that familiarity can lead to sexual avoidance, the familiarity-breeds-avoidance theory does not explain why a formal and strongly sanctioned taboo had to arise to prevent what was a natural aversion anyway. Furthermore, as a theory, it is contradicted by evidence showing that in fact incest does occur in many parts of the world. The actual occurrence of incest raises questions about whether familiarity does beed sexual aversion. Some anthropologists (and some psychoanalysts) have suggested the very opposite.

Preventing Disruption   Malinowski and Freud believed that the desire for sexual relations within the family is very strong. They suggested that the most important function of the incest taboo is in preventing disruption within the nuclear family. Malinowski argued that, as children grow into adolescence, it would be natural for them to attempt to satisfy their developing sexual urges within the group of people emotionally close to them—that is, within the family. If this were to happen, conflict would occur and the role relationships within the family would be disrupted; fathers and sons and mothers and daughters would compete. This would hinder the family in carrying out the transmission of cultural values in a harmonious and effective way. According to this theory, the incest taboo arose to repress the attempt to satisfy sexual desires within the family and to direct such desires outward.

This theory appears to make quite a bit of sense; unregulated sexual competition within the family would undoubtedly be disruptive. However, an alternative to the incest taboo could be the regulation of sexual competition among the family members. Furthermore, although Malinowski's theory suggests why the incest taboo exists between parents and children, it does not explain the prohibition of sexual relations between brothers and sisters. Regulating sexual activity within the family might solve the problem of disruption through sexual rivalry, but it would not solve the genetic problem. Only the familial incest taboo has both advantages: it prevents disruptions of the family over sexual competition and promotes outbreeding and genetic variability.

Forming Wider Alliances   Another theory, proposed most recently by Claude Lévi-Strauss (1969), stresses the importance of cooperation among groups larger than the nuclear family. The incest taboo forces people to marry outside the family, thus joining families together into a larger social community. This has undoubtedly contributed to the success of the human species. The alliance theory does not account for the origin of the incest taboo, but alliance between nuclear families certainly seems to be adaptive and can account for the persistence of the familial incest taboo and its extension to groups other than the nuclear family.

In summary, then, it does appear that the familial incest taboo has a number of advantages for the human species. In other animal species, incest is frequently prevented by expelling junior members from family groups as they reach sexual maturity. Because humans take so long to mature, the familial incest taboo seems to be the most efficient and effective means of promoting genetic variability, familial harmony, and community cooperation. These advantages can explain the spread and persistence of the taboo, if not its origins (Aberle et al. 1963).

Exogamy and Alliance

Exogamy specifies that an individual must marry outside particular groups. Because of the association of sex and marriage, prohibi-

tions on incest produce an almost universal-rule of exogamy within the primary family group of parents and children and between brothers and sisters. In every society, exogamous rules also apply to some group larger than the nuclear family. Most often, **lineages** and **clans,** which are descent groups based on a blood relationship, are exogamous.

The advantages of exogamy are similar to those proposed for the incest taboo. In addition to reducing conflict over sex within the cooperating group, such as the hunting band, exogamy leads to alliances between different families and groups. Alliance between groups larger than the primary family is of great adaptive significance for humans. Such alliances may have economic, political, or religious components; indeed, these intergroup rights and obligations are among the most important kinds of relationships established by marriage. Thus, the biblical text from Genesis "Then will we give our daughters unto you, and we will take your daughters unto us, and we will dwell with you and we will become one people" illustrates what must have seemed to be a clear alternative to primitive and ancient peoples—that between marrying out (of the family or local group) or being killed out. Early hunting and gathering bands undoubtedly exchanged women in order to live in peace with one another and to extend the social ties of cooperation.

One outstanding feature of marriage arrangements among contemporary hunters and gatherers is a system of exchange and alliance between groups that exchange wives. These alliances are important among peoples who must move around to take advantage of the availability of a food supply. Different groups take turns visiting and playing host to one another, and this intergroup sociability is made easier by exchanging wives. One consequence of exchanging women is that each hunting-gathering camp becomes dependent on others for a supply of wives and is allied with others through the bonds that result from marriage. This system contributes to the maintenance

Pictured here is a kin group among the !Kung. A characteristic feature of marriage among contemporary hunters and gatherers is a system of alliances among bands that exchange wives. This allows maximum flexibility among peoples who must move frequently to obtain food. (Courtesy of the American Museum of Natural History)

of peaceful relations among groups that move around, camp with one another, and exploit overlapping territories. It does not entirely eliminate intergroup aggression, but it probably helps keep it down to a manageable level.

The benefits of exogamy were very clear to the mountain-dwelling Arapesh with whom Margaret Mead (1963) worked. Their attitude about marriage was summed up in the following saying:

Your own mother
Your own sister
Your own pigs
Your own yams that you have piled up,
You may not eat.
Other people's mothers,
Other people's sisters,
Other people's pigs,

Other people's yams that they have piled up,
You may eat (p. 92).

Just as hoarding one's own food and not sharing or exchanging with the community is unthinkable for the Arapesh, so is keeping the women of one's group to oneself. In many societies, the very mention of incest is often accompanied by protestations of horror. For the Arapesh, incest simply does not make sense. In answer to Mead's question about incest, an Arapesh informant answered: "No, we don't sleep with our sisters. We give our sisters to other men and other men give us their sisters" (p. 92). When asked about a man marrying his sisters, the Arapesh answer was:

What, you would like to marry your sister? What is the matter with you? Don't you want a brother-in-law? Don't you realize that if you marry another man's sister and another man marries your sister, you will have at least two brothers-in-law, while if you marry your own sister you will have none? With whom will you hunt, with whom will you garden, with whom will you visit? (p. 97).

In peasant societies, rules of exogamy may apply to the village as well. In Northern India, a man must take a wife from outside his village. Through exogamy, the Indian village becomes a center in a kinship network that spreads over hundreds of villages. Because the wives in a typical Indian village may come from many different villages, the village has a "cosmopolitan" character. This also affects the quality of family life in Northern India. As we have seen in Khalapur, "peace at any price" is an important value in a household where brothers' wives are strangers to one another. The potential for conflict among sisters-in-law shapes child-rearing and personality and helps explain many rules of conduct in the North Indian family.

Village exogamy is not characteristic of all peasant societies. In Mexico, for example, women tend to marry within, rather than outside, the village. In the village of Tepoztlán, studied by Oscar Lewis, over 90 percent of marriages take place within the village, and 42 percent within the same neighborhood. This gives the Mexican village a more cohesive sense of community compared with the Indian village, where caste that cuts across villages, rather than the village community, is the most important unit of identification.

Other Kinds of Marriage Rules

Endogamy The opposite of exogamy, **endogamy** refers to marriage within one's own group, however that group may be defined. In order to keep the privileges and wealth of the group intact, blood relations may be encouraged or required to marry. This helps explain endogamy among royalty. In India, the caste is an endogamous group. An individual must marry someone within the caste or within the specific section of the caste to which he or she belongs. Although American society does not have specific named groups within which one must marry, so-called racial groups and social classes tend to be endogamous. In the past, racial endogamy was enforced by law in some states. In the case of social classes, opportunity, cultural norms, and similarity of life style all contribute to maintaining endogamy. It may be as easy to love a rich person as a poor one, but it is a lot harder to meet one unless you are rich yourself.

Preferential Marriage Rules In addition to rules about whom one may *not* marry and the group within which one *must* marry, some societies have rules about the groups or categories of relatives from which marriage partners are drawn. One of the most common is that an individual (ego) should marry a cross cousin. **Cross cousins** are people related through siblings of the opposite sex at the parental generation—that is, the child of either the mother's brother or the father's sister. In the United States, we do not distinguish our cross cousins from our **parallel cousins**, children of siblings of the same sex at the parental

generation—that is, of one's mother's sister or one's father's brother. Both relations are generally excluded from the categories of people from which a mate is selected.

Preferential cross-cousin marriage is related to the organization of kinship units larger than the nuclear family. Where descent groups are **unilineal**—that is, formed by either the mother's or the father's side exclusively—parallel cousins will be members of ego's own kinship group, but cross cousins will not. Since unilineal kinship groups are usually exogamous, a person is prohibited from marrying parallel cousins (who are frequently called and treated as "brothers" and "sisters") but will be allowed, or even required, to marry cross cousins, who are outside the kinship group. Preferred cross-cousin marriage reinforces ties between kin groups established in the preceding generation. In this sense, the adaptive value of preferential cross-cousin marriage is the same as exogamy: the establishing of alliances between groups. But where exogamy establishes alliances between a number of different groups, preferential marriage rules intensify the relationship between a limited number of groups generation after generation.

A few societies practice preferred parallel-cousin marriage. Among the Muslim Arabs of North Africa, the preference is for an individual to marry the son or daughter of the father's brother. Muslim Arab culture has a rule of **patrilineal descent;** descent and inheritance are in the male line. Parallel-cousin marriage may serve to prevent the fragmentation of family property, because economic resources can be kept within the family. A result of parallel-cousin marriage is to reinforce the solidarity of brothers. On the other hand, by socially isolating groups of brothers, parallel-cousin marriage adds to factional disputes and disunity within the larger social system.

The Levirate and the Sororate The **levirate** is the custom whereby a man marries the widow of his dead brother. In some cases, the children born to this union are considered children of the deceased man. Among the Nuer, a pastoral people of Africa, a form called "ghost marriage" exists: a man can marry a woman "to the name of" a brother who had died childless. The offspring of this union would be designated as children of the deceased. Where the **sororate** exists, the husband of a barren woman marries her sister, and at least some of these children are considered those of the first wife. The term is more commonly used to refer to the custom whereby, when a wife dies, her kin group supplies a sister as a wife for the widower.

The existence of the levirate and sororate attests to the importance of marriage as an alliance between two groups rather than between individuals, as is the case in our own society. Through such customs as the levirate, the sororate, and widow inheritance, not only are group alliances maintained, but the marriage contract can be fulfilled even in the event of death. Since marriage involves an exchange of rights and obligations, the family of the wife can be assured that she will be cared for even if her husband dies. This is only fair if she has fulfilled her part of the marriage contract by providing domestic services and bearing children.

But what if there is no one of the right relationship for an individual to marry? Or what if, as in the case of the levirate or sororate, the preferred marriage partner is already married? The point to note here is that there are often kin who are classified as equals for the purpose of marriage and who can be chosen as marriage partners. For example, if a man is supposed to marry his father's sister's daughter, the daughters of all women classified as his father's sisters, whether or not they are biologically in this relationship to the man in question, will be eligible as marriage partners.

Number of Spouses

All societies have rules about how many spouses an individual may have at one time. **Monogamy** permits only one man to be mar-

ried to one woman at any given time. Monogamy is the rule in our own society, although it is by no means the most frequent rule in the world's cultures. Given the increasing divorce rate and subsequent remarriage in the United States, perhaps the term "serial monogamy" most accurately describes the pattern in our own society. In this pattern, a man or woman has one marriage partner at a time but, because of the relatively easy divorce laws, will not necessarily remain with that partner for life.

Polygamy is plural marriage. It includes **polygyny,** which is the marriage of one man to several women, and **polyandry,** which is the marriage of one woman to several men. Most societies in the world permit (and prefer) plural marriage. In a world sample of 554 societies, polygyny was favored in 415; monogamy, in 135; and polyandry, in only 4 (Murdock 1949). Thus, about 75 percent of the world's societies prefer plural marriage. This does not mean, however, that most people in these societies actually have more than one spouse. Polygyny as a cultural ideal is related to different factors in different societies. Where women are economically important, polygyny can increase a man's wealth and therefore his social position. Also, since one of the most important functions of marriage is to ally different groups with one another, having several wives from different groups within the society serves to extend an individual's alliances. Thus, chiefs, headmen, or leaders of states may have wives from many different clans or villages. This provides leaders with increased economic resources that may then be redistributed among the people, and it also binds the different groups to the leader through marriage. Polygyny thus has important economic and political functions in some societies. Polygyny is found most characteristically in horticultural societies in which a high level of productivity is pursued. Although the most obvious advantages in polygynous societies seem to go to men—additional women in the household increase both the labor supply and productive yield, as well as the number of children—the status of females in such

Polygyny is an ideal in many societies but often cannot be realized except by those of high status. In societies with chiefs, such as this West African society, having many wives is an important economic resource for men of high rank and a way of building alliances throughout the society. (Simone Larive)

societies is not uniformly low, and in some societies women welcome the addition of a co-wife because it eases their own work load and provides daily companionship. Furthermore, although when combined with patrilineality, polygyny may mean that women are restricted by patriarchal authority, polygyny can also be combined with a high degree of sexual freedom for women.

Polyandry occurs primarily in parts of Tibet, Nepal, and India. Although the system may be an adaptation to a shortage of females in a society (this has been suggested for the Toda of Southern India and the Pahari Hindus of the Himalayan foothills), in two of these societies, the Toda and the Tibetan, it is the practice of

female infanticide that creates a shortage of women. In a society where men must be away from home for long periods of time, polyandry provides a woman with more than one husband to take care of her. In Tibet, polyandry appears to be related to the shortage of land. If several men marry one woman, this keeps down the number of children a man has to support. If brothers marry the same women, land can be kept within the family rather than fragmented over the generations.

The Toda of Southern India are a classic case of fraternal polyandry. The Toda female marries one male and at the same time becomes the wife of his brothers. If other brothers are born after the original marriage, they will also

E T H N O G R A P H Y

POLYGYNY: THE TIWI OF NORTH AUSTRALIA

Polygyny appears to be most adaptive in horticultural societies, but there are some foraging societies in which it is also adaptive. The Tiwi of Australia are one such society (Martin and Voorhies 1975).

The Tiwi live in an environment in which there is an ample supply of game and fish and an abundance of vegetable foods. Although kangaroos, lizards, fish, turtles, and geese are hunted by the men, it is the vegetable foods gathered by women that provide the staple of everyday meals. Women also make their own tools and, with their dogs, hunt small game. The major problem in the Tiwi environment is not the shortage of food, but rather the collecting of food that is abundantly available.

The Tiwi provide an excellent example of the way polygyny functions for both men and women. Earlier studies of the Tiwi were mainly done by men, and the following description of the function of polygyny in their society by the male ethnographers Hart and Pilling represents a male viewpoint on the advantages of polygyny (1960).

Among the Tiwi, as in most human groups, the male-female ratio is about equal, except that in the older age groups women tend to predominate, since they tend to live longer than men.

The location of the Tiwi.

Because the Tiwi require that every single woman must be married but do not require this of men, plural marriage is not only the cultural ideal but a reality for many Tiwi males.

A Tiwi male has the right to betroth his infant daughter to whomever he chooses (within the limits of the kinship system). In choosing a future son-in-law, men looked for their own best economic and social advantage. Hart says: "In Tiwi society daughters were an asset to their fathers and they [the fathers] invested these assets in their own welfare." A Tiwi father bestowed his daughter on a peer who was already a friend or an ally or on someone he wished to become a friend or ally. Or he might bestow his daughter on a man who had already bestowed a daughter on him. If he was looking for "old age insurance," a father might choose a man much younger than himself who showed signs of being a good hunter and fighter and who seemed likely to rise in influence. When the older man could no longer hunt, his son-in-law would still be young enough to provide him with food.

In all these cases, the future husband would be a great deal older than his young wife. The men on whom infant "wives" were bestowed tended to be in their forties or fifties or perhaps in their late twenties or thirties. As happens in our own society, where "money comes to money," a younger man who looked good to one girl's father would also be an attraction for other fathers. A man who was a "good catch" might have no wives living with him until his late twenties or thirties. Then, as his betrothed wives came of age (around fourteen), he would quickly acquire two or three. As these wives began to have children, he in turn could become an "investor": by betrothing his daughters to other men, he could acquire still more wives for himself.

In this system, many younger men, especially those who were not promising hunters, wound up with few or even no wives. These men could acquire wives by marrying older women who had been widowed. Older men who had outlived their contemporaries could marry widows, as could younger men who were not sufficiently attractive to acquire wives by bestowal of other men's daughters. Among the Tiwi, being an important, influential man required having a great many wives.

The large, multiple-wife household among the Tiwi can be regarded as an adaptation to the conditions of their existence. The more wives a man had, the more food could be collected. A Tiwi man readily admitted: "If I had only one or two wives I would starve; with ten or twelve wives they can all go out collecting and at least two or three are likely to bring back something at the end of the day so we all can eat." Because of the importance of food collecting, old wives were needed as well as young ones. An older woman knew the environment and was experienced in finding food. Younger wives served as apprentices and reinforcements for older wives. For this reason, every man who could tried to marry an older woman first. Hart found that households in which a man had only one or two wives, especially if both were young, had a much lower standard of living. From this perspective, women appear as little more than pawns in the marriage game, being distributed in a system over which they have little control. Consistent with this perspective of the female role in the marriage system was an early ethnographic emphasis on the political power and religious dominance Tiwi males had in the system.

Recent ethnographic work on the Tiwi by female ethnographers has caused a reexamination of this perspective. The work of Jane Goodall (1971) portrays Tiwi women not simply as wives but rather as women who have a fluctuating inventory of husbands. Early in her married life, the Tiwi girl is introduced to the man who will become the husband of any daughters she may bear. This relationship between a mother-in-law and her prospective son-in-law is very important in Tiwi social structure. The son-in-law must immediately begin to provide food and favors to his mother-in-law, and he often joins her camp at this time. Until a woman has her first pregnancy, she enjoys both sexual and social freedom, and Tiwi young women traditionally engage in several extramarital sexual unions with lovers of their own age, a practice that, although officially not approved of, is tolerated. When a woman gives birth to a girl, who is given to the prospective son-in-law as a wife after a few years, the son-in-law is bound to remain in his mother-in-law's residential group and serve her for life. As a woman gets older, her respect and power increase. As she moves through a series of marriages, she assumes the important role of senior wife, moving into a position of power in the domestic group. Her co-wives and their daughters form a cohesive economic and social unit, and in addition, she has considerable influence over her sons. Goodall's view is that, rather than being socially repressed by male authority as one might assume in a polygynous society, the Tiwi woman has prestige, power, and initiative based on both solidarity with other women and economic complementarity with men.

share in the marital rights. Sexual access to the wife appears to rotate rather equally, and there is little reported friction or jealousy. When all the brothers live with their wife in one hut, a brother who is with the wife will place his cloak and staff outside as a warning to others. When a wife becomes pregnant, determining the biological father is not considered necessary. Rather, a ceremony called "giving the bow," held in the woman's seventh month, assigns the child a legal or social father. This man makes a ceremonial bow and arrow from twigs and grass and presents these to the wife in front of his relatives. Usually, the eldest brother performs this ceremony, and then all subsequent children are considered his. After two or three children are born, another brother will usually "give the bow." Occasionally a woman will marry several men who are not biological brothers. When these men live in different villages, the wife will live in the village of each husband for a month. The men arrange among themselves who will "give the bow" when she becomes pregnant. Since the practice of female infanticide has largely ceased among the Toda, the male-female ratio has evened out. Due to this, as well as the influence of Christian missionaries, the Toda today are largely monogamous (Queen and Habenstein 1974).

Polygynous societies are much more frequent than polyandrous societies. But even where polygyny is preferred, the ratio of males to females may be such that few men will be able to have more than one wife, if all men are to have at least one. Furthermore, where men must exchange wealth for wives, many men will not be able to afford more than one wife and will therefore have to settle for monogamy.

In our own society, marriage is so closely tied to sexual and emotional exclusivity that it is hard for us to understand how polygynous marriages could exist without conflict and jealousy. The American reader must keep in mind, however, that sexual jealousy among women might not be a problem in societies which do not idealize romantic love and exclusive sexual rights in marriage. In some societies, in fact, sexual intercourse plays a very small role in the marriage relationship. Karl Heider (1970) reports that for the Dani of New Guinea, there is a period of about four to six years of sexual abstinence after the birth of a child. Although polygynous men may have sexual intercourse during this time with any one of their wives other than the new mother, many men appear to prefer to stay with the wife who has just given birth and forgo sexual activity. Given Heider's view that the taboo on extramarital intercourse appears to be generally taken seriously, the Dani are a good example of a culture in which interest in sex, even as an aspect of married life, is much lower than in our own. Like people of other cultures in New Guinea, most married Dani men normally sleep in the men's house, sometimes visiting their wives at night.

Even where a low level of sexual interest is not typical in a society, other kinds of mechanisms exist to minimize potential conflict between co-wives. Sororal polygyny, in which a man marries women who are sisters, is one such mechanism. Women who have grown up together may be more willing to cooperate and can get along better than women who are strangers to each other. Also, co-wives usually live in separate dwellings. A husband who wants to avoid conflict will attempt to distribute his economic resources and sexual attentions fairly evenly among his wives so there will be no accusations of favoritism. Where women's work is hard and monotonous, co-wives provide company for one another.

CHOOSING A MATE

As I have indicated, in most societies marriage is important because it links the kin groups of the married couple. This group interest in marriage frequently overrides any interest the individuals getting married have in each other, and it accounts for the practice of arranged marriages. In our own society, where marriage is primarily an affair of individuals and where

In some patrilineal societies, especially among Islamic peoples, great emphasis is put on guaranteeing a husband's control over his wife's sexuality. In order to ensure a Muslim woman's honor and that of her family, she wears a fully protective veil when out in public. (Serena Nanda)

the married couple tends to make a new home apart from the parents, families have less interest in whom their children marry and certainly less control over marriage than is the case elsewhere. Although choice is not quite as free in practice as American ideals would lead us to believe, theoretically any individual is quite free to choose a mate. Furthermore, since sexual compatibility and emotional needs are considered so important in the United States, mates are chosen on the basis of personal qualities largely having to do with physical attractiveness and that whole complex of feelings we call romantic love. Ideally, economic considerations are subordinated to the ideal of marrying for love.

In societies where the personal satisfactions of the married couple are subordinate to the needs and interests of the larger group, choosing a mate is much less of an individual, haphazard affair. The kin groups of both bride and groom have a strong vested interest in seeing that both parties fulfill their obligations, and therefore they have much more control over marriage arrangements, including the choice of a spouse for their children. An important consideration in arranging a marriage is family reputation. In Muslim societies, for example, the honor of a family is a primary consideration in its reputation. This honor is upheld both by men and women, and an individual who is disgraced brings disgrace on the family. This honor is expressed differently by men and women. For men, honor is a public matter involving bravery, piety, and hospitality; it may be lost, but it may also be regained. The honor of women involves one major consideration, sexual chastity. Once this is lost, it cannot be regained. If a woman's loss of virginity becomes known, no one of the appropriate group will want to marry her. Therefore, the family, to the extent that this is possible (and this differs among different social classes), zealously guards daughters, isolating them behind the veil or restricting their movements outside the household. This concern for female sexual chastity is prominent in societies where the children belong to the kin group of the father or where inheritance follows the male line, making the paternity of the child of paramount importance. Only if a woman is a virgin at marriage and is thereafter restricted in her movements and contacts with men can a man be sure the child she is carrying is his own.

In societies with elaborate social hierarchies, such as in India, the family's social status is also important. A marriage will typically be arranged from within the same section of the same caste, although it is the ideal that the family of the boy have somewhat higher social status than the family of the girl. In this patrilineal society, the bride's family must ritually defer and accept a subordinate status to the family of the groom. This is psychologically easier if the social position of the bride's family is a little lower than that of the groom's family. If the bride is expected to move in with her husband's family after marriage, this also shapes the personal qualities considered desirable in a potential marriage partner. Domestic abilities are considered very important—but even more important is the willingness of the girl to be obedient to her elders. A girl who shows signs of having an independent or complaining nature is viewed as a potential source of trouble by her future in-laws.

Where marriages are arranged, go-betweens are frequently used. A go-between, or marriage broker, has more information about a wider network of families than any one family can have. Furthermore, neither the family of the bride nor that of the groom will lose face if its offer is rejected by the other party. Although the arranged marriage system tends to become less rigid as societies urbanize and industrialize, it still remains true that in most societies,

families and larger kin groups have much more control over marriage and the choice of a spouse than in the United States.

TRANSFER OF RIGHTS AND EXCHANGES OF GOODS AT MARRIAGE

The essence of marriage is that it is a publicly accepted relationship that involves the transfer of certain rights and obligations among the participating parties. These rights primarily involve sexual access of husband and wife to each other, rights of the husband over any children born to the wife, obligations by one or both parents to care for children born to the union, and rights of husband and wife to the economic services of the other. Marriage may also give the families or kin groups of the bride and groom certain rights in each other for goods or services. These "relationships of affinity" may be symbolically expressed, as in India, where the family of the wife owes certain forms of deferential behavior to the family of the husband. This is true for all kin. Any person "from the girl's side" will be expected to behave in a ritually respectful manner to a person "from the boy's side."

The transfer of rights in marriage is often accompanied by an exchange of goods and services. Sometimes this exchange may be simply "presents"—that is, items customarily given as a way of winning and preserving the goodwill of those with the power to transfer marital rights, though not necessary to complete the transfer. In other cases, the exchange of goods and services is essential for the transfer of marital rights to take place. If such an exchange is not completed, the rights in marriage can be forfeited.

Three kinds of exchanges made in connection with marriage are bridewealth, dowry, and bride service. **Bridewealth** (or **bride price**) refers to goods presented by the groom's kin to the kin of the bride. **Dowry,** a rather rare practice, found in India and at one time customary in Europe, is a presentation of goods by the bride's kin to the family of the groom. The functions of dowry in India are a point of some controversy. One point of view holds that the dowry is a voluntary gift, a symbol of filial affection for a beloved daughter leaving home and a way of compensating her for the fact that traditionally she could not inherit land or property. It is also sometimes seen from this point of view as a source of security for her, as the jewelry she gets in her dowry would be hers to keep. Another point of view has it that dowry is a unilateral transfer of resources by a girl's family at her marriage to the groom's family as a recognition of the latter's generosity in taking on what is perceived as an economic liability, since upper-class and upper-caste women in India are not supposed to work. Dowry from this standpoint would be seen as a compensatory payment from the bride's family, who is losing an economic liability, to the groom's family, who is taking one on. **Bride service** refers to the practice whereby a young husband must work for a specified period of time for his wife's family in exchange for his marital rights. This practice tends to be customary in societies where accumulating material goods for an exchange at marriage might be quite difficult, and is found among some foraging societies. Among the !Kung, for example, a man may work for his wife's family for as long as fifteen years or until the birth of the third child.

The most common form of exchange of wealth is bridewealth. A major function of the payment of bridewealth is the legitimation of marriage (Ogbu 1978). This is confirmed by the fact that in societies where bridewealth is customary, an individual can claim compensation for the violation of conjugal rights only if the bridewealth has been paid. Furthermore, bridewealth paid at marriage is returned (subject to specified conditions) if a marriage is terminated. Another function of bridewealth that has been emphasized by anthropologists is that it entitles the husband to domestic and

The bride in India wears elaborate jewelry, much of which comes from her parents as part of her dowry.

sexual rights over his wife. Although this is true, marriage confers rights on the wife as well as the husband. By establishing marriage as legal—that is, recognized and supported by public sanctions—bridewealth allows wives to hold their husbands accountable for violations of conjugal rights, as well as the other way around. A third function traditionally ascribed to the payment of bridewealth is that it serves to stabilize marriage.

It is true that the exchange of goods at marriage does indicate the importance of marriage as a social, rather than an individual, affair, and it would seem to give the family of the groom a vested interest in keeping the couple together. A recent examination of cross-cultural data, however, shows that marriage may be stable for reasons other than the payment of bridewealth, and that the bridewealth payment itself does not mean that divorce will not occur. Finally, the idea that bridewealth is a payment for the loss of the woman to her husband's family is not fully supported by the cross-cultural data either. In some societies, for example, bridewealth is customary even though the husband goes to live with his wife's family or the husband assists his wife's family economically, especially as they get older. This recent reexamination of the conditions under which bridewealth is customary has also led to the reopening of the question of the relationship between bridewealth and women's status. The long-held assumption by colonial administrators, missionaries, and even anthropologists that the payment of bridewealth resulted in a lower status for women can be questioned. Ogbu (1978) argues that such payment enhances rather than diminishes the status of women, by enabling both husband and wife to acquire reciprocal rights in each other. The low status of women in parts of Africa where bridewealth is customary has nothing to do with the use of bridewealth in the legitimation of marriage.

Whatever the exact nature of the exchange of goods or services in marriage, the transfer of rights in a marriage is a "public" affair, almost always surrounded by ritual and ceremony. These ceremonies are a way of bearing witness to the lawfulness of the transaction. It is these ceremonies, publicly witnessed and acknowledged, that distinguish marriage from other kinds of unions that resemble it. "Living together," for example, may have some of the same emotional functions for the two individuals, but it does not involve obligatory economic exchanges or establish relationships between the individual and the spouse's kin.

DEFINING MARRIAGE

In a few societies, sexual rights, economic responsibilities, or socialization of children are not derived from relationships in marriage, but are part of the rights and responsibilities of groups other than those formed by husband-wife and parent-child.

The classic case presenting problems to anthropologists attempting to reach a universal definition of marriage is that of the Nayar of South India. They are a landowning caste who live in the state of Kerala. The Nayar "family" was not formed through marriage, but consisted rather of male and female kin descended from a female ancestor. This household group, called the *taravad*, typically contained brothers and sisters, a woman's daughter and granddaughters, and their children. *Taravad* property was held jointly in the name of the oldest surviving male. This type of family was related to the system of Nayar marriage.

Traditionally there were two kinds of marriage among the Nayar, the *tali*-tying ceremony and the *sambandham* relationship. Every Nayar girl had to undergo the *tali*-tying ceremony before she reached puberty; this rite marked a girl's transition to womanhood. The man with whom a girl tied the *tali* had no further rights in her nor did she have any obligations to him (except that at his death she performed certain rituals). After this ceremony, however, a girl could enter into *sambandham* unions with a number of different men of the proper caste with whom she would have children. The *taravad*, however, retained rights over a Nayar woman's procreative powers and authority over her children. Even so, for a child to have full birth rights in the *taravad*, a father had to be acknowledged. Any one of the men with whom the woman had had a *sambandham* union could acknowledge paternity by bearing certain expenses associated with the birth of the child. Where paternity was doubtful, an assembly of neighbors would attempt to coerce the current "visiting husband" to make the payments. If no man of the appropriate caste would take on the role of father, the woman and child were expelled from the *taravad* and from the caste, because it was assumed that the woman was having relationships with a lower-caste man. This was considered polluting not only for the woman, but for the entire *taravad*.

In the Nayar system, then, a woman had several "husbands" (*sambandham* unions), but the responsibility and care of children were in the hands of a group of brothers and sisters (the *taravad*). From the point of view of the polyandrous woman and her *taravad*, polyandry enhanced both individual and group prestige. Polyandry also gave the Nayar woman access to men who were in many different occupations, and their services could then be accessible to the *taravad*. The Nayar marriage and family system was well suited to the traditional Nayar occupation of soldiering. Without permanent responsibilities and permanent attachments to wife and children, a young Nayar man was free to pursue a military career. The agricultural land owned by the Nayar *taravad* was worked by lower-caste landless serfs and managed by an older male, an economic system that also freed younger Nayar men from the necessity of living in the *taravad* (Mencher 1965).

The data on the Nayar indicate that any universal definition of marriage would have to be very general indeed to cover all the known variations. Anthropologists are not so interested in such a definition as they once were. More important than establishing a definition to cover all known cases is looking at the kinds of rights that are transferred through marriage in different societies, and the kinds of families and domestic groups marriage creates. Our interest in the Nayar, then, focuses not on whether they have marriage or not, but on the way in which sexual access to women, economic responsibility, and rights over children are legitimized in Nayar society.

THE FAMILY

Two basic types of families identified by anthropologists are the elementary, or nuclear, family and the extended family. Nuclear families are organized around the conjugal tie—that is, the relationship between husband and wife. The extended family is based on consanguineal, or blood, relations extending over three or more generations.

The Nuclear Family

The **nuclear family** consists of a married couple and its children. This type of family may exist as a relatively isolated and independent unit, as it does in our society, or it may be embedded within larger kinship units. The claim of some anthropologists (Murdock 1949) that the nuclear family is a universal social institution has been disputed on the basis of some exceptional cases, such as that of the Nayar and the Israeli *kibbutz*. The independent nuclear family is the ideal in only a small percentage of the world's societies, primarily among hunters and gatherers and in modern industrialized nations, both of which require a high degree of mobility.

In our own society, the nuclear family ideally has its own residence, away from the parents of either husband or wife. Because the married couple forms a separate domestic and economic unit, the involvement of parents or other kin in mate selection is marginal. Larger kin groups are not expected to exercise control over or interfere in the affairs of the nuclear family. Although there are some ideals about the different roles that should be played by husband and wife with regard to economic support, sexual activity, and child care, these roles are not rigidly defined. Failure to carry out familial roles may result in dissolution of the nuclear family, but since larger kin groups are not involved in the transfer of rights and obligations in marriage, the dissolution primarily affects only the family members. The nuclear family may also be dissolved by the death of one of the spouses.

In our society today, many functions formerly belonging to the nuclear family have been taken over by other groups. At one time, the family in Europe and the United States was a productive unit, and this is still true of some farm families. The typical American family, however, has largely lost this function; economically, its most important function is as a unit of consumption. Once, leisure activities and recreation were also carried out primarily within the family group; today, the peer group plays a much more important role in leisure activities and in inculcating values. The state has also, through various kinds of social programs, undermined the importance of caring

Is the Nuclear Family Universal?

Many social scientists have maintained that the nuclear family, even when embedded in other kinship structures, is universal and that this universality is based on its necessity for carrying out the basic and necessary sexual, economic, reproductive, and educational functions required by every society (Murdock 1949). Although some theorists have praised this family structure as being necessary for producing healthy personalities, others have condemned it as having reactionary influences on children and as creating an oppressive situation for women. The question of whether the nuclear family structure is universal or necessary is becoming increasingly relevant in today's society, with divorce prevalent and so many families headed by a single parent. One society that has attempted to divest itself of the nuclear family is that of the *kibbutz* (Spiro 1974).

Kibbutzim are collective agricultural settlements in Israel. The *kibbutz* was created by European Jews who wanted to establish a community built on social justice and the economic principles of "from each according to his ability and to each according to his needs." Private property would be done away with; the community rather than the family would be the most important group. Women, who had been limited to a secondary role in the traditional East European nuclear family, would have a new chance to become full human beings, equal with men, working alongside them, and not limited to the private domestic sphere of family life. Although communal child rearing originally started out as an expedient to allow women to work, it has since grown into an important part of *kibbutz* ideology. The degree to which communal child rearing is considered essential varies a great deal; some *kibbutzim* adhere to a communal child-rearing policy much more strongly than others.

Typically, an infant born on the *kibbutz* is raised in an infants' house almost from birth and is cared for with several other infants by a trained nurse. The infant is regularly visited by the mother and is usually breast-fed, and the mother also comes to put it to bed. Thus, this is a time of

With the emphasis in the kibbutz on the equality of women, women working, and the attempt to play down the importance of the nuclear family, communal child living arrangements, pictured above, are an important and unique feature of kibbutz life. (William E. Grossman)

close emotional contact between mother and infant. Later, the growing child lives with its peers, again cared for by a trained caretaker. By the age of three or so, the children eat with the group, rather than their parents, feeding themselves under the caretaker's supervision. As they grow older, the peer group becomes the main factor of continuity in their life and the major agent of enculturation. The group does everything together: eating, playing, bathing, studying, and sleeping. Studies of the personalities of *kibbutz* children seem to indicate that they feel themselves to be "children of the *kibbutz*" and are regarded as such by adults. They feel that they belong not to individual families but to the whole community. There is little evidence of serious pathology, deviance, or delinquency on the *kibbutz*, and the research indicates that its children can grow up emotionally healthy and productive.

Furthermore, on the *kibbutz* the basic economic unit, both for production and consumption, is also the whole community, rather than the nuclear family. Eating is a communal activity not only for children but also for adults. Although there is a division of labor between males and females—women tend to predominate in "service" activities, such as education, washing, and cooking, and men dominate in agriculture, where heavy machinery is used and are not found at all in the educational system from infancy to junior high school (Spiro 1979)—the division of labor does not characterize the relationship that exists between couples. Each mate works in some aspect of the economy, each is an independent member of the *kibbutz* on his or her own, and each, as a member, receives his or her equal share of the goods and services that the *kibbutz* distributes. Neither engages in economic activities that are exclusively directed to the satisfaction of the needs of the mate. There are no sanctions on sexual relations among adult single members of the *kibbutz*; two single persons who wish to have a more intimate and permanent relationship request permission to share a room, and the granting of this request is the *kibbutz*'s acknowledgment that they are now "a couple." Becoming a couple, which may often not involve a marriage ceremony until the birth of the first child, does not change any of the communal economic responsibilities of the couple. Thus, it would seem that the *kibbutz* is a society in which sexual, reproductive, economic, and educational functions are met in the absence of a nuclear family structure.

Yet the issue is more complex. In spite of the absence of formal structure, the nuclear family is a recognizable unit in *kibbutz* life (Spiro 1974). Affective ties are stronger between men and women who are married to each other than between other *kibbutz* comrades. Children's affective ties to their own parents are also of a different and more intense quality than their ties to other caretakers. Furthermore, although the *kibbutz* rather than the family provides the basic necessities of life, small luxuries and extras are provided within the nuclear family. More importantly, recent research, some of it by the same anthropologist who did the earliest studies of the *kibbutz*, Melford Spiro, indicates that the absence of the nuclear family structure is keenly felt by *kibbutz* women, who are increasingly agitating for more "feminine prerogatives"—in particular, for the right to keep their children in their rooms overnight. This is consistent with the fact that the *kibbutz* has always seemed to have a "woman problem," in that men are more satisfied as members than women are, and more women than men are likely to want to leave. Women are also more likely than men to violate *kibbutz* principles regarding the family structure (O'Kelly 1980:308). Can this be explained by pointing to the importance of the nuclear family in meeting the emotional needs of human beings in a way that no other structural unit can?

Although Spiro (1979) and others see the desire to return to more of a nuclear family structure as indicative of some basic biological need in women, other anthropologists have given different answers. It appears, for example, that in spite of the *kibbutz* ideology of sexual equality, women have not, in fact, participated equally in the high-prestige positions such as agriculture, but have been placed in the more monotonous, low-prestige, nonproductive service sectors. This has resulted in less political influence and participation in *kibbutz* life. Further, the threat of warfare in Israel has led to a higher value being placed on the male-dominant values that underlie a state in which military combat has assumed a great national importance. The constant threat of war has also led to an increased emphasis on the maternal role for women, who are expected to play a supportive role for their sons. It has also led many mothers to insist on keeping their own children with them at night in response to the tensions engendered by terrorist raids. All these and other factors are contributing to the lack of success in the arena of sexual equality. Thus, many women on the *kibbutz* may feel that, since they cannot gain satisfaction from their work or contribution to the community, they should at least be able to have the satisfaction that comes from the maternal role. In short, we cannot assume that the experiment to do away with the nuclear family has failed because of some inherent factor in human nature that requires it. Rather, the *kibbutz* research stresses that rigid definitions of family types are not the most useful way of understanding the family as it exists in specific cultural contexts. It is more useful to examine the different components of the nuclear family "complex" and investigate how these various rights, obligations, activities, and functions are actually distributed—and with what costs and benefits—in different societies.

The structure and functions of the family are changing in the United States. With the increase of women working and a high divorce rate, men are taking a more involved role in child care. (Serena Nanda)

for the aged or sick person as a family function. Socialization of children, too, takes place in important ways outside the family, in school and through the mass media.

In contrast to this picture of the declining functions of the nuclear family in our own society is the increased expectation that the family will satisfy our needs for affection and intimacy. Critics of the nuclear family in the United States feel that this burden is too much for the family to bear. In an age in which personal happiness has become a primary cultural value, it is perhaps beyond the capacity of any one social group. The alienation experienced by many Americans indicates that families often do not carry out their "affective" functions very well (Bronfenbrenner 1974).

The nuclear family is adapted in many ways to the requirements of industrial society. Where jobs do not depend on family connections, and where geographical mobility may be required for obtaining employment and success in a chosen career, a small, flexible unit like the independent nuclear family has its advantages. This type of family also seems to be adaptive to the requirements of a hunting and gathering life, since more than three-fourths of foraging societies have this type of family unit. In such societies, however, the nuclear family is not nearly as independent or isolated as in our own society; the family unit almost always camps with the kin of the husband or the wife.

Composite, or **compound, families** are aggregates of nuclear families linked by a common spouse. A polygynous household, consisting of one man with several wives and their respective children, would constitute a compound family. In this case, each wife and her children will normally occupy a separate residence. The dynamics of compound families are quite different from the dynamics of a family that consists of one husband, one wife, and their children, all of whom occupy a common residence. In the compound family, for example, the tie between a mother and her children is particularly strong, and the relations between the children of different mothers by the same father is different in a number of ways from the relationship between full siblings in the typical Euro-American nuclear family. Furthermore, in analyzing the dynamics of the compound family, the interaction between co-wives must be taken into account, as well as the different kinds of behavior patterns that emerge when a man is husband to several women rather than just one.

The Extended Family

The **extended,** or **consanguineal, family** consists of two or more lineally related kinfolk of the same sex and their spouses and offspring, occupying a single household or homestead and under the authority of a household head. An extended family is not just a collection of nuclear families. In the extended family system, the ties of lineality—that is, the blood ties between the generations—are more important than the ties of marriage. In more than half of the world's societies, the extended family is the ideal.

Extended families may be organized around males or females. A patrilineal extended family (such as the Rajputs of Khalapur, India, described in Chapter Seven), is organized around a man, his sons, and the sons' wives and children. A matrilineal family is organized around a woman and her daughters and the daughters' husbands and children. The Nayar of South India represent the extreme of the consanguineal family, for the conjugal tie is for most purposes completely absent. Most extended family systems do give some recognition to the nuclear family. Thus, among the Rajputs of Khalapur, women are considered responsible for caring for their own children, and the conjugal tie is clearly recognized, if only as a potential source of trouble for the larger family group.

The Patrilineal Extended Family   A society in which the extended family was the ideal was premodern China. In China, lineal descendants from father to son to grandson were the backbone of family organization. The family continued through time as a permanent social entity. As older members were lost through death, new ones were added through birth. As in India, marriage in China was viewed more as acquiring a daughter-in-law than taking a wife. It was arranged by the parents, and the new couple lived with the husband's family. Again, as in India, the obedient relationship of the son to his father and the loyalty and solidarity of brothers were given more importance than the ties between husband and wife. In fact, in both societies the public demonstration of affection between a married couple was severely criticized. In both systems it was anticipated and feared that a man's feeling for his wife would interfere with his carrying out responsibilities to his own blood kin.

In such cultures, a good wife is one who is a good daughter-in-law. She must work hard, under the eye of her mother-in-law and her husband's elder brothers' wives. With the birth of a son, a woman gains more acceptance in the household. As the years go by, if she has

been patient and played her role well, the relationship between husband and wife develops into one of companionship and a more equal division of power. As her sons grow up, the wife achieves even more power in the household as she begins to arrange for their marriages. When several sons are married, a woman may be the dominant person in the household, even ordering her husband about, as his economic power, and consequently his authority, wanes.

The Matrilineal Extended Family   Extended matrilineal families are found among the Hopi, a Western Pueblo native American group who live in the Southwest. The Hopi household revolves around a central and continuing core of women. When women marry, their husbands come into the household and have important economic functions, though they do not participate in its ritual. Husbands are peripheral, with divided residences and loyalties. When crises arise, the father is often blamed and treated as an outsider.

The father's obligations to his sons are primarily economic. He prepares them to make a living by teaching them to farm and herd sheep, and he may go into partnership with them in herding activities. When a son marries, a father will frequently present him with a portion of the flock and a small piece of land. The economic support a son receives from his father is returned in the father's old age; a son supports his father and takes the responsibility for his funeral rites. In return for this service, the son will receive a larger share of his father's personal property than his brothers. The father's role is more that of friend and teacher, and the father-son relationship is characterized by affection and little punishment. A father's relationship to his daughter is generally affectionate but not close, and he has few specific duties in regard to her upbringing.

The mother-daughter relationship is an exceedingly close one based on blood ties, common activities, and lifelong residence together. A mother is responsible for both the economic and the ritual training of her daughters. The daughter behaves with respect, obedience, and affection to her mother and normally will continue to live with her mother and her mother's sisters after marriage. A mother also has a close relationship with her son. He belongs to her lineage and will keep much of his personal and ritual property in her home. A son shows a respect for his mother as head of the household and consults her on all important questions. The strongest and most permanent tie in Hopi society is between sisters. The foundation of the household group is the relation of sisters to one another and to their mother. The children of sisters are raised together; if one sister dies, another looks after her children. Sisters cooperate in all domestic tasks. There are usually few quarrels, and when they occur, they are settled by the mother's brother or their own brothers.

As in all matrilineal societies, the mother's brother's relation to his sister's sons is a very important one. As head of his sister's lineage and household, his position is one of authority and control; he is the chief disciplinarian and has the primary responsibility for transmitting the ritual heritage of the lineage and clan, which occupies the highest place in Hopi values. He usually selects the most capable nephew as his successor and trains him in the duties of whatever ceremonial position he may hold. A nephew is frequently afraid of his maternal uncle, in contrast to the affectionate relationship with his father. A mother's brother plays an important role at the time of his nephews' and nieces' weddings and is consulted in the choice of a spouse. It is he who instructs his nephew in the proper behavior toward his new relatives and who formally welcomes his niece's husband into the household.

The Advantages of the Extended Family   The extended family is clearly adaptive under certain economic and social conditions. Murdock's survey indicated that the extended family prevails in all types of predominantly cultivat-

ing societies. The main advantages of this type of family are economic; the extended family can provide a larger number of workers than the nuclear family. This is useful both for food production and for producing and marketing handicrafts, which are generally more well developed among cultivators than foragers. Furthermore, in stable agricultural societies, ownership of land becomes important; it is a source of pride, prestige, and power. The family becomes attached to the land, knows how to work it, and becomes reluctant to divide it. A system in which land is divided into small parcels through inheritance becomes relatively unproductive. The extended family is a way of keeping land intact, which provides additional security for individuals in times of crisis. This relationship between land and family type is supported by evidence from India showing that the higher castes, who own more land and other property, are more likely to have extended families than the lower castes.

There are also the values of companionship in the extended family as daily activities are carried out jointly by a number of kin working together. A further advantage is that the extended family provides not only economic support but also a sense of participation and dignity for the older person, who lives out his or her last years surrounded by respectful and affectionate kin. This contrasts with the independent nuclear family, in which the presumed advantages of privacy and personal autonomy are paid for as people grow old and are regarded as a burden and a nuisance if they join the household of one of their children.

Although it may be generally true that old people fare better in societies with extended family systems, the life of individuals past their prime is not always enviable, even in these societies. When sons begin to raise families of their own, extended families frequently split into parts. As the father loses his productive abilities, he is slowly divested of his former status and power. In a Fijian society studied by Sahlins (1957), the people say, "His time is up"—and an old man literally waits to die.

With increasing industrialization, there appears to be a shift to nuclear family households in many societies, such as Japan, although the ideal of the extended family remains strong. (United Nations)

Although the Fijian ideal is that an old father should be properly cared for by his brothers and sons, "actually he sinks into a pitiable position. In the old days, he might even be killed. Today he is barely kept alive, his counsel is never sought and he is more often considered silly than wise" (p. 451).

Because the independent nuclear family appears to be adapted to a modern industrialized society, many social scientists have predicted that the extended family will be modified in the direction of the independent nuclear family as modernization and industrialization spread. The corollary of this assumption is that, although the extended family has advantages among cultivators or economically marginal populations, these advantages become liabilities with urbanization and industrialization. Milton Singer (1968), an anthropologist who has studied the families of industrial leaders in the city of Madras, India, says no. He points

out that the patrilineal joint family as it exists in India is a flexible institution. The principles of mutual obligation of extended kin, joint ownership of property, and an authority structure in which the male household head takes responsibility for making decisions after consultation with junior members can easily be, and have been, successfully transferred to the management of modern corporations.

DOMESTIC GROUPS AND POSTMARITAL RESIDENCE RULES

A **domestic group,** or household, is not the same as a family. Although domestic groups most often contain related members, nonkin may also be part of the domestic group. On the other hand, members of a family may be spread over several domestic groups, or households. The composition of domestic groups is affected by the rules a society has about where a newly married couple will live. **Neolocal residence** exists when it is the norm for a married couple to establish an independent domestic unit. Only 5 percent of the world's societies are neolocal. Neolocal residence is the ideal in our own society. It is related to the high degree of mobility required in an industrial system and to a value system that makes romantic love, the emotional bond between husband and wife, privacy, and independence primary.

Most societies have a rule of **patrilocal residence.** A woman lives with her husband's kin after marriage, either in the same household or in a nearby dwelling or compound. In societies with a **matrilocal residence** rule, the husband lives with the wife's kin after marriage. If a couple has the choice of living with either the wife's or the husband's family, the pattern is one of **bilocal residence.** A fifth and rare residence pattern is called **avunculocal residence.** In this case, the married couple is expected to live with the husband's mother's brother.

In attempting to explain why a society would have a particular kind of residence rule, anthropologists have generally emphasized economic factors. It has been suggested that, where men must work cooperatively, such as in societies dependent on big-game hunting or intensive agriculture, there will be a patrilocal rule of residence. Matrilocality would appear to be adaptive in horticultural societies, where women have an important role in the economy. The cross-cultural data do not prove this reasoning to be entirely correct. Although it is true that most matrilocal societies do practice horticulture, this is also the case for the majority of patrilocal societies.

The importance of male cooperation in warfare is suggested as another reason for a patrilocal rule of residence (Ember and Ember 1971). Where fighting between lineages or villages is common, it is useful for men who will fight together to live together. Otherwise they might wind up having to make the choice between defending their wife's local group, the one with whom they live, against the families with whom they grew up. Where warfare takes place between societies, rather than within them, and where men must leave their homes to fight, cooperation among women is very important. Since common residence promotes cooperation, matrilocal residence is a functional norm where males engage in warfare that extends beyond local groups.

Residence rules are ideal or preferred norms of behavior; actual behavior is frequently different. The choices couples make about where to live after marriage depend on many individual situational factors, although they are likely to be guided by the ideal norms of the society. Because kinship ideology (to be discussed in the next chapter) is derived from both norms and actual patterns of postmarital residence, residence rules, as well as the actual choices made by individuals, are important in the social organization of a society.

SUMMARY

1. Three major functions of marriage and the family are regulating sexual access between males and females, arranging for the exchange of services between males and females, and assigning responsibility for child care.

2. Although marriage and family are rooted in the biological complementarity of male and female and the biological process of reproduction, they are cultural patterns and differ in different human societies.

3. Incest taboos are prohibitions on mating between relatives or people classified as relatives. Some theories that attempt to account for the universality of such taboos are that the taboos limit inbreeding, that they reflect the natural aversion to sexual relations between close kin, that they prevent disruption within the family, and that they force people to marry out of their immediate families, thus joining people into a larger social community.

4. Exogamy is a rule that requires people to marry outside a particular group. This rule is adaptive in forging alliances between families within a society.

5. Endogamy is a rule requiring marriage *within* a specified group. One of its functions is to keep wealth within the group or to maintain the so-called purity of the blood line.

6. All societies have rules about the number of spouses allowed a man or woman. Most of the world's societies allow some form of plural marriage (polygyny or polyandry), whereas our own society has a rule of monogamy (one spouse only).

7. Marriage, which is a publicly sanctioned relationship, most often is legitimated by the exchange of goods between the kin of the bride and the kin of the groom. The most common form of exchange is bridewealth, in which the kin of the groom gives various kinds of goods to the kin of the bride.

8. There are two basic types of families. The nuclear family is organized around the tie between husband and wife (the conjugal tie); the extended family is organized around blood ties extending over several generations.

9. The nuclear family, which is predominantly found in contemporary industrial societies and foraging societies, appears to be adaptive where geographical mobility is important. The extended family predominates among cultivators, because it provides a larger number of workers than the nuclear family and is also a means by which landholdings can be kept intact over generations.

10. A domestic group is a household; it usually, but not necessarily, contains members of a family. The composition of domestic groups is shaped by the postmarital residence rules of a society.

11. The most widespread rule of residence is patrilocality, by which the wife goes to live with her husband's family. Matrilocality, by which the husband goes to live with his wife's family, is found primarily in horticultural societies.

Neolocality, by which the married couple lives independently, is found in a relatively small number of societies, including that of the United States.

SUGGESTED READINGS

Bohannan, P., and Middleton, J., eds.
1968   *Marriage, Family and Residence.* Garden City, N.Y.: The Natural History Press. This reader includes articles on incest, marriage, family, and domestic groups from a wide variety of cultures.

Briggs, Jean L.
1970   *Never in Anger: A Portrait of an Eskimo Family.* Cambridge, Mass.: Harvard University Press. An intimate account of an Eskimo family and its relation to the author.

Fox, Robin
1967   *Kinship and Marriage.* New York: Penguin Books. A clear and readable introduction to social organization.

Leibowitz, Lila
1978   *Females, Males, Families: A Biosocial Approach.* North Scituate, Mass.: Duxbury Press. An interesting book based on lectures for an introductory course on the family, including a survey of sex and nurturing among nonhuman primates.

Stack, Carol
1975   *All Our Kin: Strategies for Survival in a Black Community.* New York: Harper & Row. A view of the black, lower-class kin group that emphasizes the adaptive nature of extended domestic networks.

CHAPTER ELEVEN

KINSHIP
AND
ASSOCIATION

▶ Why is kinship so important in
  nonstate societies?

▶ Can you explain why hunters and
  gatherers have kinship classification
  systems similar to those of
  industrialized societies?

▶ How do age and sex operate as bases
  for association in nonstate societies?

*With all beings and all things
we shall be as relatives.*
Sioux Indian

*H*uman beings are social animals, and our pattern of group living has undoubted value for our survival as a species. One way of looking at social organization is to look at the different groups that are found in a society. In societies traditionally studied by anthropologists, kinship is the most important social bond. Kin relations are the basis of group formation; relationships between individuals are mainly governed by kinship norms; and the extension of kinship ties is the main way of allying groups to one another and incorporating strangers into a group. The importance of kinship in most of the world's cultures provides an important contrast with our own society, in which other principles of social organization, such as work, citizenship, and common economic and political interests, operate to structure behavior and act as the basis on which groups are formed. This does not mean that kinship is insignificant in modern industrialized society. The nuclear family is, after all, a kin group and a core social institution in the United States. Larger groupings of relatives also become important on various ceremonial occasions. Even in the United States, a person claiming a kin relation is regarded differently from someone who is not a relative.

KINSHIP

Kinship includes relationships through blood and relationships through marriage. In every society, the formation of groups and the regulation of behavior depend to some extent on socially recognized ties of kinship. A **kinship system** refers to the totality of relationships based on blood and marriage that links individuals in a web of rights and obligations; to the kinds of groups formed in a society on the basis of kinship; and to the system of terms used to classify different kin (kinship terminology). It is because there is an interrelationship between the formation of kinship groups, the development of kinship ideology, the behavior of different kin toward one another, and the kinship terminology of a society that anthropologists refer to kinship as a system.

Although a kinship system always rests on some kind of biological relationship, kinship systems are cultural phenomena. The ways in which a society classifies kin are cultural, and they may or may not be based on a scientifically accurate assessment of biological ties. The term for father, for example, may refer to the actual biological father (*genitor*) of a child, or it may refer to a man who takes on the responsibility for the child's upbringing and/or is socially recognized as the father (*pater*). In the Trobriand Islands, for example, the biological role of the male in reproduction is not given cultural recognition, and fatherhood is established by marriage; the "father" is the mother's husband. In some polyandrous societies, such as the Toda of India, biological paternity is irrelevant; fatherhood is established by the performance of a ritual. In this and other similar cases, social fatherhood is what counts. Because kinship systems are cultural creations, there is a wide variety of ways in which both consanguineal (blood) and affinal (marriage) relatives are classified in different societies. There are also differences in the kinds of social groups formed by kinship and in the ways in which kin are expected to behave toward one another.

Culturally defined ties of kinship have two basic functions that are necessary for the continuation of society. First, kinship serves to provide continuity between generations. In all societies, children must be cared for and educated so that they can become functioning members of their society. With the possible exception of the *kibbutz* and other contemporary attempts at collective child rearing in communes of unrelated people, it is a kinship unit that is fundamentally responsible for socialization. Furthermore, a society must also provide for the orderly transmission of property and social position between generations. In most human societies, inheritance (the transfer of property) and succession (the transfer of social position) take place within kin groups.

Second, kinship defines a universe of others on whom an individual can depend for aid in a variety of ways. The minimal group of importance in mutual aid is the domestic group of a woman and her children and an adult male. In most societies, however, kin groups that include relatives beyond this minimum are very important. It is undoubtedly the adaptiveness of social groups larger than the elementary family that accounts for the fact that expanded kin groups are found in so many human societies.

RULES OF DESCENT AND THE FORMATION OF DESCENT GROUPS

In anthropological terminology, **descent** refers to the culturally established affiliation with one or both parents. In many societies, descent is an important basis of social group formation. In one sense, of course, the nuclear family is a descent group, but here we use **descent group** to mean those groups of consanguineal kin who are lineal descendants of a common ancestor extending beyond two generations. Where descent groups are found, they have important functions in the organization of

The Kinship Diagram

Kinship diagrams are more convenient than verbal explanations and allow us to see immediately how different kinship statuses are linked. In order to make a kinship diagram precise and unambiguous, all relationships in the diagram are viewed from the perspective of one status, labeled EGO. Terms of reference rather than terms of address are used—that is, terms we would use in talking *about* a relative rather than talking *to* one. In English, for example, we would refer to our "mother" but might address her as "Mom." The symbols used in kinship diagrams are these:

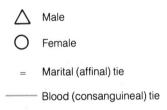

△   Male

○   Female

=   Marital (affinal) tie

———   Blood (consanguineal) tie

Using these symbols, and English terminology, a kinship diagram of the nuclear family looks like this:

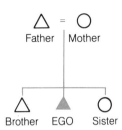

domestic life, the socialization of children, the use and transfer of property and political and ritual offices, the carrying out of religious ritual, the settlement of disputes, and political organization and warfare.

Two basic types of descent rule, or kinship ideology, operate in society. In a system with a rule of **unilineal descent,** descent-group membership is based on links through either the paternal or the maternal line, but not both. Two types of unilineal descent rules are **patrilineal descent** and **matrilineal descent.** In societies with patrilineal descent, an individual belongs to the descent group of his or her father. In societies with matrilineal descent, an individual belongs to the descent group of the mother. (There are some exceptions, as in societies with double descent, which will be described later.)

In societies with a system of **bilateral descent,** both maternal and paternal lines are used as the basis for reckoning descent and for establishing the rights and obligations of

kinship. Bilateral kinship systems are found in relatively few societies throughout the world, although they are characteristic of Western European culture and of the United States.

Unilineal Descent

The frequency of unilineal descent in the world's cultures is due to two major advantages: (1) Unilineal rules result in the formation of descent groups that can perpetuate themselves over time even though their membership changes (as modern corporations can). Corporate descent groups are permanent units and have an existence over and above the individuals who are members at any given time. Old members die and new ones are admitted through birth, but the integrity of the corporate group as a group persists. Such groups (like lineages) may own property and manage resources (just as a modern corporation does). (2) Such rules provide unambiguous group membership for every individual in the society. In short, where descent is traced through only one line, group membership is both easily and clearly defined. By knowing the descent group to which he or she belongs and the descent group of others, an individual can be sure of his or her rights of ownership, social duties, and social roles. He or she can also easily relate to a large number of known and unknown people in the society.

Although systems of unilineal descent share certain basic similarities throughout the world, they do not operate exactly the same way in every society. In addition, actual behavior in any society does not correspond exactly to the rules as they are defined in the kinship ideology. Systems of descent and kinship are basically a means by which a society relates to its environment and circumstances. As situations and conditions change, the rules of kinship, like other ideal norms, will be bent and manipulated so that a group may be successful in its environment. The accepted departures from the norm which exist in every society give unilineal systems a flexibility they would otherwise lack, a flexibility necessary for human adaptation. We will look now at some of the different types of unilineal descent groups.

Types of Unilineal Descent Groups A **lineage** is a group of kin whose members trace descent from a common ancestor and who can actually demonstrate those genealogical links among themselves. Lineages formed by descent through the male line are called **patrilineages.** Lineages formed by descent through the female line are called **matrilineages.** Lineages may vary in size from one consisting of a male or female, their children, and their children's children, to one consisting of more than three generations. Where lineages own land collectively and where the members are held responsible for one another's behavior, the lineage is considered a corporate group. In some societies the lineage functions as a corporate group; in other societies it does not.

A **clan** generally refers to a unilineal kinship group whose members believe themselves to be descended from a common ancestor, but who cannot trace this relationship genealogically. Sometimes the presumed common ancestor may be a mythological figure, and sometimes no specific ancestor will be known or named. Clans are frequently named and may have a **totem**—that is, some feature of the natural environment with which they are closely identified and toward which the clan members must behave in a special way.

Clans and lineages have different functions in different societies. The lineage is frequently a local residential or domestic group, and its members therefore cooperate on a daily basis. The lineage is also important in regulating marriage; in most societies, an individual must marry outside his or her lineage or the lineage of either parent. Clans are not generally residential units but tend to spread out over many villages. Clans therefore often have political and religious functions, rather than primarily domestic and economic ones.

One of the most important functions of a clan is to regulate marriage. In most societies, clans are exogamous. The prohibition on marriage within the clan strengthens its unilineal character. If a person married within the clan, his or her children would find it difficult to make sharp distinctions between maternal and paternal relatives. Lowie (1948:237) says of the Crow Indians of North America, among whom clans are very important, that in case of marriage within the clan, "a Crow ... loses his bearings and perplexes his tribesmen. For he owes specific obligations to his father's relatives and others to his mother's, who are now hopelessly confounded. The sons of his father's clan ought to be censors; but now the very same persons are his joking relatives and his clan." Not only would this person not know how to act toward others, but others would not know how to act toward him. Clan exogamy also extends the network of peaceful social relations within a society as different clans are allied through marriage.

Patrilineal Descent Groups   In societies with patrilineal descent groups, an individual (whether male or female) belongs to the descent group of the father, the father's father, and so on (see Figures 11.1 and 11.2). Thus, a man, his sisters and brothers, his brother's children (but not his sister's children), his own children, and his son's children (but not his daughter's children) all belong to the same group. Inheritance moves from father to son, as does succession to office.

The degree to which a woman is incorporated into the patrilineage of her husband varies in different societies. In some cases, a woman may retain rights of inheritance in her father's lineage. In general, however, in a patrilineal system a man gains some degree of control over his wife and children. Great care is taken in patrilineal societies to guarantee the husband's rights and control over his wife (wives) and children, because the continuity of the descent group depends on binding the wife and children to the husband. Patrilineal systems most often have patrilocal rules of residence, so a wife may find herself living among "strangers" (this of course would not be the case in societies where cousin marriage is practiced), and this undermines female solidarity and support. Because marriage in patrilineal systems is generally surrounded by strict sanctions and tends to be more stable than it is in matrilineal systems, anthropologists have tended to neglect the potential for disruption that derives from the discontent of women in these societies. In fact, women are not always as submissive as they have been portrayed in the anthropological literature on patrilineal societies, and their struggles against control by the husband's group are an important theme in both the reality of domestic life and in mythology and literature (Denich 1974).

The Nuer, a pastoral people who live in the Sudan in East Africa, are a patrilineal society. Among the Nuer, all rights, privileges, obligations, and interpersonal relationships are regulated by kinship; one is either a kinsman or an enemy. Membership in a patrilineal descent group is the most significant fact of life, and the father, his brothers, and their children are considered the closest kin. Membership in the patrilineage confers rights in land, requires participation in certain religious ceremonies, and determines political and judicial obligations, such as making alliances in feuds and warfare.

The patrilineage has important political functions among the Nuer. Lineage membership may spread over several villages and thus help create alliances between otherwise independent villages that contain members of several different lineages. Related lineages form still larger groups, or clans. Clans are viewed as composed of lineages, not of individuals. Each Nuer clan has its members spread out over many villages. Because an individual cannot marry someone from within his or her own lineage or clan or from the lineage of the mother, kinship relations extend widely throughout the tribe. In the absence of a centralized system of political control, kinship-based alliances are an important mechanism for keeping the peace, in view of the Nuer belief that kin should not fight with one another.

Matrilineal Descent Groups   Two fundamental ties recognized by every society are that between a woman and her children and that between siblings (brothers and sisters). In all societies, males have the responsibility of providing for and protecting the mother-child unit, and they have control over women and their children. In patrilineal societies, this control falls to the man who is designated as the child's father. In matrilineal societies, however, the major protecting, providing, and controlling male is the brother of a woman rather than her husband. A man gains sexual and economic rights over a woman when he marries her, but he does not gain rights over her children. Children belong to the mother's descent group, not the father's. Thus, the membership of a matrilineal descent group consists of a woman, her brothers and sisters, her sister's

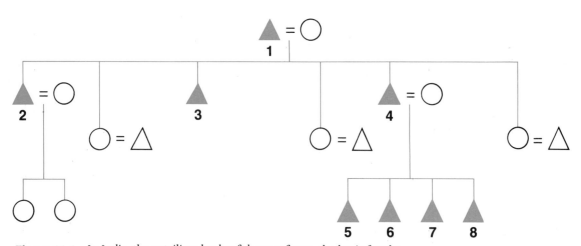

Figure 11.1   In India, the patrilineal rule of descent forms the basis for the
patrilineal joint family, which is a corporate group in that property is owned
conjointly by male members.

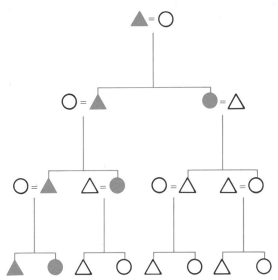

Figure 11.2 *Membership in a patrilineal descent group. In societies with patrilineal descent groups, membership is based on links through the father only. Sons and daughters are members of their father's descent group (shown in red), as are the children of sons, but* not *of daughters.*

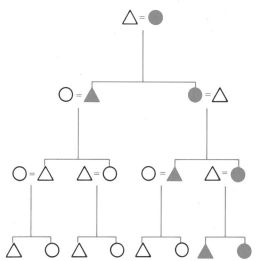

Figure 11.3 *Membership in a matrilineal descent group. In a society with matrilineal descent groups, membership in the group is defined by links through the mother. Sons and daughters are members of their mother's descent group, as are the children of daughters, but* not *the children of sons.*

(but not her brother's) children, her own children, and the children of her daughters (but not of her sons) (Figure 11.3).

Matrilineal systems tend to be correlated with a matrilocal rule of residence; a man goes to live with or near his wife's kin after marriage. This means that in the domestic group, it is the man who is among "strangers," whereas his wife is surrounded by her kin. The inclusion of a husband in the household is of less importance in a matrilineal system than in a patrilineal one, and marriages in matrilineal societies tend to be less stable than those in other systems. As we saw among the Nayar of India, it is possible for a matrilineally organized group to do away with the presence of husbands and fathers altogether, as long as there are brothers who assume responsibilities. It is important to remember that, although women usually have higher status in societies where there is a matrilineal reckoning of descent, matrilineality is not the same as matriarchy, a society in which the formal posi-

tions of power are held by women. With a few possible exceptions (Wallace 1970), the most important resources and highest political positions are in the control of males, although the male with the most power and control in matrilineal societies is not the husband (father) but the brother (uncle). The role of the mother's brother is an important or special one even in patrilineal societies, but in matrilineal societies it is particularly important. The mother's brother is a figure of authority and respect, and it is the children of a man's sister rather than his own who are his heirs and successors.

In a matrilineal society, the relationship between a man and his son is likely to be affectionate and loving, because it is free of the problems of authority and control that exist between fathers and sons in a patrilineal society. A man may feel emotionally close to his sons, but he is committed by the matrilineal kinship ideology to pass on his knowledge, property, offices, and so on to the sons of his sister. With these individuals (his "nephews"), he may have less friendly relations or even conflicts, as they are subject to his control. Thus, in a matrilineal system, a man's loyalties are split between his own sons and the sons of his sister; in a patrilineal system, this tension does not occur as part of the kinship structure.

The Hopi, a Pueblo group in the American Southwest, are a matrilineal society. The matrilineage is conceived of as timeless, stretching backward to the beginnings of the Hopi people and continuing into the future. Both male and female members of the lineage consider their mother's house their home, though men move out to reside with their wives after marriage. They return to this home for many ritual and ceremonial occasions, however, and also in the case of separation or divorce. The relationship of a man with his father's lineage and household is affectionate, involving some economic and ritual obligations but little direct cooperation or authority.

In addition to lineages, the Hopi also have matrilineal clans that extend over many different villages. A Hopi man must not marry within his own clan or the clan of his father or his mother's father. Marriage thus results in a wide range of relatives in addition to those an individual acquires through birth through the clan he (and his mother) belongs to. A Hopi has obligations to the clan of the father as well as to that of the mother and also to the clans of the person designated as the ceremonial father. Kinship terms are extended to all these individuals, leading to a vast number of potential sibling relationships and a lateral integration of a great number of separate lineages and clans. This extension of Hopi kinship relates a Hopi in some way to almost everyone in his or her village, in other villages, and even to individuals in other Pueblo groups who have similar clans. Whereas the lineage group is of particular importance to women, these larger clan groups are the arena of male activities. Here men play important political and religious roles, in contrast to the marginal positions they have in domestic life. The Hopi also extend kinship

ideology to the world of nature. The sun is called *father*, and the earth and corn are called *mother*. These phenomena in nature such as plant and animal species that serve as clan names are also referred to by kinship terminology, such as *mother* or *mother's brother* (Eggan 1950).

A number of explanations have been given by anthropologists in their attempts to understand the evolution of unilineal descent groups. Many of these explanations fail to take into account the diversity of the systems that have been lumped together as unilineal. The contemporary anthropological approach is not so much to ask: "What kind of kinship system exists in a particular society?" but rather to ask: "What are the common interests that give people a reason for joining together and defining themselves as a collective entity justified by reference to kin ties?" These interests *may* be economic, such as land or cattle or gardens; they may also be political or religious or involve warfare within the society or with other societies. As older theories of kinship lose their explanatory power under the weight of new data, rethinking kinship has become an important new focus in anthropology.

Bilateral Descent

In systems of bilateral descent, an individual is considered to be related equally to other kin through both the mother's and the father's side, although in our own society, which is bilateral, the patrilineal principle is dominant in the handing down of family names. In a unilineal kinship system, an individual is affiliated with a large number of lineally extended relations through time, but only on one side of the family. A bilateral group extends along lines established by links through both males and females, but it incorporates only relatively close biological relatives.

In bilateral (or cognatic) systems of descent, there are no clear descent groups formed in the way described for unilineal systems. The

Double Descent: The Yako of Nigeria*

When descent is traced through a combination of matrilineal and patrilineal principles, a system of **double descent** exists. In societies with double-descent systems, the individual belongs both to the patrilineal group of the father and the matrilineal group of the mother. Such societies are relatively rare, about 5 percent of the world's known cultures. In systems of double descent, matrilineal and patrilineal descent both operate as principles of affiliation, but the descent groups formed by these rules tend to operate in different areas of life.

The Yako of Nigeria are a society with a system of double descent. The Yako have full development of both patrilineal and matrilineal corporate kin groups. Cooperation in daily domestic life and continuous association are strongest among a group of patrilineally related kinsmen who live with or near one another. These men jointly control and farm plots of land, and membership in the patriclan is the source of rights over basic economic resources—farmland and forest products. Patriclan obligations include providing food at funerals. Inheritance of membership in the men's associations and the right to fruit trees are also transmitted in the male line. The arbitration of disputes is in the hands of senior patriclan members, and cooperation in ritual and succession to some religious offices are also derived from clan membership.

Matrilineal bonds and clan membership are also important in Yako society, despite the fact that matriclan members do not live near one another and do not cooperate as a group in everyday activities. The rights and duties of matrilineal kinship are different. Practical assistance to matrilineal kin, the rights and obligations of the mother's brother and his sister's sons, and the authority of the priest of a matrilineal clan are

based on mystical ideas regarding the perpetuation and tranquillity of the Yako world. The Yako believe that the fertility of crops and beasts—as well as that of humans—and peace between individuals and within the community as a whole are associated with and passed on through women. Life comes from the mother; it is by a wife that children are produced. The children of one mother are bound to mutual support and peaceful relations. The matrilineage is thus held together by mystical bonds of common fertility, and anger and violence between its members are considered sinful. These sentiments are expressed and reinforced in the cult of the matriclan spirits, whose priests are ritually given the qualities of women.

Despite their isolation from one another by the rule of patrilocal residence, matriclan relatives have specific mutual obligations. Rights in the transfer of accumulated wealth, as opposed to basic economic resources, belong to the matrilineal kinship group. It is the members of a matriclan that supervise a funeral and arrange for the disposal of the dead person's property. All currency and livestock customarily pass to matrilineal relatives, who also receive the greater share of tools, weapons, and household goods. The movable property of women passes to their daughters. Matriclans also have the responsibility for the debts of their kin, for making loans to one another at reasonable rates, and for providing part of the bridewealth transferred at the marriage of a sister's son. Thus, for the Yako, paternity and maternity are both important in descent; each contains inherently different qualities from which flow the rights, obligations, and benefits, both practical and spiritual, by which individuals are bound to one another and through which the continuity of the society is ensured.

*Based on Daryll Forde, "Double Descent Among the Yako," in A. R. Radcliffe-Brown and Daryll Forde, eds., *African Systems of Kinship and Marriage.* London: Oxford University Press, 1967 (first publ. 1950), pp. 285–332.

kin network formed by a bilateral reckoning of descent is called a **kindred.** With the exception of brothers and sisters, every individual's kindred is different from every other individual's. Since kindreds are actually overlapping categories of kin (which is why the term *kin network* rather than *group* is used), they cannot be the basis for the formation of corporate groups. This is the major functional weakness of the kindred as a cooperative, kin-based collectivity. Since it is not a group but rather an ego-centered network, it cannot own land or have continuity over time. On the other hand, bilateral systems have great flexibility. An individual can mobilize a number of relatives from either the father's or the mother's side (or both), depending on the particular enterprise being undertaken. Bilateral kinship systems appear to be particularly adaptive in societies where mobility and independence are important, and they predominate among hunters and gatherers and in modern industrial societies.

THE CLASSIFICATION OF KIN

In all societies, kin are referred to by special terms. The total system of kinship terms and the rules for using these terms make up a kinship classiciation system. An understanding of these systems is more than an interesting anthropological game; the ways in which kin are classified are associated with the roles they play in society. If, for example, an individual (called **Ego**) refers to his father and his father's brothers by the same term, the roles he plays in relation to these kin will tend to be generally similar. By the same token, if Ego's father and father's brothers are referred to by different terms, it is expected that these males will be in a somewhat different relationship to Ego. Kinship classification systems not only structure perception of the social universe; they also regulate behavior. As with other cultural norms, kinship has both an ideal and a real component. Not all individuals act according to cultural norms, and special circumstances as well as individual personality differences modify the actual relationship individuals have with their kin.

No kinship classification system has a different term of reference for each position in the kinship structure. This would require far too many terms to remember. In every kinship terminology, therefore, some relatives are classed together—that is, referred to by the same kinship term. In our own terminology, we use the term *aunt* to refer to both our father's and our mother's sisters, as well as women who marry the brother of either father or mother. In other societies, these women may be referred to by different terms. In our kinship terminology, we lump together our mother's sister and our father's sister, as well as the wives of our uncles, because their roles in relation to Ego are generally similar. In societies where the mother's sister and the father's sister have very different rights and obligations with respect to Ego, they will be distinguished in the kinship terminology.

Principles for Classifying Kin

Societies differ in the categories of relatives they distinguish and in the principles by which kin are classified. Some of the most important principles used to separate and lump together different categories of kin are the following:

1. *Generation.* In English, the kinship terms that refer to generation are those such as *father*, *uncle*, and *aunt*. These terms refer to relatives who belong to the parental generation. *Grandfather* and *grandmother* are in the generation before that. *Brother* and *sister* refer to individuals in Ego's generation; and *son*, *daughter*, *niece*, and *nephew* are in the generation below Ego.

2. *Relative age.* This criterion for classifying kin is not used in the English kinship terminology, although it is used in many other kinship systems. In North India, Ego uses different terms to refer to older brother's wife and younger brother's wife. These differences reflect the important differences in behavior that exist between Ego and these two kinds of kin. An Indian woman is expected to avoid or act with great reserve toward her husband's older brother (referred to as *jait*), but is allowed great freedom, affection and even sexual joking with her husband's younger brother (referred to as *deva*).

3. *Lineality vs. collaterality.* Lineal kin are related in a single line, such as grandfather-father-son. **Collateral kin** are related through a linking relative. An example of a collateral relation is that between Ego and father's brother or sister or mother's brother or sister. In many societies, collaterality is not distinguished in the kinship terminology. Ego refers to the father and the father's brothers as *father*. The mother and her sisters may similarly be referred to as *mother.* In these systems, parallel cousins may also be referred to by the same terms as those for brother and sister.

4. *Sex.* In English, some of our kinship terms differentiate by sex; for example, *aunt* and *uncle*, *brother* and *sister*. The term *cousin*, however, does not distinguish the sex of the relative.

5. *Consanguineal vs. affinal kin.* Some people related to Ego by blood (consanguinity) are distinguished from similar relationships by marriage. In our own society, we have *daughter* and *daughter-in-law*, *sister* and *sister-in-law*, and so forth. We do not, however, distinguish between a male of our father's generation (one ascending) in terms of blood or marriage tie. *Uncle* refers to the brother of either our father or mother and also to a man who marries the sister of either parent.

6. *Sex of linking relative.* Where collaterality is important, the sex of the linking relative may be distinguished in the kinship terminology. For example, parallel cousins are distinguished from cross cousins. Distinguishing between these types of cousins is important in societies where Ego may not marry a parallel cousin but may be allowed, or even obliged, to marry a cross cousin.

7. *Side of the family.* This basis of classification, called **bifurcation,** means that the kinship terms used for the mother's side of the family are different from those used for the father's side of the family. In societies with this principle, the mother's brother would be referred to differently from the father's brother.

Types of Kinship Terminologies

Systems of kinship terminology reflect the kinds of kin groups that are most important in a society. Anthropologists have identified six systems of kinship terminology: Hawaiian, Eskimo, Iroquois, Omaha, Crow, and Sudanese.

Hawaiian   As its name suggests, this system is found in Polynesia. It is relatively simple in that it uses the least number of kinship terms. The Hawaiian system emphasizes the distinctions between generations and reflects the relative equality between the mother and the father's side of the family in relation to Ego. All relatives of the same generation and sex—for example, father, father's brother, and mother's brother—are referred to by the same kinship term. Male and female kin in Ego's generation are distinguished in the terminology, but the terms for sister and brother are the same as those for the children of one's parents' siblings (Figure 11.4). This system correlates with ambilineality and ambilocality, which means that an individual may choose which descent group he or she wishes to belong to and will live with after marriage. By using the same terms for parents and their siblings, a closeness is established with a large number of relatives in the ascending generation, allowing a wide choice for Ego in deciding which group to affiliate and live with.

Eskimo   The Eskimo terminology is correlated with bilateral descent. It is found among hunting and gathering peoples and also in our

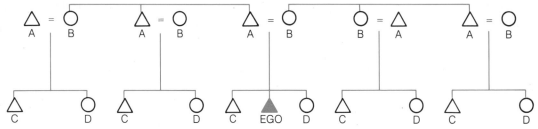

Figure 11.4   Hawaiian terminology. Symbols with the same letters underneath are referred to in the same way by Ego.

own society. The Eskimo system emphasizes the unit of the nuclear family by using terms for its members (mother, father, sister, brother, daughter, son) that are not used for any other kin. Outside the nuclear family, many kinds of relatives that are distinguished in other systems are lumped together. We have already given the examples of aunt and uncle. Similarly, all children of our kin in the parental generation are called cousins, no matter what their sex or who the linking relative is. The Eskimo system singles out the biologically closest group of relations (the nuclear family) and treats more distant kin more or less equally (Figure 11.5).

Iroquois   The Iroquois system is associated with matrilineal or double descent and emphasizes the importance of unilineal descent groups. In this system, the same term is used for mother and mother's sister, and a common term also applies to father and father's brother. Parallel cousins are referred to by the same terms as those for brother and sister. Father's

sister and mother's brother are distinguished from other kin, as are the children of father's sister and mother's brother (Ego's cross cousins) (Figure 11.6).

Omaha   The Omaha system is found among patrilineal peoples, including the native American group of that name. In this system, the same term is used for father and father's brother and for mother and mother's sister. Parallel cousins are equated with siblings, but cross cousins are referred to by a separate term. A man refers to his brother's children by the same terms he applies to his own children, but he refers to his sister's children by different terms. These terms are extended to all relations who are classified as Ego's brothers and sisters (Figure 11.7). In this system, there is a merging of generations on the mother's side. All men who are members of Ego's mother's patrilineage will be referred to as *mother's brother* no matter what their age or generational relationship to Ego. Thus, the term applied to mother's brother is also applied to the son of mother's brother.

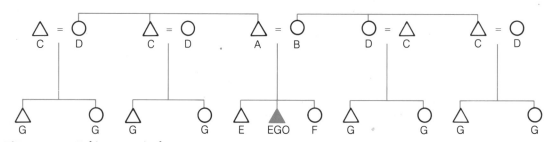

Figure 11.5   Eskimo terminology.

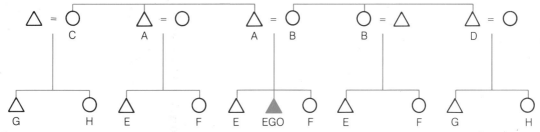

Figure 11.6   *Iroquois terminology.*

This generational merging is not applied to relations on the father's side. Although father and his brothers are referred to by the same term, this does not extend to the descending generation. The differences in terminology as applied to the father's patrilineal and the mother's patrilineal group reflect the different position of Ego in relation to these kin. Generational differences are important on the father's side, because members of the ascending generation are likely to have some authority over Ego (as his father does) and be treated differently than patrilineage members of Ego's own generation. Since the mother's patrilineage is relatively unimportant to Ego in this system, this is reflected in lumping them all together in the terminology.

Crow   The Crow system, named for the Crow Indians of North America, is the matrilineal equivalent of the Omaha system. This means that the relations on the male side (Ego's father's matrilineage) will be lumped together, whereas generational differences will be recognized in

the mother's matrilineal group (Figure 11.8). In both the Omaha and Crow systems, the overriding importance of unilineality leads to the subordination of other principles of classifying kin, such as relative age or generation.

Sudanese   The most extremely descriptive terminological systems are sometimes called Sudanese systems, after the groups in Africa, primarily in Ethiopia, that use them. The terminological types included here use different terms for practically every relative—siblings, paternal parallel cousins, maternal parallel cousins, paternal cross cousins, and maternal cross cousins. Ego refers to his or her parents by distinct terms and uses separate terms for father's brother, father's sister, mother's sister, and mother's brother (Figure 11.9). Although most groups using this system tend to be patrilineal, there is also evidence of ambilineality. This distinguishes these kinship systems from other patrilineal systems described here and may account for this distinctive and relatively rare type of terminology.

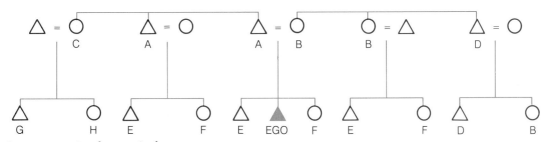

Figure 11.7   *Omaha terminology.*

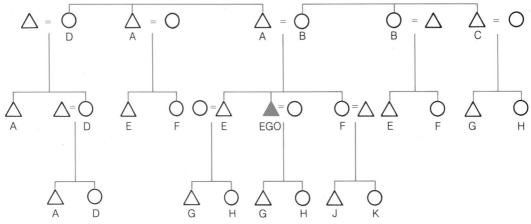

Figure 11.8   Crow terminology.

The great variety in kinship terminologies calls attention to the fact with which we began this chapter: kinship systems reflect social relationships and are not based simply on biological relations between people. Kinship classification systems are part of the totality of a kinship system. Each of the types of classification described above emphasizes the most important kinship groupings and relationships in the societies in which they are found. Thus, the Eskimo system emphasizes the importance of the nuclear family, setting it apart from the more distant relations on the maternal and paternal sides. The Iroquois, Omaha, and Crow systems, found in unilineal societies, emphasize the importance of lineage and clan. In the Hawaiian system, the relative simplicity of terms leaves the way open for flexibility in choosing one's descent group. At the other extreme, the Sudanese system, with its highly descriptive terminology, may in fact have the same function. In making sense out of kinship, including our own system, anthropologists attempt to understand the relationship between terminologies, rules of descent, and the formation of groups based on kinship and the particular ecological, economic, and political conditions under which different kinship systems emerge.

NONKIN FORMS OF ASSOCIATION

Although kinship is of great importance in structuring social relations and as a basis for the formation of groups in all societies, other principles of association are also important. In this section, we will look at nonkin groups and relationships, and the roles such associations play in traditional societies.

Groups Based on Age

All societies recognize at least three social categories based on age: children, adults, and the aged. Each category has its own role, and in some societies, groups based on age are extremely important. Age as a basis of social groups reaches its most elaborate development among certain tribes in Africa. Most of these age-based groups are made up of males and have military and political functions, such as among the Karimojong, the Masai, and the Nandi of East Africa. A society for which age is the most important principle of social organization is the Nyakyusa, who have been studied by Monica Wilson (1963).

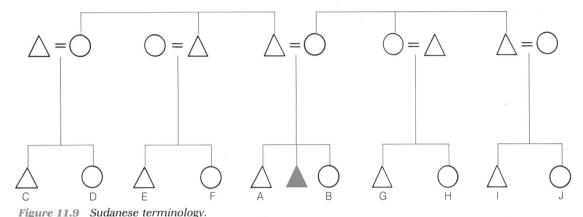

Figure 11.9   Sudanese terminology.

Associations Based on Sex

Sex—that is, being male or female—provides an obvious basis for solidarity. In some societies sex is a very important principle upon which associations are formed. Most anthropological attention has been paid to male associations, probably because more societies have such groups than have comparable ones for females. Age grading, for example, is largely a male phenomenon, with women apparently tacked on through marriage.

In Melanesia, Australia, and among some South American Indian groups, men's associations and cults are prominent in social and religious life. Adolescent boys are initiated into the men's cult and thereafter spend most of their lives in the men's house, only visiting their wives, who live with the children in their own huts in the village. These men's cults are closed to women and surrounded by great secrecy. The men's house itself is usually the most imposing structure in the village, and in or near it are kept the sacred musical instruments and paraphernalia of the cult. The musical instruments, which are often flutelike (shaped like the male genitals) are the symbolic expressions of male dominance and male solidarity in opposition to women. Often, and

especially in Australia, these cults are associated with circumcision rites for newly initiated boys, after which the initiates are considered men and introduced to the secrets of the cult. Frequently associated with these cults is a mythology of how the cults came into being and an "explanation" of why women are not allowed in them. These myths may also "explain" why women are socially inferior to men and why men and women have different roles in society.

Some social scientists give psychological interpretations of these cults. The cults are viewed as unconscious defenses against the males' recognition of their own vulnerability in relation to women. Men, after all, are born of women and nurtured by them; only women have the creative power of childbirth. Many of the rituals associated with men's cults appear to be reenactments of childbirth. The very secrecy with which men's cults are surrounded, the phallic shape of the musical instruments, and the associated mythology seem to make sense as an expression of the ambivalence men have toward women, who give them life and from whom they must ultimately break away if they are to become truly men (Bettelheim 1962; Murphy and Murphy 1974). The solidarity of women in these soci-

E T H N O · G R A P H Y

AGE VILLAGES AMONG THE NYAKYUSA*

The Nyakyusa are cattle owners and cultivators living in the Great Rift Valley at the north end of Lake Nyasa in Southeastern Africa. Before the coming of the Europeans in the late nineteenth century, they had no centralized political authority and were divided up into a number of small, independent chiefdoms. The Nyakyusa are patrilineal and patrilocal. Although the patrilineage is important as a group has a common interest in cattle, patrilineal kinsmen do not live together. Rather, the Nyakyusa village consists of a group of age mates with their wives and young children. It is the forma-

*Adapted from Monica Wilson, Good Company: A Study of Nyakyusa Villagers. Boston: Beacon Press, 1963.

tion of age villages that distinguishes the Nyakyusa from other culturally similar African groups who also have age-based forms of organization.

The age village starts when a number of boys about ten years old build huts together at the edge of their fathers' village. The boys go to live in their new huts, sleeping and spending their spare time in them as well. They continue to eat in their mothers' huts. A group of boys will eat together, taking turns visiting the mother of each member of the "gang." For the Nyakyusa, eating with one's age mates is highly valued, and a boy who often comes home to eat by himself will be severely scolded. The boys' village starts out small, with perhaps a dozen members,

but it grows larger as young boys from the fathers' village or other villages in the neighborhood become old enough to join it. When the original members are about fifteen years old, the village is closed to any more ten-year-olds, who will then form a new village on their own. The boys in an age village live together throughout their lives. When they marry, they bring their wives to the village. As their sons grow up, they form new villages. Daughters may move out if they marry men in other villages, but since they frequently marry one of their father's age mates, they may remain within the village in which they were born.

Once in each generation, there is a great ritual at which

eties is not formalized in cults or associations but is based on the actual cooperation of domestic life and strong interpersonal bonds among female kin.

In many native American societies, associations based on sex were also prominent. A few of these associations were exclusively for women, and their activities involved the performance of rituals to make the corn grow and to increase the buffalo herds. Most of the clubs were for men, however, although they had purposes and social functions different from those of the men's cults described above. Typ-

ical were the military associations among the Crow and Cheyenne. For the individual, the association was like a social club; many of its activities were recreational. These societies fostered the idea of the brave warrior, and membership was limited to those of outstanding military achievement. Exceptionally brave men were chosen as officers and were allowed to wear special ornaments and dress as a sign of their bravery. Although the activities of these societies provided public entertainment, they also had more important functions. At the time of the communal buffalo hunts, when bands

the elders hand over administrative power and military leadership to the younger generation. At this time, land is also transferred from the village of the fathers to the village of the sons. One of the members of the sons' village is appointed headman by the retiring chief and the headmen of the villages of his generation. At any one time, then, Nyakyusa social organization includes three different age grades: the old men, who are retired from administration and military duties; the ruling generation, which is responsible for administration and defense; and the young men and boys, who have not yet "come out" but who may be called upon to fight.

The age village is the group around which the good life is organized for the Nyakyusa. The good life consists of the enjoyment of the company of equals. A man learns law, logic, and manners in the company of his peers, and a social isolate is likely to be accused of witchcraft or think himself bewitched. Because kinsmen of different generations cannot communicate easily due to the respect juniors must show for their elders, it is the age village, not the kin group, that is the most important center of sociability. Nor can the nuclear family be the center of the good life; women are fit for lovemaking, not for friendship.

This unusual form of social organization raises some questions about its origin and functions. The Nyakyusa explanation is that age village organization inhibits incest between father-in-law and daughter-in-law. "Once, they say, a certain chief looked upon his son's wife and saw that she was beautiful and said, 'she is fit to be a queen,' and took her; and men thought that was very bad and said henceforth fathers-in-law should never see their daughters-in-law lest they be tempted to commit incest with them. And so fathers and sons live in different villages." Furthermore, the Nyakyusa believe that sexual activities of parents should be kept separate from children. This is a common belief in many societies, including our own, and is particularly prominent among East African peoples. The Nyakyusa have reached a solution to these two problems that seems quite reasonable to them, although it represents a rare case from a cross-cultural perspective.

Wilson suggests that the regulation of sex may indeed play a role in Nyakyusa social organization. The Nyakyusa do not have male initiation rites or any formal recognition of male adulthood. Therefore, any young man past puberty is a potential mate for a woman of his own age. Since the Nyakyusa are polygynous, a grown son may be a potential lover of his father's junior wives. Furthermore, the Nyakyusa, who practice the levirate, permit a son to inherit his father's wives when his father dies (with the exception of his own biological mother). These cultural patterns give some basis to the jealous fears fathers have of their sons in this society, a source of potential disruption for which age villages are a solution.

gathered together, the military societies acted as police, keeping order and punishing those who broke the law (Lowie 1963).

In West Africa, many kinds of associations with important social functions existed for both males and females. Two of the most well-documented of these societies are the Poro and the Sande, which are the male and female associations among the Kpelle of Liberia. Both societies had the initiation of the young as one of their primary purposes, but they had many other functions as well. The Poro (male) society had important political functions beyond the local community, and it extends even today into national politics. Although Sande power was more limited, there was in the past a female head of the entire tribal Sande. In Sierra Leone, where the Sande organization includes over 90 percent of rural women, men are discouraged from marrying uninitiated women. The Sande organization has power through its transformation of girls into marriageable women. Madam Yoko, a woman who became very powerful in Sierra Leone in the late nineteenth century, effectively utilized her role within the Sande organization to build the

A men's house in Ponape, Micronesia. In societies with men's cults, the men's house is often the most imposing structure in the village. (Raymond Kennedy)

political network on which her leadership was based. Sande dancers achieve great prestige, and Madame Yoko was an outstanding dancer. She also sponsored the initiation of many girls into Sande and arranged marriages for them in ways that would advance her own political career. Even today, women in Africa use the Sande organization to establish alliances and further their political careers (Hoffer 1974).

In relatively small and technologically primitive societies, associations such as we have been describing appear to be organized for recreation and the distinction of rank. They also may have religious functions. In some cases, these societies are for healing, and only individuals who have recovered from serious illness can become members and are then called upon to practice their arts on others. In tribal societies, associations that go beyond

kinship as a basis for membership have important political functions. Among the Plains Indians, they keep the peace during communal hunts and also provide entertainment. In other cases, they resolve disputes, protect members against both supernatural and human harm, and integrate different segments of a tribe beyond the local level. The presence of societies in West Africa, for example, corresponds with an absence of age-group organizations; where one is absent, the other fulfills similar political and social functions. Many of these associations are based on ascribed statuses such as sex or age, but others are voluntary, and still others require certain achievements for membership. It is under conditions of modernization and urbanization that voluntary associations increase dramatically and play important roles in social change, and these organizations will be discussed in Chapter 16.

A drawing by Jesse Cornplanter of the False Face Society among the Iroquois. Such associations had important curing, religious, and political functions among many native American peoples and served as mechanisms of pan-tribal integration. (Courtesy of Museum of the American Indian Heye Foundation)

SUMMARY

1. Kinship systems are cultural creations that define and organize relatives by blood and marriage. A kinship system includes the kinds of groups based on kinship and the system of terms used to classify different kin.

2. The functions of kinship systems are to provide continuity between generations and to define a group of people who can depend on one another for mutual aid.

3. In traditional societies, kinship is the most important basis of social organization. This contrasts with industrial states, in which principles of social organization, such as citizenship, social class, and common interests, become more important than kinship.

4. In many societies, descent is important in the formation of corporate social groups. In societies with a unilineal rule of descent, descent-group membership is based on either the male or female line. Unilineal systems are found among pastoral and horticultural societies.

5. A lineage is a group of kin whose members can actually trace their descent through a common ancestor. A clan is a group whose members believe they have a common ancestor but cannot trace the relationship genealogically. Lineages tend to have domestic functions, clans to have political and religious functions. Both lineages and clans are important in regulating marriage.

6. In patrilineal systems, a man's children belong to his lineage, as do the children of his sons but not of his daughters. Husbands have control over wives, and children and marriage are surrounded by strong sanctions. The Nuer and the Rajputs of India are patrilineal.

7. In matrilineal systems, a woman's children belong to her lineage, not that of their father. The mother's brother has authority over his sister's children, and relations between husband and wife are more fragile than in patrilineal societies. Matrilineal systems contain a contradiction, in that men are reluctant to give up control over their sons to the lineage of their wives. The Hopi are a matrilineal society.

8. Patrilineality grows out of patrilocality, which is based on the common economic interests of brothers. Matrilineality grows out of matrilocality, which arises under special circumstances; when these conditions disappear, the kinship system tends to change.

9. In systems of double descent, Ego belongs to both the patrilineage of the father and the matrilineage of the mother. Each group functions in different social contexts. The Yako of Nigeria have a system of double descent.

10. In bilateral systems, Ego is equally related to mother's and father's kin. A bilateral rule of descent results in the formation of kindreds, which are ego-centered kinship networks, rather than a permanent group of kin. Bilateral kinship is found predominantly among foragers and in modern industrialized states.

11. Kinship terminology lumps together and distinguishes relatives according to various principles such as generation, relative age, lineality or collaterality, sex, consanguinity or affinity, bifurcation, and sex of the linking relative. Different societies may use all or some of these principles in classifying kin.

12. The six types of kinship classification systems defined by anthropologists are the Hawaiian, Eskimo, Iroquois, Omaha, Crow, and Sudanese. Each reflects the particular kinship group that is most important in the society.

13. Although kinship groups dominate in most structurally simpler societies, other forms of association are also found. Some of the nonkin groups in tribal societies are based on age. One example is the age villages found among the Nyakyusa of East Africa.

14. Groups based on sex may also be important. In many parts of Melanesia and South America, men spend most of their time in association with other men and live in a special men's house. In other societies, notably those of West Africa, men's and women's associations are also important in religious, political, and social life.

15. In complex societies and those undergoing social change, kinship groups often become weaker, and voluntary associations based on economic and political interests become more important, though kinship relationships are still relevant.

SUGGESTED READINGS

Bohannan, P., and Middleton, J., eds.
　1968　*Kinship and Social Organization.* Garden City, N.Y.: The Natural History Press. Classic articles on kinship and kinship terminology.

Pasternak, Burton
　1976　*Introduction to Kinship and Social Organization.* Englewood Cliffs, N.J.: Prentice-Hall. Just what it says—a good introduction for the beginning student.

Schneider, David M.
　1968　*American Kinship: A Cultural Account.* Englewood Cliffs, N.J.: Prentice-Hall. A look at kinship in the United States and what it suggests about our culture.

Schneider, David M., and Gough, Kathleen, eds.
　1961　*Matrilineal Kinship.* Berkeley: University of California Press. An examination of a variety of matrilineal systems and how matrilineality may be related to subsistence, productivity, and political organization.

Schusky, E. L.
　1965　*Manual for Kinship Analysis.* New York: Holt, Rinehart and Winston. An introduction to the basics of kinship, including exercises for the student in analyzing kinship terminology.

Wilson, Monica
　1963　*Good Company: A Study of Nyakyusa Age-Villages.* Boston: Beacon Press (first publ. 1951). An interesting study of an African society with an unusual form of social organization.

CHAPTER TWELVE

SOCIAL RANKING AND STRATIFICATION

▶ Are there any societies in which all people are equal?

▶ What are the differences between a class and a caste system?

▶ Does the culture of poverty mean a poverty of culture?

> *"Hell . . . nobody knows everything. One man is a doctor, so he talks about surgery. Another man is a teacher, so he talks about books. But doctors and teachers don't know anything about concrete. You're a cement finisher and that's your specialty."*
>
> *"Maybe so, but when was the last time you saw anybody standing around talking about concrete?"*
>
> Tally, from *Tally's Corner* by Elliot Liebow

One important difference in the way societies are organized is the degree to which individuals within the society have equal access to prestige, power, and the resources necessary to sustain life. Although it is clear that not all human beings are equally endowed with talents, appearance, and skill, not all societies formally recognize this inequality. In approaching this aspect of social reorganization, anthropologists have distinguished three basic types of societies: egalitarian societies, rank societies, and stratified societies. Each of these three principles of social organization is tied up with economic and political organization. The economies of egalitarian societies are primarily organized through reciprocity, those of rank societies through redistribution, and those of stratified societies through market exchange. Similarly, as we will see in Chapter Thirteen, egalitarian societies have little specialization of political roles; rank societies are characterized by chiefs as the ruling powers; and stratified societies are correlated with a particular kind of political organization known as the state. Although for some purposes, economics, social status systems, and politics can be separated, they are in fact all interrelated.

EGALITARIAN SOCIETIES

In **egalitarian societies,** no individual or group has more access to resources, power, or prestige than any other. This does not mean that in such societies all members have equal prestige. In addition to age and sex differences, individual differences in skill at a variety of tasks will always be recognized. Some individuals are better hunters; others are regarded as more skilled at a craft; others are singled out for their healing ability; still others are acknowledged as knowing more or speaking in a more expressive manner than the ordinary person. In an egalitarian society, however, no individual, no matter how high or low in esteem in the group, is denied the right to make a living or is subject to the control or exploitation of others. Furthermore, whatever prestige an individual gains on the basis of ability is not transferable to his or her heirs or relatives. There is no fixed number of positions that are ranked and for which individuals must compete. The prestige attached to being a good hunter, for example, will go to as many good hunters as there are in the group.

Hunting and gathering societies are characteristically egalitarian. Factors preventing any permanent and unequal distribution of wealth are the lack of land ownership; the relatively low technological level, which inhibits storing up large quantities of food; the need for mobility, which inhibits the accumulation of material goods; and the obligation to share food. The activity of hunting and foraging itself does not require a permanent leader, and food-getting activities are often carried out individually or in groups in which individuals are organized as equal, cooperating members. Even when hunting societies have a headman, this position carries no real power or economic advantage and is not inherited or inheritable. But not all foraging societies are equally egalitarian. Among some Inuit groups, for example, differences in wealth did develop. In groups where whaling was important, a successful whaler accumulated more wealth than others

and often distributed it in such a way as to control the less successful men. The fishing groups along the Northwest Coast of America were not egalitarian at all, and in fact they exhibited a higher degree of ranking than many horticultural societies.

RANK SOCIETIES

In **rank societies,** there are formal differences in prestige but no important restrictions on access to basic resources. There is an inherited position of chief, and his prestige is linked to the redistribution of goods, frequently in the form of competitive feasts and religious ceremonies. But although chiefs in such societies may have great prestige and certain privileges, they do not accumulate food and goods for their own use. Their basic standard of living does not differ from that of the ordinary members of the society. Rank societies have not only the high-prestige position of chief but also ranking of kin groups. Kin groups closest to the chief genealogically have the most prestige, and in some rank societies order of birth is important as a criterion of social status.

Rank societies are mainly found among cultivators and herders, though simple ranking also exists among some hunting groups. The Siriono of eastern Bolivia, for example, have a simple ranking system (Holmberg 1969). In spite of its simple technology, this impoverished society does have the office of chief, which is generally passed on from father to son. But the Siriono chief has few privileges: the main ones are that only he is allowed more than one wife, and his family occupies the center of the communal dwelling in which the Siriono extended families live. As chief, he is entitled to be called *ererekwa*, but this title is also used by women generally to refer to their husbands. Since the chief is usually a better hunter than the others, he uses his position to distribute meat and build up obligations from others. Because chiefs "know more about things and are able to do them better than anyone else," they are given

In rank societies, the chief is a source of supernatural power. Here a chief on the island of Ponape, Micronesia, is being served kava, a ceremonial drink. The server's head is turned away, as no one may look directly at the chief. (Raymond Kennedy)

more respect than the average man. Some prestige is gained among the Siriono by being a close relation to the chief, but an individual's position depends much more on ability to provide food than on any other factor.

The most complex ranking systems were found in Polynesia and among the Indian societies of the Northwest Coast of America. These societies consisted of a series of individual positions, all ranked in order; no two individuals were precisely equal. Among the Nootka, rights to manage all economic resources, such as fishing, hunting, and gathering grounds, were held by individuals, although a relative could not be prevented from using them. Inheritance of these rights passed only through the line of the eldest sons. The same was true for the office of chief. The line that went through lesser sons was ranked lower than that of eldest sons, and these differences in rank were typically expressed in terms of wealth. This wealth consisted only partly of important economic resources; it was also symbolic, as in the right to use special names, perform certain ceremonial functions, sponsor potlatches, and wear certain items of clothing and decoration. Only chiefs, for example, were allowed to wear abalone shell jewelry and sea-otter fur on their robes. The right of directing the use of economic resources supported the symbolic ranking system. As manager, a chief of a kin group received resources that formally acknowledged his rank—the first of the salmon catch, the best parts of sea mammals that had been killed, blankets, and furs. It was from this source that a chief could sponsor a potlatch at which most of these goods were given away.

A similar ranking system existed in Tahiti, although that society could be divided into the Ari'i, who were the immediate families of the chiefs of the most important lineages in the larger districts; the Ra'atira, who were the heads

This San Blas Kuna woman of Panama wears gold jewelry that represents the wealth of her family. Although there are differences in wealth and prestige in rank societies, no individual or group is denied access to basic resources. (United Nations/ Jerry Frank)

him. Thus, in some Polynesian islands, the highest chief was kept completely away from other people and even used a special vocabulary that no one else was allowed to use.

Rank societies, then, are organized by kinship. Rank is based on position (birth order and genealogical closeness to the chief) within the kinship system, and membership in the kinship group entitles each individual to access to basic resources. No one group of people is exploited in order to maintain a ruling class exempt from food production. Even in ranked societies where slaves existed, they were actually individuals attached to wealthier families and not an exploited class on which the economy depended. In these ways, rank societies are distinguished from societies with social stratification.

STRATIFIED SOCIETIES

A **stratified society** has formal, permanent social and economic inequality. Some individuals and groups (over and above those defined by age and sex) are denied access to the basic resources necessary for survival and well-being. Stratified societies have relatively permanent and wide differences between groups in terms of standard of living, security, prestige, political power, and life chances. These major dimensions of social stratification are usually analyzed in terms of power, wealth, and prestige. Anthropologists are interested in studying the relationships among these dimensions within a society and in comparing stratification systems in different cultures.

One important distinction that is made in comparing systems of social stratification is whether they are based on ascription or achievement. In a stratification system in which ascription is important, an individual's **status,** or position in the system, is mainly determined by birth. **Ascribed statuses** are those social positions to which an individual is born. Sex, race, and ethnic group are examples of ascribed statuses in American society. Kinship

of less important lineages and their families; and the Manahune, which included the remainder of the population. Social rank in Tahiti had an economic, political, and religious aspect. Mana, a spiritual power, was possessed by all individuals, but in different degrees depending on rank. The Ari'i had the most mana because they were closest to the ancestral gods from which mana comes. An elaborate body of taboos separated those with more mana from those with less and also regulated social relations between individuals in the three ranks. Higher-ranked people could not eat with those of lower rank; and because men had higher rank than women and children, they could not eat with them. The highest-ranking Ari'i was so sacred that anything he touched became poison for those below

group and caste membership are other examples of ascribed statuses. In a stratification system based on achievement, an individual's position is largely determined by his or her own efforts. **Achieved statuses** are those an individual chooses or achieves on his or her own. Wife, doctor, criminal, and artist are examples of achieved statuses in the United States. In simpler societies most statuses are ascribed, although in some of them individual achievement plays an important role, and there are some opportunities for moving up in society through a combination of skill and hard work.

Although different systems of social stratification can be described as based primarily on ascription (closed systems) or achievement (open systems), most societies contain both. Anthropologists are interested in the many kinds of statuses, both ascribed and achieved, and the ways in which individuals are chosen to fill social positions.

The stratification system in the United States includes elements of both ascribed and achieved status. Color is an ascribed status, which affects an individual's placement in the system no matter what other status he or she achieves. The position of shoeshine man is an achieved status that places an individual low in our class hierarchy. (Serena Nanda)

Power, Wealth, and Prestige

Power is the ability to produce intended effects on oneself, on other human beings, and on things. Power thus means the ability to make and carry out decisions affecting one's own life, to control the behavior of other human beings, and to transform objects or resources. Power used with the consent of the members of a society is called **authority** and is legitimate. Power may also be illegitimate, exercised without the approval of society. The powerful individuals or groups in a society are best able to act on their perceptions of where their self-interest lies. In stratified societies, this frequently means at the expense of the goals of other individuals and groups. From an anthropological standpoint, our interest is in knowing who has the power in a society, through what channels it is exercised, and what its sources are. As one example, we might compare power in the United States as it rests with corporation presidents, elected public

officials, movie stars, or the heads of organized crime families. From a cross-cultural perspective, we might compare the sources and management of power of an American president, a Bantu chief, and the head of the Communist Party in the Soviet Union.

Wealth as an aspect of social stratification is the accumulation of material resources, or access to the means of producing these resources. Many social scientists believe that wealth is the most important aspect of social stratification and the foundation on which the other dimensions, such as power and prestige, rest. For Karl Marx and those who follow his thinking, the basic principle of social organization is the system by which resources are produced and allocated to provide for the satisfaction of basic human needs. Marx differentiated between two main strata in society: the capitalists, who own the means of production, and the workers, who are employed by others. According to Marx, it is this relationship to the means of production that is important in determining not only how much power and prestige one has but also one's chances to survive. One need not be a Marxist to see the obvious ways in which wealth can translate into power. Rich men are more likely to run for political office and win than others, and wealthy capitalists can influence government in ways that are in their own self-interest.

Prestige, or social honor, is a third dimension of social stratification. Complex societies, which are occupationally specialized, contain a number of different positions that are ranked high or low in relation to one another. Occupations are ranked somewhat differently in different societies. We will see, when we look at the Hindu caste system, that one criterion for ranking occupations in India has to do with the level of ritual purity or pollution. Although this exact concept does not exist in the United States, we do have the idea of a "dirty job" ranked lower than jobs that are not dirty. Generally speaking, white-collar occupations carry more prestige than blue-collar occupations. As socioeconomic conditions change, the value system that supports a particular system of prestige will also change. Different occupations may gain or lose prestige. In ancient China, for example, the intellectual had high status; in modern China, an attempt is being made to raise the prestige of the worker, and the intellectual is regarded as a parasite.

The prestige given different occupations is related to the power inherent in such occupations, the income derived from them, and their importance to the society, among other factors. Although income is a basis for prestige in American society, the ways in which that income is earned and wealth is accumulated also have to be taken into account. People who earn their incomes illegally, generally speaking, have less prestige in the community than those whose incomes are legally earned. Who do you think has more prestige in our society—a baseball player who signs a $2 million contract, a heart surgeon who earns $200,000 a year, or the head of an illegal gambling syndicate whose profit runs to millions? On the other hand, money eventually buys high social position, at least in our society. Sending one's children to the best schools, buying a home in the best neighborhood, joining the right clubs, and so on give individuals the chance to interact socially with others in high social positions. All these opportunities cost money. The social status of a family can thus improve dramatically over just a few generations. Some families now prominent in United States political life, for example, made their fortunes in ways that today would be considered deviant or illegal.

The question of whether prestige or class is more important as a basis for protecting one's self-interest has long been argued by social scientists. Two opposing views on this question are those of Marx and Max Weber, a German sociologist of the late nineteenth century. Whereas Marx saw people as conscious of themselves as a group mainly in terms of similar economic interests, Weber believed that people may value prestige and the symbolic aspects of status even more than money. Weber further argued that political action can be motivated by a group's desire to defend its social position as well as, or even in opposition to, its economic self-interest. For example, poor whites in the American South may refuse to join poor blacks in working for improvement of their common economic position because they are more interested in maintaining the status differences based on color.

SOCIAL CLASS

The two basic forms of social stratification are class and caste. In a **class system,** the different strata (classes) are not sharply separated from one another but form a continuum. **Social mobility** (movement from one class to another) is possible. An individual born into one social class can, through various means (education, marriage, good or bad luck, hard work) move into another.

Social Class in America

The United States is said to have a relatively open class system; one's position depends largely on achieved statuses such as occupation, education, and life style, and there is a relatively good chance for upward mobility. The open class system of our society is part of our mythology and is based on the democratic principle of equality and opportunity for all. Many people in the United States find it difficult to accept the evidence that this equality has not yet been fully realized and that, in fact, social class is an important aspect of social organization in our nation. Many studies have shown that social class membership does appear to correlate with various attitudinal, behavioral, and life style factors, testifying to the reality of social classes.

Anthropological research indicates that social class is more than an economic phenomenon. A social class is also a **subculture;** its members share similar life experiences, occupational roles, values, educational backgrounds, associational affiliation, leisure activities, buying habits, and political views. Beyond being linked by these shared traits, members of a social class tend to associate more with one another than with people in other classes. Studies of social stratification in many societies show that informal social interaction such as visiting most frequently involves members of the same class. Thus, the life style and interactional dimensions of social class reinforce one another. Through interaction based on common residence and schooling, for example, individuals learn the life style of their social class. Since life style is an important part of sociability, people with similar life styles tend to associate with one another.

Social Class and Life Chances

Some social scientists argue that approaches to social stratification that emphasize life style, cultural patterns, and prestige obscure important economic and power differences in American society. Another way to look at social class that brings economic factors and power into sharper focus is to examine the differences in life chances among social classes. **Life chances** refer to an individual's opportunity to fulfill or fail to fulfill his or her potential in society. An individual's life chances include the chance of survival, opportunities to obtain an education that will help maximize intellectual and creative potential, opportunities to participate in associations and cultural life, and opportunities to live in comfort and security.

An individual's life chances are linked to his or her position in the stratification system. Although the American myth of equality includes the belief that "anyone can become president," the relationship between life chances and social mobility does not uphold this idea. Social mobility is also a life chance that depends on where one already is in the class system. Individuals born into positions of wealth, high status, and power strive to maintain those positions, and because of their high social class frequently have the means to keep others from achieving mobility. People born into the middle class have a better chance of improving their life chances than people born into a poor class. The very poor and those who belong to minority groups that are discriminated against in our culture have lower life chances than the middle class. Low social position tends to negate not only one's own life chances but also those of one's children. Poverty tends to perpetuate itself through generations, calling into question the openness of the American class system.

The Culture of Poverty

The self-perpetuating nature of poverty has attracted the interest of both social scientists and policymakers. A number of anthropologists, notably Oscar Lewis, argue that poverty is not just an economic condition but a way of life that tends to perpetuate itself by failing to provide its members with the values and skills necessary to be successful in the larger society. According to Lewis (1966), the **culture of poverty** is an adaptation of the poor to their marginal position in stratified, capitalistic societies. Some of the characteristics of this "culture" are lack of participation in the cultural and social institutions of the larger society, chronic shortage of cash and the absence of savings, low levels of education, mistrust of government and fear of the police, early experience with sex, consensual marriages and a high rate of children born out of wedlock, and families centered on the mother, with fathers weak or absent.

The matrifocal, or mother-centered, family, in which there is no economically productive husband and father, has been one of the main points of the culture of poverty debate. The term "matrifocal" became popular with the publication of the Moynihan Report, written in 1965 by the then assistant secretary of labor, Daniel Moynihan. In it he attempted to demonstrate that the matrifocal family was the "cause" of the high incidence of crime and social disorganization in lower-class black communities. The report held that the matrifocal family is disorganized and "pathological" and is unable properly to socialize or control its children. Individuals brought up in this kind of family are said to develop strong feelings of inadequacy, have poorly developed egos, be fatalistic about the future, and live for the moment, rather than being able to defer gratification for the sake of future rewards and achievement. These personality traits appear to be internalized by the age of six or seven and inhibit the ability of these individuals to take advantage of opportunities to improve their position when and if these become available. These traits thus account for the continuation of poverty over generations as well as for the criminal and pathological behavior that is the result of improper and inadequate socialization.

Lewis's concept of the culture of poverty appears to place much of the blame for the conditions in which the poor live on the poor themselves. Critics of the concept say it obscures the role of social, political, and economic forces in the larger society that create and maintain a class of poor people and that need to be changed if the poor are going to change their lives. Among these critics is Charles Valentine (1971), an anthropologist who has studied a poor community in the United States. Valentine offers an alternative interpretation of the behavior patterns of the poor in America. He suggests that whatever is distinctive about social life at the lowest economic levels of society is determined primarily by the socioeconomic and political structure of the larger society. According to Valentine, the poor have the same values and desire the same things as other people, but the constraints of poverty do not allow them to realize the values and behave in the same way as the middle class. The mother-centered family, for example, can be viewed as an adaptation to economic conditions that prevent adult males from obtaining decent jobs. Males prevented from having adequate access to jobs are unable to carry out the economic aspects of the roles of husband and father. Furthermore, the system of welfare does not allow for child support if an able-bodied man is living in the household. Among lower-class black populations, both the greater availability of work for females as compared with males and the economic independence from males provided by welfare allotments give women an extra economic value that leads to their becoming the center and power in the household.

In addition, recent research has indicated that the picture of the matrifocal family presented by the Moynihan Report does not give a full picture of lower-class black family life. Carol Stack, for example, in a book called *All Our Kin* (1974) shows that the basis of familial structure and cooperation in these communities is not the nuclear family but an extended cluster of relatives related chiefly through children but also through marriage and friendship. These people carry out the

Some characteristics defined as part of the "culture of poverty" are mother-centered families, low income, large numbers of children, low educational levels, and a lack of participation in political institutions. The culture of poverty is an adaptation to the marginal position of the poor in stratified societies, such as Mexico. (Bernhard Krauss)

whole range of domestic and child-care functions. This domestic network spreads over several kin-based households formed around women and based on the role of women in child care, but men also play important roles. They contribute to the networks of both the mothers of their children and their own mothers. The shifting of residences and "elastic boundaries" of households are adaptations to the crises and calamities that are always part of life among the poor.

Critics of the culture-of-poverty concept hold that the lack of motivation of poor children in school is based on a realistic perception of the fact that, where jobs are not available, doing well in school means nothing. Fear and mistrust of government, including the police, are based on the reality of government neglect and police bru-

tality. The inability to defer gratification is based on the fact that the future offers very little. *Tally's Corner*, a study of the world of black street-corner men in the inner city of Washington, D.C., written by Elliot Liebow (1967), gives an interpretation of unemployment among lower-class black males that contradicts the popular explanation of "laziness." Liebow shows that it is not unwillingness to work that explains high male unemployment but rather a combination of the exploitation of these men when they do find work, the lack of self-esteem that stops them from taking work opportunities, and the culture of the street-corner group, which gives emotional support only for failure.

In the United States, a man is "worth" what he is paid. The self-worth of the street-corner man is constantly under attack because he cannot often get work and because much of the work he is offered is low paying, psychologically unrewarding, physically difficult, and intermittent. Those who hire the street-corner man often justify the low wages they pay on the ground that these men steal from them, thus making the material rewards of the job actually much higher than the standard salary. But it is in terms of salary that an American man measures his self-worth. What is stolen from the job does not count in society's terms, and it also leaves the worker vulnerable to the wishes of an employer who might want to fire him or exploit him in other ways. The poor, black, inner-city male is seen by himself as a failure; in this he reflects society's view of him as a failure because of his marginal work role. The street-corner society is participated in by men who are all failures; success pulls the man out of the only group from which he has received psychological

support. The dependency of the poor black family on welfare further undermines the male's self-esteem and the stability of the family. Thus, the entire social structure, cultural values, male-female relations, and the psychological components of dependency have to be viewed as an integrated whole if poor people are to become self-supporting.

Valentine suggests that by focusing on the weak, dependent personality that is said to be created by the culture of poverty, the strength and vitality of the many poor people who manage to survive under the worst conditions have been overlooked. For Valentine and other critics of the culture-of-poverty concept, values and psychology are not the heart of the issue. Rather, these are rationalizations for a society that discriminates against the poor and that has failed to provide the kinds of employment necessary to give all its citizens a reasonable standard of living.

CASTE

In contrast to class systems, which are based primarily on achieved statuses, a caste system is based on birth. An individual belongs to the caste of his or her parents and cannot move from one caste to another. In a class system, individuals from different classes may marry (and marriage is one route to upward social mobility). In a caste system, an individual can marry only within the caste. Caste, in other words, is hereditary and **endogamous.** The castes, however many there are, are ranked in relation to one another and are usually associated with a particular occupation. A **caste system,** then, consists of a ranked and culturally distinct number of interdependent endogamous groups. Unlike class systems, in which no clear boundaries exist between the different classes, a caste system has definite boundaries between castes. Many of the social rules in a caste system are directed toward maintaining social distance between castes.

Some anthropologists (Dumont 1970) define

caste only as it exists in India, where it is firmly embedded in the Hindu religion. Others view caste as a system of stratification that is found in a number of societies outside India, for example Japan and parts of Africa. A cross-cultural definition of caste has also been applied to the relations between whites and blacks in the United States, particularly in the South until very recently. The castelike aspects of this social system included membership based on birth (one was born white or black and remained in that category for life), marriage within the caste, cultural distinctiveness of the two groups, traditional occupations each group could enter or was prohibited from entering, and a rank order in which white was superior. Many of the norms of behavior in the old South revolved around keeping "blacks in their place" and preventing blacks and whites from mixing except under certain conditions. Like a caste system anywhere, this system had a full-fledged mythology associated with it, an attempt to "explain" and justify the inferior position of the lower caste. Ultimately, this system, like other caste systems, was maintained by physical force, which came into the open whenever the status quo was threatened. In writing of the South in the 1930s, John Dollard (1937), in his *Caste and Class in a Southern Town*, demonstrated that, although social classes existed within the two castes, a castelike line was drawn between blacks and whites. No matter how high a position a black reached, he or she could not cross the caste barrier. In a comparison of caste in India and the United States, Gerald Berreman (1959) demonstrated convincingly not only that castelike features operated in the United States but also that classlike features operated in the Indian caste system.

Apartheid, or separateness, is the official state policy of the Republic of South Africa, and it illustrates the extremes to which stratification may lead. Here, workers in the Elsies River Plant of the Chrysler Corporation must leave their work by segregated exits. (United Nations)

The Caste System in India

The unique elements of the Indian caste system are its complexity, its relation to Hindu religious beliefs and rituals, and the degree to which the castes (or more properly subcastes) are cohesive and self-regulating groups. The Hindu belief about the division of society is that there are four caste categories, called *varna*. The *varna* are ranked according to their ritual purity, which in turn is based on their traditional occupations. The Brahmins, who are ranked highest, are priests and scholars; the Kshatriyas, or warrior caste, are second; the Vaisha, or merchants, are ranked third; and the shudras, or menial workers and artisans, are ranked fourth. Below these four *varna* is a fifth group, called the untouchables. The untouchable castes, who perform the polluting work of cleaning latrines or working with leather, are considered so ritually impure that just their mere touch contaminates the purity of the higher castes. An individual's birth into one of these *varna* is said to be a reward or punishment for the quality of his or her actions in a previous life.

Many traditional rules of behavior in India are designed to maintain the boundaries between castes. Members of different castes do not eat with one another, and a higher-caste person will not accept most kinds of food or drink from a lower-caste person. Untouchable castes are segregated in their own part of the village and are not allowed to drink water out of the same wells as higher castes. Before recent laws establishing legal equality, marriage and sexual relations between castes were forbidden. Each caste has distinguishing cultural features, and the higher castes more nearly approximate Hindu religious ideals in their behavior. This includes vegetarianism, a taboo on alcohol, and the prohibition of remarriage for widows. Only high castes are allowed to perform certain rituals, such as the tying of the sacred thread on young boys, which symbolizes a second birth. Formerly, Brahmin priests would not minister to the religious needs of the untouchables and lower castes, and untouchables were not allowed to enter village temples.

Caste in India is tied up, especially in the village context, with the exchange of goods and services. Families of various artisan and serving castes, such as carpenters, potters, black-

In India, the caste system is an important means of regulating the exchange of goods and services. Barbering, for example, is an activity traditionally performed in exchange for grain and clothes, rather than cash. (Serena Nanda)

smiths, water carriers, leather workers (who remove dead cattle from the fields), barbers, and washermen, perform necessary services for families of high-caste landowners and in return receive food from them. In addition, landowning families may pay serving-caste families with grain, clothing, fodder for animals, and animal products such as butter and milk. The landowning castes may also give the serving castes small amounts of cash, free rent, or the use of tools. This client-patron, or *jajmani*, relationship is often carried on over several generations between the same families. The serving castes also exchange goods and services among themselves. Thus, at the village level, the different castes form an interdependent, organic whole.

This view of the caste system emphasizes its integrative function and the way caste benefits society as a whole, showing how it pro-vides benefits to both the high-caste landowning families and the serving castes. Landowners get a steady supply of workers and can maintain a high-status life style; they need not perform menial and ritually polluting work. The serving castes, in turn, are assured economic security. This description, however, is a somewhat idealized one; many anthropologists have argued that the benefits of the system are much greater for the high castes than the low castes and that social integration in the Indian village is due as much to physical coercion and the absence of alternatives for the lower castes as it is to the integrating force of reciprocity.

The Dynamics of Caste

Idealized views of the caste system, which emphasized its stability, were obtained by anthropologists mainly from high-caste Hindus. New studies of caste in rural and urban areas reveal a dynamism that earlier studies overlooked. Lower- and middle-ranked castes frequently do not accept their position and use a number of strategies to rearrange their rank. Efforts by untouchable castes to change their rank often bring a violent reaction from the higher castes, who want to preserve their own prestige, wealth, and power.

Social mobility in the caste system is a group rather than an individual effort. A caste that has achieved a certain amount of economic success might try to raise its prestige by adopting the customs of a higher-caste group and claiming a new rank for itself. An upwardly mobile caste attempts through its caste council to change the behavior of its members, getting them to conform to high-caste behavior patterns. A lower caste might also, as part of its strategy, invent a myth for itself showing that it originally came from one of the higher-ranked *varna*.

With the achievement of Indian independence in 1948 and the creation of a democratic constitution, caste in India has both weakened and gained strength. The Indian government, in an attempt to make up for past discrimination and suffering, has reserved special jobs and places in the universities for members of untouchable and lower castes. The advantages to be gained by claiming membership in one of these castes may therefore be substantial, and a number of caste associations have grown up to help members use these new opportunities. Discrimination against untouchables was also outlawed, although as we have seen with race relations in the United States, this is difficult to enforce at the local level. The vote has been extended to all castes, and low castes now have a potential for political power through elected representation. These factors have somewhat altered the strategies of upward mobility for some low castes.

Owen Lynch (1969) has described these changes in strategy for the Camars, an untouchable caste of leather workers in the city of Agra. Camars have traditionally been

This woman is a sweeper, a member of one of the previously called untouchable *castes in India. Although the Indian government has taken a strong stand on affirmative action and reserved places in schools and jobs for members of these oppressed castes, they still suffer economic and political burdens derived from their low status in the caste and class hierarchy. (Serena Nanda)*

shoemakers, and because of the increased demand for shoes both in India and abroad, some of them have become fairly wealthy. Changes in the economic conditions of the Camars, as well as political circumstances, have stimulated them to try to raise their position in the caste system. They claimed to be Kshatriyas (the warrior caste), and in an effort to get this claim accepted by the higher castes, they outlawed the eating of beef and buffalo and adopted some high-caste rituals, such as the tying of the sacred thread. These efforts, however, were not successful. Under the leadership of an untouchable, Dr. B. R. Ambedkar, who was educated in England and the United States, the Camars are now trying a different strategy, that of conversion to Buddhism. Unlike their earlier attempts to raise their status within the caste system, this move is an attempt to improve their position by putting themselves outside the caste system altogether. At the same time, they wish to retain their status as a special caste in order to be eligible for the benefits of affirmative action undertaken by the Indian government.

The Camars of Agra offer a good example of the dynamics of caste and how it is both weakened and perpetuated in modern India. The study also invites comparison with similar efforts by other groups in other societies—for example, among blacks in the United States.

Although Indian castes are ranked on the basis of prestige rather than wealth, the gains of high-caste position are not just symbolic. The higher castes also benefit materially from their higher status and are in a better position to exercise political power in their own self-interest. The lower castes appear to accept their low position without question, but their conformity actually hinges a great deal on their awareness that economic sanctions and physical force will ultimately be used against them if they dare to try and break out of their low place. Members of the upper castes, whether in India or the United States, have long used the rationalization that the lower strata of their society are "happy where they are." That this is not the case is clear from the protest movements by the poor and oppressed in both India and the United States.

One of the problems with much of the social science work done on caste in India is that most studies, unlike Lynch's, cited above, are done from the viewpoint of members of the highest castes. Joan Mencher (1980) is another anthropologist who has studied the Indian hierarchy from the point of view of untouchables, or Harijans, to use the word coined by Gandhi, which means "children of God." Mencher's work suggests that the untouchable castes are caught in a circular bind of stigmatized identity (that is, they are viewed as polluting) and economic exploitation. Although the Indian government has outlawed untouchability, there has not been the kind of radical economic reform that would eliminate the economic barriers to their mobility, and without economic improvement there can be no change in the stigmatized aspect of their identity. At the same time, without a change in their stigmatized identity as untouchables, it is very difficult for any radical economic change to take place (p. 262). Furthermore, although high-caste Indians frequently refer to the religious basis of caste as a justification for the social hierarchy, lower caste informants almost universally explain their low status by referring to economic factors, such as the concentration of land or capital in the hands of the elite. In examining the contemporary political/economic scene in India, Mencher raises the question of why caste has continued to play such an important role in social identity and politics. Her conclusion is that richer members of the high castes emphasize the importance of *caste* status in order to inhibit poorer members of the high castes from uniting economically with members of lower castes, and thus threatening the dominance of richer, capital and land owning upper caste members. As long as members of untouchable castes continue to be socially stigmatized, this will inhibit the formation of classes and class consciousness in India, an obvious advantage to those at the top.

SEXUAL STRATIFICATION

Sexual stratification refers to one aspect of the relations between the sexes: equality (or inequality). Because we live in a society in which sexual inequality predominates, we may tend to assume that male dominance is universal; and we may think it is inherent in the biological or role differences between men and women. Thus, it is important for us to look at other cultures in which this aspect of male-female relations is different, in order to see the culturally determined nature of sexual stratification and the conditions under which it arises and is maintained. Furthermore, a cross-cultural perspective will uncover societies that are much more egalitarian than our own and reveal the conditions under which such egalitarianism exists.

There are some societies, including our own, that we can call male dominated. In this type of society, both people's ideology and practices, or behavior, involve sexual stratification. Males have control over the most important resources in society, and they are believed to be both different in nature from and superior to women. Some societies considered to be clearly male dominated are India, Muslim Middle Eastern societies, and some Mediterranean societies—for example, Sicily. Even in societies that appear to be strongly male dominated, however, women do not simply or easily adapt to their subordinate status but attempt to check male dominance in some way and thereby achieve a measure of autonomy or even influence of their own (Schlegal 1977). For example, in many of the lower strata of male-dominated socities—such as among the lower castes in India, in Sicily, or among the Ladinos of Guatemala (Maynard 1974)—there are existential conditions that ameliorate the actual power men have. In the case of India, lower-caste women work. In Sicily, the men's farm work keeps them too busy to deal with the bureaucratic authorities, so that women have to take over this job. Furthermore, the cultural ideal of male infallibility makes men especially sensitive to the humor that women use to undermine their egos. Among the Guatemalan Ladinos, the frequency with which lower-class men abandon their families leaves the wives in actual control of the household. Where male dominance is rigid, men and women often have very separate spheres of activity, and this means that there are female domains—notably the household and even certain kinds of economic activities—where women derive social and emotional satisfaction. This is true, for example, of high-caste Indian women in villages. Although they may be subject to male control, they can exercise some substantial power as mothers-in-law and mothers.

Among many tribes in New Guinea, the inequality between the sexes is expressed in the idea that men can be polluted and contaminated by the touch of women. This Gururumba man is inducing vomiting by swallowing a three-foot length of cane, which will rid him of the polluting effect of women. (Courtesy of the American Museum of Natural History)

In a second type of society, which has qualified, or modified, male dominance, women have some important political roles or some access to resources of their own. They can use these to advance their position in the home and the position of their kin and to extend and enhance their own social networks. This type of society is characteristic of many cultures of West Africa, where women not only produce but also market and control the resources from certain crops. Women in West Africa may also be politically active through their control of female initiation societies, similar to those of young men.

In a third type of society, the egalitarian, the ideology of male dominance is absent or very

In many parts of West Africa, women both produce and sell their products in the marketplace. This control over important economic resources improves their position in society. (United Nations)

weak. Women have the means to gain access to important economic resources and to occupy decision-making roles and positions. Egalitarianism between men and women may be based on a complementarity of roles; it does not necessarily mean, as we tend to mean in the West, that women and men do the same things. Thus, in some foraging societies, such as the !Kung, the fact that men hunt and women gather does not mean a system of male dominance. A more recent look at some societies, such as the Inuit, that on the basis of male ethnographies were held to be male dominated suggests that they, too, may be egalitarian in practice, in spite of a slight ideological bias toward male dominance based on hunting of big-game animals (Briggs 1974). In socialist societies, such as the Soviet Union, China, and Israel, there is a strong ideology of sexual egalitarianism. Although the reality may not have matched the ideal, women in these societies make important contributions to the economy and hold political office,

and behavioral equality is upheld by law and by social norms.

An important factor in sexual stratification is the relation of women to the production and distribution of goods. A major question affecting women's status is: "Who will care for the children?" In no society have men taken over child care, or even a substantial proportion of it. Where governments have made communal child care available, women's ability to involve themselves productively in the economy has raised their status; where child care is not addressed, no ideology of equality alone can be sufficient for egalitarianism.

Another factor affecting sexual stratification is the nature of the social institutions. Where the household organization is the central social unit and social groups beyond the household are weak, women's position is likely to be higher than in societies where there are well-organized groups outside the household. The household tends to be the most important unit in a society where production is for subsistence or small-scale exchange and the society's members are not engaged in complex and long-distance trade networks. Furthermore, where the needs of defense or military expansion require male-centered military organizations, or where there are important civil or religious bureaucracies, women's status tends to be lower than otherwise. The influence of Westernization, including European missionary activity and the international market economy, has almost always had the effect of undermining women's status in previously more egalitarian societies (Leacock 1981).

Finally, it must be understood that the particular relationship of the sexes in any society is an outcome of the mingling of many forces—political, economic, social, and ideological—over time. It is through ethnographic detail and analysis of these forces that we can come to see that sexual stratification is not a biological, or even cultural, universal in human societies, but rather a problem to be analyzed and explained.

This infant and child-care center is part of the International Instruments factory in Bangalore, India, which employs a great many female workers. The availability of economically feasible child-care centers is an important factor in allowing women to participate in and benefit from economic development in a society. (Serena Nanda)

PERSPECTIVES ON SOCIAL STRATIFICATION

Social stratification results from the unequal distribution of goods and services within a society. The basic questions here—who gets what and why—depend on cultural values, the organization of production, and the access different individuals and groups within a society have to societal goals. Social scientists approach the understanding of social stratification from two major theoretical perspectives: functionalism and conflict theory.

Functionalism stresses the integrative functions of social stratification and the contribution such systems make to social order, stability, and social functioning. Functionalists hold that the existence of every complex society depends on the regular performance of specific tasks that require special training and intelligence. If the most intelligent, talented, and best-trained individuals are to perform these tasks, they must be motivated by a system of rewards. The assumption is that, if you pay a surgeon the same as a sanitation worker, no one will be a surgeon, since it takes long years of training and involves enormous responsibilities. Thus, a major function of social stratification is that it provides a system of rewards, both material and symbolic, so that all the necessary jobs in society will be filled. From a functionalist perspective, social stratification also contributes to the social order by integrating groups that have common economic and political interests when kinship no longer plays an important integrating role. A system of social stratification is seen as inhibiting social conflict between individuals and groups; social inequality is the price of social stability.

Critics of functionalism point out that societies do not always reward individuals who fulfill the most essential roles. Such vital roles as nurse and schoolteacher, for example, do not carry material or symbolic rewards equal to those of a baseball player or television personality in our own society. Furthermore, a stratification system prevents many intelligent and talented people who are members of low-prestige and powerless groups from gaining access to the training and opportunities that lead to the more highly rewarded occupations and positions in society.

Conflict theory holds that the natural condition of society is change and conflict, not order and stability. From this perspective, social stratification results from the constant struggle for scarce goods and services that takes place in all complex societies. Stratification exists because those who have acquired power, wealth, and prestige exercise their power to keep what they have. This is accomplished not only by the threat of force or the use of force but also by social values and beliefs that justify the present system of inequality in the minds of those in the lower social positions. Conflict theorists contend that stratification not only results from but *generates* conflict, because the interests of the different social classes are opposed. They tend to view conflict and change in a more positive light than functional theorists, since they see progress that results from conflict as better for a society than maintaining the status quo. Thus, conflict theory is useful in calling attention to conflict and change as universal aspects of human life and society. In examining social phenomena such as class and caste, for example, we can look at them from two perspectives: (1) How do such systems contribute to social integration and social order? (2) How do they reflect conflict and stimulate social change?

SUMMARY

1. Social ranking is an important feature of variation in social organization. Anthropologists have identified three types of social systems: egalitarian, rank, and stratified. Egalitarian systems, which are found among hunters and gatherers, give every individual and group in society equal access to basic resources, power, and prestige.

2. Rank societies, or chiefdoms, recognize differences in prestige among individuals and groups, but no one is denied access to the resources necessary for survival. Like egalitarian societies, rank societies are still organized along kinship lines. The ruling family maintains its position largely through the distribution of goods and food throughout the entire society, rather than through force.

3. In stratified societies, social, political, and economic inequality is institutionalized and maintained through a combination of internalized controls, political power, and force. Kinship ties between the upper and lower strata are no longer recognized, and there is a wide gap between them in standard of living. Some of the productive efforts of the lower strata go to support the life style of the upper strata, who control the basic resources but are themselves exempt from food production.

4. The three major dimensions of social stratification are power, wealth, and prestige. Power refers to the ability to control people and things, wealth to accumulation of economic resources, and prestige to the way in which an individual is socially evaluated by others. The particular value system of a culture determines the ways in which power, wealth, and prestige interact to determine where a person will be placed in the stratification system.

5. Two major types of stratification systems are class and caste. In a class system, social position is largely achieved, though it is also determined partly by the class into which a person is born. People may move between social classes, which form a continuum from bottom to top.

6. Social classes can be viewed as subcultures, each characterized by a particular life style. The identification of a culture of poverty has been used by some anthropologists to explain the perpetuation of poverty over several generations. Critics of this concept point out that it is not the culture of poverty that makes people poor, but rather that poor people are excluded from access to the political and economic resources with which they could improve their position.

7. In a caste system, social position is ascribed (based on birth.) Boundaries between castes are sharp, and there is no intermarriage. The Indian caste system is the most complex and is based on Hindu ideas of ritual purity and pollution. Aspects of a caste system are also said to exist in the relations between blacks and whites in the traditional social system of the United States.

8. Sexual stratification and sexual egalitarianism can both be explained by a complex mix of social, economic, political, and cultural institutions. Sexual stratification tends to develop where societies are engaged in complex economic relations with outsiders and in expansionist military activities.

9. Social stratification can be viewed as functional for the social order, because it motivates people to undertake all the jobs necessary for the society to survive. Social stratification can also cause conflict, however; different social strata, with opposing interests, can clash with one another over goals and resources.

perspective that women are universally subordinate to men is derived from the sexual stratification of our own society.

Mills, C. Wright
   1956   *The Power Elite.* New York: Oxford University Press. A well-known conflict theorist puts forth his view that power in the United States is in the hands of top corporate, military, and government leaders.

Ogbu, John
   1974   *The Next Generation: An Ethnography of Education in an Urban Neighborhood.* New York: Academic Press. A Nigerian anthropologist views American education from the perspective of minority groups in the socially stratified society of the United States.

Valentine, Betty Lou
   1978   *Hustling and Other Hard Work.* New York: Free Press. An immensely valuable and readable work with case studies of three families in a poor, black ghetto in the United States. Based on five years of fieldwork by a sensitive and perceptive ethnographer.

Warner, Lloyd W.
   1963   *Yankee City* (abridged edition). New Haven, Conn.: Yale University Press. A readable and interesting work on social class in a New England city.

Wiser, William, and Wiser, Charlotte
   1971   *Behind Mud Walls, 1930–1960.* Berkeley: University of California Press. A classic description of an Indian village, showing the workings of the *jajmani* system. A sequel follows the changes up until 1970.

SUGGESTED READINGS

Leacock, Eleanor Burke
   1981   *Myths of Male Dominance.* New York: Monthly Review Press. A collection of articles by the author. It cogently and persuasively makes the case that the

CHAPTER THIRTEEN

POLITICAL SYSTEMS AND SOCIAL CONTROL

► What happens when people break the rules of their society?

► How do hunters avoid conflict?

► Why do so many tribal societies engage in warfare?

► How can we account for the origin of the state?

The eye of the dove is lovely, my son, but the sky is made for the hawk. So cover your dovelike eyes and grow claws.

A Swat Pukhtun proverb*

All human societies must coordinate and regulate the behavior of their members; all need mechanisms for making and enforcing decisions. At the beginning of this chapter, we will look at two ways in which societies organize and regulate themselves. One is **political organization,** the patterned ways in which legitimate power, or authority, is used to coordinate and regulate behavior; the other is law. Later in the chapter, we will look at the forms of politi-

*Quoted in Charles Lindholm, *Generosity and Jealousy: The Swat Pukhtun of Northern Pakistan*. New York: Columbia University Press, 1982.

cal organization found at different levels of social complexity: band societies, tribal societies, chiefdoms, and states.

REGULATING HUMAN BEHAVIOR

Political Organization

In most societies, the authority to make decisions that affect the public interest is placed in some part of the social system, such as kinship, economics, or religion. Group leaders can rule by virtue of their

Political leaders surround themselves with elaborate symbols of office in order to help legitimize their control. (United Nations)

positions as heads of families, lineages, or clans. In other cases, rulers base their claim on divine ancestry. In some societies, the coordination and regulation of behavior are in the hands of a religious practitioner. If supernatural intervention is an important aspect of the decision-making process—where to hunt, when to move camp, how to find a thief—those who have access to supernatural power will have important political roles in society. If political authority is based on the distribution of goods and services, as it frequently is, leadership will be embedded in economic roles and modes of exchange.

Legitimate power, or authority, means power exercised with the approval of the community. In cases of the legitimate use of power, people obey because they expect that eventually they will benefit from the exercise of that power. We may not like to pay taxes, but we do recognize the right of our government to collect taxes and consider it one of the prices we have to pay for the benefits of government in general. The shared values and beliefs that legitimatize the distribution and uses of power in a particular society make up its **political ideology.** If power is not legitimate, it is coercive; people obey because they are afraid of some immediate, direct, and specific punishment. Although some political systems rest more on

Political processes are the ways in which different, and often conflicting, interest groups mobilize resources to achieve their goals. Shown in this photograph is the peaceful protest by homosexuals in New York City aimed at getting passage of a gay rights bill. The Hassidim, an orthodox Jewish sect, along with other conservative religious groups, demonstrate against the bill. (John McCabe)

coercion than others, both coercion and political ideology play a role in maintaining order in a society.

Up until 1940, anthropologists were primarily interested in how political institutions—the structure of status roles through which legitimate power is exercised in a society—worked to maintain stability. More recently, they have turned their attention to **political processes,** the ways in which groups and individuals mobilize support and use power to achieve a variety of public goals. These goals include changing the relationships between groups in society—for example, the redistribution of material resources or the right of access to political office. Another goal may be changing the relationship of the group to its environment, such as building a road or clearing public land. Political goals may also involve changing the relationship of the group to other groups, such as waging war, making peace, or gaining independence from a colo-

nial power. The motivations behind these goals are many; although all political behavior affects the public interest, it is not always in the public interest. Groups and individuals may be motivated by self-interest, a desire for economic gain, or a need for prestige; they may also be motivated by altruism and idealism.

The study of political processes focuses on political activities and events and the ways in which groups compete with one another for control. Anthropologists look for sources of power outside formal political institutions. One is factions, or informal systems of alliance within well-defined political units such as lineages or villages. Another is leadership, which may depend partly on political office but also on the manipulation of kinship networks or wealth in order to build a following. The study of political processes emphasizes how power changes hands in society and how new kinds of political organization develop.

Political processes are thus not just activities that support the social order, avoid or resolve conflicts, and promote the general welfare. The political goals of a group within a society may, in fact, be to promote conflict, change some of the basic aims of existing political institutions, or even destroy the existing social order. Groups or factions within a society may use illegal or informal means to gain their ends—terrorism, for example—but this does not make these activities any less political. On the other hand, conflict and violence are not *necessarily* destructive. In many societies, violence is a legitimate means of dealing with conflict, as in the case of blood feuds in tribal societies. Conflict may actually support the social order; competition for legitimate goals makes those goals seem worth fighting over. The violent conflict that may occur over succession to office does not destroy the power of the office being sought. The struggle itself emphasizes that the conflicting groups see the office as something worth struggling for. Thus, there is a difference between **rebellion,** the attempt of one group to reallocate resources *within* the existing political structure, and **revolution,** an attempt to overthrow the existing form of political structure and put another type of political structure in its place.

Law

In no human society does life move along in peace and harmony at all times. Individuals do not always do what they are supposed or expected to do, and they frequently act in ways that disrupt the social order. For a society to function adequately, there must be some conformity among its members. An important—perhaps major—basis for conformity in most societies is the internalization, or learning, of norms and values. Most people comply with authority, and most societies do not rely on force to maintain order.

But what happens when people do not want to conform or, rather, want to do things that do not follow the norms and values of their society? Every society has developed mechanisms to deal with this situation. Many of these mechanisms are informal; gossip and ridicule, for example, are important ways of regulating human conduct. Since most individuals value the esteem of others, the fear of being gossiped about or made fun of is a powerful way of ensuring conformity. Witchcraft accusations are another control mechanism. Anyone who stands out in society, is malicious, or has a nasty temper may be accused of being a witch and suffer punishment. Just the fear of being accused exerts pressure on individuals to conform. Avoidance is another informal way of dealing with social deviants. In small societies, where activities are cooperative, an individual who is shunned by others is in a very bad way, both psychologically and economically. Even in our own society, avoidance is a powerful way to get people to conform. One of the strongest expressions of anger, and one often used by small children who have few resources at their command with which to control others, is to say, "I'm not going to talk to you anymore."

Supernatural sanctions are also important in regulating human behavior. A sin is a deviant behavior that is believed to call forth punishment by supernatural forces. In the Trobriand Islands, incest is a sin; an individual who engages in this behavior is punished by a divinely imposed skin affliction. Supernatural forces that punish social deviants are found in every culture; there are ghosts, spirits, giants who eat little children—even a Santa Claus who does not give presents to children who do not behave.

But what of those who just will not conform? Every society has such people. What is to be done with them? This is where law comes in. In *The Law of Primitive Man*, E. Adamson Hoebel (1974) defines **law** as "those social norms whose neglect or infraction is regularly met, in threat or in fact, by the application of force by an individual or group who have the socially recognized privilege of acting this way" (p. 28). In every society, some offenses are considered so disruptive that force or the threat of force will be applied. It may be applied by official representatives of the community, such as judges, courts, police, and jails. It may also be done by individuals with community approval; kin of a murdered man may be allowed, or even expected, to revenge him by killing someone from the murderer's kin group. The control of deviant behavior is therefore a major function of law in all societies.

Law also operates to resolve conflicts that would otherwise be disruptive to community life. In politically complex societies such as modern states, crimes against the state are differentiated from grievances that individuals have against one another. In structurally simpler societies, disputes between individuals may be handled by the community in the interests of maintaining order. Conflicts between individuals may involve the whole community as judge, as in Inuit song duels. Or a go-between may try to get the complainants to settle. In some societies, go-betweens have the authority to enforce their decisions; in others, they can only persuade the parties

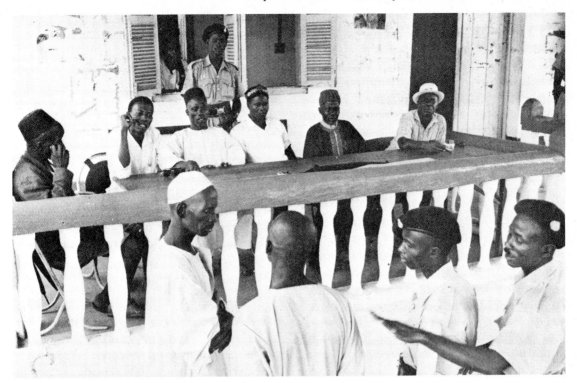

The village court in Sierra Leone is administered by a tribunal of local leaders headed by the chief. The defendant (center with shaved heads) faces the tribunal on charges of possessing stolen goods at the time of his arrest. The chief's police officer (left, with white skull cap) acts as defender for the accused. In this case, the defendant was given three months at hard labor and a fine. (United Nations)

to resolve their differences peaceably. In still other cases, supernatural powers are called upon—for example, in cases of trial by ordeal.

The anthropology of law, like political anthropology, has also redefined its emphasis in the last twenty years. Now the focus is more on the informal and formal ways in which behavior is regulated and conflicts are resolved in a society than on the formal legal institutions with which we are familiar. At one time, there were heated arguments over whether primitive societies, with no formal institutions for regulating behavior, could be said to have law. Such questions are no longer of interest to most anthropologists. All societies have "trouble cases," incidents of individual behavior that contradict important social norms or conflicts between individuals that cannot be settled informally between themselves. Every society includes patterned ways of responding to these cases, and it is in this response that law is found. Because political organization includes both the ways in which public policy is made and the ways in which it is enforced in a society, our study of political organization also includes the study of law.

Kinds of Political Organization

Political organization and law exist in all societies, but not all societies have specialized, formal mechanisms through which authority is exercised and law is enforced. The main point about variation in political organizations is, in fact, the degree to which political roles, institutions, and processes are differentiated from other aspects of social organization. A second important aspect of variation is the degree to which authority is centralized or diffused throughout society. Both aspects of political variation, in turn, are related to social complexity, the number of different *kinds* of groups in a society and the ways in which they are connected to one another. Using social complexity as a standard, anthropologists have defined four major types of political organization (Service 1971). In order of their complexity, these are band societies, tribal societies, chiefdoms, and states. Each type tends to be correlated with a particular way of making a living, population size and density, economic system, and pattern of social ranking. Of course, these exact types are not always found in the real world; many societies have some but not all the characteristics of an ideal type.

BAND LEVEL SOCIETIES

Band organization, which is the least complex type of society, is characteristic of hunters and gatherers. Reciprocity is the dominant economic pattern in band societies. There is no concept of private ownership of basic resources, such as land or water, although bands may be loosely identified with certain territories. Band societies are egalitarian; there is little role specialization and little difference among the members in terms of wealth, prestige, or power.

Political Integration

A **band** is a relatively small group of people (twenty to fifty) made up of nuclear families who live together and are loosely associated with a territory on which they hunt and gather.

Bands are relatively independent of one another. There are few higher levels of control or centralized mechanisms of leadership.

Bands are exogamous (people must marry out), and ties between bands are established mainly by marriage. Because a bilateral kinship system is characteristic of band societies, an individual is linked to many different bands through ties of blood and marriage. Bands may also be linked through the trading relations of some of their members. Membership in bands is quite flexible, and individuals may change their residence from one band to another fairly easily. The flexibility of band organization is particularly adaptive for the hunting and gathering way of life and low population densities.

Leadership

There is no formal leadership in band societies. Leaders in foraging bands are usually older men whose experience, knowledge of group traditions, and success in hunting are the source of their respect by others. Leaders have no way of enforcing their views; decisions are usually made by all adult men in the group, and leaders can only persuade. Others follow them if they have been successful in the past. Among Inuit groups, for example, the local level leader is called "The One to Whom All Listen," "He Who Thinks" or "He Who Knows Everything Best." Successful Inuit whaling captains who do not generously distribute their accumulated wealth among the group are called merely "rich men" and are distinguished from those whose superior ability and generosity make them respected leaders in the village.

The !Kung of the Kalahari in Africa also have headmen, and among some groups this office is passed from father to son. The band headman is not necessarily the group leader, however; members may turn to any individual of intelligence and skill for guidance. Neither headman nor leaders gain any political or economic advantage from their position: "Every person does his own work, carries his own load and shares meat." Nothing special in the way of wealth or status marks them out from others. The main duty of a !Kung headman is to manage the band's resources, primarily water and vegetable foods, and to plan where the band will migrate within its territory. Visitors to the band must ask his permission before gathering plant foods and taking water, although, as one informant told Laura Marshall, an anthropologist who worked among the !Kung, "If you are very thirsty, you have no time to ask permission" (1967).

Social Control

In band societies, social order is maintained informally by gossip, ridicule, and avoidance. In extreme cases, an individual may be killed or driven out of the community. Among the !Kung, for example, the sharing of meat is so strongly established that they can hardly conceive of an individual's not doing this. When Marshall tried to suggest that an individual could hide with his family in order not to share meat with others, the !Kung "howled with laughter. They said that a man would be very bad to do that. He would be like a lion. They would have to treat him like a lion by driving him away or teach him manners by not giving him any meat . . . not even a tiny piece." Stealing is another crime among the !Kung, although it occurs rarely. An individual's footprints are as recognizable as his face, and a thief can easily be detected. In the one case of stealing recounted to Marshall, a man who stole another's cache of honey was killed by the owner.

Although theft and the refusal to share food are serious offenses in most band societies, not all are as successful as the !Kung in regulating them. The Siriono, a hunting society of the Amazon, have a similar norm, but it is recognized more in the breach. Siriono frequently attempted to hide food, and families would

steal off to the forest in the night to eat in order to avoid sharing. Unlike the !Kung, however, the Siriono live in a difficult environment and are constantly on the brink of starvation (Holmberg 1969). Where food is very scarce, social norms about sharing may break down altogether, as illustrated by the selfishness of the Ik of Uganda, described by Colin Turnbull (1972). Theirs is a truly frightening story of a society in which almost perpetual starvation led children to take food from the mouths of their old parents, and people who shared were ridiculed as fools.

Among the Inuit, supernatural sanctions are an important means of social control. Violations of norms are considered sins, and offenders may be controlled through ritual means. Public confessions are directed by the shaman. The offender is defined as a patient, rather than a criminal, and is led to confess all the taboos he or she has violated. The local villagers form the audience and participate as a background chorus. These confessions are mainly voluntary, although a forceful shaman may denounce a member of the community he feels has engaged in acts repulsive to the spirits and is therefore dangerous to the whole group. A person who fails to obey the orders of the shaman may be driven from the community.

Conflict Resolution

Although the need for cooperation and reciprocity minimizes conflicts between individuals in band societies, they do occur and may even become quite violent. Under the conditions of band society, where the effective social unit is a small group of persons in face-to-face contact, quarrels and conflicts between individuals have a way of involving many other group members. Though few formal institutions exist for resolving conflicts, social mechanisms do operate to prevent them from seriously threatening the social order.

The Mbuti of the Ituri forest, for example, have a process called flux (Turnbull 1968). Among the Mbuti, there is great flexibility in the composition of local groups; individuals may change their residence quite easily, and bands regularly break up into smaller units and reform into larger ones throughout the year. Breaking the band down into smaller units always separates individuals who have been in conflict with one another, thus preventing prolonged hostilities.

Among some Inuit groups, disputes between individuals are resolved through various kinds of contests. Some of these are physical, such as head butting or a kind of boxing. Others are verbal, like the famous song duels, where the weapons are words—"little, sharp words like the wooden splinters which I hack off with my ax" (Hoebel 1974:93). Although murder is normally resolved by a killing, a man may choose to revenge his kin in a song duel if he feels too weak to kill his opponent, or if he knows he will win the song contest. Each contestant in a song duel tries to deliver the traditional compositions with the greatest skill. The one for whom the audience claps the loudest is the winner. Winning the song duel has little or nothing to do with the facts of a dispute. But it does resolve the quarrel and restore normal relations between those who have become hostile toward each other. The original complaint is laid to rest, and a "judgment" is laid down that is accepted by the contestants.

There is fighting in band societies, both verbal and physical. Violent aggression of an individual nature is not infrequent, and it can result in death or serious injuries. But warfare or armed conflict between socially defined groups of people is not formalized in most band societies because of the low level of technology and simple political organization. Among band level hunting and gathering societies, war usually takes the form of family feuding that may continue for generations. There is no formal organization for war and no position of warrior. Military activity is contained within the patterns of kinship. There is little production for warfare and little organized social mobilization to support armed combat. In band societies, the primary objectives of war are likely to be personal; the motivations for fighting are the personal grievances of one individual or a small group of people. Fighting takes place in short skirmishes. Where band societies come into contact with technologically and culturally more dominant groups, the bands tend to retreat into marginal areas rather than fight. They isolate themselves or form peaceful relations with their neighbors (Harrison 1973:42).

TRIBAL SOCIETIES

A **tribe** is a culturally distinct population whose members think of themselves as descended from the same ancestor or as part of the same "people." Tribes occur primarily among pastoralists and horticulturalists, and they are integrated economically by both reciprocity and redistribution. Like bands, tribes are basically egalitarian, with no important differences among members in wealth, status, and power. Also like bands, tribes do not have a separate and distinct set of political roles and institutions. Tribes are usually organized by unilineal kin groups. It is these groups that are the units of political activity as well as the "owners" of basic economic resources. The emergence of local kin groups larger than the nuclear family goes with the larger populations that develop in horticultural and pastoral societies.

The effective political unit in these societies is a shifting one. For most of the time, local units of a tribe operate independently. They come together in response to external conditions—either the threat of attack or the opportunity to attack others. Otherwise, little tribal-level organization exists. In fact, under certain conditions, segments of a tribe may be in a state of perpetual violent conflict. As is the case with bands, tribal political organization and mechanisms of social control are embedded in institutions such as kinship or religion. Political functions and roles are not specialized.

Political Integration

The major difference between band and tribe is that a tribal society contains mechanisms that integrate the local segments of the society. Age grades are one kind of association; military societies (clubs) or secret societies also cut across and integrate the segments that make up a tribe. The clan is a form of tribal association based on kinship, and clans may even link members of different tribes.

One form of tribal integration that clearly shows the shifting nature of the political unit in tribal society is a **segmentary lineage system.** In this system, individuals belong to multiple descent units, or segments, that form at different genealogical levels and function in different contexts. Among the Nuer of East Africa (Figure 13.1), for example, there are about twenty clans, each of which is divided into lineages. Below the level of the clan are segments called maximal lineages, which are themselves broken down into major lineages. Major lineages are, in turn, subdivided into minor lineages, and minor lineages are made up of minimal lineages. The minimal lineage contains three to five generations and is the basic permanent descent group that functions in day-to-day activities. Members of a minimal lineage live in the same village and regard one another as the closest relatives. The minimal lineages are politically independent, and there is no formal or centralized leadership above this level.

Only when there is conflict between two minimal segments does the higher order of lineage structure come into play. Minor, major, and maximal lineages are not groups; they are alliance networks that emerge only in opposition to one another. In a serious dispute between members of different minimal lineages, other groups take the side of their nearest kin. The conflict thus becomes one that matches the highest-order lineages involved. Anthropologists call this kind of political structure complementary opposition (Evans-Pritchard 1968). Marshall Sahlins (1961) suggests that the

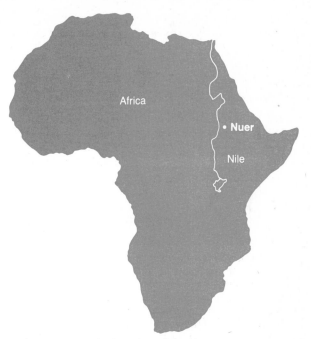

Figure 13.1   *The location of the Nuer.*

segmentary system allows stronger tribes to expand into nearby desirable territories held by weaker groups. Complementary opposition directs the energies of the society upward, away from the competition between kin, to the outside enemy. Lineage segments on the borders of other tribes know that, if they attack an enemy, they will be helped by other lineages related to them at the higher levels of organization.

Tribes with segmentary lineage systems are expanding populations. The Nuer have expanded at the expense of the Dinka, a neighboring pastoral group that originally inhabited the grasslands desired by the Nuer for pasturing their livestock. Because the Dinka were the first in this area and had neither enemies to fight nor neighbors to push back, they did not develop strong mechanisms of tribal integration. The Nuer were the invaders in this area. Their segmentary lineage system developed in response to the need for expansion, and they have, in fact, been successful in pushing the Dinka off much of their land.

In social systems based on complementary opposition, such as that of the Swat Pukhtun of Northern Pakistan, brothers and cousins are often pitted against each other in the struggle for power. In Pukhtun society, therefore, friendship between two unrelated males is highly idealized. (John Gregg)

Leadership

Like bands, tribal societies have leaders but no centralized leadership and no formal offices that are a source of political power. Among the Nuer, for example, the head of the minimal descent group can use his authority to threaten members of the local group with banishment if they do not agree to settle a dispute. Among many native American populations, there were different kinds of leaders for different kinds of activities. The Cheyenne had war chiefs and peace chiefs. Among the Ojibwa of Canada, there were war leaders, hunting leaders, ceremonial leaders, and clan leaders. Europeans who first came in contact with the Ojibwa frequently misinterpreted the system and imposed on the Ojibwa the concept of a supreme leader or chief. A much better translation of tribal leader in many of these groups is "big man." When the Canadian government insisted that the Ojibwa must have a chief, the Ojibwa coined a native word, *okimakkan*, which is best translated as "fake chief."

Under certain ecological and social conditions, a more substantial kind of political leadership may emerge in tribal societies. In areas with predictable climate and relatively abundant resources, strong authority roles or true chiefs emerge. The Basseri of Southern Iran are a tribe of pastoral nomads with a strong chieftaincy. On their migrations, the Basseri move through areas used by other tribes. To avoid exhaustive grazing of an area, famine of the flocks, and intertribal fighting, the Basseri must stick to their migration schedules and fixed routes. One of the important functions of the Basseri chief, therefore, is to coordinate the movements of the tribe.

The Basseri chief's strength rests not only on the need for a strong authority to coordinate migration movements but also on the role he plays in mediating between the tribe and the settled agricultural populations with whom the Basseri interact. The Basseri must pass through land inhabited by farmers under centralized bureaucratic control. They negotiate contracts with these agriculturalists for using pastureland, and they also exchange products with them. These interactions can result in conflicts; for example, a nomad's herds may damage a farmer's crops. Because the nomad and the farmer operate within two different social systems, informal mechanisms of conflict resolution cannot be used to settle their differences. Furthermore, the nomad, because he must be on the move, cannot take the time to become involved in lengthy court proceedings, which are a regular way of settling disputes among farmers. The nomad may not even be able to respond to a court summons without hardship. Violence is, of course, a solution, one that has been used frequently in the past. But for peaceful resolution of farmer-nomad conflicts, other political mechanisms must come into play. This is provided by the institution of centralized chieftaincy. The chief represents a fixed point in the nomadic community on which the farmer can fix his grievance. Because a chief has a domestic staff and is relieved from the actual duties of pastoral-

ism, he has the time to work at conflict resolution and can represent the interests of his
tribe. Nomads recognize the need for a chief
in these situations and have a great feeling of
respect for him and awareness of their dependence on him, all of which strengthen his power
(Barth 1964).

Another kind of tribal leader is characteristic of societies throughout Melanesia and New
Guinea. This is the big man, a self-made leader
who gains power through personal achievements rather than through holding office. He
begins his career as the leader of a small, localized kin group. Through a series of public
actions, such as generous loans, the big man
attracts followers within the community. He
skillfully builds up his capital and increases
the number of his wives. Since women take
care of pigs, he can increase the size of his pig
herds. He distributes his wealth in ways that
build his reputation as a rich and generous
man: by sponsoring feasts, paying subsidies to
military allies, purchasing high ranks in secret
societies, and paying bridewealth for young
men seeking wives. By giving generously, he
places many other people under obligation to
him. Big men command obedience from their
followers through this personal relationship of
gratitude and obligation.

The activities of big men do provide leadership above the local level, but this integration is fragile. It depends not on the creation
of permanent office, but on the personality and
constant striving of an individual. Big men rise
and fall. With their deaths, their faction may
dissolve, or other ambitious men may undermine their power. Most important, however,
the big man must spur his local group on to
ever greater production if he is to hold his own
against other big men in the tribe. To maintain
prestige, he must give his competitors more
than they can give him. This means the big
man must begin to withhold gifts to the followers who are producing for him. The discontent this brings may lead to the defection
of the followers or even the murder of the big
man. A big man cannot pass on his status to

*It may be that native American tribal "chiefs" were
created by Europeans who projected their own
systems of centralized political office on groups
with whom they came in contact. Dealing with one
leader was easier than dealing with a collective
body. (Courtesy of the American Museum of
Natural History)*

others; each individual must begin anew to
amass the wealth and forge the internal and
external social relationships on which big man
status depends (Sahlins 1971).

Social Control and Conflict Resolution

Tribes, like bands, depend a great deal on
informal ways of controlling deviant behavior
and settling conflicts, but they have also developed more formal mechanisms of control. The
Cheyenne were particularly successful in
peacefully resolving intratribal conflict and in
controlling individual behavior when this was
necessary for the common good. Their relatively formal structure of social control came
into play during the summer season, when
Cheyenne bands came together for great communal buffalo hunts and tribal ceremonies.
Order was necessary to prevent disputes, and
strict discipline was required on the buffalo

ETHNOGRAPHY

THE KPELLE MOOT: THE INFORMAL SETTLEMENT OF DISPUTES IN AN AFRICAN SOCIETY*

Many traditional societies in West Africa are known for their high development of law and legal procedures. In addition to these formal procedures and courts, however, there are also informal, quasi-legal procedures for settling disputes. One such procedure, found among the Kpelle of Liberia, is called the moot, or "house palaver." The Kpelle are rice cultivators who live in Central Liberia (see map on p. 277). The most important kinship group is the patrilocal polygynous family; several of these families form the core of a residential group, known as a village quarter, headed by a quarter elder. In Liberia the highest official court is that of a paramount chief; there are also official courts of the district chief. There are also unofficial town chief, or quarter elder, courts, and in addition, grievances are settled informally at moots. Kpelle courts are basically coercive and handle best those types of cases, such as assault or theft, in which the litigants are

*Based on James L. Gibbs, Jr., "The Kpelle Moot: A Therapeutic Model for the Informal Settlement of Disputes," in Johnetta B. Cole, ed., *Anthropology for the Eighties.* New York: The Free Press, 1982.

not linked in a relationship that must continue after the trial. The courts are not effective, however, in the many matrimonial cases brought before them, because the courts' harsh and official tone tends to drive spouses apart rather than reconciling them. Kpelle courts customarily treat matrimonial cases by granting the couple a divorce. The moot, on the other hand, tends to reconcile the couple; it is successful in doing this because it is not only conciliatory but also therapeutic.

The Kpelle moot takes place before an assembled group that includes kinsmen of the litigants and neighbors from the quarter where the case is being heard. The cases before it are usually domestic matters: alleged mistreatment by a spouse, an attempt to collect money from a kinsman for a job not completed, or a quarrel among brothers over the inheritance of their father's wives. The moot is most often held on a Sunday—a universal day of rest among the Kpelle—at the home of the complainant, the person who calls the moot. The mediator at the moot is selected by the complainant. He is a kinsman who also holds an office, such as

quarter elder, and thus has experience in handling disputes. The proceedings begin with one of the group elders pronouncing a blessing on the complainant and his relations. The elder does this dramatically, walking up and down, waving a fly whisk, and demanding that the assembled group join him. The effect is to unite those attending in common action before the hearing begins and to focus attention on the concern with maintaining harmony and the well-being of the group as a whole. The litigants and spectators, including the elders, sit crowded together, in sharp contrast to the spatial separation between litigants and judges in a courtroom. The mediator, though a chief, wears ordinary clothing.

The complainant speaks first and may be interrupted by the mediator or anyone else present. After he or she has been thoroughly questioned and is also questioned by those present. The two parties question each other directly and question others in the room. The meeting is spirited and lively, but order is maintained by the mediator. The mediator and others point out the various faults committed by both parties. After everyone has been heard, the mediator expresses the consensus of the group. The person held to be mainly at fault then formally apologizes to the other person. This apology takes the form of giving token gifts such as clothing, a few coins, or some rice to the wronged person. The winning party, in accepting the gifts of apology, is expected to give, in return, a smaller token to the loser to show good will. The losing party must also present beer to the mediator and the spectators, and it is then consumed. The elder again pronounces a blessing, offers thanks for the restoration of harmony within the group, and asks that all continue to act with good grace and unity.

A comparison with a court case highlights the therapeutic effectiveness of the moot. Whereas in a courtroom, grievances can be only partially aired, in the moot, there is a much fuller airing of the issues, and the range of relevant material is very broad. This fuller airing results in catharsis; if the solution to a dispute reached in the moot is to be lasting, it is important that there should be nothing left unsaid that will embitter either party and undermine the decision.

Secondly, the resolution of the case is not a solution imposed by a judge, but is based on consensus. There is no unilateral ascription of blame, but an attribution of fault to both parties. The ritualized apology symbolizes concretely the consensual nature of the solution. The public offering and acceptance of the tokens of apology indicate that neither party has

any further grievances. The parties and the spectators drink together to symbolize the restored solidarity of the group and the rehabilitation of the offending party. This group support, which is heightened by the opening and closing blessings, is very important in indicating to both parties that they have a real problem, but that others are concerned and willing to help them. This support motivates the participants to speak freely and thus move toward a lasting resolution of their problems. Furthermore, in the moot, the litigants are allowed to say things to each other that would probably result in a citation of contempt and possible jail sentence if they were in a court. In hurling recriminations, litigants invite response from the spectators, who frequently gently reprimand them for being in the wrong. Thus, the litigants are able to see that their own perspective may not be based in reality and are moved to reconsider their position. Finally, just as the patient is coaxed to conformity by the granting of rewards in the therapeutic situation, so the reward of group approval is granted publicly in the moot, both to the wronged person who accepts an apology and to the person who is big enough to make one. In this way, the wrongdoer is restored to good grace; since blame is typically spread around, he or she is not singled out and isolated in being labeled deviant. Moreover, the "fines," or token gifts, are not so expensive as to give the loser additional reason for anger directed at the winning party. The rewards of the moot are

positive, in contrast to the negative sanctions of the courtroom. The deviant is pulled back into a relationship with the wider group; if the moot is successful, reconciliation will be achieved with no residue of bitterness or resentment. In the case of married couples, then, the successful moot results in reconciliation, not divorce; in other relationships that must continue outside the case, it is hoped that the moot will finish off people's quarrels and abolish bad feeling.

The moot and similar institutions in other societies are mechanisms of social control that break the progressive alienation of the deviance cycle, something that is normally not achieved in a more formal court proceeding. The model of the West African moot has become the basis for a reexamination of many court procedures in the United States. As courts become more crowded and inaccessible for various kinds of disputes between parties who are in relatively long-term relationships, the process of mediation, or informal dispute resolution, has mushroomed all over America (Tomasic and Feeley 1982). Legal and social reformers are hoping that these new neighborhood justice centers, which utilize the "house palaver" model, will make justice more responsive to people's needs.

hunt. An individual hunter could ruin the hunt for others by alarming and scattering the buffalo. These tribal gatherings and communal hunts were policed by members of military associations. The associations not only punished offenders but also tried to rehabilitate the guilty parties by bringing them back within the tribal structure. The function of the police was not revenge, but getting the deviant to conform to tribal law in the interest of the welfare of the tribe. Individuals were punished by a variety of methods. Sometimes their teepees were ripped to shreds, or the ears of their horses were cut off, a mark of shame. Offenders might also be whipped. If they resisted, they might be killed on the spot. If, however, they accepted the punishment and appeared to have learned a lesson, they were accepted back into the group, and their belongings were often replaced. But the Cheyenne military societies operated only during the hunt period. At other times, more informal sanctions and leadership operated at the band level.

Another means of regulating behavior in tribal societies is through the use of go-betweens. Among the Nuer, a Leopard Skin chief acts as a mediator, particularly in cases where a killing takes place. As in other tribal societies, when one person kills another, retaliation can be expected from the dead person's kin and may begin a true feud. After a killing, the killer may seek sanctuary in the home of the Leopard Skin chief. The chief goes to the home of the slayer's family and gets the family to promise to pay a certain number of cattle to the dead person's family. He then goes to the family of the victim and tries to get them to accept this compensation. The Leopard Skin chief can only mediate, however; he cannot compel either of the families to accept the settlement. In the case of other kinds of disputes, such as that over ownership of cattle, the chief and perhaps other respected elders in the community may attempt to get the two sides to make a settlement through public discussion. There is no means of enforcing their suggestions, however. Although go-betweens have little or no authority to enforce their decisions, they express the general interest of society in ending tension, punishing wrongs, and restoring social stability. Go-betweens, with the power of public opinion behind them, are usually effective. But if a settlement cannot be agreed upon, a feud will begin, undertaken by the aggrieved party.

Formal, complex, and specialized systems for resolving conflicts and regulating behavior are particularly well developed in West Africa. Among the Ibo, for example, the body of elders met in a central council to act as mediators and referees in settling disputes. In these courts, or councils, the senior elder opened the proceedings by a prayer to the gods to enable them to come to the right decisions and punish anyone who attempted to pervert justice or any witness who gave false evidence. In some towns, a council elder was first made to swear that he would not make decisions in secret, take sides in disputes, appropriate communal or other property by force, or use public monies for his own purposes.

All offenses did not result in a trial. A criminal might be punished by the family or by the person against whom he or she had committed the crime. Murderers could hang themselves or get a relative to substitute, and the case would be considered closed. Trials were held when a case was in doubt. The elders who tried cases took into account the social position of those accused, the strength of their kin relations, and whether they were useful members of society, as well as the seriousness of the offense. If after the evidence was heard, the case was still in doubt, it was decided by an oath or an ordeal. An **ordeal** is a means of determining guilt or innocence by having those who are accused submit themselves to dangerous or painful tests believed to be under supernatural control. Among the Ibo, the drinking of poison was an ordeal. The use of ordeals means that judges do not have to put their own prestige on the line in every judgment. Where there is no central political authority to enforce decisions, mediators need the extra weight of supernatural backing to ensure that people will comply (Meek 1972).

Nomadic pastoralists, like horticulturalists, also have a tendency to engage in feuding and warfare. Warfare among pastoralists is most frequently associated with raiding other groups for animals, a way of bringing about a balance between population and resources. The approach to warfare that stresses the interrelationship among ecology, social structure, level of sociocultural complexity, and conflict is a good example of the kinds of understanding anthropologists seek. The studies of Harris (1976), Vayda (1976), and others indicate that warfare can be explained *not* by attributing it to some human instinct for aggression, but rather by understanding its relationship to other ecological and sociocultural factors—that is, as part of a total sociocultural system.

The function of warfare in regulating the balance between population and resources in tribal populations is related to the absence of strong mechanisms for tribal integration through peaceful means, and to the absence of strong motivations to produce food over and above immediate needs. An economic surplus, which can support more specialized and centralized political authority really emerges with the level of sociocultural integration called a chiefdom.

CHIEFDOMS

Two main characteristics distinguish chiefdoms from tribes. Unlike a tribe, in which all segments are structurally and functionally similar, a **chiefdom** is made up of parts that are structurally and functionally different from one another. A ranking system means that some lineages, and the individuals in them, have higher or lower social status than others. As we saw for Polynesia and the Northwest Coast of America, rulers, nobles, and commoners may be distinguished from one another by genealogical closeness to the chief. There may also be geographical units within a chiefdom, each of which has its own chief or council.

The second difference between tribes and chiefdoms is that a chiefdom has a centralized leadership that consists of an *office* of chief (as opposed, for example, to the individualistic and self-made leadership provided by a Melanesian big man). The rise of a centralized governing center—that is, the chief and his political authority—is closely related to redistributive exchange patterns. Goods move into the center (the chief) and are redistributed through the chief's generosity in giving feasts and sponsoring rituals. The economic surplus created by the chief level of organization is used to benefit the whole society, though at the same time it is the primary support of the chief's power and prestige.

An economic surplus gives members of a chiefdom a greater measure of security than is possible in a tribal society. The chief can distribute labor as well as food. In addition, centralized authority prevents the outbreak of violence between segments of the society, and at the same time it gives the society a greater degree of military power vis-à-vis other societies than tribes are able to muster. Chiefdoms are found mainly in pastoral societies or those in which intensive agriculture is practiced, though they also existed among the hunting and fishing societies of the Northwest Coast of America.

Regulation of Behavior and Conflict Resolution

Internal violence within chiefdoms is reduced, because the chief has authority to make judgments, to punish deviant individuals, and to resolve disputes. In the Trobriand Islands, the power of a chief to punish people is achieved partly by hiring sorcerers to kill the offender by black magic. The greatest power of the Trobriand chief lies in his power to control garden magic. As "garden magician" he not only organizes the efforts of the villagers under his control but also performs the rituals considered necessary for success at every step—preparing the fields, planting, and harvesting.

Warfare in Tribal Societies

As we have seen earlier (Chapter Five), the idea that aggressive instincts provide the basis for war has tended to wither under the impact of ethnographic evidence of war-free societies, as well as primate studies. Anthropological explanations of war have generally accepted the theory that aggression is learned and have attempted to understand war in terms of the social and ecological contexts in which it occurs. One view has been to link warfare to aspects of social structure such as patrilineality and patrilocality, which by promoting male solidarity make the resort to force to solve conflicts more feasible than in matrilineal and matrilocal societies, which undermine fraternal solidarity and engender conflicting loyalties among males. On the other hand, patrilocality and matrilocality may develop out of societies that have different types of warfare. When warfare is carried out over long distances, for example, matrilocality favors domestic harmony when the warriors are away.

Although anthropologists may not agree about the specific causes of warfare, one area of wide agreement is that war is grounded in material, or ecological, conditions. In tribal societies, particularly, most recent theories of warfare stress important elements of competition over resources or point to warfare as a way of regulating the relations between human populations and resources. One of the earliest proponents of this view (Hunt 1940) convincingly demonstrated, for example, that the wars of the Iroquois were a struggle to control the fur trade. This perspective is consistent with research over the last twenty years that has attempted to show that warfare may be adaptive in a number of ways in tribal society—for example, in redistributing land or animal protein (see Rappaport's study in Chapter 14). One of the most elaborate and controversial theories to explain the prevalence of warfare in tribal society was developed by William Divale and Marvin Harris (1976). Although they used ethnographic material from the Yanomamo, the "fierce" people studied by Napoleon Chagnon, Divale and Harris believe that their theory can be generalized to many other tribal, tropical-forest horticulturalists.

Figure 13.2   The location of the Yanomamo.

Feuding and warfare appear to be constant in many tribal societies. Among the Yanomamo (Figure 13.2), intertribal hostility and warfare are almost a way of life. Yanomamo villages organize and conduct war parties against one another not for land, but to steal each other's women. In a Yanomamo raid, as many men as possible are killed, and as many women as possible are captured. According to their ethnographer, Chagnon (1977), the constant warfare and militant ideology of the Yanomamo are a way of preserving village autonomy. Because the Yanomamo have not been able to control conflict within villages, fights often break out among individuals. This leads to the division of villages into independent and hostile camps. In order to be able to survive as an independent unit in an environment of constant warfare, members of a village adopt a hostile and aggressive stance toward other villagers. Yanomamo aggressiveness is encouraged from childhood and reinforced by a cultural pattern that demands a display of ferocity on the part of males. This ferocity is demonstrated not only in the fights between men but also in the way husbands treat their wives.

Warfare among the Yanomamo, as well as among other horticultural groups, has been explained as a way of controlling population. Divale and Harris (1976) argue that war regulates population indirectly by leading to female infanticide, not by causing deaths in battle. In societies where warfare is constant, there is a cultural preference for fierce and aggressive males who can become warriors. Since male children are preferred over females, female infants are frequently killed. Among the Yanomamo, the shortage of women that results from female infanticide appears as a strong *conscious* motivation for warfare, thus providing a continuing "reason" for the Yanomamo to keep fighting among themselves. In the absence of effective contraception and abortion, the most effective and widespread means of regulating population growth is reducing the number of fertile females.

However persuasive Divale and Harris's argument is for the Yanomamo, it is not necessarily valid for all tribal groups in which war is a predominant feature. Andrew Vayda (1976) has suggested that a critical factor is the fact that most of these societies practice slash and burn horticulture. Because it is much harder to clear forest for cultivation than to work land that has already been used, a local group may prefer to take land from other groups, by force if necessary, rather than expand into virgin forest. This sets up a condition in which warfare is a way for societies that have experienced a decrease in food supplies due to population increase, or that have reached the limits of expansion into unoccupied land, to expand. Where there are effective nonwarlike ways in which population can be redistributed within the total territory of the tribe, tribes may not be warlike or may direct their aggressive activities outward toward other tribes. According to Vayda, the Maori of New Zealand are an example of the first model, and the Iban of Sarawak are an example of the second.

Warfare in tribal societies seems to be correlated with the absence of overarching, formal, conflict-resolving mechanisms, although even among the fierce Yanomamo, for example, various informal mechanisms inhibit most small hostilities from escalating into full-fledged warfare between villages. This raises the question of the relationship between political evolution and warfare. Warfare can be examined as part of the process of political evolution; it often, though not inevitably, tends to lead to increased political centralization through the increased need to regulate daily life, especially the suppression of internal conflicts. Further, since waging war is costly, it often leads to increasingly centralized control over production. In contrasting war in tribal, egalitarian societies with war in our own society, a major issue is that warfare in tribal societies must essentially be carried out by the voluntary contribution of adult males. In a state society, coercion replaces voluntariness. Furthermore, although in tribal societies, it is possible that some individuals benefit more than others from going to war, in state societies, it becomes clear that there are divergent interests in going to war, and that some economic and political groups benefit much more than others. It is when this fact is perceived that coercion replaces voluntariness. As Brian Ferguson so aptly states in his introduction to a comparative study of warfare (1984), the view that warfare is not universal or inevitable but arises from a complex interaction of factors, including competition over scarce resources, need not mean that modern states are destined to wage war over raw materials and cheap labor. Rather, this viewpoint directs our attention to the economic and political interests of those who decide military policy. The costs and benefits of warfare in modern states are unequally distributed. The myth of instinctive and inevitable human aggression as a cause of warfare is an important prop of militarism in the United States, and it is congenial to some of our most important cultural values. Anthropologists, in uncovering the "hidden agenda" in warfare in a wide range of societies, including our own, can make a real contribution to understanding what circumstances engender in people the motivation to go to war and perhaps, ultimately, contribute to controlling warfare in the future by illuminating its causes in the past.

Among pastoral tribes the office of chief is an important one. This Bedouin
sheikh is shown with his two sons. (United Nations)

The ultimate power of the chief is his magical
control of rain; if he wishes, he can produce a
prolonged drought, which will cause many
people to starve. This power is used when the
chief is angry as a means of collective punishment and enforcement of his will.

Among the Basseri, the chief, or *khan*, has
great power in settling disputes. Disputes come
to the chief only after informal methods within
the camp have failed to achieve a settlement.
Once a dispute is brought to the chief, he can
dispose of the case at his will. His decisions
must be obeyed, and an individual who does
not comply is beaten with a pole. In other societies, even where chiefs have equally strong
powers, they choose to rule with tact and
kindness, rather than by the use of force. Clellan Ford (1938:545) describes the actions of a
wise Fijian chief in the following case:

*A woman had gotten angry at her husband, who
had failed to fix their leaky roof. One rainy night
she threatened to kill him with a knife. She
chased him around the room and finally aimed
a blow at his head. The husband grabbed a mat
from the floor to use as a shield. The knife struck
the mat and rebounded on the woman's head,
resulting in a deep cut. On hearing of this, the
chief called both parties together, and listened
with great seriousness to their arguments. The
wife complained her husband was lazy and spent
all his time drinking* **kava.** *The husband complained his wife neglected her duties and seldom cooked for him. The chief could easily have
disposed of the matter by fining the husband
and the wife for causing trouble. Instead, he
sensed an underlying tension in the relationship, of which this fight was only a symptom.
He called members of the village and heard
their testimony. It appeared that the woman
thought herself too good for her husband, and*

he felt and resented this. The chief got the husband and wife to admit this. He then ordered the woman to be a better spouse and sent the man off to work in his garden, warning him that any future trouble would result in his exile from the village. The chief then gave a gift to the male members of the village and asked them to repair the roof. After settling the dispute, the chief held a feast for the village.

Social order in chiefdoms is maintained through fear and through genuine respect for and loyalty to the chief. As our examples illustrate, the chief's authority is backed by his control of symbolic, supernatural, administrative, economic, and military power. This permits more stability in chiefdoms than in tribes, though sometimes violent competition for the office of chief occurs. Chiefs generally suppress any attempt at rebellion or threats from competitors and deal harshly with those who try to take their power. To emphasize the importance of this office for the society, offenses against the chief are punishable by death.

STATE SOCIETIES

The most complex political organization is the state. A **state** can be defined as a hierarchical, centralized form of political organization in which a central government has the legal monopoly over the use of force. In addition, states are characterized by social stratification. In most cases, state societies rest on a system of intensive agriculture, the productivity of which allows the development of cities, economic and occupational specialization, and extensive trade. It has been suggested that one of the most important characteristics of the state is its ability to expand indefinitely without splitting, through the incorporation of a variety of political units and ethnic groups. Thus, states can become much more populous, heterogeneous, and powerful than any other kind of society.

Social Stratification

As it does with chiefdoms, the rise of a centralized ruling authority creates an economic surplus. But in state societies, only a part of the surplus created by intervention in the economy goes back to the people directly; some is used to support the activities of the state itself, such as maintaining administrative bureaucracies, standing armies, artists and craft workers, and a priesthood. Part of the wealth produced in states is also used to support the ruling class in a luxurious style. Only the ruling class has unlimited access to basic resources. The power of the state is used to maintain this unequal access and to collect food surpluses through taxation.

In chiefdoms, ranking is based on kinship. In state societies, kinship does not regulate relations between the different social classes. Instead, each class marries within itself, and kin ties no longer extend throughout the whole society. This contributes to the widening of the gap between the classes.

Centralized Government

The state as a form of political organization is characterized by a high degree of functional specialization. Social order is maintained through government, an interrelated set of status roles that became separate from other aspects of social organization, such as kinship. The components of a state are no longer kinship groups; other kinds of groups and relationships, particularly those based on territory, become more important. A person becomes a member of the society through citizenship rather than kinship, and the sense of being "one people" is no longer limited to those who recognize ties of blood and marriage. The administrative divisions of a state are territorial units, cities, districts, and so on. Each unit has its own government, though these governments are not independent of the central government.

In state societies, government performs the functions that keep the society going. The state, for example, intervenes in every aspect of the economic process. Through taxation, it stimulates the agricultural production of households. It also controls labor; it can order people to work on roads and buildings and to serve in armies, thus affecting the work force available for agriculture. The state also intervenes in the exchange and distribution of goods and services through complex market networks. It protects distribution by making travel safe for traders as they move their goods from one place to another and by keeping peace in the marketplace. The state may also intervene in the consumption process. It can pass laws regarding which people are allowed to use which goods—for example, by reserving for the elite such items as gold, silk, or other costly symbols of high status. These complicated exchanges and rules brought a need for record-keeping. Systems of writing arose in some states, as well as systems of weights and measures. In some states, cities arose as administrative, religious, and economic centers. It was in these centers that important cultural achievements in science, art, architecture, and philosophy were stimulated.

The Monopoly of Force

The major defining characteristic of state societies is the government's monopoly over the use of force. A state uses a code of law to make clear how and when it will use force and forbids individuals or groups to use force. Written laws are passed by authorized legislative bodies and enforced by formal and specialized institutions of law enforcement. Courts and police forces, for example, have the authority to impose all kinds of punishments: prison, confiscation of property, fines, and even death.

In state societies, the fact that only the state has the authority to use force does not mean that force is used only by the state. In fact,

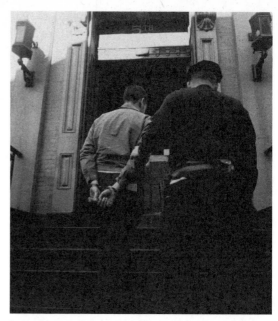

In a state society, monopoly over the use of legitimate force rests in the hands of the state. (United Nations)

many states are plagued by the illegal use of force and violence, which may take many different forms. Sometimes force occurs as disputes between individuals; sometimes, as the terrorizing of the population by bandits or outlaws; sometimes, as rebellion directed at overthrowing those who control the government; and sometimes, as revolutionary attempts to overthrow the entire structure of government. The state is constantly on the alert to ward off threats to depose the government or outbreaks of violence that might result in civil war. To the extent that a state wins the loyalty of its people by its ideology and effective protection of their economic and political rights, the constant use of force will not be necessary. It is always there in the background, however, as an instrument of social control. In addition to suppressing internal disorder, the state also defends itself against external threats. More than any other form of political organization, the state can mobilize to carry out military action or war for both defensive and offensive purposes.

The Rise of State Societies

The formation of a state is the result of a number of interrelated events feeding back on one another in complex ways. Ecological and historical circumstances, population pressure, long-distance trade, warfare and military organization, conquest, internal competition between groups, the maintenance of private property and the privileges of elite classes, and the necessity for more integrated management of public works such as irrigation all may play a role in the emergence of the state (Cohen and Service 1978).

Theories of state formation tend to emphasize either conflict or integration as the dominant factor. A conflict theory proposed by Morton Fried (1967) focuses on the centralization of government power as a response to social stratification. In Fried's view, as population increases, different parts of a population begin to compete for access to scarce resources. Ultimately, one group becomes dominant, and that group then wants to protect its superior position. In order to do this, it centralizes the institutions of government, particularly those that give a monopoly on the use of force. For Fried, the function of the state is first and foremost to protect the system of social stratification.

Elman Service (1971), on the other hand, stresses the integrative functions of the state. He emphasizes the positive benefits of the state as a form of sociopolitical integration and points out that all its citizens tend to regard it as legitimate and even good. There are many examples in history of states ruled by a monarch who was despotic and even cruel and who nevertheless was perceived by the people as deserving of respect and loyalty. For Service, the main functions of the state are protecting the rights of citizens, providing effective mechanisms for the peaceful settlement of disputes, and promoting the ability to substantially increase food production, thus offering a greater measure of economic security than other forms of organization. Social stratification, in Service's view, is a result rather than a cause of state formation; conditions leading to centralized government bring with them the development of a ruling class.

Within this opposition between the conflict and integrative approaches to state formation are theories that emphasize more specific factors. V. Gordon Childe (1936), an archeologist, sees the state developing automatically with the invention of agriculture. As the domestication of plants increases the surplus of food, some individuals are able to take on full-time occupational specialties. This creates a more complex division of labor, out of which develops the complex form of political integration called the state. One criticism of this view is that increased food production does not automatically create a surplus. Rather, a food surplus tends to be created by social mechanisms, such as the rise of centralized political institutions or the introduction of a cash economy.

Another theory stresses large-scale irrigation as the main factor leading to development of the state. This theory attempts to demonstrate that under certain ecological conditions, large-scale irrigation is perceived as conferring definite economic advantages on a population. But building irrigation projects and keeping them in repair require much coordination as well as more complex decision-making processes, because conflict can easily arise over who receives what benefits. The need to regulate rights to water and to manage human labor leads to the centralization of political power and ultimately results in the formation of a state. Critics of this theory point out that, although large-scale irrigation does lead to some political centralization, it does not necessarily lead to formation of a state. Furthermore, a number of large-scale states, such as China, Mesopotamia, and Mexico, developed before the development of large-scale irrigation. On the whole, however, centralized political authority does seem to be adaptive in an economy dependent on irrigation.

Another theory, developed by Robert Car-

A view of Machu Picchu, the site of a pre-Columbian Peruvian state. Like other indigenous states, this one arose in an area of circumscribed agricultural land. (United Nations/A. Jongen)

neiro (1970), sees the state resulting from warfare under certain ecological conditions—where there is a limit on the agricultural land available to expanding populations. As an example of this theory, Carneiro describes the rise of the state in pre-Columbian Peru. The independent, dispersed farming villages of Peru were confined to narrow valleys bounded by the sea, the desert, or mountains. As the population grew, villages split and population dispersed until all the available agricultural land was used up. At this point, more-intensive methods of agriculture were applied to land already being farmed, and previously unusable land was brought under cultivation by means of terracing and irrigation. As population continued to increase, more pressure was brought on the land, and war over land was the result. Because of the environment, vil-

lages that lost wars had nowhere to go. The price of a defeated population remaining on its land was acceptance of a politically subordinate role. As a number of villages were defeated, the political organization of these areas became more complex and developed into chiefdoms. The warring units were now larger. As conquest of larger areas continued, centralization of authority increased, until finally the entire area was under the control of one chief. The next step was the conquest of weaker valley chiefdoms by stronger ones until powerful empires emerged. The Inca Empire of Peru is a notable example of this process of state formation.

As a form of sociopolitical organization, the state is one of humankind's most important cultural achievements. Philosophers as well as anthropologists have been fascinated by what induces human beings to give up part of their freedom to the control of the state. In seeking the answer to this question, anthropologists have examined the available evidence, both for ancient and contemporary states, and have developed various theories. It is now generally agreed that no theory that limits state formation to one single chain of cause and effect is a sufficient explanation. A newer approach sees the origin of the state as involving a different interaction of factors in different circumstances. Prestate societies in various situations respond to different selective pressures by changing some of their internal structures, by subduing a competing group, by gaining control of water resources, or by establishing themselves as dominant in a region. This initial shift sets off a chain reaction of other changes that leads ultimately to the state. The state thus emerges as a cultural solution to various kinds of problems that demand more centralized coordination and regulation of human populations.

SUMMARY

1. Political systems, which include law, function to solve the problems of coordinating and regulating human behavior. The major political processes in any society are making and enforcing decisions affecting the common good and resolving conflicts.

2. Both informal and formal mechanisms of social control regulate human behavior. Informal social control is achieved through gossip and ridicule. Formal sanctions include exile, death, and punishment as meted out by judges, courts, and police.

3. Political organization varies according to the degree of specialization of political functions and the extent to which authority is centralized. These, in turn, vary with the degree of social complexity. Four basic types of political organization are bands, tribes, chiefdoms, and states.

4. In a band society there is little integration of groups at a level higher than the band and no centralization of leadership or social control. Band level political organization is characteristic of hunting and gathering societies.

5. Tribal organization occurs mainly among horticulturalists and pastoralists. Most frequently, localized kin groups, which are the typical political units in tribal society, act independently. But under certain social conditions, such as the threat of attack, these units may come together in collective action. Tribal societies contain some mechanisms of organization, such as age groups, clans, and associations, that integrate all the local segments of the tribe.

6. Although tribal societies often have some centralized form of social control that inhibits violent conflict between segments, warfare is frequent. Warfare may be adaptive in these societies as a way of limiting population growth or redistributing land.

7. In a chiefdom, kinship is the most important principle of social organization. Unlike the tribe, this form of society has an office of chief, which is a socially recognized position of leadership and authority. An important support of the chief's power is his role in the redistribution of goods through feasting.

8. A state, which is a hierarchical, centralized form of organization in which a central government has a legal monopoly over the use of force, is the most complex of the four types of political organization. States are characterized by social stratification. But unlike chiefdoms, in which social ranking is based on kinship, the state incorporates groups and classes that have no kinship ties with one another.

9. A number of theories deal with the rise of the state. Some emphasize the conflict created by the existence of social classes; others emphasize the integrative functions of the state, such as protecting the rights of citizens, providing for the peaceful resolution of conflict, and promoting increased food production.

10. If we examine the various factors associated with the rise of states in different parts of the world and at different times, it appears that the state is a cultural solution to a number of *different* problems, all of which demand more centralized coordination and regulation of human populations.

SUGGESTED READINGS

Cohen, Ronald, and Service, Elman R.
1978   *Origins of the State: The Anthropology of Political Evolution.* Philadelphia: Institute for the Study of Human Issues. A series of articles on the rise of the state in different parts of the world. A good introduction summarizes anthropological theories of state formation.

Harris, Marvin
1977   *Cannibals and Kings: The Origins of Cultures.* New York: Random House. In his usual interesting style, the author discusses, among other things, the rise of states and warfare in preindustrial societies.

Hoebel, E. A.
1968   *The Law of Primitive Man.* New York: Atheneum (first publ. 1954). Interesting ethnographic material showing the relationship of law to other aspects of society among groups at different levels of sociocultural integration.

Lindholm, Charles
1982   *Generosity and Jealousy: The Swat Pukhtun of Northern Pakistan.* New York: Columbia University Press. A fascinating account of a society where husbands and wives, fathers and sons, brothers and cousins all are opposed to each other, and the guest and the friend are idealized.

CHAPTER FOURTEEN

RELIGION

▶ Why is religion a universal human institution?

▶ What are some of the religious beliefs and rituals found in different cultures?

▶ What are the differences between shamans and priests? cults and congregations?

> *The anthropological study of religion is therefore a two-stage operation: first, an analysis of the system of meanings embodied in the symbols which make up the religion proper, and second, the relating of these symbols to social-structural and psychological processes.*
>
> Clifford Geertz*

*From *The Interpretation of Cultures,* p. 125.

Our discussion in this chapter will view religion as "the beliefs and practices concerned with supernatural beings, powers and forces" (Wallace 1966). *Supernatural* refers to those powers, events, and experiences that are beyond ordinary human control and the laws of nature and outside reality as normally experienced. Every society has some set of beliefs and practices that centers on the relationship of humans to the supernatural. Religion, which goes back to the beginnings of the human species, is a true cultural universal. The antiquity and universality of religion have led many anthropologists to speculate about its origins and functions. Although the search for origins no longer dominates anthropological thinking as it once did, anthropologists are still interested in the many functions religion serves in human society. Some of the most important functions of religion will be discussed in the following section. They will come up again as we look at the variety of religious beliefs and practices throughout the world's cultures.

THE FUNCTIONS OF RELIGION

The Search for Order and Meaning

One of the most important functions of religion is to give meaning to and explain those aspects of the physical and social environment that are not fully understood through normal experience and thought. In every society, religion deals with the nature of life and death, the creation of the universe, the origin of society and groups within society, the relation of individuals and groups to one another, and the relation of humankind to nature. This whole cognitive system is called a **cosmology,** or world view. In the absence of full understanding about themselves and the world, humans create an image of reality peopled with supernatural beings and supernatural forces. This image serves as a framework for interpreting events and experiences, particularly those that are out of the ordinary, or "unnatural." When humans reach the limits of their intellectual capacities, their powers of endurance, or the limits of their understanding of the relation between what they try to do and the success they have, beliefs and practices relating to the supernatural emerge as a way of imposing order on the universe, of giving humans the feeling that they have some measure of control.

Science and religion are similar in that both involve "the quest for unity underlying apparent diversity; for simplicity underlying apparent complexity, for order underlying apparent disorder; for regularity underlying apparent anomaly" (Horton 1973). But there is also a major difference between science and religion. Science is an open system of thought, religion a closed system. Science provides explanations that are not considered to be absolutely valid but rather are open to new data. In science, there is an awareness of alternative theories or explanations; ideally, as old explanations are found to be invalid, new ones will be accepted. Religion, on the other hand, is a closed system of beliefs. Religious beliefs are sacred; they are not to be questioned and are not open to empirical testing.

The separation between religion and science in our own society corresponds to our sharp separation of the supernatural and the natural. In other societies, these two concepts are less sharply separated. The supernatural can be seen as part of the natural and as intervening in all aspects of life. Thus, the kin group includes both living relatives and dead ancestors; power and leadership are often believed to have divine origins; rules of behavior are given divine sanction, and breaches are punished by the gods. The success of even ordinary undertakings in the physical world is ensured by enlisting the help of supernatural powers. Natural disasters, illness, and misfortune are believed to be caused by extrahuman or supernatural spirits. Natural and supernatural, human and natural, past, present, and future may be perceived as a unity in a way that violates the logic of Western thought. This makes it difficult for us to understand many non-Western religions and accounts for our ethnocentric labeling of them as "irrational," "contradictory," or the products of faulty thinking.

Reducing Anxiety and Increasing Control

Many religious practices are aimed at ensuring success in carrying out a wide variety of human activities. Prayers and offerings are made to supernatural beings in the hope that they will aid a particular individual or community. Rituals are performed to call on supernatural beings and to control forces that appear to be unpredictable, such as those in the natural environment upon which humans depend for survival. One of the widespread practices used to control supernatural forces is magic. Although magical practices exist in many societies, magic seems to be more prominent in those in which there is less predictability in the outcome of events and thus less feeling of being in control of the social and physical environment. In the Trobriand Islands, for example, magic is not used for ordinary canoe trips within the lagoons, but only when the Islanders undertake the long-distance and dangerous canoe trips to other islands in their kula trade. Magic is also prevalent in sports and games of chance.

Even if magic cannot "work" from the standpoint of Western science, it may be effective in achieving results indirectly, mainly by reducing the anxiety of the individuals and groups that practice it. This reduced anxiety allows them to proceed with more confidence, and the confidence may lead to greater success. Where technological advance and science are able to increase predictability and control over events and human relations, magic tends to become less important.

Maintaining the Social Order

Religion has a number of important functions that either directly or indirectly help maintain the social order and the survival of a society. To begin with, religious beliefs about good and evil are reinforced by supernatural means of social control. Thus, religion is a powerful force for conformity in a society. Furthermore, through myth and ritual, social values are given sacred authority and provide a reason for the present social order. Religious ritual also intensifies solidarity by creating an atmosphere in which people experience their common identity in emotionally moving ways. Religion is also an important educational institution. Initiation rites, for example, almost always include the transmission of information about cultural practices and tradition.

By supporting the present social order and defining the place of the individual in society and in the universe, religion also provides people with a sense of personal identity and belonging. When individuals have lost a positive identity, or when life has no meaning because of the disintegration of a traditional culture, religion can supply a new and more positive identity and become the basis for a new and better culture. Religion can also provide an escape from reality; in the religious beliefs of an afterlife or the coming of a Messiah, powerless people who live in harsh and deprived circumstances can create an illusion of power through the manipulation of religious symbols. Religion in these circumstances is an outlet for frustration, resentment, and anger and is a way of draining off energy that might otherwise be turned against the social system. In this way, religion indirectly contributes to maintaining the social order.

In summary, religion has both instrumental and expressive functions. The instrumental aspect of religion has to do with actions performed in the belief that, if people do certain things, they can influence the course of natural or social events to their advantage. The expressive aspect of ritual refers to the ways in which religious symbolism is used to express ideas about the relation of humans to nature, self to society, or group to group. In its expressive aspect, religion is an important force for social integration.

RELIGION AND SYMBOLISM

Because religious ideas are always expressed through symbolism, anthropologists today are also interested in studying the meanings of religious symbolism and the logic that connects symbols to religious beliefs. Religious symbols may be verbal, such as the names for gods and spirits and certain words, phrases or songs that are believed to contain some supernatural power. **Myths,** or sacred narratives that tell how the world came to be created through the agency of semidivine heroes, are powerful symbolic communications of religious ideas.

E T H N O G R A P H Y

RELIGIOUS RITUAL AND ADAPTATION

Recent research has shown that religious belief and ritual not only indirectly contribute to the survival of a society but may also directly affect the relationship between a social group and its physical environment. A study by Roy Rappaport (1967) of the Tsembaga of New Guinea shows how religious belief and ritual may produce "a practical result on the external world."

The Tsembaga, who live in the valleys of a mountain range in New Guinea, are swidden cultivators who also raise pigs. Small numbers of pigs are easy to keep, as they eat anything and help keep residential areas free from garbage. Although pigs can ruin gardens in the early stages of planting, after the trees are well established, pigs are allowed to root in the gardens where they actually help cultivation by eating seeds and tubers (sweet potatoes). If pig herds grow very large, however, feeding them becomes a problem, and it becomes necessary for extra food to be harvested just to feed the pigs. Furthermore, when pig herds become too large, they are more likely to invade gardens and require more supervision. The Tsembaga kill pigs only on ritual occasions—either at pig feasts or in times of misfortune such as illness, death, or warfare.

The Tsembaga have a ritual cycle that they perform, they say, in order to rearrange their relationships with the supernatural world. This cycle can be viewed as beginning with the rituals performed during warfare. In Tsembaga warfare, opponents generally occupy territories next to each other. After hostilities have broken out, each side performs certain rituals that formally designate the other group as the enemy. Fighting may continue on and off for weeks, sometimes ending with one group's being routed. In this case, the survivors go to live with their kinsmen, and the victors destroy the losers' gardens, slaughter their pigs, and burn their houses. The victors do not occupy their land, however, as this is believed to be guarded by the ancestors of the defeated group.

Most Tsembaga warfare ends in truce, however, with both groups remaining on their territory. When a truce is declared, each group performs a ritual called "planting the rumbin." The rumbin is dedicated to the ancestors, who are thanked for helping in the fight. At this ritual planting, there is a wholesale slaughter of adult pigs. Some of the meat is eaten by the local group itself, and the rest is distributed to other groups that have helped it fight. After this feast, there is a period in which the fighting groups are still considered to be in debt to their allies and their ancestors. This period will not end until the rumbin plant is uprooted. This ritual also requies a pig feast and occurs when there are sufficient pigs.

The question is: How many pigs are sufficient? It is when pig herds reach over four per woman caretaker that they

Myths are not merely explanatory stories of the cosmos, but rather have a sacred power in themselves that is evoked by telling the myths or acting them out ritually. Myths may tell of what *really* happened, though they are clothed in poetic and sometimes esoteric language. Religious symbolism may also be expressed in material objects—in masks, statues, paintings, costumes, body decorations, or objects in the physical environment.

Religious ideas are also acted out, in dance, drama, and physical movements. In religious ritual, all these symbolic means are used to express religious ideas. It is because religious ideas are so complex and abstract that they require symbolic representation in order to be

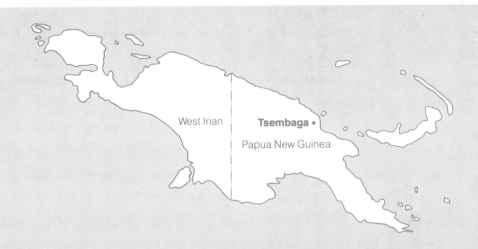

West Irian

Tsembaga •

Papua New Guinea

become too troublesome to manage and begin to compete with humans for food. Thus, it is the wives of the owners of large numbers of pigs who begin agitating for the ritual to uproot the rumbin. This ritual, which is followed by a pig festival lasting about a year, involves much entertaining among villages. Food is exchanged, and hosts and guests spend the nights dancing. At this time, future alliances may be set up between hosts and guests. At this time, also, much trade takes place, involving such items as axes, bird plumes, and shell ornaments. For one festival, Rappaport observed that

between 4,500 and 6,000 pounds of pig meat were distributed over 163 occasions to between 2,000 and 3,000 people in seventeen local groups. The pig festival ends with another pig slaughter and the public presentation of a salted pig belly to one's allies. This concludes the ritual cycle. A local group would now consider itself free to attack its neighbors, knowing that assistance from both human allies and ancestors would be forthcoming because their obligations to feed them pork had been fulfilled.

This ritual cycle among the Tsembaga shows a number of functions of religion. It adjusts

the man-land ratio, as survivors in a defeated group seek refuge in other local groups. It also facilitates trade through the markets and exchanges that take place during the year of the pig festival. Most directly in terms of survival, however, it assures the distribution of local surpluses of pig meat, which is a source of high-quality protein throughout the whole Tsembaga region. The ritual cycle also helps to maintain an undegraded environment, as pigs are killed when there get to be too many of them and when they threaten the source of human food.

grasped by the ordinary person. The Christian ritual of the communion service, for example, itself symbolizes the New Testament myth of the Last Supper, which communicates the difficult idea of "communion with God." This idea is present in other religions but is represented by different symbolism. In Hinduism, for example, one of the most popular representations of communion with God is the love between the divine Krishna, in the form of a cowherd, and the gopis, or milkmaids, who are devoted to him. In the dramatic enactment of the stories of Krishna, and in the singing of songs to him, the Hindu religion offers a path to communion with God that can be understood by ordinary people.

In Hinduism, the classic theme of the God and Goddess appears very frequently and is enshrined in many artistic forms. The God, or male, symbolizes the passive aspect, or Eternity; the Goddess, or female form, symbolizes the activating energy, or dynamism of time. They appear to be opposites but are in essence one. Just as the God has his living counterpart in every man, so does the Goddess have her living counterpart in every woman. The two together represent the oneness or the unity of the divine essence. This sculpture is from the temples of Khajuraho in India. (Serena Nanda)

One anthropological approach that is particularly interested in religious symbolism is called **structuralism.** Structuralists, among whom the most well known is Claude Lévi-Strauss, aim to discover the rules by which meanings are attached to symbols and ultimately to discover the laws of human thought. Because the freest thought takes place in myth and ritual, these are the main materials analyzed by structuralists.

Structuralists hold that human experience is fundamentally conceived of as contrasts—between life and death, male and female, nature and culture, humans and God. The function of myth, ritual, and other elements of culture, particularly religion, is to reestablish a bridge between the oppositions. This bridge is established by the introduction of a third category, which partakes of both of the oppositions and is thus in itself abnormal. It is this mediating category that is the focus of religious awe and all ritual and taboo. A structural analysis of the Hebrew taboo on pork, for example, centers on the pig as an animal that partakes of two animal categories; it has cloven hoofs, as do cattle, but does not chew cud. Being neither here nor there, it is unclean (in a spiritual or symbolic sense) and thus tabooed (Douglas 1970). The structuralist approach also helps explain the widespread use of such symbols as hair (which is part of the human body but can be separated from it), ashes (which are both matter and nonmatter), the color white (which is all colors and no color), and the mythological use of "monsters" or figures with bodies of animals and heads of humans.

STRUCTURE AND ANTI-STRUCTURE

Victor Turner (1969) has extended the concept of structuralism to explain the function and symbolism of a wide variety of roles and activities in different societies. Turner goes back to the work of Arnold van Gennep (1961), who noted a similarity in many rituals in human societies, particularly those rituals he called *rites of passage*. Rites of passage are rituals that accompany every change of social status by individuals or groups. Van Gennep identified three phases in such rites: The first phase is separation, which serves to detach the individual or group from a former status. The second, or liminal, phase is one in which the ritual subject is "in limbo," having been detached from the old status but not yet attached to a new one. The third stage is reincorporation, where the passage from one status to another is symbolically consummated. Now the ritual subject is in a new status by virtue of which he or she takes on rights and obligations binding on incumbents in the new position. We shall see further on in the chapter how these phases are applied to the transitions from childhood to adulthood in many societies.

Turner is most interested in the liminal stage. The symbols of this stage are often those of "nothingness," or ambiguity, representing things that are "neither here nor there," betwixt and between. This stage is often associated with danger or supernatural power and sacredness. A main characteristic of the liminal stage is that it involves a dissolution of many of the structured and hierarchical classifications that normally separate people in society—for example, caste, class, or kinship categories. Another characteristic of the liminal stage is that it involves the ritual subjects in a relationship of oneness, or what Turner calls "communitas." Communitas is a genuine human bond that puts all persons in the same, relatively undifferentiated category. Communitas can be expressed in different ways in different societies, in a variety of activities in which the low become high and the high become low or structure is dissolved temporarily for a festival or ceremony or through certain kinds of performances in which mediating figures are dominant. Communitas, or anti-structure, alternates with structure in the form of communal rituals.

As society becomes more complex and differentiated, some institutionalized liminal statuses emerge in society. These statuses are part of the anti-structure and function as representatives of communitas, or as the medium for bringing it about. These sources of communitas are most often persons or groups that share the characteristics of liminality; they are outlaw, or of low status, or of ambiguous nature. It is their very marginality or low status or ambiguity that is, paradoxically, the source of

their power. For example, the *hirjas*, or men/women of India described in Chapter 4, are in between the classifications of male and female; it is because of their sexual ambiguity that they are believed to have the power to confer blessings for fertility. The restoration of political or economic equilibrium in society is often brought about by outlaws, such as Jesse James, who stole from the rich to give to the poor. Similarly, in Western fairy tales we hear of simpletons, or "little tailors," who strip off the pretensions of the powerful and bring them down to common humanity. Turner views the hippies and other counterculture groups of the '60s as emphasizing their marginality as a way of enhancing their own sense of communitas, as well as a way of undermining the structure of society.

Turner explains a great many seemingly diverse roles in different cultures by the concept of communitas: the Catholic monastic orders, Hindu mendicants, medieval court jesters, prostitutes with a heart of gold—all these roles marginal to the structure of society represent humanity or communitas versus the special interests of high placed groups within the normative structure. All these structurally marginal roles represent an open morality or anti-structure as against the closed morality and structure of the larger society. In representing communitas, these individuals and groups attempt to capture the spontaneous, immediate, and concrete nature of the human bond, as opposed to the norm governed, institutionalized, and abstract nature of society. If structure is a set of classifications, for example, into male and female, then communitas breaks in at the margins of the classification system, in the form of bisexuals or transvestites, who are sacred and have power because they transgress or dissolve structure.

Communitas is the source of much myth, art, symbol, and ritual. Turner concludes from his cross-cultural study of communitas that humans need this bond and that social life is a process of moving between structure and anti-structure. Humans need structure to pro-

The flowering of cults and other communal groups in the United States, such as the Hare Krishna cult pictured here, can be viewed as the search for communitas. In India, the cult of Krishna is also a manifestation of communitas, as it involves the breaking down of structured separations—between persons of different castes and between humans and the divine. (Serena Nanda)

vide order, but as Turner says, "Beyond the structural lies not only the Hobbesian 'war of all against all' but also communitas . . ." (p. 131), the dissolution of structure aimed at transcending structure and thus more fully realizing the oneness of the self and the other.

KINDS OF BELIEFS: ANIMISM AND ANIMATISM

A basic distinction in types of religious beliefs is that between animism and animatism. **Animism** is the belief that not only living creatures but also inanimate objects have life and personality; these supernatural persons are referred to as spirits, ghosts, or gods. Such beings are believed to behave as people do: they are conscious, they have will, and they feel the same emotions as human beings. Such spirits may reside in features of the physical environment, such as trees or stones, or they may reside in animals. In hunting societies— for example, the Lele of Africa and the Inuit— the spirits of animals are worshipped because it is believed that a hunt will be successful only if an animal allows itself to be killed. Souls, which may also reside in human bodies, are believed to be able to leave the body at will, temporarily during sleep or permanently as in death. Spirits or souls that leave the body at death turn into ghosts, which come in a variety of forms and relate in various ways to the living in different cultures.

The distinction between a spirit and a god is mostly one of scale. A god is a supernatural being of great importance and power; a spirit is a lesser being. **Polytheism** is the term used for a religion with many gods, and **monotheism** refers to a religion with only one god. Things are not quite this clear in real cultures, however. In so-called polytheistic religions, the many gods may be just so many aspects of the one god. In India, for example, it is said that there are literally millions of gods; yet even an uneducated Indian will understand that in some way (which does not confuse him or her, though it may confuse us), these are all aspects of one divine essence.

The Nuer are another culture in which the distinction between the Great Spirit and lesser spirits is fuzzy to the outsider. The Nuer, of course, have no difficulty in understanding the different contexts in which different aspects of the Great Spirit are invoked. E. E. Evans-Pritchard (1968) describes a ceremony held to end a blood feud. All the speakers, representing both clans and including the Leopard Skin chief, addressed the various gods: Great Spirit, spirit of the sky, spirit of our community, spirit of the flesh (this refers to the divine power of the Leopard Skin chief), and spirit of our fathers. Each clan representative appealed to God not only as God but also as God in relation to the group he represented. The Leopard Skin chief referred to God in his special relation to his religious role as mediator, as well as to the priestly lineage he belonged to.

Just as in polytheistic religious, in which all gods and spirits may be reflections of one god, so in monotheistic religions, the one god may have several aspects. In the Roman Catholic religion, for example, there is God the Father, the Son, and the Holy Ghost, in addition to a number of lesser supernatural spirits such as the saints, ghosts, the devil, and the souls of people in heaven as well as the souls of those living on earth.

Animatism is the belief in an impersonal supernatural power. *Mana* is perhaps the most widely known term for this power. **Mana,** or supernatural power, may be inherent in the universe but may also be concentrated in individuals or in objects. We have seen earlier that Polynesian chiefs had a much higher degree of *mana* than ordinary people. *Mana* is the key to success, but it can also be dangerous. That is why the belief in *mana* is so frequently associated with an elaborate system of taboos, or prohibitions. *Mana* is like electricity; it is a powerful force, but it can be dangerous when not approached with the proper caution.

A cross-cultural approach seems to indicate that *mana*, or power, is very often found in those areas (spatial, temporal, verbal, or physical) that are the boundaries between clear-cut categories. Hair, for example, is believed to contain supernatural power in many different cultures (remember the Old Testament story of Samson and Delilah). Hair is a symbol of the boundary between the self and the not-self. It is both part of a person and can be separated from the person. Hence its ambiguity, and its power. Doorways and gates are also familiar symbols of supernatural power. They separate the inside from the outside and can thus serve as a symbol of moral categories such as good and evil, pure and impure. Because these symbols of boundaries contain supernatural power, they are frequently part of religious ritual and are surrounded by religious taboos.

PRACTICES AND RITUALS

A religious **ritual** is a patterned act that involves the manipulation of religious symbols. Most religious rituals use a combination of the following practices to contact and control supernatural spirits and powers: prayer, offerings and sacrifices, manipulation of objects, telling or acting out of myths, altering the physiological state of the individual (as in trance and ecstatic experiences or through drugs), music, dance, and drama (Wallace 1966).

Prayers and Offerings

Prayer is any conversation held with spirits and gods. Prayer can involve a request or a pleading; it can be in the form of a bargain or consist of merely praising the deity. In many

Body Ritual among the Nacirema*

The anthropologist has become so familiar with the diversity of ways in which different peoples behave in similar situations that he is not apt to be surprised by even the most exotic customs. In fact, if all of the logically possible combinations of behavior have not been found somewhere in the world, he is apt to suspect that they must be present in some yet undescribed tribe. This point has, in fact, been expressed with respect to clan organization by Murdock. In this light, the magical beliefs and practices of the Nacirema present such unusual aspects that it seems desirable to describe them as an example of the extremes to which human behavior can go.

Professor Linton first brought the ritual of the Nacirema to the attention of anthropologists twenty years ago, but the culture of this people is still very poorly understood. They are a North American group living in the territory between the Canadian Cree, the Yaqui and Tarahumare of Mexico, and the Carib and Arawak of the Antilles. Little is known of their origin, although tradition states that they came from the east. . . .

Nacirema culture is characterized by a highly developed market economy which has evolved in a rich natural habitat. While much of the people's time is devoted to economic pursuits, a large part of the fruits of these labors and a considerable portion of the day are spent in ritual activity. The focus of this activity is the human body, the appearance and health of which loom as a dominant concern in the ethos of the people. While such a concern is certainly not unusual, its ceremonial aspects and associated philosophy are unique.

The fundamental belief underlying the whole system appears to be that the human body is ugly and that its natural tendency is to debility and disease. Incarcerated in such a body, man's only hope is to avert these characteristics through the use of the powerful influences of ritual and ceremony. Every household has one or more shrines devoted to this purpose. The more powerful individuals in the society have several shrines in their houses and, in fact, the opulence of a house is often referred to in terms of the number of such ritual centers it possesses. Most houses are of wattle and daub construction, but the shrine rooms of the more wealthy are lined with stone. Poorer families imitate the rich by applying pottery plaques to their shrine walls.

While each family has at least one such shrine, the rituals associated with it are not family ceremonies but are private and secret. The rites are normally only discussed with children, and then only during the period when they are being initiated into these mysteries. I was able, however, to establish sufficient rapport with the natives to examine these shrines and to have the rituals described to me.

The focal point of the shrine is a box or chest which is built into the wall. In this chest are kept the many charms and magical potions without which no native believes he could live. These preparations are secured from a variety of specialized practitioners. The most powerful of these are the medicine men, whose assistance must be rewarded with substantial gifts. However, the medicine men do not provide the curative potions for their clients, but decide what the ingredients should be and then write them down in an ancient and secret language. This writing is understood only by the medicine men and by the herbalists who, for another gift, provide the required charm.

The charm is not disposed of after it has served its purpose, but is placed in the charmbox of the household shrine. As these magical materials are specific for certain ills, and the real or imagined maladies of the people are many, the charm-box is usually full to overflowing. The magical packets are so numerous that people forget what their purposes were and fear to use them again. While the natives are very vague on this point, we can only assume that the idea in retaining all the old magical materials is that their presence in the charm-box, before which the body rituals are conducted, will in some way protect the worshipper.

*From Horace Miner, "Body Ritual among the Nacirema." Reproduced by permission of the American Anthropological Association from *The American Anthropologist*, 1956, 58:503–507.

Beneath the charm-box is a small font. Each day every member of the family, in succession, enters the shrine room, bows his head before the charm-box, mingles different sorts of holy water in the font, and proceeds with a brief rite of ablution. The holy waters are secured from the Water Temple of the community, where the priests conduct elaborate ceremonies to make the liquid ritually pure.

In the hierarchy of magical practitioners, and below the medicine men in prestige, are specialists whose designation is best translated "holy-mouth-men." The Nacirema have an almost pathological horror of and fascination with the mouth, the condition of which is believed to have a supernatural influence on all social relationships. Were it not for the rituals of the mouth, they believe that their teeth would fall out, their gums bleed, their jaws shrink, their friends desert them, and their lovers reject them. They also believe that a strong relationship exists between oral and moral characteristics. For example, there is a ritual ablution of the mouth for children which is supposed to improve their moral fiber.

The daily body ritual performed by everyone includes a mouth-rite. Despite the fact that these people are so punctilious about care of the mouth, this rite involves a practice which strikes the uninitiated stranger as revolting. It was reported to me that the ritual consists of inserting a small bundle of hog hairs into the mouth, along with certain magical powders, and then moving the bundle in a highly formalized series of gestures.

In addition to the private mouth-rite, the people seek out a holy-mouth-man once or twice a year. These practitioners have an impressive set of paraphernalia, consisting of a variety of augers, awls, probes, and prods. The use of these objects in the exorcism of the evils of the mouth involves almost unbelievable ritual torture of the client. The holy-mouth-man opens the client's mouth and, using the above mentioned tools, enlarges any holes which decay may have created in the teeth. Magical materials are put into those holes. If there are no naturally occurring holes in the teeth, large sections of one or more teeth are gouged out so that the supernatural substance can be applied. In the client's view, the purpose of these ministrations is to arrest decay and to draw friends. The extremely sacred and traditional character of the rite is evident in the fact that the natives return to the holy-mouth-men year after year, despite the fact that their teeth continue to decay.

It is to be hoped that, when a thorough study of the Nacirema is made, there will be careful inquiry into the personality structure of these people. One has but to watch the gleam in the eye of a holy-mouth-man, as he jabs an awl into an exposed nerve, to suspect that a certain amount of sadism is involved. If this can be established, a very interesting pattern emerges, for most of the population shows definite masochistic tendencies. It was to these that Professor Linton referred in discussing a distinctive part of the daily body ritual which is performed only by men. This part of the rite involves scraping and lacerating the surface of the face with a sharp instrument. Special women's rites are performed only four times during each lunar month, but what they lack in frequency is made up in barbarity. As part of this ceremony, women bake their heads in small ovens for about an hour. The theoretically interesting point is that what seems to be a preponderantly masochistic people have developed sadistic specialists.

The medicine men have an imposing temple, or *latipso*, in every community of any size. The more elaborate ceremonies required to treat very sick patients can only be performed at this temple. These ceremonies involve not only the thaumaturge but a permanent group of vestal maidens who move sedately about the temple chambers in distinctive costume and headdress.

The *latipso* ceremonies are so harsh that it is phenomenal that a fair proportion of the really sick natives who enter the temple ever recover. Small children whose indoctrination is still incomplete have been known to resist attempts to take them to the temple because "that is where you go to die." Despite this fact, sick adults are not only willing but eager to undergo the protracted ritual purification, if they can afford to do so. No matter how ill the supplicant or how grave the emergency, the guardians of many temples will not admit a client if he cannot give a rich gift to the custodian. Even after one has gained admission and survived the ceremonies, the guardians will not permit the neophyte to leave until he makes still another gift.

The supplicant entering the temple is first stripped of all his or her clothes. In everyday life the Nacierema avoids exposure of his body and its natural functions. Bathing and excretory acts are performed only in the secrecy of the household shrine, where they are ritualized as part of the body-rites. Psychological shock results from the fact that body secrecy is suddenly lost upon entry into the *latipso*. A man, whose own wife has never seen him in an excretory act, suddenly finds himself naked and assisted by a vestal maiden while he performs his natural functions into a sacred vessel. This sort of ceremonial treatment is necessitated by the fact that the excreta are used by a diviner to ascertain the course and nature of the client's sickness. Female clients, on the other hand, find their naked bodies are subjected to the scrutiny, manipulation and prodding of the medicine men.

Few supplicants in the temple are well enough to do anything but lie on their hard beds. The daily ceremonies, like the rites of the holy-mouth-men, involve discomfort and torture. With ritual precision, the vestals awaken their miserable charges each dawn and roll them about on their beds of pain while performing ablutions, in the formal movements of which the maidens are highly trained. At other times they insert magic wands in the supplicant's mouth or force him to eat substances which are supposed to be healing. From time to time the medicine men come to their clients and jab magically treated needles into their flesh. The fact that these temple ceremonies may not cure, and may even kill the neophyte, in no way decreases the people's faith in the medicine men.

There remains one other kind of practitioner, known as a "listener." This witchdoctor has the power to exorcise the devils that lodge in the heads of people who have been bewitched. The Nacirema believe that parents bewitch their own children. Mothers are particularly suspected of putting a curse on children while teaching them the secret body rituals. The counter-magic of the witchdoctor is unusual in its lack of ritual. The patient simply tells the "listener" all his troubles and fears, beginning with the earliest difficulties he can remember. The memory displayed by the Nacirema in these exorcism sessions is truly remarkable. It is not uncommon for the patient to bemoan the rejection he felt upon being weaned as a babe, and a few individuals even see their troubles going back to the traumatic effects of their own birth.

In conclusion, mention must be made of certain practices which have their base in native esthetics but which depend upon the pervasive aversion to the natural body and its functions. There are ritual fasts to make fat people thin and ceremonial feasts to make thin people fat. Still other rites are used to make women's breasts larger if they are small, and smaller if they are large. General dissatisfaction with breast shape is symbolized in the fact that the ideal form is virtually outside the range of human variation. A few women afflicted with almost inhuman hyper-mammary development are so idolized that they make a handsome living by simply going from village to village and permitting the natives to stare at them for a fee.

Reference has already been made to the fact that excretory functions are ritualized, routinized, and relegated to secrecy. Natural reproductive functions are similarly distorted. Intercourse is taboo as a topic and scheduled as an act. Efforts are made to avoid pregnancy by the use of magical materials or by limiting intercourse to certain phases of the moon. Conception is actually very infrequent. When pregnant, women dress so as to hide their condition. Parturition takes place in secret, without friends or relatives to assist, and the majority of women do not nurse their infants.

Our review of the ritual life of the Nacirema has certainly shown them to be a magic-ridden people. It is hard to understand how they have managed to exist so long under the burdens which they have imposed upon themselves. But even such exotic customs as these take on real meaning when they are viewed with the insight provided by Malinowski when he wrote:

"Looking from far and above, from our high places of safety in the developed civilization, it is easy to see all the crudity and irrelevance of magic. But without its power and guidance early man could not have mastered his practical difficulties as he has done, nor could man have advanced to the higher stages of civilization."

religions, it is common to make a vow in which the individual promises to carry out a certain kind of behavior, such as going on a pilgrimage or building a temple, if the gods will grant a particular wish. Other forms of prayer are less familiar to the Westerner. In some cultures, gods can be lied to, commanded, or ridiculed. Among the many Northwest Coast tribes of North America, the insulting tone used to one's political rivals was also used to the gods. In these ranked societies, the greatest insult was to call a man a slave; when calamities fell or their prayers were not answered, people would vent their anger against the gods by saying, "You are a great slave" (Benedict 1961:221).

Making offerings and sacrifices to supernatural beings is also a widespread religious practice. Sometimes these offerings consist of the first fruits of a harvest—grain, fish, or game. Sometimes the offering of food is in the form of a meal for the gods; among the Hindus, the gods are given food that they eat behind a curtain. After the gods have eaten, this food is distributed among the worshippers.

In some societies, animals or humans may be sacrificed as an offering to the gods. Among cattle pastoralists of East Africa, such as the Nuer and the Pokot, cattle sacrifices are an important part of religious practices. The essence of the East African "cattle complex" is that cattle are killed and eaten only in a ritual and religious context, which seems to be an inefficient use of resources. This ritual use of cattle in sacrifice has always been of interest to anthropologists, and at one time it was given as a common example of how religious practices interfere with rational exploitation of the environment. More recent research has shown, however, that the sacrifice of cattle in a ritual context may be quite adaptive. Cattle sacrifices are offered in community feasts that occur on a fairly regular schedule, averaging out to once a week in any particular neighborhood. The feasts are thus an important source of meat in the diet. Furthermore, the religious taboo that an individual who eats ritually slaughtered meat may not take milk on the same day has the effect of making milk more available to those

Offerings to the gods are frequently used to gain their helpful intervention in human affairs. Here a Ponapean pounds the root for making kava, a ceremonial drink that is offered to the deities. (Raymond Kennedy)

who have no meat, or conserving milk which can be consumed as sour milk on the following day. In addition, the Pokot prefer fresh meat, which is also healthier than meat which is not fresh. Since one family could not consume a whole steer by itself, the problem of how to utilize beef most efficiently without refrigeration techniques is solved by offering it to the community in a ceremonial setting. In this way, meat can be shared without fighting over the supply, because the portions are distributed according to age and sex by a rigid formula (Schneider 1973).

In cultures where animal sacrifice occurs, only certain animals are considered appropriate offerings. Among the Nuer, for example, only animals that have been neutered, particularly oxen, are used in religious ritual. In sacrificing an ox, a parallel is being made between symbolic and social categories. Among the Nuer, certain problems involve the restraint of sexuality and the role of women. The ideal norms of Nuer society require loyalty of brothers to the partilineage. In reality, however, it is the brothers by the same mother who are most loyal to one another and may be in competition with their half-brothers (the Nuer are

*The religion of post-classic Maya, like the Aztec, involved human sacrifice.
Pictured is a temple at the Mayan site of Chichén Itzá, in Yucatán, with its steep
steps down which the sacrificial victims were thrown. (Serena Nanda)*

polygynous). An important source of conflict in Nuer society thus centers on women. Furthermore, there is conflict between the cooperation demanded by loyalty to the patrilineage versus the individual ambitions a man can realize through his wife and his sons. Thus, Nuer women are divisive on two counts—as wives and as mothers. These conflicts are projected onto women, and women are blamed for the conflicts between men. The aggressive aspects of sexuality are seen as responsible for the failure of Nuer men to live up to their moral obligations. Cattle are important religious symbols for sexuality and social relations. Bulls represent the attributes of maleness and vitality, which are admired but which, it is recognized, contain elements of ambition and aggression that are socially disruptive. The castrated ox, on the other hand, represents the subordination of sexuality and disruptiveness to social ends and thus symbolizes the

Nuer moral ideal. This makes the ox the most suitable animal for ritual sacrifice (Beidelman 1966).

Human sacrifice has also been a widespread practice, although it was often stamped out by European colonial governments. The Aztecs of Mexico, for example, had a religion in which human sacrifice was an important element. The Aztec gods, such as the jaguar and the serpent, were bloodthirsty and fierce and required human victims to appease their appetites. The victims, most of whom were captured in war, were ritually killed at the top of a pyramid built for this purpose. Their hearts were torn out and offered to the sun, and their blood was offered to the idols representing gods. The corpse was then tumbled down the pyramid, which with its very steep steps was efficient for this purpose. An attendant dismembered the body, and the arms and legs of the victim became the central dish in a feast given by the man who had captured him. Although Aztec cannibalism was limited to the ruler, nobles, and those who had captured victims in a war, it was practiced on a rather grand scale, perhaps totaling about 20,000 victims a year.

Michael Harner (1977) has recently proposed an ecological interpretation of Aztec sacrifice and cannibalism. He holds that human sacrifice was a response to certain diet deficiencies in the population. In the Aztec environment, wild game was getting scarce, and the population was growing. Although the maize-beans combination of food that was the basis of the diet was usually adequate, these crops were subject to seasonal failure. Famine was frequent in the absence of edible domesticated animals. To meet essential protein requirements, cannibalism was the only solution. Although only the upper classes were allowed to consume human flesh, a commoner who distinguished himself in war could also have the privilege of giving a cannibalistic feast. Thus, although it was the upper strata who benefited most from ritual cannibalism, members of the commoner class could also benefit. Furthermore, as Harner explains, the social mobility and cannibalistic privileges available to the commoners through warfare provided a strong motivation for the "aggressive war machine" that was such a prominent feature of the Aztec state.

Other interpretations of Aztec cannibalism have also been offered. To begin with, there is even some question that the Aztecs practiced ritual cannibalism, and there is no agreement about the extent of this practice. Harner, for example, bases his arguments on the evidence from early Spanish chroniclers such as Cortez, who wrote journals and letters describing Mexican customs. But as one critic (Ortiz de Montellano 1978) points out, the Spanish conquistadors did not necessarily write straightforward accounts of what they saw; they slanted their descriptions to make the Aztecs seem like barbarians in order to convince the king of Spain to support the conquest and undertake a large conversion effort by the Church. Ortiz de Montellano further argues that Aztec cannibalism can be fully explained by religious ideology and the desire to achieve status. He holds that neither the need for a dietary supplement nor the significance of the dietary contribution of human flesh has been convincingly demonstrated by Harner. The point here is not to prove one side of the argument or the other but to indicate some of the ways in which even the most bizarre religious practices can be made to "make sense" in terms of the sociocultural system of which they are a part.

Magic

Magic is an attempt to mechanistically control supernatural forces. In performing magic, human beings are expressing their belief that they may directly affect nature and one another, for good or ill, by their own efforts. Magic is thus different from other religious practices, such as prayer and offerings, in which the gods are *asked* to help bring about some condition. Magic involves specific ritual procedures that, if done correctly, will compel a specific and predictable result. In imitative magic, the procedure performed resembles the result desired. Imitative magic may go back thousands of years; pictures of bleeding animals painted on cave walls suggest that imitative magic was used to ensure success in hunting. Imitative magic may make use of verbal elements as well. Among the Cherokee, a spell for minor burns is:

Water is cold
Ice is cold
Snow is cold
Rime is cold
"Relief!" I will be saying.

Here the spell invokes four cold things. Along with saying the spell, cold water is also blown onto the burns, and this probably has some healing power of its own. Contagious magic uses something that has been in contact or

Divine intervention may be invoked to cure illness. A Navajo curer, Grey Squirrel, attempts to cure a patient by administering herbs, which is one element in the curing ceremony. The patient sits on a sand painting. (Museum of the American Indian, Heye Foundation)

will be in contact with whatever the magician wishes to influence. In contagious magic, the part may represent the whole; for example, sorcerers use the hair or fingernails of their intended victims to work their magic against them.

In many cultures, magical practices are part of most human activities. Among the Asoro of New Guinea, when a child is born, its umbilical cord is buried so that it cannot later be used by a sorcerer to cause harm. In order to prevent the infant's crying at night, a bundle of sweet-smelling grass is placed on the mother's head, and her wish for uninterrupted sleep is blown into the grass. The grass is then crushed over the head of the child who, in breathing its aroma, also breathes in the mother's command not to cry. When a young boy kills his first animal, his hand is magically "locked" into the position of the successful kill. When he later tries to court a girl, he will use love magic, which in a particularly powerful form will make

him appear in front of her with the face of another man to whom she is known to be attracted. Both magical and technical skills will be used to make gardens and pigs grow. One technique is to blow smoke into the ear of a wild pig to tame it. This is based on the belief that the smoke cools and dries the pig's "hot" disposition. Magical techniques are used for serious illness—blowing smoke over the patient to cool a fever (which is hot) or administering sweet-smelling leaves with a command for the illness to depart.

Divination, a magical practice directed toward obtaining useful information from a supernatural authority, is found in many societies. Flipping a coin is an example of divination in our own culture. Divination is magical in that it is a mechanical procedure for picking one of a set of alternative solutions, no one of which appears on the basis of available evidence to be preferable to the other. The practice of divination makes people more confident in their choices when they do not have all the information they need or when several alternative courses of action appear equal. Divination may also be practiced when a group decision has to be made and there is disagreement. If the choice is made by divination, no member of the group feels rejected.

Among the Naskapi, who hunt caribou on the Labrador peninsula, a form of divination called scapulomancy is used for hunting. In the divination ritual, a shoulder blade (scapula) of a caribou or other animal is scorched by fire. The scorched bone is used as a map of the hunting area, and the cracks in the bone are read as giving information about the best place to hunt. Naskapi scapulomancy may be adaptive because it randomizes the choices of location, a strategy that modern game theorists know results in the least chance of repeated failures.

Some farmers in the United States use a divination technique called "water-witching" or "dowsing" to find sources of well water where scientific opinion offers no certainty about where water will be found. In one technique, the dowser holds a forked willow branch (a willow is a tree found by river banks and is "sympathetic" to water) in his hands as he walks over a property. When he stands above water, the wand is supposed to bend downward. The effect of this ritual is to help a homesteader make a decision and be able to move forward confidently in developing his farm. In fact, because of the great variability of the water table, the method of the dowser appears to be no more or less reliable than scientific techniques in determining which spots will have water.

Sorcery

Magic may be used to benefit the community or an individual, or it may serve antisocial purposes. **Sorcery** is the use of magic with the intent of harming another person. Bone-pointing is a magical technique of sorcerers in Melanesia and is described by Malinowski for the Trobriand Islands. The sorcerer ritually imitates throwing a magical stick, either an arrow or the spine of some animal, in the direction of the person the magic is intended to kill. For the magic to work, the sorcerer must perform the procedure with an expression of hatred. He thrusts the bone in the air, twists it as if in anger in the wound, and then pulls it out with a sudden jerk. Both the physical act and the emotional state of passion have to be imitated to achieve results.

Cases of magical death, or death from sorcery, have been observed by anthropologists in a number of parts of the world. A classic case is that described by Cannon (1942), in which he observed an Australian aborigine who sickened and died after believing himself the victim of sorcery. Sorcery, like the other forms of magic discussed above, achieves its results indirectly by affecting the individual's emotional state. The effectiveness of sorcery depends on the awareness of the victim that a magical ritual is being performed against him

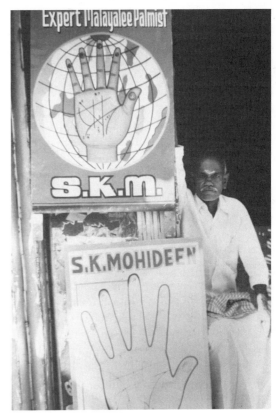

The popularity of astrology and fortune telling, as a way of predicting and thereby controlling the future, can be seen as an indication that many persons feel that they are not really in control of their lives. (Serena Nanda)

or her. If the victim is psychologically vulnerable to begin with and believes in the effectiveness of sorcery, he or she may exhibit a stress reaction that consists of the disordering of various physiological functions. The intended victim may despair, lose his or her appetite, and slowly starve to death, unable to overcome the inertia caused by realizing he or she is a victim.

The use of magic and sorcery appears to be attracting an increasing following in our own society, where it also achieves its results through exploiting the vulnerability of people who feel they have little control over their lives. Edward J. Moody (1974) describes a witch cult in San Francisco in which a great many ritual and magical practices are believed to give the cult members control over others and help them achieve success in life. A frequently used magical ritual is the "curse." If a member of the cult feels he has been hurt by another individual, he can bring his case to the high priest and the congregation. If they agree he has been unjustly treated, they will perform a ritual curse on the offender. The name of the intended victim is written on the skin of an unborn lamb and burned in the altar flame while the member speaks the curse, commanding that the victim be tormented in a variety of horrible ways. In one case described by Moody, a letter was sent to the victim informing him that a curse had been placed on him, and then a death certificate filled out in his name was mailed to him. After several weeks, the man in fact entered the hospital with a bleeding ulcer; when he recovered, he left San Francisco permanently. Although this victim may not have believed in the power of magic, he already had a bleeding ulcer, a failing business, and hypertension, a combination that made him vulnerable to the cult's efforts against him. Moody's description of the cult members suggests that, when people feel that they are losing control over their lives and are unable to make changes through manipulation of the real world, they will turn to the manipulation of the supernatural. Marvin Harris (1975) has also suggested that this is one explanation of the increase in the popularity of magic and witchcraft in contemporary American society.

Witchcraft

Witchcraft, like sorcery, is an attempt to harm another person through supernatural means. Unlike sorcery, which requires actual material substances, witchcraft is a quality of an individual, and witches operate only through psychic means. Sorcerers consciously undertake the kinds of actions they know will harm another; the power of witches may be an invol-

untary one. Our understanding of witchcraft will best be furthered by looking at the way it operates in a particular human society, in this case the Azande of Africa, who have been intensively studied by the anthropologist E. E. Evans-Pritchard (1958).

The Azande believe witchcraft to be a physical condition of the intestines that allows the soul of the witch to go out at night and harm others. Although the Azande believe that witchcraft can enter into every misfortune that befalls them, they do not live in constant terror of witches. After some misfortune occurs, they blame it on a witch. The Azande know that misfortunes are part of life: canoes are overturned, people become ill, houses burn down. The questions the Azande ask, which are the basis of the belief in witchcraft, are "Why me?" and "Why now?" Witchcraft in one sense is thus a theory of causation; what Americans might attribute to coincidence or bad luck, the Azande blame on the activities of a witch. Where a belief in witchcraft pervades a society, it becomes the first explanation when misfortune occurs. The Azande understand perfectly well that sometimes a lack of skill or a lack of morality is the cause of misfortune. A careless potter whose pots break will have a hard time getting others to accept witchcraft as the cause. Similarly, the Azande do not believe that witchcraft causes a person to lie or steal, and they hold the individual responsible for such moral lapses.

The Azande believe that witches are motivated by hate, envy, and spite against a specific person. Thus, an Azande man who believes that witchcraft has been worked on him looks around for the person with whom he has quarreled or who may have reason to be jealous of him. If the misfortune is a significant one, such as an illness or blight on his crops, the man takes action in a number of ways. He may try using magic to stop the witchcraft or call in a diviner to find out who the witch is so that he or she can be persuaded to call off the evil. In extreme cases, he may kill the alleged witch.

Witchcraft as it operates among the Azande indirectly helps to maintain the social order. It provides an explanation for what would otherwise be unexplainable and therefore gives support to the established pattern of culture. The procedures involved in handling witchcraft also help prevent the open disruption of established social relations, since an oracle must be consulted to divine who the witch is. Action is taken only with the support of the group; one person does not carelessly accuse another of being a witch. Witchcraft also serves as a leveling mechanism among the Azande, as it does in other societies. Since it is primarily a man who has repeated good fortune or who acquires more than the normal amount of wealth who is believed to become the target of witchcraft, individuals rarely attempt to outdo their neighbors by producing more than what is required for their own needs. Furthermore, witchcraft helps reinforce Azande ideas about morality; it defines the good man and the evil man. The person who is jealous, spiteful, and envious knows that he is most likely to be accused as a witch, and this expectation will bring his behavior more into conformity with the norms. In this way, witchcraft is a means of controlling behavior considered harmful and disruptive to the society. These functions of witchcraft are not unique to Azande society; they have been found to operate in many other societies as well.

THE ORGANIZATION OF RELIGION

Like other human behavior, religious behavior is patterned and organized. A useful way of examining religious organization is in terms of the degree of specialization of religious personnel—those who conduct ceremonies and perform rituals. On this basis, Anthony Wallace (1966) identifies four patterns of religious organization: individualistic cults, shamanistic cults, communal cults, and ecclesiastical cults. Although all patterns can be found in complex societies, simpler hunting and gathering societies may have only individualistic and shamanistic cults. Communal cults are characteristic of horticultural and tribally organized societies, and ecclesiastical cults are found in state societies.

Individualistic Cults

In **individualistic cults** each person may be a religious specialist, seeking contact with the supernatural directly according to his or her own experience and psychic needs. An example of an individualistic religious cult is the *vision quest*, a pattern of seeking contact with the supernatural found among many Indian groups of North America. In these cultures, an individual was able to develop a special relationship with a particular spirit that would give the person power and knowledge of specific kinds. The spirit acted as a personal protector, or guardian. The vision seeker was under a strong emotional impulse and by various means, such as fasting, isolation in a lonely spot, or self-mutilation, intensified his or her emotional state.

The Thompson Indians of Western Canada had a vision quest that included most of the traits typical of this pattern. When a boy, usually between the ages of 12 and 16, became old enough to dream of an arrow, a canoe, or a woman, he began his search for a guardian spirit. Before the actual quest itself, the boy had to run, with bow and arrow in his hands, until he was exhausted. Then he was made to plunge into cold water. He did this four times a day for four days. His face was painted red, and he put on a headband of cedar bark and tied ornaments made of deer hoof to his knees and ankles. He also wore a skin apron decorated with symbols of the life occupation for which he sought the spirit's assistance. The nights prior to undertaking the quest were spent in dancing, singing, and praying around a fire on some nearby mountain peak.

The boy then went on lonely pilgrimages into the mountains, eating nothing for several days on end. He intensified his physical suffering by sweating himself with heated rocks over which he threw water and also by whipping his body with nettles. During all this time he also threw rocks and ran for miles to ensure against disease, laziness, and bad luck. This strenuous regime continued until the boy had a dream of some animal or bird and received the inspiration for a spirit song that he would then always use to call upon his protector. He also prepared a medicine bag of the skin of the spirit animal and filled it with a variety of objects that had taken on symbolic significance for him during his quest. These became the symbols of his power (Pettitt 1972).

Although the vision quest was an intensely individual experience, it was nevertheless shaped by culture in a number of ways. Among the Crow Indians, for example, several informants related the same vision and interpretation to the anthropologist Robert Lowie (1963). They told of how on their lonely vigil they saw a spirit or several spirits riding along, and how the rocks and trees in the neighborhood turned into enemies who attacked the horsemen but were unable to inflict any harm. They interpreted this to mean that the spirits were making the visionary invulnerable. This motif is part of Crow mythology and is unconsciously worked into their experience by the vision seekers. Another cultural influence is that most Crow Indians obtained their spiritual blessing on the fourth night of their seclusion, and four is considered a mystical number among the Crow.

Shamanistic Cults

A **shaman** is socially recognized as having special supernatural powers that are used on behalf of clients for a variety of activities: curing, divination, sorcery, and reading fortunes, among others. Among Inuit coastal communities, the shaman's most important service is

to make a yearly spiritual trip to the bottom of the sea to persuade the sea goddess (Sedna), who is the keeper of the sea animals, to release the game so that the Inuit can live through one more year. Inuit shamans are also frequently called upon to cure illness; this is done by discovering which supernatural being has been offended by a broken taboo and caused the illness. Frequently, the illness is treated by extracting a confession from the victim, and through a ritual procedure the possessing spirit is then exorcised.

A typical shamanistic curing performance among the Netsilik Inuit is described by the ethnographer Asen Balicki (1963:385):

The shaman, adorned with his paraphernalia, crouched in a corner of the igloo ... and covered himself with a caribou skin. The lamps were extinguished. A protective spirit called by the shaman entered his body and, through his mouth, started to speak very rapidly, using the shaman's secret vocabulary. While the shaman was in trance, the **tupiliq** *(an evil spirit believed to be round in shape and filled with blood) left the patient's body and hid outside the igloo. The shaman then dispatched his protective spirits after the* **tupiliqs;** *they, assisted usually by the benevolent ghost of some deceased shaman, drove the* **tupiliqs** *back into the igloo through the entrance; the audience encouraged the evil spirits, shouting: "Come in, come in, somebody is here waiting for you." No sooner had the* **tupiliqs** *entered the igloo than the shaman, with his snow knife, attacked them and killed as many as he could; his successful fight was evidenced by the evil spirits' blood on his hands.*

In case the patient died, it was said that the *tupiliqs* were too numerous for the shaman to kill or that after the seance evil spirits again attacked the patient.

Shamanistic activity has important therapeutic effects for individual clients, who are often relieved of illness through the cathartic effects of the ritual. Shamanism also has important integrating functions for the society. Through a wide variety of symbolic acts, shamanistic performances bring together various beliefs and religious practices in a way that dramatically expresses and reinforces the values of a culture and the solidarity of a society. Such performances frequently involve participation by the audience, whose members may experience various degrees of ecstasy themselves. These performances are cathartic in the sense that they release the anxiety caused by various disturbing events affecting individuals or the community as a whole. The forces of nature and the supernatural, which have the power to do evil in a society, are brought under control; seemingly inexplicable misfortunes are given meaning within the traditional cultural pattern; and the community is better able to carry out its normal activities.

Communal Cults

In **communal cults,** groups of ordinary people hold rituals or ceremonies for the total community or parts of it—for example, age groups, sex groups, kinship groups, castes, or neighborhoods. These ceremonies may use ritual specialists, but the basic responsibility lies with ordinary people who on this occasion take on specialized sacred roles and perform sacred acts. Communal cult institutions include many different kinds of rituals. Some are not connected with the supernatural, such as Fourth of July celebrations in the United States. Most of these rituals can be conveniently divided into rites of passage and rites of intensification.

Rites of Passage   **Rites (rituals) of passage** mark the transition of an individual from one social status to another. One of the most important functions of religion is to help individuals and society deal with the crises of life. In almost all societies, transitions in social status—conception, birth, puberty, marriage, death—are surrounded by religious ritual. As we mentioned earlier in the chapter, rites of passage tend to have three phases: separation, transition, incorporation. In the separation

phase, the individual is removed from his or her old group or status. The rituals of this phase symbolize the loss of the old status or personality—having the head shaved or casting off one's old name. In the transition stage, the individual is between stages; although cut off from the old status, he or she has not yet been incorporated into the new one. At this point, the individual may be treated as sacred, in recognition of the power and the danger of this in-between position. In the third stage, the individual is incorporated into the new group or status. The rituals and symbols of this stage frequently are those of rebirth.

The Kaguru, a matrilineal tribe living in East Africa (Beidelman 1971), have initiation rites for both boys and girls. The Kaguru view initiation as necessary in order to convert irresponsible, immature minors into morally responsible adults. Kaguru male initiation includes both circumcision and moral instructions. Kaguru initiates learn how they will be expected to conduct themselves as adults. The physical distress of initiation makes the difference between the old life of the child and the new life of the adult more dramatic and leads to a greater acceptance of a new code of behavior.

Ideally, a group of boys is initiated together, both to increase the prestige of the ceremony and to divide the costs; also it is felt that the boys will bear the pain of circumcision and learn better if they are in a group. The most important persons in charge of putting the boy through initiation are his father and his mother's brother, who plays an important role in all matrilineal societies. A professional circumcisor is hired for the operation. He is chosen for his skill in cutting and the effectiveness of his medicines, which protect the boy from both physical and supernatural dangers.

The themes of danger and vulnerability are dominant in the ritual. On the announced day, the boys, some senior male kin, and their circumcisor are led into the bush. The boys are stripped of their clothing and shaved of all body and head hair. This symbolizes the separation

Among the Gururumba, when a person dies his or her physical body ceases to function but the vital essence that animated the person continues in the form of a ghost. If the ghost has not been treated with sufficient respect in the form of burial ritual, it will come back to perform disruptive acts on the living. This Gururumba woman is covered with white clay, a symbol of mourning. (American Museum of Natural History)

from their previous statuses. The boys are told that they may die from the circumcision. The boy's elder kinsmen hold him down in a sitting position while he is circumcised. It is considered admirable not to flinch or cry out, but those who do so are not condemned. The cutting is accompanied by songs and ritual. The foreskin is cut off, removing the "low, dirty," femininelike part of the boy. The bloodied objects are buried secretly. The boys are led to a shed to rest and be fed by elders. During the healing time, they are considered to be helpless, like babies.

When the boys recover physically, each day they are allowed to go farther back into the camp. The boys are told that if they reveal the

secrets of initiation, they will be devoured by wild beasts. During this time, the kin of the boys are also on their best behavior, because their actions may supernaturally endanger the boy's life. When the boys have finally recovered, they are sent out into the forest to perform some task. Everything in the initiation camp is then burned or buried. When the boys return, they are told that the elders have swallowed everything. After staying up all that night, the youths, singing to show they have "conquered" the bush, are led out of the camp the next morning by their friends and kinsmen. After a feast and dance, the boys will be considered fully initiated. During this feast, the boys are blessed and given new names associated with certain kinsmen, both living and dead. The youth is now considered a full social person. He may engage in an adult sex life, court girls, and consider marriage. He will require a full funeral when he dies and become a true ancestral ghost.

Funerary rites from our own and other societies indicate that death is a rite of passage. Rituals of the first stage, in which grief may be demonstrated by family and friends, mark the loss of the social person. In this stage, the remains of a deceased person may be buried. In the transitional period, the soul of the dead, as well as the corpse itself, is believed to be dangerous. It can take the form of a ghost and can wander among the living and cause illness and other misfortunes. In the third stage, the deceased is ritually removed from isolation or "limbo" and incorporated into its new status, perhaps as an angel in heaven, or as reunited with ancestors. This stage is marked in some societies by unearthing the bones of the dead, ritually treating them, and burying them again. With this phase of the ritual, the deceased is no longer dangerous to the living.

Rites of Intensification **Rites of intensification** are directed toward the welfare of the group or community, rather than the individual, and have rather explicit goals: increasing the fertility of the land in agricultural societies

Initiation rituals use many kinds of religious symbolism. Here white pipe clay is being applied as part of an Australian ritual. (American Museum of Natural History)

or the availability of game among hunting and fishing groups. These rites are also performed when there is a crisis in the life of the group, as in the transfer of power or in the loss caused by death. Funerary rites directed at moving the deceased individual from death to a new life have corresponding rituals that must be observed by the survivors. In the first stage, the survivors ritually express their bereavement for the loss of the deceased; in the interim stage they are in a period of limbo (mourning); finally, with the performance of rituals that end the mourning period, they resume normal social activity. Rites of intensification are also carried out to maintain the ties between the dead and the living, as in the case of ancestor worship, or to express the unity between humans and nature, as in the case of totemism.

Totemism is a prominent feature of the reli-gion of the Australian aborigines, who believe that people and nature share a common life and belong to one moral order. Just as human society is divided into mutually dependent and reciprocating groups, so too is nature. Each human group is linked with some species or object in the natural environment, which is its totem and with which it is mutually interde-pendent. By rules of birth and locality, people are grouped into "societies" or "lodges," each of which is associated with a different totem. This totem is their Dreaming. The Dreaming refers to the name of the totem species, to a cult hero, to the myths that tell of the deeds and sacred places of the totem species or hero, and to the rituals organized to represent the myths. In order to join the cult for which he is eligible, each male must undergo an initia-tion symbolizing death and rebirth. Only after this is knowledge of the myth, ritual, and sacred objects that make up the Dreaming gradually given to him. The chief object is the bull-roarer, the symbol and voice of the sky hero or of the totemic Dream Time heroes. In desert areas, the most important rites are for the increase of the totemic species. These rites are connected with centers associated with the cult heroes. Natural objects, mostly rocks, are said to be transformed bodies or parts of heroes or totemic species that appear in the cult myths. Myths are sung, actors re-create the heroic scenes, and human blood is applied to the stone symbol. As a result, the natural species increases, as the spirits of the species go forth to be reincarnated. Except for an annual ritual occasion, the members of a totemic group do not eat its totem species, although members of other totem groups are allowed to do so. Thus, each group denies itself one type of food and depends on other groups for the ritual increase of foods it does eat. In addition to increasing rites, there are also ceremonies held at temporarily sacred places. Here the past of the Dream Time heroes is reenacted. As they realize the presence of the Dreaming, onlookers and performers become carried away in a state of ecstasy. Through these rituals, the community maintains continuity with the past, enhances the feeling of social unity in the present, and renews the sentiments on which cohesion depends (Elkin 1967).

The totem rites of the Australians clearly point up the social functions of religion. According to Emile Durkheim (1961), a French sociologist, it was this function of religious ritual that was most important. When people worship their totem, which is a symbol of their common social identity, they are actually worshipping society—the moral and social order that is the foundation of social life. Durkheim believed that totemism was the origin of religion, because the aboriginal populations of Australia are technologically among the world's simplest societies. Although this aspect of his theory is no longer thought to be correct, his analysis of the social function of religious rites

in terms of heightening social solidarity is an important contribution to anthropology.

Religious ritual can also promote social solidarity by channeling conflict so that it does not disrupt the society. In all societies there are conflicts of interest and unconscious hostility between groups who are in unequal power relationships. Many societies have *rituals of reversal* during which people in the different groups ritually reverse their relationships. In the Zulu society in Africa, one day in the year women act as men and men act as women. The women chase and beat the men and act sexually aggressively toward them. In India, the celebration of Holi, which is primarily a harvest festival, includes a ritual reversal between dominant and inferior castes, as well as between men and women.

We are familiar with such reversals in Sadie Hawkins Day and Leap Year rituals, when in our own society it is considered permissible for women to ask men to marry them. In many high schools and colleges, one day is set aside when freshmen are allowed to harass the senior class, or students take over the classrooms and teachers take the role of students. Rituals of reversal contribute to social stability by allowing the channeled release of tensions that build up when one group of people is in a permanently subordinate position to another.

Ecclesiastical Cults

An **ecclesiastical cult** has a professional clergy that is formally elected or appointed and that devotes all or most of its time to a specialized religious role. These people, called priests, are responsible for performing certain rituals on behalf of individuals, groups, or the entire community. Individuals have access to supernatural power only through these intermediaries. Where ecclesiastical cults exist, there is a rather clear-cut division between the lay and priestly roles. Laypeople participate in the ritual largely as passive respondents or audience, rather than as managers or performers.

In ecclesiastical religions, priests and other kinds of intermediaries are required to carry out religious ritual. These specialists are also more knowledgeable than the ordinary person and act as teachers, as does the Buddhist priest in Katmandu, Nepal. (United Nations)

Ecclesiastical cults are most frequently associated with gods who are believed to have great power; these cults may be part of a religion that worships several such high gods, as in the religion of the ancient Greeks, Egyptians, and Romans, or just one high god, as in the Judeo-Christian tradition and Islam. Ecclesiastical cults are usually found in politically complex state societies. In these socially stratified societies, the elite may invoke religious authority in order to control the lower classes. The priesthood and religion act not only as a means of regulating behavior, which is a function of religion in all societies, but also as a way of maintaining social, economic, and political inequalities.

In societies where an ecclesiastical cult is the established religion of the state or the upper classes, the religious practices and beliefs of the poor or lower classes may be quite different from those of the elite. Powerless segments of society may use religion to rationalize their lower social position, and they may place more

emphasis on an afterlife in which they will receive more rewards than those who had power. Sects and cults among the poor may have a millenarian outlook—they may be focused on the coming of a messiah who will usher in a utopian world. In many of these cults, members participate in rituals that give individuals direct access to supernatural power by experiencing states of ecstasy heightened by singing, dancing, handling of dangerous objects such as snakes, or the use of drugs. There are many such sects and cults in the United States.

One of the most well known is that of the serpent handlers, whose churches are spread over Southern Appalachia. Serpent handling is justified in these fundamentalist congregations by reference to Mark 16:17–18, in the King James Bible:

And these signs shall follow them that believe: In my name shall they cast out devils; They shall speak with new tongues; They shall take up serpents; *and if they drink any deadly thing, it shall not hurt them; They shall lay hands on the sick, and they shall recover.*

For those who are the members of these churches, the above signs are demonstrations of the power of God working in those individuals who, through their belief, become his instrument. When a person receives the power of the Lord, he or she is able to handle poisonous snakes without being bitten. In these church services, members of the congregation pick up handfuls of poisonous snakes, thrust them under their shirts or blouses, hold on to them while dancing ecstatically, and even wrap them around their heads and wear them like crowns. The ritual of serpent handling takes up only part of the service, which includes in addition the singing of Christian hymns, dancing, spontaneous sermons, faith healing, and "speaking in tongues," all of which are part of the Holiness movement in Appalachia.

Weston LaBarre (1969), writing about these churches in *And They Shall Take Up Serpents*, suggests that to the extent that these religious experiences create an illusion of power and stop people from making real changes in their lives, these sects and cults are maladaptive. They are adaptive at the level of the whole society, however, because they channel dissatisfaction and anger so that the larger social structure is left intact.

REVITALIZATION MOVEMENTS

In many parts of the world, groups of people have experienced rapid disintegration of their culture through contact with the West. Culture loss, and the subsequent loss of a positive personal identity, have led to the emergence of **revitalization movements,** consciously organized efforts to construct a more satisfying culture. Some of these movements aim to restore a golden age believed to have existed in the past; others look toward a utopian future in which roles will be reversed and the lowly

will be in power. Sometimes, these movements reject all elements of the old cultural systems under which they suffer; in other cases, they attempt to combine new customs with the old and dissolve the social boundaries between the dominant and powerless groups in society. Even when a revitalization movement may be relatively ineffectual in bringing about the desired changes, it can still bring a sense of salvation and a more positive identity to people afflicted with feelings of conflict, inadequacy, and alienation from themselves and society.

In our own society, cultural loss, economic oppression, and powerlessness experienced by different lower-class and minority groups have also led to religious revitalization movements, such as the Ghost Dance among the native Americans in the 1880s and the Black Muslim movement in contemporary America. Two hundred years of slavery and a hundred and fifty years of prejudice and discrimination have left blacks in America economically deprived and burdened with a sense of racial inferiority. Various religious revitalization movements have appeared from time to time in the black community as a response to the stress of deprivation and the inability to forge a positive identity within American culture and society. The Nation of Islam, also known as the Black Muslims, is a contemporary revitalization movement that appears to be somewhat successful, both in attracting members and in changing their lives (Parenti 1967).

The Black Muslims advocate racial separation in a nation of their own and obedience to the messianic and authoritarian leadership of the "messenger," Elijah Muhammad. The movement contains many religious elements drawn from Islam and rejects many cultural patterns that are part of black life in the United States. The Black Muslims do not for the most part seek violent confrontations with whites in order to create their new world, but rather attempt to change the behavior of blacks in a way that will endow their life with meaning and purpose. The movement offers hope in a future in which blackness will no longer be despised.

The success of this movement with blacks for whom all hope of rehabilitation had been dismissed—drug addicts, criminals, alcoholics, unemployed slum dwellers—has been impressive. They have become obedient to the teachings of Elijah Muhammad, abstaining from drink, drugs, tobacco, gambling, promiscuity, stealing, and idleness. Muslims are forbidden to spend money frivolously and are committed to pooling their resources to help themselves and one another. They have created Muslim-owned schools and businesses. Muslim men must dress conservatively in suits and ties. Muslim women are supposed to wear a full white robe covering their arms and legs, and a white headdress. The dress of both men and women represents a break with the stereotype of the flamboyantly dressed lower-class black in America. The woman's dress in particular symbolizes a new relationship between men and women; women are protected, secluded, and obedient to males and are expected to be devoted to their homes and families.

The foods prescribed by the Nation of Islam are wholesome (whole wheat rather than white bread), and those that are forbidden include both the traditional Islamic taboos on pork and sea food, as well as "soul food" or the standard southern fare reminiscent of the past, such as corn bread, black-eyed peas, collard greens, and opossum. There is only one daily meal, which the family eats ceremoniously together. These patterns do not merely symbolize a new and positive identity for Black Muslims; they also have had a strengthening effect on health and family life.

The Black Muslim movement is a clear example of the ways in which the construction of a collective identity through the use of myth, symbol, and organization revitalizes the identity of the individual. The movement suggests that the seeking of change through secular political organization has not made a sufficient impact in restructuring American society to include a positive identity for all its citizens. Where politics fails, religious revitalization movements fill the gap.

This discussion of the Black Muslims again raises the question of whether religion may be more adaptive for some groups in society than for others. Where religious myths justify social stratification, elite groups obviously benefit more than others. Where the resentment of oppressed or subordinate groups is drained off in religious ritual, the resulting social stability would seem to be most advantageous to those already in the dominant positions. Although religion allows an illusion of control, this illusion may not be adaptive for many peoples in the long run. It remains to be seen whether political revitalization and participation will undermine the power of religious beliefs and rituals to alleviate the stresses caused by culture contact, modernization, and social inequality in the contemporary world.

SUMMARY

1. Religion is the beliefs and practices of a society concerned with supernatural beings, powers, and forces. Religion is a universal culture pattern and goes back to the beginnings of the human species.

2. Religion has many functions. Some of the most significant are explaining aspects of the physical and social environment, reducing anxiety in risky situations, increasing social solidarity, education, ensuring conformity, maintaining social inequalities, and regulating the relationship of a group of people to their natural environment.

3. Religious ideas are always expressed through symbols in which things stand for other things. Religious ideas are also acted out in ritual, and ritual reinforces beliefs.

4. Two widespread kinds of religious beliefs are animism and animatism. Animism is the belief that inanimate objects as well as living creatures have life and personality. Animatism is the belief in an impersonal supernatural power.

5. Many kinds of religious rituals are used to manipulate and control supernatural powers: prayer, offerings and sacrifices, telling and acting out of myths, music, and altering emotional states through physical suffering or drugs.

6. Magic is an attempt to control supernatural forces mechanically. Magic may be used for good or antisocial purposes; sorcery, however, is the use of magic with the intent of harming another person.

7. Beliefs about witchcraft have a number of functions in society. They ensure conformity, explain unpredictable events, prevent open social conflict, and act as a leveling mechanism.

8. Religious behavior is almost always organized. Four types of organization have been defined, based on the degree of specialization of religious personnel.

9. In individualistic cults, each individual may be his or her own religious specialist and have direct contact with supernatural power.

10. Shamanistic cults involve the use of shamans, who are socially recognized as having special powers that they exercise on behalf of their clients and groups in society.

11. In communal cults, groups of ordinary people hold rituals for the welfare of the whole community or of groups within the community. Two kinds of communal rituals are rites of passage, which mark the transition of individuals from one social status to another, and rites of intensification, which are directed toward the welfare of the community.

12. Ecclesiastical cults are characterized by a professional group of religious specialists who are responsible for performing rituals on behalf of individuals or the community. Only these specialized practitioners have access to supernatural power. This kind of religious organization is characteristic of complex and socially stratified societies.

13. Religious revitalization movements are consciously organized efforts to construct a new culture and personal identity. These movements arise in situations in which a group of people has been oppressed and has suffered cultural loss and loss of personal identity.

SUGGESTED READINGS

Daner, Francine
    1976   *The Children of Krishna.* New York: Holt, Rinehart and Winston. An anthropologist looks at the Hare Krishna cult in the United States and some of the ways it has adapted to Western culture and the identity needs of young adults who are alienated from the larger society.

Fried, Martha N., and Fried, Morton H.
    1980   *Transitions: Four Rituals in Eight Cultures.* New York: Norton. A readable examination of four life cycle rituals in eight widely differing cultures.

Leslie, Charles, ed.
    1960   *Anthropology of Folk Religion.* New York: Random House. A collection of interesting articles on religious beliefs and rituals from Africa, India, the South Pacific, and Mexico.

Lessa, W. A., and Vogt, E. Z., eds.
    1971   *Reader in Comparative Religion: An Anthropological Approach* (3d ed.). New York: Harper and Row. An excellent collection of articles on many different aspects of religion.

Myerhoff, Barbara
    1976   *Peyote Hunt: The Sacred Journey of the Huichol Indians.* Ithaca, N.Y.: Cornell University Press. A fascinating account of the search for Peyote, which figures prominently in the annual rituals of the Huichol Indians of Northern Mexico.

Victor Turner
    1977   *The Ritual Process: Structure and Anti-Structure.* Ithaca, N.Y.: Cornell University Press. A discussion of the roles and rituals that represent communitas in different societies, with a case study from the Ndembu of south-central Africa by a leading figure in symbolic anthropology.

CHAPTER FIFTEEN

The Arts

▶ What does Ice Age art suggest about the earliest human societies?

▶ Is music a universal language with many dialects?

▶ How is dance an adaptive aspect of human culture?

▶ What does folklore communicate about human society and social status?

> *The well-educated are those who are able to sing and dance well.*
>
> Plato

Much of what human beings do, as we have seen, they do to survive. And yet it is also true that human life everywhere consists of more than just survival. In every society, people apply imagination and skill to matter, movement, or sound to express emotions and values and to give one another pleasure. The forms of this creative activity include the graphic and plastic arts, such as painting, sculpture, carving, pottery, or weaving, and the structured use of sound in music, song, poetry, and folklore. In the movements of the human body—in dance, sport, and games—we also see the appli-cation of imagination, beauty, skill, and style that goes beyond the merely practical. **Art,** then, refers to both the process and the products of human skill applied to any activity that meets the standards of pre-ferred form or beauty in a particular society. In this sense, for example, tea drinking is an art form in Japan but not in the United States. This broad definition of the arts allows us to consider games and other forms of popular entertainment in some of the same ways that we consider arts in the more tra-ditional sense.

Masks are an important art form in parts of Africa. When used in ritual they are believed to take on the supernatural power of the spirits they represent. By confining supernatural power in a mask, or other material form, such power is more easily controlled and manipulated. (Serena Nanda)

ANTHROPOLOGICAL PERSPECTIVES

Because art in its broadest sense is a universal aspect of human experience, it is worthy of study by anthropologists and by those who wish to understand our species more completely. It is also humans' great variety of artistic forms and styles that makes the study of the arts so rewarding. Because artistic endeavors express some of the basic themes and values of a culture, they are an important way to gain insight into cultural patterning in different societies and into the different ways in which peoples perceive reality.

Anthropological discussion of the arts ordi-

narily divides them into four types: plastic and graphic arts; music; dance; and folklore (consisting mainly of oral tradition). Certain general approaches in cultural anthropology can be applied to the study of all these arts, but because of their different natures, they are usually studied by specialists. Some of the generalized approaches to the study of the various arts consider (1) content, themes, or subjects; (2) style; (3) changes over time; (4) social and psychological functions; (5) relationships with other aspects of culture and society; and (6) the creative process and the interaction of artists and their audience. Before looking at the various forms of human art, we will first examine the functions of art in society and the place of art within culture.

The Symbolic Nature of Art

One way of analyzing art is in terms of how it functions as a form of symbolic communication in society. In the first place, art can be seen as communicating direct meaning. For example, some dance movements attempt to imitate the movements of animals, and the contents of some paintings are believed not merely to represent, but to be—to partake of the spirit of—the thing visualized. Masks used in ritual are often believed to take on the supernatural power of the spirits or beings they represent. By being given a form, as in a mask, a painting, or a sculpture, the spirit can be more easily manipulated and controlled by humans. Among the Kalabari of Africa, for example, spirit beings are represented by sculptures. Offerings are made to them, and the sculptures are the center of ritual action. The more sophisticated individuals in the culture recognize that the statue is not the actual spirit; they consider it a confinement of the spirit. The point of confining, or localizing, the spirit in material form is to manipulate it for human ends.

A second way in which art is symbolic is that particular artistic elements reflect particular emotions or meanings. In this case, the symbolism is culturally specific, and one needs a knowledge of the particular cultural meanings assigned to a particular artistic element. In Western music, for example, the use of the minor scale conveys the emotion of sadness, and various other musical forms are traditionally associated with particular emotions. The traditional element is important in evoking the emotion, because individuals in that culture have been taught the association. In our own culture, the phrase "Once upon a time" signals to us that this is not going to be a story about "real" events and people and sets the stage for us to respond emotionally in certain ways.

A third way in which the arts are symbolic is that they reflect certain kinds of social behavior or social structure. The totem poles of the Northwest Coast Indians reflect the importance of social hierarchy. Stories of traditional dance dramas deal with religion. The organization of ritual using dance and music reflects the division of society into various kinship units or ethnic groups. Art styles may also reflect cultural values or patterns. In a study of Navajo music, for example, David McAllester showed that it reflected values in several ways. The characteristic Navajo cultural value on individualism is reflected in the attitude that what one does with one's music is one's own affair. Second, the Navajo are essentially a conservative people and believe that "foreign music is dangerous and not for Navajo." Third, the Navajo value of formalism is expressed in the belief that there is only one right way to sing every kind of song (one can contrast this with the value of innovation expressed in improvisation in music—for example, jazz).

The arts may also be symbolic on a deeper level; that is, they represent certain universal aspects of human thought, needs, and emotions. Freudian psychology, for example, assigns certain universal meanings to certain kinds of symbols. The widespread plots of myths having to do with incest might appear to reflect the unconscious working out of the Oedipal complex; the shape of the flute as a musical instrument and its association with men's cults in many culture areas have been interpreted as having phallic significance; certain colors have been interpreted as expressing universal physiological processes: red for blood or white for semen or breast milk.

The Integrative Function of the Arts

The symbolic nature of the arts in communication is related to what is undoubtedly their most important function—that of integration. Through the arts, the beliefs, values, ethics, knowledge, emotions, and ideology and world view of a culture are expressed and communicated. The art forms of a society do not merely reflect culture and society. Participation in cultural performances fosters the unity and harmony of a society in a way that is intensely *felt* by its members. It is perhaps the primary social function of the arts to produce this condition. The art forms of a society take up cultural themes and individual emotions—death, masculinity, pride, chance, relations between male and female, aggression, social cooperation—and present them in ways that make their essential nature understandable, even if it cannot be consciously articulated. Art makes dominant cultural themes visible, tangible, and thus more real. Thus, art is a means of expression that not only heightens emotions associated with cultural themes, values, and goals but also serves to display them in ways that are emotionally compelling.

In many cultures, including our own, games and sports are emotionally compelling and symbolic in a way that make us think of them, at least in their function, as like traditional art forms. Using this perspective, let us look in the accompanying box at the American game of football and see what it may symbolize about our society.

Football in the United States

According to Arens (1976), the popularity of football in the United States (which is unique among the countries of the world in its attachment to this game) derives from the fact that football contains characteristics particularly important in our society: technological complexity, coordination and specialization, as well as the tendency to violence, although that violence is expressed within the framework of teamwork, specialization, and mechanization. From this view: "The football team looks very much like a small scale model of the American corporation: compartmentalized, highly sophisticated in the coordinated application of a differentiated, specialized technology, turning out a winning product in a competitive market" (Montague and Morais 1976:39). Thus, the football game is a model of the most important productive unit in our society—the business firm. By watching football, we are watching a model of the way our world works. It is because football is a small-scale model of our world that it allows us to understand that world. It "renders visible and directly comprehensible a system that is far too large and complex to be directly comprehended by any individual." How many of us can understand the interconnections between all aspects of the American economic system?

Beyond this, however, football is a model of the traditional route to success in our society. Dedication, hard work, and self-sacrifice for the good of others (here, the football team) are held up as the basic principles on which success is based and are the characteristics most praised in individual players. Football is the staging of a real event in which the principles of success are shown to work. The success model is also illustrated in football commentary or sportscasting. The accomplishments of each player are compared with those of others, and the rewards of the system—money and recognition—are then extended to the players on the basis of their performances. To the extent that football is a model of the real world, the audience sees the actors being evaluated according to objective criteria and rewarded according to performance. It is this process that is at the ideological core of the traditional culture of the United States and that is ultimately related to the productive process in our society. Surely football is an example of the statement that "art" serves to display the cultural themes of a society in ways that make them emotionally compelling. As for its integrative function, Arens notes at the very beginning of his article that 79 percent of American households were tuned in to the first Super Bowl game on TV, indicating that this entertainment cuts across all the divisive aspects of our social structure—race, ethnicity, income, political affiliation, and regionalism.

The Arts in Cultural Context

The study of art largely divorced from its cultural context reflects to some extent an ethnocentric point of view that "art for art's sake" exists in all cultures. In fact, the opposite is true. Art in most societies is in fact *not* manufactured (or performed) solely for the purpose of giving pleasure. The separation of art from other activities and the separation of a class of objects or acts labeled "art" is characteristic only of modern societies. It is an extension of their tendency toward less cultural integration than is generally found in preindustrial societies. In modern societies, for example, even bad art is distinguished from other cultural products. In preindustrial societies, art is embedded in all aspects of culture; no separate class of material products, movements, or sounds is created solely to express esthetic values.

The Inuit, for example, who are considered by anthropologists to have a highly developed artistic skill, do not themselves have a separate word for art. Rather, all "artificial" objects are lumped together as "that which has been made," regardless of the purpose of the object. This does not mean that Inuit do not have esthetic values, but rather that their plastic art is applied to the manufacture of objects that have primarily instrumental value, such as tools, amulets, or weapons. It should not surprise us, then, that the Inuit, like most other preindustrial societies, do not make a distinction between artist and craftworker, a distinction that does exist in our society. Similarly, many skills—dancing, weaving, singing, playing a musical instrument—that in our own society are performed as a special category of behavior called the arts are in other societies skills that most people use in everyday life. In all societies, some individuals are recognized as more competent in these skills than others, but this competence does not necessarily translate itself into the specialized role of artist.

Because art is so embedded in cultural traditions, many anthropologists tend to believe that it may be difficult to measure esthetic values and styles according to any universal standard. What is beautiful in one culture may not be in another. Each culture has developed its own traditions of content and style, to which individuals in that culture conform in their application of creative imagination and skill. The appreciation of art in terms of values and forms that are not our own is difficult to achieve, although this can partly be overcome by attempting to understand the cultural context of art. One of the difficulties is that in the United States today, originality and innovation are an important part of our artistic standards. But art, which is a creative process, is not necessarily an innovative one. Artists in other societies may be very conservative, and archeologists provide evidence that the artistic styles of cultures remain stable over very long periods. Furthermore, the integration of art with religion in non-Western societies may limit the range of variation that individual artists display. Where religion and art have become sep-

A typical house style with rather elaborate decoration in a Paramacca Maroon village in Surinam, South America. Each man ideally carves his own house decoration, and the excellence of the craftsmanship is a source of prestige. (John Lenoir)

arated, as is now true in much of the contemporary world, experimentation, innovation, and real change in artistic endeavor are much more likely to occur.

Cultures differ not only in their esthetic preferences but also in the attention they give to various types of art. In some cultures, masks and painting are the most important media for the expression of esthetic values and technical skill. In other cultures, verbal skills are more important, with a wealth of myths, folktales, and word games and relatively little painting, sculpture, or pottery. Although every culture has dramatic performances as part of its religion, some cultures have developed this skill more than others. We do not know of any human culture, no matter how simple its technology or how difficult its environment, that does not have any form of art. In fact, when we look at cultures in which making a living is not easy and in which social structure is relatively simple, such as Inuit and aboriginal

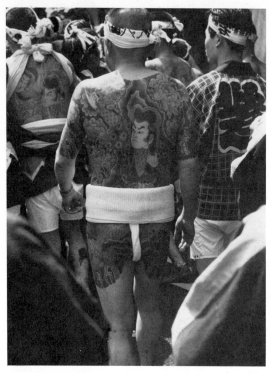

Tattooing in Japan may have begun with fishermen who believed that tattoos of dragons and demons would scare off sharks, or it may have its origins in the branding of criminals. Swashbucklers of feudal times adorned themselves with a more terrifying air. Ultimately, this practice spread to other social classes, including, today, wrestlers and members of organized-crime associations. (Sheldon Brody)

Australian groups, we find that art has an important place in the culture and that skill in a variety of art forms is of a very high level. We may thus speculate that art is essential in human society and may even have very important adaptive functions.

GRAPHIC AND PLASTIC ARTS

Many skills come under the heading of graphic and plastic arts: painting; sculpture and carv-

ing in wood; work in precious metals, bone, ivory, and horn; pottery and work in clay; basketry; weaving and embroidery; architecture; the tailoring of skins and other materials for clothing; and tattooing and other kinds of body ornamentation. The major anthropological emphasis on the arts in small-scale societies has been on the study of graphic and plastic arts. This may be due to the fact that such arts result in products that can be dealt with on their own, removed from their cultural setting, in a way that nonmaterial products such as dance or musical performance cannot. Plastic and graphic forms of art, for example, can be collected and exhibited in museums and art galleries, illustrated in books, and photographed easily. This allows them to be fairly easily compared with one another—in chronological sequences, in terms of stylistic variation, or as representative of the work of individual artists. An artistic product has a permanence that a performing art does not have, and this also makes it easier to study.

Style and Society

Interpreting Ice Age art (see accompanying box) is just one example of how art can lead us to an understanding of culture and how culture can influence art. Another fascinating attempt in this direction is the work of John Fischer (1961). Fischer's theory is that certain aspects of artistic style "say something" about sociocultural reality, and that this reality in turn shapes the kinds of fantasies that provide psychological security and thus esthetic satisfaction for the artist. Using a cross-cultural sample of relatively homogeneous societies, Fischer tested several hypotheses relating artistic style to the development of social hierarchy. First, he distinguished two major types of societies: authoritarian (hierarchical) and egalitarian.

In authoritarian societies, social hierarchy is positively valued. Society is viewed as divided into groups in higher and lower statuses. Each group has a set of rights and responsibilities in relation to those above and below. Those lower than Ego serve him, and he must help and protect them; Ego must serve those higher than he, who will in turn help and protect him.

The opposite ideal type is the egalitarian society, in which hierarchy as a principle of organization is rejected. Although differences of prestige do exist, these are not emphasized or even explicitly recognized. Work is seen as cooperative, rather than involving power differences between people working together. Individuals who attempt to control others are not valued as leaders; in fact, they are likely to be seen as a threat to society.

Fischer hypothesized that hierarchical and egalitarian societies would have different art styles, and he specifically related four aspects of style to emphasis on social differentiation.

Traditional art forms may use contemporary subject matter. Here a lady driver is expressed in the "X-ray" style characteristic of much of Australia and New Guinea. Note the repetition of simple elements in the art of egalitarian societies. (Serena Nanda)

1. Designs that included the repetition of a number of simple elements would be characteristic of egalitarian societies, whereas designs integrating a number of unlike elements would be characteristic of hierarchical societies. This hypothesis was based on the idea that security in egalitarian societies depends on the number of comrades (equals in social status) that Ego has. The multiplying of the same design elements is the symbolic representation of peers. In the hierarchical society, security depends on relationships with individuals in a number of differentiated positions. In design, these are symbolized by the integration of a variety of distinct elements.

2. Designs with a large amount of empty (irrelevant) space should characterize egalitarian societies; designs with little irrelevant space should characterize hierarchical societies. This hypothesis was based on the assumption that in egalitarian societies people relate to others as equals or do not relate at all. Security in egalitarian societies is found in isolation from other groups. In hierarchical societies, security is produced by incorporating strangers into

the hierarchy in a position of relative dominance or submission. This tendency for incorporation would be expressed in designs having little empty space.

3. Symmetrical designs should characterize egalitarian societies; the designs of hierarchical societies should tend to be asymmetrical. Symmetry is a special case of repetition; asymmetry expresses difference.

4. Figures without enclosure should characterize egalitarian societies; enclosed figures should predominate in the designs of hierarchical societies. The lack of enclosure in egalitarian societies symbolizes their face-to-face interaction on an equal basis. The enclosures in the designs of hierarchical societies symbolize the importance of social boundaries between individuals of different ranks.

Fischer's hypotheses were all supported, and this suggests that he is indeed on to something in his view that in the field of visual design, at least, art styles may be seen as "cognitive maps" of a sociocultural system.

Art in Culture: Interpreting Ice Age Art

One early anthropological interest in the graphic and plastic arts was an attempt to apply to them the evolutionary perspective that was being applied by nineteenth-century anthropologists to other aspects of culture. One of these evolutionary theories held that there was a progression of abstract art, characteristic of "primitive" cultures, to the naturalistic or realistic art found in Western civilizations. This theory was undermined by the discovery of Paleolithic, or Ice Age, art, much of which consists of paintings of animals on cave walls. The images are realistic and complex and show a high degree of delicacy, skill, and stylistic variation. When this art was first discovered in France and Spain, it was hard to believe it had been created by human beings living 30,000 to 15,000 years ago. The fact that this art was in no way primitive and yet was made by the earliest modern ancestors of our species underlines the difficulty of trying to establish an evolutionary perspective in the development of art styles. Contemporary anthropologists have thus attempted to study this art from a different perspective: that of what it can tell us about the ideology and life styles of the humans who created it.

Although it is impossible to know for certain, comparison with the art of contemporary hunting and gathering societies suggests that some Ice Age art had a close association with hunting ritual and with a world view that is particular to hunting societies (Levine 1957). In these societies, dependence on nature leads to an intense and intimate relationship with the natural setting. Given the technology of hunting peoples, the hunt is difficult, and killing big animals may even be dangerous. Although hunting peoples are extremely knowledgeable about their environment, unexpected natural phenomena can produce crises in their lives. Even when the food supply is abundant, unpredictability and the resistance of game to the hunter's purpose create anxiety. This anxiety and uncertainty are expressed by an ideology that perceives nature as active and personal. The peopling of the universe with gods or spirits that can take helping action allows hunting societies to have some control over their situation. It is believed that nature can be appealed to, by humans. One of the ways this is done is by ritually compensating nature for what humans must take from it.

These themes are associated with certain attitudes and patterns of behavior toward art. The main belief in this connection is that a work of art *is* what it represents. From this belief stems the idea that art objects themselves have *mana*-like power. Thus, hunting peoples who make artistic products often do so ritually—that is, as a way of satisfying and appealing to nature. Some aspects of Ice Age art may be interpreted in this way. Many of the drawings of animals, for example, show signs of having been superimposed; it is possible to interpret this superimposition as

MUSIC

The Conceptual Basis of Music

All cultures have their own traditional way of using the voice and instruments in structured ways to produce song and music. But the variety in musical systems is not limited to the different ways in which sound is structured; different conceptualizations underlie and shape musical systems. Although music is sound, not all sounds are music. Knowledge of a culture from the inside is required to understand the culture's conceptualizations, which are part of its musical behavior. A description of the conceptual basis of music of the Basongye people of the Republic of the Congo by Alan Merriam (1964) serves as an excellent example. The Basongye see music as something uniquely

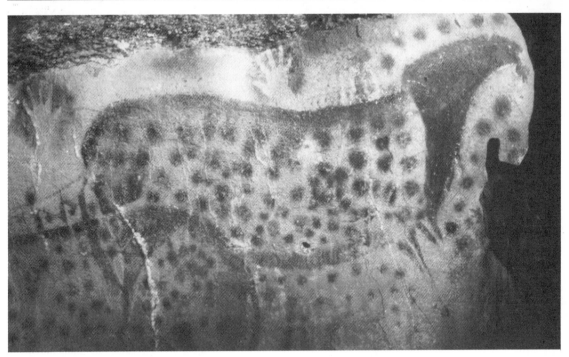

Figure 15.1   *Analysis of a horse, found in a cave in France and dated about 14,500* B.C., *indicates that the outline was filled with spots over a period of time, and the hand prints above the horse, and more spots, were added later. These superimpositions support the argument that such paintings had ritual value for the peoples who made them.*

being part of a restitution ritual (Figure 15.1). Whenever an animal was killed, its essence was restored to nature by a ritual drawing of the animal's image at a sacred spot. If restitution to nature is believed not only possible but also necessary, drawing images is one way that this can be accomplished. Taking a life is dangerous; ritual art, dedicated to the powerful spirits who protect life, is one way of lessening the danger.

human. They do not consider as music the sounds made by birds or animals or such natural sounds as the wind whistling through the trees. But all human sound is not music either. The Basongye say: "When you are content, you sing; when you are angry, you make noise. When one shouts, he is not thinking; when he sings, he is thinking. A song is tranquil; a noise is not." Furthermore, the Basongye consider that sound, in order to be music, must be organized. Thus, a single tap on a drum is not considered music, but drums played together in the traditionally patterned form drummers use are music. For sound to be considered music, it must continue over time. Thus, striking all drums once together does not produce music.

Focusing on the conceptualization of music in a particular culture leads us to understand why some avant-garde or controversial music elicits such resistance, even in our own culture. In a book significantly called *Silence* (1961), John Cage, a composer who is original, even "shocking," in his conception of music, advocates some new understandings. Cage, unlike the Basongye, wants to work out compositions according to the idea that "nothing takes place but sounds"; he wants to include in musical compositions those sounds that just happen to be in the environment. A composer who makes a musical composition out of twelve radios playing simultaneously challenges us to consider our own conceptualization of music in the same way that musical behaviors from another culture do.

Variation in Culture Areas

Although the variety of conceptualizations of music has not been explored by anthropologists, the variety of musical forms and instruments has been well documented. We are fond of saying that music is a universal language, but it may be more correct to say that music is a language consisting of a number of dialects, some of them mutually unintelligible. Several musical culture areas of the world can be differentiated, though all culture areas show significant internal differences in details and have several rather than only one musical tradition.

The Northeast Asian area includes China, Mongolia, Korea, and Japan. The music of this area is essentially melodic rather than harmonic. Melodic instruments in the early Confucian orchestra consisted of sets of like units: a set of tuned metal bells for chimes, stone slabs for stone chimes, a set of strings on a zither. In contrast to the Western idea of an ensemble in which all instruments sound together as one, each instrument in this music maintains its own identity. Divergence in time, pitch, and ornamentation of several instruments simultaneously playing the same basic melody gives the music a highly stylized quality.

In the Southeast Asian area, percussion, made with gongs, xylophones, cymbals, and bells, predominates. Here the orchestra is not a group of musicians, but a set of instruments unified by their physical appearance and common tuning system. In Indonesia, for example, the *gamelan* (orchestra) is unified by the proper relative sizes of the instruments, the themes and motifs of the decorative carving, and the particular color combinations of paints on the instruments. There is no standard tuning; only instruments belonging to the same orchestra or made by the same maker are in tune with one another. Thus, unlike in the West, musicians do not bring their own instruments to a concert. Each instrument has a function in the orchestra; some lead, others carry the theme, and others accentuate the theme. This is also in contrast to the Western symphony orchestra, in which one instrument may do several of these things at various times during the performance.

In South Asia (India and Sri Lanka), there are many traditions: tribal music, folk music, commercial film music, and a classical tradition that grows out of religion and philosophy of the Vedic period, going back several thousand years. In the classical tradition, music is seen as a path to self-realization; the texts of classical songs are prayers to the gods. The human voice is the primary instrument. Vocal style is basic to all melody, whether sung or played on an instrument. If an ensemble includes a vocalist, her or his role is preeminent. What is sung is more important than how it is sung. The music is essentially melodic, and improvisation has a significant place in performance.

Music in Africa is part of community life. The most important general characteristics of African music are its rhythmic complexity, a call and response pattern, the constant use of percussive devices such as hand clapping and foot stomping, improvisation, interesting vocal effects such as falsetto, and the simultaneous sounding of different pitches by singers or instrumentalists. A great variety of materials is

Among tribal nomadic peoples of North Africa and Western Asia, major musical forms include the solo song, recitation of epics, and group dances with modest instrumental accompaniment. Women use tamborines to accompany their own songs. These women of Targuist, Morocco, are singing the song of the Rif. (United Nations)

used for musical instruments—clay, metal, gourds, bamboo, tortoise shells, hides, skins, seeds, stones, and palm leaves. Wind and string instruments are found in Africa, but it is the drum that has always attracted the attention of students of African music. Drums are used to talk to spirits, to communicate between people, and to provide accompaniment for dancing. The important factor in the "talking drums" for which Africa is famous is that the drums create a sound that will carry for long distances. Although in some tribes arbitrary signals are used to symbolize words and concepts, more frequently the sound system of the drum is tied into the pitch structure of a language. Most African languages are tonal, which means that each syllable of a word has a prescribed tone or pitch. In order to be understood, a speaker must use the proper pitch and syllable. With drums on which the

pitch can be changed, the tones and rhythms of these languages can be played and understood.

Among the Indians of North America, music is essentially used in connection with religious ceremonies. It is largely vocal, with flutes, drums, and rattles used to accompany the voice. There is a wide variety of vocal styles. The Pueblos of the Southwest prefer deep male choruses; Plains tribes and the Navajo have a piercing falsetto tradition. In South America, where complex civilizations developed, orchestras and musical drama predate the Spanish conquest. Some of these forms spread into the countryside in the form of folk versions of urban music. Orchestral and choral effects are quite unlike anything in North America. Contemporary urban music often includes aboriginal influences in both melody and instruments.

In contemporary music in the Americas, the

influence of the African tradition is important—particularly rhythmic sophistication, call and response patterns, and the use of improvisation. African musical styles have continued with the least change in the dance and cult music of Brazil and the Caribbean, and they blend in with Hispanic styles in the rhumba and conga of Cuba and the steel band music of Trinidad. The steel band instruments, however, are a local invention and use a previously unknown principle of instrument construction. In the United States, spirituals and blues and jazz, from which rock and roll is derived, also have their origins in Afro-American music.

The music of the islands of Polynesia shows great variation, with a few common stylistic features. For the most part, traditional music was restricted to chantlike recitations and employed relatively few pitches. The complex manner of singing used trills, different tempos, shouts, and variations in breathing that were often more significant than tonal range or song structure. Traditional chant songs consisted of genealogies, accounts of mythological events, war songs, and love songs. The number of instruments was relatively small: drums, slit-gongs, and bamboo pipes. For making the rhythm of dance movements audible, shells or animal teeth were strung together and worn on the body. Before European contact, stringed instruments were scarce; today, two imported string instruments—the ukulele and the guitar—are among the most popular in all Oceania.

Music and Human Adaptation

Documenting the wide variety of musical styles and instruments is, of course, only the beginning in the science of ethnomusicology. Music, like the other arts, can be said to represent the "soul," or cultural identity, of a people in a highly condensed and emotional form. An important aspect of studying music, then, is in an attempt to understand the culture of a particular people. And like other art forms, music plays an important indirect role in human adaptation, primarily perhaps by contributing to the integration of society.

One of the most ambitious attempts to document the more direct ways in which music enters into human adaptations has been carried out by Alan Lomax and his colleagues (1968). One obvious relationship is the way in which music is used as an accompaniment for the procurement of food and natural resources and the processes of preparing them for human use. Lomax demonstrates that there is a direct correlation between the ways in which people work and their song style. Individualized song performances are correlated with several work situations, such as the voluntary and temporary work teams found in simple band societies and the small family work teams found in societies with plow agriculture. In horticultural societies—where work groups are relatively permanent, cohesive groups of age mates, clan brothers, or extended families—group singing predominates. Thus, the individualism characteristic of many aspects of life in hunting societies has its correlate in individualized song performance. The solidarity and cohesiveness of kin groups in horticultural societies is reflected in the communal or group nature of their singing. In industrial societies, where the individual or individual family is separated from the others, individualized song performance again emerges as important.

DANCE

Dance is a form of human behavior composed of culturally patterned, purposeful, and intentionally rhythmical body movement and gestures that are not part of ordinary motor activities and that have an esthetic value. Dance appears in every human culture and is also universally combined with other kinds of media—music and song, for example. It also

Music and dance are often combined to produce trance experience, which is one mode of gaining supernatural powers. At the Bab Segma in Fez, Morocco, on Sundays, hundreds of people gather to watch and listen to storytellers and boys who fall into a trance after hours of dancing. (United Nations)

involves supplementary materials added to the human body, such as decoration, costume, and masks.

Dance, like the other arts, is also symbolic behavior. It carries meanings that are arbitrary and culturally specific in the same way that human speech does. In dance, as in other kinds of human behavior, social learning is important. It is this aspect of human dance that differentiates it from biologically programmed ritual movements among nonhuman animals, such as the "dance" of honeybees or the mating movements of birds. Dance in human societies is used to communicate a variety of ideas and emotions (information), but the meaning of human dance is not self-evident; it depends primarily on the meanings assigned to it in different societies.

Because of its physical nature and its ability to elicit intense emotions, dance is often associated with the kind of excitement that signals special events in the lives of individuals or groups. Thus, dance is often involved in rites of passage, which mark changes in social status. Because the physical behavior involved in rhythmic and energetic dance may alter various physiological processes, such as the production of adrenaline, dance is also an important way of altering states of consciousness. In this connection, it may be part of rituals that involve trance and other states of emotion that transcend everyday experience. Through dance, an individual and a group can *feel* the qualitative shift in the normal pattern of mental functioning through a disturbed sense of time, a loss of control, perceptual distortion, a feeling of rejuvenation, a change in body image, or hypersuggestibility.

The study of dance suggests that it appears to be rooted in human capabilities for imposing order on the universe and may be adaptive for human societies as a way of conveying information about this universe. Dancing may also be adaptive in that, like the other arts, it is a form of exploratory, novel, even playful behavior. Novelty and play are also important adaptive aspects of other primate species. Dance teaches coordination and the skills that are involved in hunting, agriculture, and war. Ordinary movements used in procuring food may be incorporated into dance. Dance (and music) are used in many cultures to stir up feelings that can then be directed toward dealing more effectively with one's environment or coping with particular social problems. War dances, for example, may rouse men to the proper pitch of excitement and confidence so that they can act more effectively in battle. Dance also provides a protected situation in which human beings can experience forms of disorientation that could not be tolerated in everyday life. These may keep alive the capacity for new orientations to reality that at some point may be critical in a group's ability to adapt and thus to survive.

FOLKLORE: FORMS AND FUNCTIONS

Folklore includes myths, which are stories about supernatural characters and events; legends, which concern historical persons and events; and other kinds of oral traditions, such as riddles, proverbs, poetical compositions, and word play.

Myth

Myths are "sacred narratives" telling of supernatural beings and heroes and of the origin of all things. By explaining that things came to be the way they are through the activities of sacred beings, myths validate or legitimatize beliefs, values, and customs, particularly those having to do with ethical relations. As Bronislaw Malinowski pointed out over half a century ago, there is an intimate connection between the sacred tales of a society, on the one hand, and its ritual acts, moral deeds, and social organization on the other (1954). "Myth is not [merely] an idle tale," wrote Malinowski, "but a hard-worked active force; the function of myth, briefly, is to strengthen tradition and endow it with a greater value and prestige by tracing it back to a higher, better, more supernatural reality of initial events" (p. 146).

A clear example of what Malinowski meant is provided by the origin myth of the Yanomamo described by Napoleon Chagnon. The Yanomamo call themselves "the fierce people." Not only do warfare and other forms of violence such as club fights and wife beating play an important role among them; they also make frequent reference to their masculine cultural ideal as one of aggressiveness and fearlessness. They justify both this ideal and the violent activity in which they engage in terms of their origin myth.

According to the Yanomamo belief, Periboriwa, the spirit of the moon, had a habit of coming down to earth to eat the souls of children. One day, two brothers, Uhudima and Suhirina, who lived on earth, got so angry at Periboriwa for doing this they decided to shoot him. One of the brothers shot a bamboo-tipped arrow at Periboriwa while he was overhead and hit him in the stomach. Blood spilled from the wound, and as it hit the earth it changed into men. This was the beginning of the Yanomamo population; it is because they have their origin in blood that they are so fierce and are continuously making war on one another (1977:48). It is easy to see how this myth functions as a "social charter" for society. In the telling of such myths and in the ritual reenactments that often accompany them, social tradition is reinforced and solidarity enhanced.

Folktales

Although folktales may contain a supernatural element, they are not sacred in the same way as myths. Folktales are told mainly for enjoyment, although they often have important educational functions. Most folktales and other verbal arts, such as riddles and proverbs, have a moral. Oral traditions are thus important in the socialization process of every society, and especially in societies without writing. Folklore can tell us much about the cultural values of a society, because it reveals which actions are approved and which are condemned. The heroes in folktales give us clues to characteristics considered admirable in a particular culture. The audience is always led by the way the tale is told to know which characters and attributes are a cause for ridicule or scorn and which are to be admired. Thus, in studying folklore, the cultural context of its telling is an important clue to understanding the tale itself.

Folklore and Social Protest

Another important way of understanding folklore is in terms of its psychological and social functions in society. Folklore provides a socially acceptable outlet for emotions that might otherwise be disruptive to the social order. Through humor, fantasy, and the creative use of imagination, oral traditions provide a channel through which hostility, ambivalence, distress, and conflict can be released. Thus, folklore is an important channel of social protest.

Folktales often embody conflicts that are part of a shared experience; the conflict of heroic folk figures symbolically touches on and communicates what the audience feels but cannot articulate. Folklore resolves in fantasy issues that are problems in real life. This function is illustrated by the studies of Roger Abrahams (1970) of the various oral traditions among urban blacks in the United States. One of the most common figures in this oral tradition is the

Be good, loyal and work hard
and you will get your just reward !!!

Figure 15.2   Humor in folklore is one way of releasing tension when protest cannot be expressed openly. This anonymous bit of folklore from urban life is a protest against the unfairness of the system of rewards in contemporary bureaucracies.

"trickster," or "clever hero." The trickster, who is usually smaller and weaker than those against whom he is matched, triumphs through his wits rather than through force. This folklore hero is known in the United States through the Br'er Rabbit tales—a set of stories in which small animals are constantly getting the better of larger ones. The popularity of trickster tales in the Old South seems to have an obvious relationship to social relations between blacks and whites before the Civil War. The trickster tales can be seen as a veiled reaction or protest against domination and as a way of presenting feelings of protest in a nonthreatening way. For blacks in the United States, the trickster may represent the hero who can be in control of his world only through cleverness. The humor of these tales serves to release tension in a situation in which open rebellion seems futile.

Abrahams points out that, as the social situation has changed for blacks in the United States, their folklore has also changed. In urban black ghettos, the "badman" has supplanted the trickster as a hero. The badman, unlike the trickster, is consciously rebelling against authority. He is arrogant and virile and unlike the manipulative and sly trickster, the badman is manliness openly displayed. The emergence of the badman hero would appear to relate to the recognition of a more open environment in the urban North and of the greater possibility of resisting authority than was true in the Old South.

THE ARTIST IN SOCIETY

In studying the artist in society, anthropologists have been somewhat limited by the relative lack of good ethnographic data. Part of the reason for this is that in many small-scale societies, the artist as a specialist does not exist. Even if certain individuals are recognized as exceptionally skilled, they may not be full-time artists but rather combine artistic specialties with other kinds of activities. As already noted, artistic skill may be applied to the manufacture of objects for everyday use. Various other artistic skills, such as in dance and music, are usually embedded in the role of religious specialist.

Furthermore, in Western society we tend to define the artist as an innovator. The importance we place on being "original" has blinded us to some extent to the role of the artist in societies where the artistic product appears

to conform much more to cultural tradition and is less likely to stand out. The emphasis on innovation and difference has led us, in general, to see the artist as a special person, often a deviant, working alone and often in opposition to rather than in harmony with society. Artists in other societies do not always have this deviant or marginal status; their personalities may also be much closer to the cultural norm than is true in the West. The importance of designating a particular individual as the creator of a particular work of art is also not universal. Much artistic production in non-Western societies has a collective and thus anonymous quality. Folk art has traditionally been defined, in fact, as productions in which the individual creator is not known or has faded out of memory. As folk art becomes commercialized, however—as is the case all over the world today in places where there are tourist markets—individual artists emerge as specialists. They have been created by market forces; the work of certain individuals is in greater demand than that of others.

In an ambitious attempt to explore the role of the artist in society, Dennison Nash (1968) developed a model that raises some questions that lend themselves to cross-cultural research. Although Nash was specifically interested in the role of the composer in society, his framework can be applied to other kinds of artists as well. Nash concentrated on the social factors operating in recruitment to the artistic role, personality, and the role of the audience.

Although people with artistic talent may appear in either sex and in any social class, societies, through their cultural definitions of ascribed status, may inhibit or prevent these talents from developing and thus not use the gifts of talented individuals to their full potential. Art, for example, is often limited to either males or females in a particular society. Kinship status may define who fulfills artistic roles. Artistic roles may be inherited in families, clans, or castes. Where art is family property, such as in the songs owned by kinship groups among Northwest Coast Indians, the singing of these songs is limited to members of the group. In India, to give another example, certain art forms are practiced only by the members of certain castes. For a long time in India, certain forms of a classical dance called *bharatnatyam* could be performed only by women of a particular caste. These women were called *devadasis*, and they were attached to temples and ceremoniously married to temple deities. Their female children also became *devadasis*, while their male children became musicians and music teachers. Often people who are marginal in a culture are its performers. In Europe and Asia, for example, gypsies play an important role in musical performances. It is possible that marginal peoples are more able to be innovative because of their marginality.

Where religious activity, such as shamanism, incorporates artistic performance, it may be that essentially unstable personalities are attracted to artistic roles. The idea of the artist as separated from, and at odds with, the world, is a Western conception. We might expect to find, therefore, that the personality of the Western artist does differ in important respects from that of the nonartist. A study of avant-garde painters in the United States in the 1960s showed that they had a variety of personality characteristics, but a common thread was a profound quest for autonomy and alienation from middle-class life. Perhaps only when music or the other arts become vehicles for altered states of consciousness do the arts attract particularly unstable personalities, although they may always attract those with an exceptional innate talent and a drive that sets them apart from others in the culture.

The widespread Western idea that the essence of art consists in artists "expressing themselves" in some unique and innovative way appears to contain a culturally specific value of individualism. Certainly, the situation for some kinds of art among the Tiv of Africa would be very foreign to us. According to Paul Bohannan (1971), art among the Tiv is a secondary aspect of other facets of life—play, religion, social status. Much of Tiv art is com-

In tribal and peasant societies the artist seeks not so much to express herself in a unique and individualistic way as to recreate traditional designs that are pleasing but well within the traditional limits of the group. (United Nations)

munal; the artist, as an individual, is unimportant. In making various products out of wood, such as walking sticks or stools, one man may start a design or carving. If for some reason he has to leave it for a while, another person may add a few strokes and then in turn hand the object to a third person. It may take several people to finish it. In Tiv society, then, the audience, or critics, of some kinds of art may also play a role in creating it. This situation contrasts with our view that art should be a thoroughly individual product.

In music, dance, and drama, the communal nature of the arts is much more apparent in traditional, small-scale societies than in modern industrial nations. Creation, performance, and audience reaction tend to merge and feed back into one another. For a performer's activity to be socially significant, it must carry some meaning to an audience, and thus such performances are always carried out within certain cultural traditions. Even in the West, however, where innovation is an important artistic value, composers and artistic performers have written and performed largely for their own times and within the framework of the musical conventions of their culture. If there is no writing system for recording or notating music, dance, and drama, this is even more likely to be true. If the audience does not understand or like one's artistic activity, there will be little chance for it to become part of the culture; and without becoming part of the culture, there is little chance of its being preserved for posterity.

SUMMARY

1. Art refers to both the process and products of human skill applied to any activity that meets the standards of beauty in a particular society. For convenience, the arts can be divided into the graphic and plastic arts, music, dance, folklore, and games and sports.

2. Art is a symbolic way of communicating. One of the most important functions of art is to communicate, display, and reinforce important cultural themes and values. The arts thus have an integrative function in society.

3. The arts should be studied in their cultural context; the separation of a class of objects or activities labeled "the arts" is mainly characteristic of modern societies and reflects the general tendency toward the separation of many kinds of activities from one another.

4. The comparative evaluation of esthetic values and artistic styles is difficult, if not impossible. Each culture has its own standards of beauty and its own artistic traditions. Cultures also differ in the degree to which they have developed different art forms. It is thus generally agreed by anthropologists that art should be studied in its cultural context.

5. Because they are easily separated from their cultural context, most attention has been given to the study of the graphic and plastic arts. These arts can be examined in terms of their stylistic variation, as a way of understanding a particular culture, or as a cognitive map of a sociocultural system.

6. Music is a universal language with many different dialects. Each musical culture area of the world has its own characteristic way of structuring voice and instrument sound. Music has many functions in culture, and it may have a directly adaptive role in its relation to the nature of work in different societies.

7. Dance is a universal form of human behavior in which meaning is attached to specific movements. Dance and music are frequently associated with altered states of consciousness and are used in ritual and other performances that mark exceptional events in the life of the individual and the group. Both are frequently associated with religion.

8. Dance may also be directly adaptive in teaching physical coordination and in building skills necessary in productive work and in warfare.

9. Folklore refers to oral traditions, particularly myth and folktales. Myths are sacred narratives that function as social charters, validating the beliefs and social structure of a society. Folktales, though told primarily for entertainment, also have important functions in society. They serve to educate, to release tension and act as a channel for social protest, and to integrate society by displaying cultural themes in a dramatic setting.

10. In small-scale societies, the artist is rarely a full-time specialist, and art is much more of a communal or anonymous endeavor. The importance of innovation as a part of artistic judgment is more characteristic of Western culture than of other cultures.

11. Although people with artistic talent may appear in any segment of society, most societies restrict the artistic role to certain individuals, using criteria of sex, kinship status, or social class. Sometimes those who fill artistic roles are cultural outsiders or members of culturally marginal groups.

12. Where art is a vehicle for altered states of consciousness—for example, where it is tied in with religion—the artist may have a personality that is strikingly different from that of other members of society. Even where the artist is an exceptional personality, however, he or she tends to operate within the traditions of society.

with articles ranging from those that are a good introduction for the beginning student to those that require some background in the field.

SUGGESTED READINGS

Dundes, Alan, and Pagter, Carl R.
1975   *Urban Folklore from the Paperwork Empire.* Austin, Texas: American Folklore Society. A very funny book that looks at the typewritten and photocopied folklore that emerges as a way of protesting against the urban bureaucracy.

Graburn, Nelson H. H., ed.
1976   *Ethnic and Tourist Arts: Cultural Expressions from the Fourth World.* Berkeley: University of California Press. An extremely interesting collection of articles on various kinds of folk art that have become popular commercially. Very good illustrations.

Keil, Charles
1966   *Urban Blues.* Chicago: University of Chicago Press. An outstanding book on the blues and bluesmen favored by black urban audiences and the ways in which such music relates to urban culture and society.

Marriott, Alice
1948   *Maria: The Potter of San Ildefonso.* Norman: University of Oklahoma Press. A book based on first-person observations and interviews with a well-known native American potter, written in a personal way that will capture the beginning student's attention.

Otten, Charlotte M., ed.
1971   *Anthropology and Art: Readings in Cross-Cultural Aesthetics.* Garden City, N.Y.: The Natural History Press. Covers all areas of the plastic and graphic arts,

CHAPTER SIXTEEN

CULTURAL CHANGE IN THE CONTEMPORARY WORLD

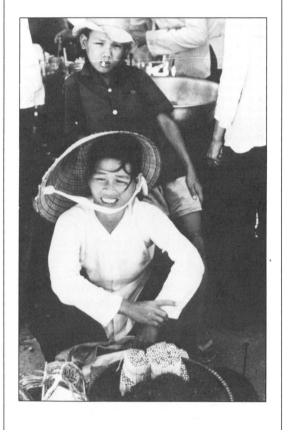

▶ What are the most important factors in cultural change in the contemporary world?

▶ How can a change in the economy lead to other changes in society?

▶ Because things change, does it mean they are getting better?

In the beginning God gave to every people a cup of clay, and from this cup they drank their life.
Proverb of Digger Indians

They all dipped in the water, but their cups were different. Our cup is broken now. It has passed away.
Ramon, a chief of the Digger Indians, as told to Ruth Benedict*

Our world is one of rapid change. Although cultural change has been continuous over the history of the human species, the *rate* at which changes are occurring today is faster than in any earlier period of human existence. With the exception of a few small populations in remote regions, no society today is unaffected by other social groups and the stream of current events. Furthermore, the very attitudes toward change itself are changing among many traditional and peasant populations. Although adherence to tradition and reluc-

*From Ruth Benedict, *Patterns of Culture*. Boston: Houghton Mifflin, 1934, p. 22.

tance to take risks are still strong, some of the changes introduced by modern industrial nations have been welcomed. Whether welcome or not, however, the initial changes have almost always had an impact on traditional peoples far beyond what was anticipated, both by the people themselves and by those who brought the changes.

CULTURAL CONTACT AND CULTURAL CHANGE

In Chapter Four, we discussed the idea that cultures are always changing, if they are to survive, in response to changes in the physical and social environment. We also introduced some of the processes by which cultures change, notably **innovation** and **diffusion.** If the contact between two societies is prolonged, so that one or both change substantially, we use the term **acculturation** to describe what happens. Acculturation did not begin with the age of Western exploration and colonialism, but the impact of these encounters on non-Western societies has been more radical in its consequences than anything previously known. The West, too, has been affected by contact with other cultures, though in less drastic ways. The channels through which cultural contact occurs and the processes of acculturation have not been the same everywhere. In some cases, the agents of cultural change have been primarily Christian missionaries; in other cases, commercial interests have brought traditional peoples into a world market economy. Industrialization and urbanization have been greatly accelerated since World War II, and the military operations of this and other wars have also played their role in cultural change. Since World War II, we can also include tourism as an important form of cultural contact.

Not all traditional cultures have been equally affected by contact, nor have the cultural responses been identical. In some cases, as we saw with the Yir Yoront, native cultures came close to disintegration. In other cases, revitalization movements arose, as with the cargo cults of Melanesia (see accompanying box).

Some tribal peoples have been relatively successful in keeping their traditional systems almost intact or have been able to synthesize new elements with the old in ways that have minimized personal and cultural disorganization. A case of successful resistance to the impact of Western culture, described by Robert Tonkinson (1974), involves a group of Australian aborigines called the Jigalong Mob, who live around the Jigalong Mission Station in Western Australia. The Jigalong had traditionally lived as hunters and gatherers, moving around in pursuit of the game and roots and

fruits that formed the basis of their subsistence. With the establishment of the mission station, some of the group settled down nearby to work for wages and to be near their children, whom they sent to the mission school. Although this led to some changes in local organization and economic life, the Jigalong Mob continued their traditional religious rituals and their complex kinship system. They exploited the opportunities to earn a living afforded by the mission, expending as little effort as possible and working only to satisfy their limited wants. Communication between missionaries and aborigines was limited; the missionaries visited the aborigine encampment only for prayer meetings, and the aborigines excluded the missionaries from their own religious ceremonies. The mutually unfavorable conceptions each group had of the other also acted as a barrier to meaningful social interaction. The aborigines associated the fundamentalist Christian missionaries with the absence of smoking, drinking, and sexual joking, while the missionaries saw the aborigines as children of the Devil and stereotyped them as lazy, deceitful, and depraved.

A number of factors help explain the successful resistance of the Jigalong Mob to cultural change. Their relative isolation at the mission contributed to their feeling of group solidarity, and they made a self-conscious effort to maintain their cultural traditions. In rural Australia, there is a generally laissez-faire attitude toward the activities of the aborigines outside the work situation, and this too contributed to the maintenance of the aborigines' cultural autonomy. Furthermore, because of their geographical isolation, this particular group had not been subject to the racial prejudice of white Australians, which led to feelings of inferiority and loss of identity among other aboriginal populations.

The experience of this particular group under the impact of cultural contact is instructive, because it shows that contact does not affect every population in the same way. Neither, it might be added, does it affect every

In efforts at modernization, traditional forms of communication are used to convey new ideas. Here a traditional Balinese song and dance drama presents the theme of family planning. (United Nations/Ray Witlin)

individual in the society in the same way. The physical location of a population, the nature of its traditional relationship with its environment, the degree to which the traditional culture is highly or loosely integrated, the nature of the contacting institution, and the mechanisms that stimulate or inhibit meaningful social contact between the populations must be considered before making any grand generalizations about the impact of cultural contact. Where traditional cultures are able to withstand disintegration and resist change, a number of factors may be at work. As we saw for the Amish in Chapter Four, it was also a particular combination of factors that allowed this group to resist change relatively successfully in spite of strong pressures from United States culture and society.

MODERNIZATION AND CHANGE

Modernization refers to processes by which traditional societies move in the direction of taking on the technological and sociocultural systems characteristic of industrialized nations. Modernization includes advanced machine technology, industrialization of the production process, urbanization, a market economy, centralized and bureaucratic structures of political administration, a growth of nonkinship social groupings, and an attitude that favors innovation and change. Whereas individuals in traditional societies are most often conservative and innovation is inhibited both because of traditional values and the leveling mechanisms of society, modernization requires

Cargo Cults in Melanesia

The anthropologist Peter Worsley describes cargo cults as they have operated in Melanesia (1959). For the last 400 years, Western culture has been spreading through the islands of Melanesia. Initially, the Melanesians were receptive to Western culture, which primarily reached them through trade goods, called "cargo" in Pidgin English, and Christianity, which was introduced by missionaries. They believed they would receive cargo and the riches of the Europeans through the missions, but they found that accepting Christianity did not bring the cargo any nearer. The Melanesians were discriminated against because of their color, and they realized that the preaching of Western religion was different from its practice.

With the expansion of the plantation economy in the islands, the enthusiasm of the Melanesians for Western culture began to wane. The Europeans removed men from their villages to work on plantations in Fiji and Australia. This trapped them into a worldwide community market in copra and rubber in which the prices, and thus wages, changed every month. These tribal peoples searched for an answer to the power of the white man and concluded that it rested on magic, which was the basis of power in their own societies. This made sense in terms of their observation of the whites: Whites did not work; they merely wrote "secret signs" on scraps of paper for which they were given shiploads of goods, whereas the Melanesians, who worked so hard, got nothing. Plainly, the whites who knew the secret of cargo were keeping it from the islanders.

Cargo cults began to appear in all parts of Melanesia. The central theme of the cults was based on the Christian idea of the millennium; in native belief, the world was about to end in a terrible catastrophe. Then God (or the ancestors, or some local culture hero) would appear, and a paradise on earth would begin. The riches (cargo) of the white man would come to the Melanesians. When Australian government patrols arrived in one part of the New Guinea highlands in 1946, they found themselves viewed as the fulfillment of a prophecy—the sign that the end of the world was at hand. The natives butchered all their pigs in the belief that after three days of darkness, "great pigs" would appear from the sky. Food, firewood, and other necessities were stockpiled to see the people through until the great pigs arrived.

In other places, native prophets announced that Europeans would soon leave, abandoning their property to the natives. In Guadalcanal, native peoples were preparing airfields, roads, and docks for the magic ships and planes they believed were coming from America. In Dutch New Guinea, where the Dutch had been driven out by the Japanese, it was believed that on the return of Mansren, the native culture hero, the existing world order would be reversed. White men would turn black like the Papuans, Papuans would turn white, root crops would grow in trees, and coconuts would grow on the ground. In some cults, the believers sat around tables dressed in European clothes, making signs on paper, in the belief that these mysterious customs were the clue to the white man's extraordinary power over goods and people.

Worsley emphasizes that, although the Europeans viewed these cult activities as "madness," they were rational attempts to make sense out of a more open attitude toward change. The typically fatalistic and conservative attitude toward experimentation that characterizes peasant and tribal societies gives way, although in most cases very slowly, to an achievement orientation, as it becomes more and more possible to acquire newly created wealth and status in the wider society through the changes modernization brings.

The response of a society to modernization depends on complex interrelationships among the physical environment, the traditional sociocultural system, and the particular modernizing influences it experiences. Although

Copra is one of the important cash crops of New Guinea. The involvement of native New Guinea populations in processing raw materials for colonially dominated markets led to the emergence of cargo cults. As indigenous peoples gain more control over their own economies, it is likely that the cargo cults will fade away. (Office of information, Port Moresby, Papua New Guinea.)

a seemingly chaotic and senseless social order, whose economy, politics, and society were beyond the comprehension of the tribal peoples caught up in them. The cargo, of course, never arrived, and old cults and leaders gave way to new ones. With the incorporation of Melanesian cultures and peoples into the political life of their newly independent nations and their participation in political institutions such as trade unions and native councils, the cargo cults died out.

many of the changes that are part of modernization tend to occur together, they need not necessarily do so. Industrialization may occur without large-scale urbanization, and urban migrants may be attracted to cities even in the absence of enough industrialization to give them employment. Entry into the market system may also be achieved without local industrialization—as, for example, in the case of tribal peoples who are induced by worldwide market demands for local natural resources, such as rubber, to produce for the market while not themselves becoming factory workers. Because change in one part of the sociocultural system leads to changes in other parts, many of the results of specific social changes that accompany the entry of traditional peoples into the modern world are unanticipated. These results are also not always positive for the society. But whether through the gradual voluntary acceptance of industrialization and urbanization under capitalism or through rapid reorganization under totalitarian state control, the traditional social and cultural orders of peasant and tribal societies are being changed, often drastically and irreversibly.

Technology, Economy, and Change

The essential element in modernization is the application of machine technology and scientific knowledge to the production process. Along with modern technology come changes in the traditional patterns of work: an increase in occupational specialization, the separation of production from kinship units, and the substitution of cash wages for traditional forms of exchange. As a result, social inequalities frequently develop where they had not existed or been important. In socially stratified societies, technological improvements often lead to even wider gaps between social classes as the benefits of technology are not equally realized by all groups within the society. (See Ethnography on pp. 352–353.)

Entry into World Markets

In the desire for manufactured goods made available by industrialization, many preindustrial peoples are drawn into worldwide market economies. Consumer goods such as electrical appliances, new clothing, bicycles, and many other gadgets become available to tribal and peasant populations, stimulating them to look for new economic opportunities. The market economy, with its commercialization of exchange and the use of all-purpose money, penetrates the tribal and peasant household or subsistence economy. Soon, even the most geographically remote peoples become caught up in market networks that extend not only to nearby urban centers but also to other societies thousands of miles away. In order to obtain the cash necessary for participation in the market economy, they commercialize agriculture. Production of cash crops equals or even outdistances production for use. We have already seen that participation in world markets they neither controlled nor understood was one of the factors that led to the rise of cargo cults among various peoples of New Guinea. This is but one of many examples of the effects of such participation on local economies.

Another example, with somewhat different effects, was the introduction of the growing of sisal in the Sertao in northeastern Brazil (Gross 1973). Peasants had traditionally subsisted on cattle raising and small-scale growing of beans and maize. In the 1930s, sisal, which is used to make rope, was introduced as a cash crop. When World War II cut off the supply of hemp from the Philippines, the price of sisal rose dramatically in the world market. Sisal was hailed as "green gold," and both large and small landholders planted all their land with sisal in the expectation of great profits.

Sisal crops take four years to harvest, however. The world price for sisal dropped dramatically after the war, and many small landholders found that they could not realize a profit on their harvest. As they no longer had any land to use for the growing of traditional crops with which to feed themselves, many small landowning peasants were forced to work for wages processing sisal for the large landowners who had bought processing machines and thus could still make a profit. Machine processing of sisal involves enormous amounts of manual labor, including shifting thousands of pounds of fiber per hour. Because the workers were paid on a production basis, they worked long hours to make ends meet in order to buy the food they could no longer grow. Food had to be imported into the region, which now produced only sisal, and a new social class of well-to-do shopkeepers grew up upon whom the peasants were economically dependent.

A study of the economic and social changes resulting from sisal growing was made by Daniel Gross, an anthropologist, in collaboration with a nutritionist. These researchers studied household budgets and caloric intake and measured physical growth and health among peasant families. They found that households that depended on wages from sisal work spent nearly all their money on food, most of which was needed to sustain the energy level of the wage earner so that he could adequately perform his demanding job. As a result, children in the households of sisal workers were being deprived of sufficient calories to maintain good health and normal rates of growth. The economic gains of the higher social classes, on the other hand, were manifested in a marked improvement in their nutritional state and that of their children. Sisal had brought prosperity to only a favored few; for most peasants, it only increased their poverty and intensified their misery.

Many non-Western nations have become dependent on one crop that is produced for a world market. Coffee is one of the most important cash crops in Rwanda, and most of it is grown by individual farmers. The farmer shown here is putting coffee beans out to be dried by the sun. (United Nations)

Tourism and Change

Since World War II, there has been an enormous increase in the number of Europeans and Americans visiting what were previously remote areas of the world. With greater accessibility, primarily through the development of airports, islands in the middle of the Indian Ocean, villages in the center of deep jungle in South America, and Inuit villages in the Canadian and American arctic are feeling the impact of tourism. Although 90 percent of the world's tourists both come from and visit countries in Europe, the United States, and Japan, tourist spending is often a major part of the economy in developing nations.

On the positive side, it is maintained that tourism can have a beneficial impact on developing nations through providing foreign exchange to pay for needed imports; creating

jobs; generating taxes; stimulating activity, particularly in the commercial and industrial sectors of the economy; and fostering foreign and local investment and capital formation. Some of the noneconomic advantages claimed for tourism are that it contributes to international understanding and peace and respect for other cultures. On the negative side, tourism that is unplanned and is controlled by outsiders can lead to overcrowding in tourist areas, rapid urbanization, labor shortages in nontourism sectors, prostitution and other demoralizing forms of "hustling," hostility towards tourists' affluence, and an increase in crime and violence. Although tourism can support and reaffirm cultural identities by reviving respect for traditional art forms, it can also degrade and parody cultural differences, lead to envy for Western goods and a Western life style, and intensify cross-cultural conflict. Perhaps one of the inevitably damaging aspects of tourism is that it "remains a statement of

E T H N O G R A P H Y

THE SKOLT LAPPS

An excellent study of some of the kinds of changes that result from technological improvements is presented by Pertti J. Pelto, who studied the effects of the snowmobile on the sociocultural system of the Skolt Lapps of northern Finland (1973). Lapp economy is based on reindeer herding, and reindeer were important for both subsistence and transportation in this arctic environment. Skolt Lapp males took great pride in their abilities as reindeer herders. The society was basically egalitarian; most individuals had equal access to basic economic resources, and there was little opportunity for social and economic differences to develop. Although the Lapps had obtained some material goods, such as flour, sugar, and various metal objects, from the outside world for centuries, the energy sources on which their subsistence depended were locally available, and they were essentially an autonomous society.

Snowmobiles were first introduced in Finland in 1962. They caught on very swiftly, and by 1971, practically all Lapp households owned at least one snowmobile and used it for transportation, hauling, and herding reindeer. Reindeer-drawn sleds, the traditional means of transportation, had completely disappeared. Many families sold their sled reindeer to finance the purchase of snowmobiles. Mechanized reindeer herding appeared to be a success; it made herding physically easier and economically more productive for the families who were the first to take advantage of the new technology.

The snowmobile has brought significant changes in Skolt life, most of which, from the point of view of Pelto, the anthropologist, are not without great disadvantages to the society as a whole. From being economically independent, the Skolt Lapps are now dependent on external and commercially distributed sources of energy for transportation, which is the critical factor in the reindeer herding economy. The management of resources now requires new skills, including reading and writing, and the use of money, as well as the technical skills involved in repairing and maintaining the snowmobiles. These skills were not equally present in all Skolt Lapp families.

Because of the initial cash outlay required to purchase a snowmobile, the families who were somewhat better off had a head start in making the transition to mechanized herding. They also gained additional income by providing transportation to families without snowmo-

fundamental inequality, whereby the 'haves' can travel halfway around the world for pleasure, while the 'have nots' struggle for subsistence beneath their noses" (Callimanopulos 1982). The control of tourism can thus be seen as another aspect of a fundamental issue: minorities' rights to self-determination.

Anthropologists have only recently begun to look at the effects of tourism on traditional cultures and economies. Consistent with the anthropological approach of examining cultural change in depth and, as much as possible, from the point of view of the recipients of change, research on tourism's impact often raises issues ignored by foreign investors interested only in their own profits. The economic benefits of tourism, first of all, very often do not go to local people. Secondly, although it is true that tourism brings in hard currency, it is also true that much of this money has to be spent in order to import things that tourists want and are not available locally. In the Seychelles, an island nation in the Indian Ocean where tourism is the main industry, food

biles. This initial advantage was a critical factor in subsequent economic success. The accumulation of resources could be used to expand into other opportunities, such as acting as tourist guides or even freeing adult males for wage work. Not all families are equally able to keep up in the snowmobile revolution. Those with lesser skills, cash, and flexibility have dropped out of herding altogether and have become dependent on the Finnish government for welfare payments and training for new kinds of employment. Although no strong system of social stratification has yet developed, Pelto predicts that the social differentiation between successful snowmobile herders and families marginal to the herding economy will become greater.

Pelto concludes that, although the snowmobile revolution has brought some economic advantages for some families, it has substantially increased dependency for all families. Even those that are succeeding are dependent on external sources of credit, for example. With the loss of the old skills

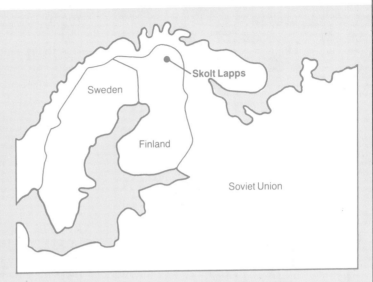

involved in nonmechanized reindeer herding, the diminished prestige accorded traditional herding activities and skills, the complete abandonment of sled reindeer for transportation, and the loss of control over the reindeer themselves, which have become more fearful of humans as a result of the noise and speed of the snowmobile, a complete return to the presnowmobile economy is not feasible. The Skolt Lapps themselves are somewhat divided on how they view the changes in their society. Those in the younger generation and those older men who have been successful tend to regard the snowmobile revolution positively. Looking at it in a more objective light and with an eye to the long-run changes, Pelto concludes that it has substantially decreased the autonomy and adaptive flexibility of the Skolt Lapp sociocultural system as a whole.

imports increased 1,400 percent over a period of 15 years, during which the number of tourists rose from a little over 500 to about 80,000. Because of the tourist demand for seafood, coastal waters have been fished out, and fish imports nearly doubled in one year, from 1978 to 1979.

Tourism almost invariably results in harm to the environment, some of it irreversible. In Bali, for example, many coral reefs are being destroyed as coral is used for building roads and making concrete. The reefs used to break up the surf, but now they are being taken away, and pollution is preventing new ones from replacing them. Thus, a severe storm would probably have a devastating effect on the economic system as well as on nearby inhabitants (McKean 1982). In the American Southwest, giant hotels use more water in one month—for swimming pools, lawn sprinklers, washing machines, and the like—than a local town and the hinterland formerly used in a year (Smith 1982). As a result, water for agriculture is disappearing or becoming so costly that small

The advertising copy for this photo reads: "Aloha from Hawaii—That's the message behind the warm smile of Rose Marie Alvaro, the Hawaii Visitors Bureau poster girl. This five-foot four-inch beauty, a beguiling blend of Hawaiian, Portuguese, Chinese, and English ancestries, is an accomplished hula dancer and Island entertainer" (Courtesy of Hawaii Visitors Bureau). Critics of the effect of tourism on indigenous populations point to the denigrating effects tourist imagery creates as it tries to capture the fantasies, often sexual, of Western, industrialized nations.

farmers and ranchers cannot afford to sink deeper wells, and many must give up their livelihood. In the mountains and forests, thousands of acres are burned annually by careless tourists. In the desert of the Sinai, which became a very popular tourist destination for campers and skin divers, many palm trees have died because ignorant tourists built fires in their midst, burning their roots. This has adversely affected the life style of the Bedouin nomads, for whom these date palms are an important part of the traditional economy (Zito 1982).

Although it is true that tourism does initially create jobs, many of these are low-skilled jobs in the service sector of tourism. The local population is expected to serve the personal needs of the tourists by cleaning their hotel rooms or waiting on tables or to amuse them in exotic ways. Thus, a class of "beach boys" has developed on some Caribbean Islands to "cater to North American women who have been steeped in the myth of black virility and come to the Caribbean to experience it" (Manning 1982). In Bangkok, tourist publicity geared to the "single man" of both Europe and Japan advertises the availability of females for sexual companionship in massage parlors, teahouses, nightclubs, and disco-restaurants (Phongpaichit 1900). Granted that these "jobs" offer a source of income, they would not seem to fit the aim of the World Tourism Organization to "create jobs that are not mechanical or alienating but based on reciprocal relations and help in integrating the individual in a more balanced society." Neither would such intercultural relations seem to foster "international understanding and respect for other cultures."

From a cultural perspective, tourism is selling fantasy, which very often involves turning a traditional culture into a spectacle for the benefit of a tourist audience. Frequently, in order to increase the flow of tourist revenue, artificial and inauthentic "folk culture" performances are invented for the tourist. Among the Eastern Cherokee of North Carolina, for example, during the tourist season a certain number of males

are self employed in the colorful business of "chiefing." These men dress in pan-Indian garb and post themselves in front of the tourist shops as an attraction. They specialize in having their pictures taken.... Tourists seem willing to accept the vulgar Indian stereotype the "chiefs" present for it fits in with their own preconceived ideas of what an Indian is (Hodge 1981:127–29).

Not all of the impact of tourism is so negative on indigenous culture. In Bali, for example, the interest of tourists in cultural performances has stimulated an improvement in the artistic quality of some of the dance and dramatic performances. The economic boost from tourist patronage of these performances has allowed local troupes to buy new instruments for their gamelan orchestras and new costumes, and it has encouraged the opening of schools and institutes throughout Indonesia for training in traditional art forms. An expert and professional group of Indonesian artists has maintained tight control over performances and is acting to conserve the quality of the arts. Similarly, the interest in tourism as a source of income among the Inuit of Greenland has led to a revival of ethnicity, which had almost disappeared, and to a desire to establish cultural ties with other Inuit throughout the United States and Canada.

Anthropological research seems to suggest that tourism is like all other forms of social change. When it is introduced gradually and controlled by local people, it can serve indigenous needs and improve some aspects of life. Mass tourism is an element of life that many non-Western cultures are having to deal with, whether they like it or not. It would seem to be in their interest to gain control of this process of "development" so that they can use it to serve their ends and not be manipulated by it.

Political Modernization and Planned Change

Politically, modernization refers to the growth of centralized and bureaucratic structures of political administration and law that extend down to local levels, both undermining local and traditional mechanisms of social control and filling in where such control mechanisms have been eroded by other processes of social change. New political ideologies emerge as the nation-state becomes the overriding structure of social integration. Previously autonomous cultural groups are drawn into national networks and brought (with varying degrees of success) under control by the state. The elite groups that control new nation-states in Asia, Africa, and Latin America are committed to

ideas of progress and development and are deliberately trying to transform their rural populations through programs of planned change.

The ways in which this happens are extremely variable, and precise formulas are not very useful. As Clifford Geertz points out, modernization is not just the replacement of the traditional and obsolete with the imported and up-to-date. The new nations of the world have the double goal of seeking to remain themselves and at the same time adapting to the requirements of the twentieth century: "There is no simple progression from 'traditional' to 'modern,' but a twisting, spasmodic, unmethodical movement, which turns as often toward repossessing the . . . past as disowning [it]" (Geertz 1973:319).

The success of new national governments in building modern and stable societies is intricately tied up with their ability to plan successfully for change in the hundreds and thousands of peasant villages of which most new nations are composed.

Peasant Society and Change

Most of the world's population today lives in peasant villages throughout Asia, Africa, and Latin America. In these villages, about 2 billion people are engaged mainly in intensive agriculture, farming primarily to feed themselves and to trade in local markets as well as producing for nonlocal cash markets. Peasants, as these people are called, are not, like tribal peoples, autonomous. Rather, they should be viewed as subordinate elements in the state societies of which they form a part. Peasants have a dependent relationship to the elites of their societies, whereas tribes are culturally and politically autonomous. (This statement is, of course, no longer strictly true but rather describes the major conceptual difference between peasants and tribes. Tribes today are very much influenced culturally by the larger sociocultural systems of which they are a part and are to a greater or lesser degree politically subordinate to national elites.) Although there are peasants in some highly industrialized countries such as France, Germany, and Japan as well as some countries in Eastern Europe, the majority of peasants live in the developing nations of the Third World, where they form a majority of the population of their countries. In India, for example, about 80 percent of the population lives in peasant villages.

As we saw in Chapter Nine, there is a great effort involved in peasant villages in meeting the material demands of religious observance and social position. This works as a leveling mechanism; that is, if people must take on social obligations that involve personal expenditure, it becomes difficult for any one family or individual to accumulate a great deal more than anyone else. But whether peasants are "spending" on ritual and social life or saving their small cash or food surplus, agricultural surpluses are *not* used to improve food output or to foster "economic growth." Thus, underproduction is one way of viewing the problems of peasants; there may not be enough to eat because not enough food is being grown. Production is also low because technology is often antiquated. Furthermore, agriculture is subject to many environmental hazards, such as weather or animal diseases, over which the peasants have no control. Unlike many tribal peoples, who have a very diversified diet and can adjust more easily to adverse effects on one food source, peasants tend to depend on a small number of crops and may be devastated if these fail.

Although the peasant village has often been seen by anthropologists as a closed entity, it always has a number of important links to the outside world. Some of these links, as in the case of marriage networks, may be to other villages. Other links are political and economic and are related to external sources of power. Traditionally, many of the links between peasants and the nonpeasant elite have been exploitative. Through taxes, rents, forced labor,

and other mechanisms, the surplus of the peasantry has been extorted by the elite for their own purposes. Thus, there has often been little abundance, and even great poverty, in peasant villages. Peasants appear to have a fear of outsiders, very often with good reason.

Peasant culture is basically an adaptation to the unpredictability of life, and peasants thus often seem conservative and resistant to change when it is introduced. Most of the developing nation-states have ambitious programs for changing peasant villages, particularly in increasing the amount of food production and trying to keep down the rate of population growth. Some of these changes succeed, and a cautious introduction of new technology suited to peasant farming and closely adapted to environmental conditions can bring about substantial improvements in peasant villages (Schumacher 1975). On the other hand, many of these technological changes have unintended consequences, not all of which can be regarded as progress, as we have seen in this chapter. Furthermore, many of the changes, both technological and social, that are introduced into peasant villages are not accepted. One of the important roles of applied anthropology is aiding planners in predicting what changes will be accepted and what their long-range impacts will be. Planned change in peasant villages is one of the important ways in which national governments in countries with large peasant populations are attempting to gain legitimacy and loyalty.

COMMUNITY DEVELOPMENT AND ANTHROPOLOGY: PLANNED CHANGE IN PEASANT COMMUNITIES

The community development movement is an attempt by the United States and other Western nations, as well as the United Nations, to promote economic growth and Western political democratic forms throughout the world. Community development tries to help people help themselves to improve the material and nonmaterial conditions of their lives. This self-help aspect means encouraging community autonomy and self-sufficiency. The assumption underlying community development among peasants is that the attitudes, values, and beliefs—in short, the culture—of peasants are resistant to change and that it is these peasant traditions that are themselves the primary determinants of change. Community development projects, whether fostered by outside agencies or by national governments, are aimed at changing attitudes of community members, so that they may develop confidence and competence to help themselves. Development aims at helping a community realize its own goals by using its own human resources, recognizing that some outside support, both material and technical, will be needed along the way. Part of the methodology of community development is to discover the "felt needs" of the population at the local level and work through these to achieve improvements. Although it is the community as a whole that is the focus of development, the assumption is that peasant communities are relatively homogeneous, and little attention is given to social stratification or conflicts of interest within peasant villages. The assumption is that development will benefit the whole community.

The community development movement as described above was consistent with a once prevailing anthropological view of the peasant community as a closed, isolated, functionally integrated whole. In their role as planners and evaluators of community development projects, anthropologists cautioned that without the holistic view of these "folk" communities and without proper attention being paid to local culture, community development projects were bound to fail.

An important project involving anthropologists in this model of community development was the Joint Cornell-Peru Project. Allan Holmberg and a team of anthropologists from Cornell University were given the charge of managing Vicos, a hacienda in the Andes in Peru, worked by Indian peasants who had been exploited by outsiders—whether Spanish or Peruvian—for centuries. In 1951, the Peruvian government, interested in bringing their Indian and peasant populations into the modern world, leased the hacienda to the project in an attempt to improve the life of the Vicosinos and at the same time to serve as a model for other, similar projects in Peru and elsewhere.

One of the major barriers to improving the material and social conditions of life in Vicos was the Indians' belief that they could not change the unequal relationship between them and the owners and managers of the large, semi-feudal estates, of which Vicos was one. The bosses, or *padrones*, saw no reason to educate their serfs, and the Vicosinos had little motivation to educate themselves. Both classes viewed formal education as a privilege of the dominant class. Although a school had been established in Vicos in 1940 by a government at least ideologically committed to equality, practically no students were enrolled, and the school had made no Vicosinos literate in its 11 years of operation. Thus, one of the high priorities of the Cornell intervention team was to promote education. Upon taking over the managerial control of Vicos, the project assigned the Indian labor force to build a new school building that could hold the hacienda's school-age population. Profits from commercial farming were invested in building materials, and the labor was provided by the peasants themselves. The Vicosinos had been promised before that the profits earned by their labor would be put back into their community, but this was the first time they actually saw it happen. When they became convinced that these new padrones meant what they said about helping the Vicosinos, motivation increased. School attendance jumped, especially when a hot lunch program was put in, which not only met the needs of the children, who were severely undernourished, but also further convinced

Modernization involves the use of machine technology, often as a substitute for traditional hand labor. The sewing machine, which has been introduced as part of community development programs in Mexico, is regarded as a useful tool in many peasant villages and lessens their dependence on buying goods from outside merchants at high prices. (United Nations)

the Vicosinos that things could really change for the better (Dobyns et al. 1962).

Similar successes were experienced in the areas of economics and social structure. The introduction of fertilizers and insecticides under the careful supervision of the anthropological team improved the potato crop. In the past, the Vicosinos had been forced to work on the owners' land for several days a week or to hire on voluntarily several days a week as farm laborers, for a pittance of a salary. With the new increase in productivity made possible by modern farming techniques, the Vicosinos now prefer to spend all their time work-

ing their own land. The Vicosinos had also been exploited by the mestizo merchants from whom they had to buy wheat and maize, since they did not grow enough to feed themselves. With the aid of the project's technical assistance, food surpluses were produced that were sold within the community at half the market price. An indigenous and democratically selected council began functioning, and Vicos itself became a center of exporting community development projects to other nearby communities. In 1962 the families living on the hacienda bought it and have since run it as a collectively managed and worked commercial enterprise (Dobyns 1972). The economic successes of Vicos also led to a change in the social structure of the area. Previously, Vicosinos were expected to be obedient to the big landowners and were forced to perform all sorts of menial activities at their command. With growing self-sufficiency and autonomy came a new dignity, and the Vicosinos now refuse to act obedient and subservient to the upper classes and mestizos. It is very clear that the intervention by anthropologists in the Cornell-Peru project resulted in substantial benefits for a previously impoverished and exploited peasant class. Whether similar projects, conducted without the dedication and expertise of the anthropologists assigned to manage Vicos, can succeed as well has not yet been established. After two decades of great idealism about community development projects, questions are being raised about its underlying assumptions, as well as about the usefulness of its operational methods in leading to substantial improvements in the lives of peasants.

The major conceptual criticism of the community development approach of the 50s and 60s is that the focus on the detailed, holistic local context directed attention away from the impact of external forces. Community structures were viewed as if they were explanations for behavior when, in fact, many of the community structures and constraints on peasant behavior come from the interaction of the "little" community with its physical environment and with the larger political forces of nation and world market. A new emphasis in development anthropology stresses the economic and ecological context of peasant decision making and its political links outside the community. The focus in this new approach is less on the local community as a closed, integrated culturally stable system than on the links between the peasant community and larger structures. The diversity within and between local communities, hierarchical differences and conflicts within communities, and national systems of power are emphasized.

Economic, social, and other decisions made by peasants are now seen not merely as a matter of cultural tradition but rather as rational and necessary, given available economic resources and environmental constraints. For example, it had frequently been assumed in developing nations that traditional pastoral economies were wasteful and that pastoralists were lacking in innovation, which is why they continued with an economy that appeared, in the eyes of development experts, to consist of "a herder seated in the shade of a tree while his animals graze; of women poking at a desperately poor piece of ground to raise a few uncertain crops and of an almost total lack of the outward material show associated with more settled cultures" (Baker 1981:66). We are now becoming more aware that pastoral societies have developed patterns of animal management over long periods of time, which are adaptive in minimizing most of the risks of overgrazing in the very marginal physical environments in which pastoralists live. Attempts at "development," which increase herd sizes with an eye to commercialization and build water tanks and wells without considering the potential effects of increased numbers of animals on limited grazing areas, have upset, sometimes irreversibly, the delicate ecological balance that traditional pastoral cultures have achieved.

A second major focus of the new development anthropology gives prominence to power and coercion and the ways in which these dimensions impact on different kinds of local communities, as, for example, under revolutionary governments. In the previous community development view, the failure of peasants to solve their own problems was attributed to a lack of solidarity and motivation within the community. Yet it can also be said that development is inhibited at the local level because of a lack of national resources and national bureaucratic mismanagement. This approach also stresses the importance of peasants as social classes, rather than merely isolated subcultures. It argues that power is an essential factor in sociocultural change and that this must be recognized if the peasants are to take control of their own lives. Toward this end, conflict has a positive effect, as it can be used to heighten a shared class consciousness among peasants. Similarly, the concept of Indian, in the Latin American context, is used as a culturally differentiating and stigmatizing term and may be seen as a way national elites maintain control over Indians. Recent development theory holds that Indians and mestizos should also be regarded as economic classes as well as ethnic groups. This point of view would tend to undercut the traditional development view that cultural integrity must always be attended to and furthered.

Finally, the newer development anthropology focuses on intracommunity differences rather than holding an assumption of community homogeneity. Empirical work has shown that responses to new economic opportunities in peasant communities depend on one's wealth and rank in the stratification system, which relates to the willingness to take the economic risks that development requires. For example, as part of the "Green Revolution," which involved the introduction of new, high-yield wheat strains into peasant villages in India, it soon became apparent that these new strains were superior only if planted in heavily irrigated fields and intensively treated with chemical fertilizers and pesticides. It was thus mainly those richer farmers, who already owned the more heavily irrigated fields and could afford to pay for the very expensive chemical fertilizers, that benefited from this development project. The attempt to introduce these wheat strains, produced in the West and capable of fulfilling their potential only with Western chemicals and the hardware necessary to run large farms, was of major benefit to the multinational companies who produced the chemicals and the hardware and to the richer farmers and merchant classes (Mencher 1974).

Revolutionary Change in Peasant Societies

In some cases, the social changes planned by modern governments may take place through peaceful, democratic means. The transformation of peasant societies may also occur through more violent alternatives, as in the case of revolutionary movements in China, the Soviet Union, North Korea, North Vietnam, and Cuba, in which peasants took an active part. These movements or revolutions are quite different from the peasant rebellions of the past, which were violent outbursts that did not fundamentally change the social structure of the larger society. In modern peasant revolutions, which are supported by a coherent ideology and an effective organizational framework, the social structures of some traditional societies have been almost completely destroyed and new socialist states created in their place.

The most dramatic example of revolutionary changes is provided by the People's Republic of China. A concise view of these changes is presented by Jack M. Potter (1967). In 1949, when the Chinese Communist party took power, China was an overpopulated, poverty-stricken country with more than 80 percent of its people living in rural villages. Many farms were small and inefficient, and technology had changed little in 2,000 years. Most villagers made hardly enough to meet their basic needs, and any surplus went into the ceremonial activities—funerals and marriages—necessary to maintain a family's status. Much of the surplus capital was siphoned off by landlords in the form of rents and exorbitant interest rates on loans. The landlord-scholar-government official class dominated the entire society. Traditionally, government intervened little in village life; its primary functions were maintaining order and collecting taxes. The nation was exploited economically by foreign powers and almost totally disrupted by the Japanese invasion in the late 1930s. An important basis of the achievement of the Communist government in reorganizing the society was the view that only through modernization and industrialization could China regain its national dignity.

The new government intervened in every aspect of peasant life in order to control the peasants and mobilize them to work in the interest of the state. The first order of business was land reform. Through government-supervised peasant associations, land and property were taken from wealthy landlords and redistributed to the peasants. The destruction of the landlord class, which had been the main buffer between the peasants and the government, now left the way open for direct government intervention in the villages. The ultimate aim was the establishment of total collectivization of village life. This process was to be achieved by stages. The first involved the reorganization of peasants into mutual aid teams in which villagers retained absolute control over their property but worked together, pooling farm tools, draft animals, and labor. In the second stage, land was still privately owned but was placed in a collective pool along with farm equipment, cattle, and labor and was worked on a collective rather than an individual field basis. When crops were harvested, some of the yield was set aside for taxes and some for the collective purchase of fertilizer, machinery, and so on; the remainder was divided among the members in proportion to their investment. In the third stage, the village was turned into a social cooperative. Tools, animals, and land were made the permanent property of the cooperative; members received no compensation for what they contributed, but derived their income only from labor points. In every stage of reorganization, there were heavy propaganda campaigns and educational meetings in order to commit the peasants to the goals of the government and a collectivized society.

By 1958, when almost all peasants had been organized into socialist cooperatives, the Great Leap Forward into the commune stage began.

These communes were multifunctional organizations covering an area including about twenty villages. The communes operated small factories and ran banks, commercial enterprises, schools, and the local government. In this stage, houses, trees, domestic animals, and garden plots, which the peasants had earlier been allowed to own and work privately, were confiscated. Women were mobilized to work alongside men, and common mess halls, kindergartens, and old-age homes were built to take over many functions previously performed by the family.

The Great Leap Forward is now acknowledged to have failed. The labor resources devoted to industry left a shortage of agricultural labor; confiscation of garden plots substantially decreased production by reducing incentive on the part of peasants; communal family activities demoralized the population. The government began a retreat to less radical forms of collective organization, and since the end of 1960, private garden plots have been returned to the peasants along with their houses and kitchens and domestic animals. Industry is giving greater attention to producing consumer goods. With these modifications, economic conditions seem to have improved considerably.

The lack of anthropological studies in China since 1945 has hindered our ability to understand fully many of the changes that have occurred there. In 1956, an anthropologist named William Geddes got permission to visit a village that had been studied before the revolution. Comparing what he was able to observe and the information gained through intensive questioning in the few days he was there with the earlier study, Geddes (1963) summarized the changes in the following ways: Women had generally achieved a higher status, and now voted. Marriages were no longer arranged. There was a lessening of the importance of kinship ties beyond the household and a decline in the authority and status of the aged. This correlated with the decline of the ances-

A work brigade on a commune in Yunnan Province, People's Republic of China.
The thresher is collectively owned and would be beyond the reach of any
individual farmer. (John Gregg)

tor cult, which had been at the center of Chinese religion and kinship. The government did not encourage religion, but had substituted new collective festivals that had a political orientation for the traditional village activities. The government had made strong efforts to promote literacy for both children and adults, and Geddes estimated that most adults could probably now read and write at a simple level. The changes initiated by the government were organized around improving the economic conditions of the population; all aspects of the new social order served this goal. In this area the government has been successful, although Geddes reminds us that the peasant acceptance of government control was prepared by armed revolution and sustained to an unknown degree by force and interference with basic freedoms.

Geddes and other observers of contemporary Chinese society point out that the success of the Communist system is due to the com-pleteness of reorganization and change; material changes and ideological commitment were mutually reinforcing. The very completeness of the system raises questions that ultimately have to do with values: To what extent does the new system allow for freedom and individuality and artistic creativity? How important is this to the people themselves compared with the dramatic improvement in the material conditions under which they live? But however we evaluate the changes that have occurred, an understanding of them would seem essential to our understanding of the transformation of peasant societies generally. This understanding has direct relevance to the formation and execution of public policy in the United States regarding its political and economic commitments to developing nations. It is to be hoped that anthropologists, who are trained to look at whole systems, can make an important contribution to these policies, which ultimately involve questions of cultural change.

Urbanization and Change

In many of the nations of Asia, Africa, and Latin America, spontaneous and voluntary migration of peasants to urban centers is one of the most, if not the most, important mechanisms of change. Although cities had important cultural roles in preindustrial societies, in the contemporary world urban migration has increased dramatically. Rural people come to cities seeking jobs and the social, material, and cultural advantages they perceive to be related to urban living. There are many different ways in which urbanization affects traditional societies. One anthropologist has characterized the adaptations of traditional societies to urbanization as a "three-ring circus," referring to the three arenas within which adaptations to urbanization take place: among the members of the home community left behind, among the urban migrants themselves, and within the urban host community to which the migrants go (Graves and Graves 1974).

Many of the migrants who leave their local communities do so only temporarily. They return to their places of origin to participate in a variety of economic or social activities and maintain important ties with those left behind. The degree to which urban migration is permanent depends partly on the personal involvements of the migrating individual within the local rural community, partly on the ability of the local community to reabsorb its returning migrants, and partly on the barriers to assimilation the migrant group meets in the urban area.

In a study of outmigration from Vasilika, a Greek village, Ernestine Friedl (1974) showed how a variety of factors led to a high degree of permanent migration to Athens, the Greek capital. Vasilika, like other peasant villages all over the world, had a labor surplus. At the same time, there were job opportunities in Athens. Furthermore, Vasilikans had a positive view of living in Athens; city living carried more prestige than village life. Rural families would support one of their sons who went to Athens to get an education, a usual first step toward obtaining a job in government service. In return for the family's support, the migrant generally gave up his rights to his share of village land, an economic benefit for those who remained. This loss of one's share in village property is a strong factor in permanent migration. Furthermore, since Vasilikans were not an ethnic or racial minority group in Athens, there were few barriers to assimilation. The Vasilikans lived throughout the city and had a wide range of social contacts with urban people. Many of them married nonvillagers, which also contributed to the permanence of urban migration.

Whether temporary or permanent, however, urban migration is both a direct and an indirect source of change in traditional societies. Not only are urban migrants themselves changed in the process of adapting to urban life, but the communities of origin are also changed. Most modern influences enter the countryside through urban centers, either by mass communication, as radios and movies become available in villages, or through the links between urban migrants and those who remain at home. Not only modern consumer goods but also new ideas, knowledge, and values are passed on to villagers through urban migrants. These modern influences permeate the village only slowly, however; material culture is affected first, and then social organization and ideology.

Ruth and Stanley Freed (1978), who studied a village close to New Delhi, the Indian capital, found that in spite of the large numbers of villagers who worked in the city, village social organization and culture remained largely traditional. Although some urban-oriented men were more relaxed about requiring the isolation of women and *purdah* (veiling), role behavior in the family did not change substantially. The basic features of the caste system were also not much changed. Two important changes that did occur were a decrease in prohibitions on lower-caste use of public facilities and a transformation of *jajmani* relationships into "fee-for-service" arrangements.

The migration of land poor peasants to cities often results in squalid living conditions, such as this slum in Santiago, Chile. (United Nations)

The prohibitions on untouchability were due more to new laws passed by the national government than urbanization itself, but the transformation of the *jajmani* system was clearly the result of the alternative of urban jobs for landless laborers who preferred to work for cash.

In summing up the trends they believed were due to urbanization, the Freeds listed the following factors, which would probably apply in a general way to other urbanizing societies as well: (1) an increasing modernization of material culture; (2) an increase in the number of villagers earning a living from modern industrial and commercial jobs instead of traditional crafts and farming; (3) less dependence of landless laborers on large landowners; (4) more casual social interactions across caste boundaries; (5) an emphasis on various features of Hinduism that were more in accord

with city life than rural life; (6) a rising level of education; and (7) more exposure to the wider world through mass communications.

Urbanization and Voluntary Associations
With urbanization, a great variety of social groups based on voluntary membership develop. These groups are generally called **voluntary associations.** Voluntary associations are adaptive in helping people organize to achieve their goals in complex and changing societies, and especially in helping migrants make the transition from traditional, rural-based society to a modern, urban, industrial life style. Although not all voluntary associations formed in newly urbanized societies have goals that are directly economic or political, these associations frequently serve as vehicles through which such goals can be achieved.

Voluntary associations that emerge among

newly urbanized populations may serve as mutual aid societies, lending money to members, providing scholarships for students, arranging funerals, and taking care of marriage arrangements for urban migrants. Some of these voluntary associations develop along kinship or tribal lines that were relevant in the traditional culture, but others, such as labor unions, are based on relationships deriving from new economic contexts and have no parallel in traditional rural society. Voluntary associations help migrants adjust to city living, and they provide the basis for political organization through which the interests of different groups in newly emergent states can be served. Such associations are also training grounds for new skills that are useful in industrial and urban contexts, such as electing officials, speaking before a group, and the use of a language other than one's native tongue. Because these associations often award prestige based on modern rather than traditional role achievements, they ease the transition from traditional to modern identities.

Voluntary associations can also help members move beyond narrow local identities based on kinship, village, caste, and tribe to wider identifications more relevant in modern nation-states, such as those of citizen or worker. Some urban voluntary associations are based on traditional statuses. These include tribal and regional associations found in West Africa, caste associations in India, and the kinship-based associations found among the Batak peoples who have migrated to cities in Indonesia. These associations have a dual function, however. On the one hand, they provide continuity with traditional sources of identity and culture; on the other, they also socialize their members into city ways, serving as a link between traditional and modern structures.

During my fieldwork in India, I studied a voluntary association in Bombay formed by women who had originally come from villages and small towns in northern India. These women were drawn together by their common language and culture, which was distinct from that of the majority ethnic group in Bombay. They belonged to the same category of high castes and were upper middle class; their husbands were professionals and businessmen. The women began their group about twenty-five years ago, meeting once a week mainly for the purpose of holding religious ceremonies and participating in the devotional singing that is an important feature of contemporary Hinduism. In their ritual activity, they attempted to re-create the social and religious life of their native region. Although this is the reason they organized, their association now has other purposes and functions as well. Through the informal exchange of gossip in the group, new patterns of behavior are introduced, discussed, evaluated, and diffused. For example, if a woman's son marries a Westerner, the group will discuss this and its implications for their own lives. In this way, the association provides a kind of emotional support system that helps the women adjust to change. Through informal discussion, new fashions and new ideas are introduced and slowly become part of an upper-middle-class urban life style.

Because high-caste Indian women are not encouraged to work, women's associations play a very important role in widening their cultural horizons and their social circle within the appropriate caste, ethnic, and class groups to which they belong. Women's groups in northern India tend to be age-graded; through participation in such a group, a young daughter-in-law can escape, at least temporarily, from the supervision of her mother-in-law and find solidarity with other women of her own age. For older women whose sons and daughters are ready to be married, these associations provide access to a network within which marriages can be arranged with some confidence.

Voluntary associations are an important part of the adaptive strategies of urban migrants, because they can be based on an almost infinite number of interests and serve a wide range of purposes. In West Africa, for example, urban women's associations are much more directly concerned with political goals and economic interests, reflecting the fact that their membership is made up of working women. The importance of these associations reflects the important economic and political roles women in West Africa traditionally play. The importance of voluntary associations in the nations of Asia, Africa, and Latin America is paralleled by the importance of similar associations among immigrant groups in the urban centers of the United States.

Informal Association in Complex Societies: Social Networks

A **social network** refers to a set of both direct and indirect links between an individual, who is at the center of a network, and other people. Unlike a social group, such as the voluntary associations discussed above, a social network is really a framework for understanding social relationships imposed by the outsider. Networks are a useful way to study social organization in cities and in complex societies, where social organization consists less of closed, kin-based, corporate groups and more of links between individual actors who share only a part of their lives with a great many other individuals in a number of situations.

One of the important points of comparison among networks is the degree of connectedness or density of the network. In a highly connected, or dense, network, the individuals with whom Ego is connected are also connected to one another. In a low-density, or dispersed, network, Ego is connected to other people who do not know one another (see Figure 16.1). Comparison of network density and structure has been used to explain a number of kinds of social behavior—for example, communication of gossip, diffusion of norms, and pressures for social control. One of the earliest uses of social networks was in the study of urban families in England (Bott 1957). Among other things, **network analysis** showed that, although many urban families are not contained within organized groups (such as a corporate kin group, for example), they do have many external rela-

In complex societies, informal relationships become important as frameworks for social activity. Network analysis is useful for studying urban life, pictured here in San Juan, Puerto Rico, where both friendship and kinship are organizing factors in social life. (Bernhard Krauss)

tionships with individuals and institutions who are not, however, linked. Network analysis opens up a new perspective on the urban family; it allows us to see that the urban family is not necessarily isolated, as is often claimed, but rather is involved in a more or less dispersed network of social relations without which it could not survive.

Not all the individuals with whom Ego is connected have the same relationship to him or her. In some of the relationships, Ego will be related to an individual in a number of ways—friend, kin, neighbor, co-worker. In other relationships, Ego may be linked to an individual in one role only—say, as a co-worker. Furthermore, Ego uses different parts of his or her network depending on the situation. Some individuals may be mobilized when it comes to finding a job, others in times of personal crisis, still others in building up a power base.

As people in traditional societies move out of their relatively self-contained communities of kinship and local groups and expand their social ties in new situations, new methods of anthropological analysis become appropriate.

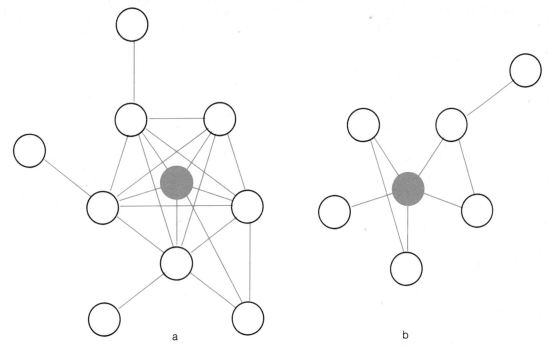

Figure 16.1   *A comparison of a highly connected network (a) and a dispersed network (b).*

Network analysis is one of these methods. Its increasing use is an example of the ways in which anthropology is adapting to social change in the contemporary world.

A LAST WORD

In this chapter we have been concentrating on change in tribal and peasant societies in the contemporary world. But it is not only other societies that are changing but our own as well. Anthropology began as a discipline with the aim of looking at other cultures so that we might eventually look more objectively at ourselves. More and more anthropologists are beginning to do ethnography in the United States and to apply the principles and theories of anthropology to our own social problems. America as a culture is becoming subject to the kind of scrutiny anthropologists previously reserved for other cultures. With this

increased objectivity, we can begin to embark on the path laid out by Edward Tylor, the founder of anthropology as a discipline, who said that we have in anthropology the means of leaving the world a better place than we found it.

SUMMARY

1. The contemporary world is affected by rates of change unlike those in any earlier period of human existence. An important source of this change is the contact between modern industrial nations and traditional nonindustrial societies.

2. One important aspect of change in the contemporary world is the application of machine technology and scientific knowledge to the production process. These technological changes can lead to significant changes in culture and social organization, many of which are unanticipated. An example is the effect of the snowmobile on the society of the Skolt Lapps in Finland.

3. Entry into worldwide market systems is another powerful factor of change in the contemporary world. Although such participation may increase the number of consumer goods available to tribal and peasant peoples, it does not necessarily raise their basic standard of living. Furthermore, it leads to a dependence on often unstable world markets over which traditionally autonomous populations have no control.

4. Tourism is a special kind of entry into world markets. Although many economic advantages are claimed for tourism, these are often more apparent than real. Tourism, although it may promote cultural identity and intercultural understanding, may also promote a loss of cultural integrity and intercultural conflict.

5. Although much contemporary change is unplanned and unanticipated, many politically modernizing nation-states are also attempting to introduce planned changes consistent with ideas of progress and development while at the same time retaining aspects of traditional culture that are important in forming national identities and ideologies.

6. Where governments are not successful in bringing about change voluntarily, there may be peasant revolutions, as in the People's Republic of China. The new socialist government intervenes in every aspect of the people's lives in order to increase productivity and through modernization and industrialization restore China to a respected place in the world community of nations.

7. Urbanization is yet another important process of change. The migration of rural peasants to cities affects not only the lives of those who migrate but also the culture and social structure of the rural areas they leave. Because of the rapid rate of urbanization in the contemporary world, the study of urban adaptations has become an important subject of anthropological research.

8. In complex societies and those undergoing social change, kinship groups often become weaker and voluntary associations based on economic and political interests become more important.

9. Anthropologists have developed a method called network analysis to study some of the informal social relationships that become increasingly important in contemporary societies. In network analysis, the links between Ego and other individuals, some of whom are in contact with one another, are examined.

10. Few anthropologists have looked at American society from a holistic anthropological perspective. This approach suggests itself as one way in which we can sharpen anthropology as a tool to improve life in our own society.

SUGGESTED READINGS

Brady, Ivan, and Isaac, Barry
  1975   *A Reader in Culture Change.* Volume II: Case Studies. Cambridge, Mass.: Schenkman. An anthology of readings on culture contact and planned change in a wide variety of societies in the contemporary world.

Bodley, John H.
  1982   *Victims of Progress.* Menlo Park, Calif.: Benjamin/Cummings. An outstanding book that persuasively details the ways in which autonomous tribal societies have become the victims of industrialization and the expansion of the state.

Harris, Marvin
  1981   *America Now: The Anthropology of a Changing Culture.* New York: Simon and Schuster. A flawed, but nevertheless provocative and useful analysis of the interlocking of various changes in American society—feminism, violent crime, the rise of cults—from a materialist point of view, written in Harris's usual lively and contentious style.

Murphy, Yolanda, and Murphy, Robert

1974   *Women of the Forest*. New York: Columbia University Press. An account of how
rubber tapping has changed the lives of
a group of horticulturalists in South
America, and particularly how these
changes have affected the lives of
women.

Spindler, Louise S.
1977   *Culture Change and Modernization: Mini-
Models and Case Studies*. New York: Holt,
Rinehart and Winston. An introduction
to the subject that includes discussion
of theories of change and case studies of
change among particular human populations both within and outside the
United States.

GLOSSARY

Acculturation   The process that takes place when contact between two societies is so prolonged that one or both cultures change substantially.

Achieved status   A social position that an individual chooses or achieves on his or her own.

Adaptation   The ways in which living populations relate to the environment so that they can survive and reproduce.

All-purpose money   Money that serves as a means of exchange, a standard of value, and a means of payment for a wide variety of goods and services.

Animatism   The belief in impersonal supernatural power (sometimes called *mana*).

Animism   The belief that living creatures and also inanimate objects have life and personality, referred to as spirits, ghosts, or gods.

Anthropology   The comparative study of humankind.

Applied anthropology   The organized interaction between professional anthropologists and both private and public policy-making bodies.

Archeology   A specialized field of cultural anthropology focused on human cultures that have existed in the past and for which there are no written records.

Art   The process and products of human skill applied to any activity that meets standards of beauty in a particular society.

Ascribed status   A social position an individual is born into.

Authority   Power exercised with the consent of the members of the society (legitimate power).

Avunculocal residence rule   System under which a married couple resides with the husband's mother's brother.

Balanced reciprocity   An exchange of goods of nearly equal value, with a clear obligation to return them within a specified time limit.

Band   The basic social unit in many hunting and gathering societies, made up of fewer than 100 people related to one another through blood ties or marriage.

Behavioral norms   The typical behavior that people who share a culture actually engage in.

Bifurcation   A principle of classifying kin under which different kinship terms are used for the mother's side of the family and the father's side of the family.

Bilateral descent rule   System under which both maternal and paternal lines are used in reckoning descent.

Bilocal residence rule   System under which a married couple has the choice of living with the husband's or wife's family.

Bride service   Work that the groom performs for his bride's family for a variable length of time either before or after the marriage.

Bridewealth   Goods presented by the groom's kin to the bride's kin to legitimize a marriage.

Call system   Form of communication among nonhuman primates composed of a limited number of sounds that are tied to specific stimuli in the environment.

Capital   Goods used to produce other goods, or wealth invested to purchase capital goods.

Capitalist society   A society in which people work for wages, land and capital goods are privately owned, and capital is invested for individual profit.

Caste system   A system of stratification based on birth and in which movement from one stratum (caste) to another is not possible.

Chiefdom   A society with social ranking in which political integration is achieved through an *office* of centralized leadership.

Clan   A unilineal kinship group whose members believe themselves to be descended from a common ancestor but who cannot trace this link genealogically.

Class system   A form of social stratification in which the different strata form a continuum and in which social mobility is possible.

Cognition   The ways in which human beings perceive, understand, and organize their responses to the universe.

Cognitive anthropology   A theoretical approach that defines culture in terms of the rules and meanings underlying human behavior, rather than behavior itself.

Collateral kin   Kin related through a linking relative, such as a man and his father's brother.

Communal cult   A type of religious organization in which ordinary people hold rituals for the community or segments of it.

Communication   The act of transmitting information that influences the behavior of another organism.

Composite (or compound) family   An aggregate of nuclear families linked by a common spouse.

Configurationalism   The theory that holds that each culture is a unique configuration or pattern of elements and values.

Conflict theory   A theory of social stratification that holds that the natural condition of society is constant change and conflict. The inequality in systems of social stratification is considered evidence of this conflict.

Consanguineal family   Individuals who are related by birth and descent.

Controlled cross-cultural comparison   An anthropological method that uses comparable ethnographic data from many societies and tests particular hypotheses.

Cosmology   The system of beliefs that deals with fundamental questions in the cosmic and social order.

Cross cousins   Individuals related through siblings of the opposite sex at the parental generation.

Cultural anthropology   The study of human behavior that is learned, rather than genetically transmitted, and that is typical of a particular human group.

Cultural ecology   A theoretical approach that regards cultural patterns as adaptive responses to the basic problems of human survival and reproduction.

Cultural evolution   The process by which new cultural forms emerge out of older ones.

Cultural integration   The tendency of the parts of a culture to be consistent or in harmony with one another.

Cultural relativity   An attempt to understand cultural patterns from the "inside" and to see the traits of a culture in terms of the cultural whole.

Culture (general)   The learned and shared kinds of behavior that make up the major instrument of human adaptation.

Culture (particular)   The way of life characteristic of a particular human society.

Culture area   A broad geographical area in which a number of societies make similar adaptations to a particular ecological zone and through diffusion come to develop similar cultural patterns.

Culture of poverty   The name given by Oscar Lewis to the constellation of cultural traits that emerge as a reaction and an adaptation of the poor to their poverty and lack of power in the larger society.

Descent   The culturally established affiliation between a child and one or both parents.

Descent group   A group of kin who are lineal descendants of a common ancestor, extending beyond two generations.

Deviance   Departures from cultural norms regarded negatively by society.

Diffusion   The spread of cultural elements from one culture to another through cultural contact.

Divination   A magical practice directed at obtaining useful information from a supernatural authority.

Domestic group   A household unit that usually, but not always, consists of members of a family.

Dominance hierarchy   A form of social structure, found among baboons, in which each adult male animal knows where it fits in relative to other males and generally accepts the situation.

Double descent   The tracing of descent through both matrilineal and patrilineal links, each of which is utilized for different purposes.

Dowry   Presentation of goods by the bride's kin to the family of the groom or to the couple.

Ecclesiastical cult   A type of religious organization in which access to supernatural power is mediated by a professional and specialized clergy.

Economic system   The norms governing production, distribution, and consumption of goods and services.

Economizing   Choosing a course of action that maximizes the well-being and material profit of the individual.

Ecosystem   Term referring to the interaction between human populations and their environment.

Egalitarian society   A society in which no individual or group has more privileged access to resources, power, or prestige than any other.

Enculturation   A term referring to the specific ways in which human infants and children learn to be adult members of their society.

Endogamy   The rule prescribing that marriage must be *within* a particular group.

Ethnocentrism   Perceiving and judging other cultures from the perspective of one's own culture.

Ethnography   The major research tool of cultural anthropology; includes both fieldwork among people in society and the written results of fieldwork.

Ethos   The dominant theme or value of a culture.

Exogamy   A rule that specifies that an individual must marry outside the group covered by the rule.

Extended family   Family based on blood relations extending over three or more generations.

Extensive agriculture   See Horticulture.

Folklore   Primarily oral traditions that have anonymous authorship and include at least two variations of the same form.

Foraging   See Hunting and gathering.

Formal economics   Theory holding that human material wants are unlimited but the means for achieving these wants is finite, and that people make choices among alternative courses of action in a rational manner.

Functionalism   The anthropological theory that culture functions to serve the needs of individuals in society.

Gender   The social classification of masculine and feminine.

Generalized reciprocity   A distribution of goods with no immediate or specific return expected.

Government   A social institution specifically concerned with making and enforcing public policy.

Horticulture   Production of plants using a simple, nonmechanized technology; fields are not used continuously.

Hunting and gathering   A food-getting strategy that does not involve food production or domestication of animals; also called foraging.

Ideal norms   The ideas a society has about what *ought* to be done.

Ideology (political)   The shared values and beliefs that legitimize the distribution and use of power in a particular society.

Incest taboos   Prohibitions on sexual relations between relatives or persons classified as relatives.

Independent invention   The process whereby similar cultural features develop without involving cultural exchange.

Individualistic cult   A form of religious organization in which each person may be her or his own religious specialist.

Initiation rite   A ritual that marks the passage from childhood to adult status.

Innovation   A new variation on an existing cultural pattern that is subsequently accepted by other members of the society.

Intelligence   The many skills and capacities that are part of the adaptive responses human beings make to their environment.

Intensive agriculture   A form of food production in which fields are in permanent cultivation using plows, draft animals, and techniques of soil and water control.

Invention   New combinations of existing cultural elements.

Kindred   A descent group made up of all the people related to an individual.

Kinship   A culturally defined relationship established on the basis of blood ties or through marriage.

Kinship system   The totality of kin relations, kin groups, and terms for classifying kin in a society.

Kula   A pattern of exchange among trading partners in the Trobriand Islands and other islands that are part of the kula ring.

Law   Those social norms whose neglect or violation is regularly met by the application of force by those in a society who have the socially recognized privilege of doing so.

Leveling mechanism   A practice, value, or form of social organization that results in an evening out of wealth within a society.

Levirate   The custom whereby a man marries the widow of a deceased brother.

Life chances   The opportunity of an individual to fulfill his or her potential in society.

Lineage   A group of kin whose members trace descent from a known common ancestor.

Linguistics   A field of cultural anthropology that specializes in the study of human languages.

Magic   An attempt to mechanistically control supernatural forces.

Mana   Sacred force, associated with Polynesian nobility, causing them to be taboo.

Market exchange   A system in which goods and services are bought and sold at a money price determined by the impersonal forces of supply and demand.

Marriage   The customs, rules, and obligations that establish a special relationship between a sexually cohabiting adult male and female, between them and any children they produce, and between the kin of the bride and groom.

Matrilineage   A lineage formed by descent in the female line.

Matrilineal descent   A rule that affiliates an individual to kin related through the mother only.

Matrilocal residence rule   System under which a husband goes to live with his wife's family.

Modernization   The process in which traditional societies move technologically and socially in the direction of industrialized nations.

Monogamy   The rule that permits a person to be married to only one other person at a time.

Monotheism   The belief in one god.

Morpheme   The smallest unit of a language that has a meaning.

Myth   A narrative that tells of the creation of the universe through the agency of supernatural beings.

Neanderthal   A variety of *Homo sapiens* that lived about 90,000 years ago. They were big game hunters, had completely upright postures and big brains, and quite possibly had a complex oral communication system, as well as an efficient technology.

Negative reciprocity   Exchange between equals conducted for the purpose of material advantage and the desire to get something for nothing.

Neolocal residence rule   System under which a couple establishes an independent household after marriage.

Network analysis   An approach to understanding the informal and fluid social relations that are typical in complex societies by mapping the links individuals have with others.

Niche   Specialized adaptation to a local environment by a group of people.

Nomadism   The constant mobility of human groups in pursuit of food (as in foraging) or a form of pastoralism in which the whole social group (men, women, and children, and animals) move in search of pasture.

Norm   An ideal cultural pattern or behavioral expectation in a culture.

Nuclear family   The family organized around the conjugal tie (the relationship between husband and wife). A nuclear family consists of a husband, a wife, and their children.

Ordeal   A means of determining guilt or innocence by having an accused party submit to tests believed to be under supernatural control.

Paleontology   The discipline that traces the evolution of humankind in the fossil record.

Parallel cousins   The children of siblings of the same sex at the parental generation.

Pastoralism   A good-getting strategy that depends on the care of domesticated herd animals. It occurs in areas where, for a variety of reasons, large human populations cannot be supported through agriculture.

Patrilineage   A lineage formed by descent in the male line.

Patrilineal descent rule   A rule that affiliates children with kinsmen of both sexes related through males only.

Patrilocal residence rule   System under which a bride goes to live with her husband's family.

Peasants   Food-producing populations that are incorporated politically, economically, and culturally into nation-states.

Phoneme   The smallest significant sound unit in a language. A phonemic system is the sound system of a language.

Phonetic laws   Regularities in sound changes that can be traced by linguists.

Physical anthropology   The study of human evolution and the biological processes involved in human adaptation.

Political ideology   See Ideology (political).

Political organization   The patterned ways in which authority is used to coordinate and regulate human behavior in the public interest.

Political process   The ways in which individuals and groups use power to achieve public goals.

Polyandry   The rule permitting a woman to have more than one husband at a time.

Polygamy   The general term for the rule allowing more than one spouse.

Polygyny   The rule permitting a man to have more than one wife at a time.

Polytheism   The belief in many gods.

Potlatch   A form of competitive giveaway practiced by the Kwakiutl and other groups of the Northwest Coast of North America.

Power   The ability to produce intended effects on oneself, other human beings, and things.

Prayer   Any conversation held with spirits or gods.

Prestige   Social honor or respect.

Primate   The *order* within the mammalian *class*, which includes monkeys, apes, and humans.

Psychic unity   The anthropological proposition that all human groups have the same mental capacities and ability to think logically.

Races   Human populations that differ in the relative frequencies of some genes.

Racism   The belief that some human populations are superior to others because of inherited, genetically transmitted characteristics.

Rank society   A society in which there are institutionalized differences in prestige but no important restrictions on access to basic resources.

Rebellion   The attempt of a group within society to force a redistribution of resources and power.

Reciprocity   A mutual give and take among people of equal status.

Redistribution   A form of exchange in which goods are collected from or contributed by members of the group and then redistributed to the group, often in the form of ceremonial feasts.

Religion   The beliefs and practices concerned with supernatural beings, powers, and forces.

Religious revitalization movement   A consciously organized effort to construct a more satisfying culture based on religious beliefs and practices.

Revolution   An attempt to overthrow the existing form of political organization.

Rites of intensification   Religious rituals directed towad the welfare of a group or society.

Rites of passage   Rituals that mark the transition of an individual from one social status to another.

Ritual (religious)   A patterned act that involves the manipulation of religious symbols.

Segmentary lineage system   A form of sociopolitical organization in which multiple descent groups (usually patrilineages) form at different levels and function in different contexts.

Semantics   The subsystem of a language that relates form to meaning.

Sex   The biological difference between male and female.

Shaman   A person who is socially recognized as having special supernatural power used on behalf of human clients.

Slash and burn   See Swidden.

Social function   The contribution a cultural trait makes to the maintenance and solidarity of a social system.

Socialization   The learning processes through which human cultural traditions are passed on from one generation to the next.

Social mobility   Movement from one social class to another.

Social network   A set of direct and indirect links between an individual and other people.

Social stratification   A system of institutionalized inequalities of wealth, power, and prestige.

Society   A group of people who are dependent on one another for survival or well-being and who share a particular way of life.

Sociobiology   A new interdisciplinary field that attempts to apply the perspective of evolutionary biology to human behavior.

Sociocultural system   The social enactments of designs for living (culture) in particular environments; incorporates both behavior and the rules of behavior as the subject matter for cultural anthropology.

Sociolinguistics   An anthropological specialty interested in speech performance.

Sorcery   The use of magic with the intent of harming another person.

Sororate   The custom whereby, when a man's wife dies, her sister is given to him as a wife.

State   A hierarchical and centralized form of political organization in which the central government has a legal monopoly over the use of force.

Status   A social position within a social structure; a role is the behavioral norms associated with a social status.

Stimulus diffusion   Process by which the general idea of an alien culture trait is borrowed, but the specific form of the trait is a local invention.

Stratified society   A society with formal, permanent social and economic inequality, in which some individuals are denied access to basic resources.

Structural-functionalism   An anthropological theory developed by A. R. Radcliffe-Brown that emphasizes the ways in which different structural elements in a social system contribute to social solidarity.

Structuralism   A theoretical perspective in anthropology that attempts to analyze the deep meanings underlying cultural elements and the rules by which cultural meanings are produced.

Subculture   A system of perceptions, values, beliefs, and customs that is significantly different from the larger, dominant culture.

Substantive economics   The study of economic systems as part of a total sociocultural system.

Swidden   A form of cultivation in which a field is cleared by felling the trees and burning the brush (sometimes called slash and burn cultivation).

Symbolic anthropology   An approach that focuses on culture as a system of shared meanings and symbols.

Syntax   That part of grammar that has to do with the arrangements of words to form phrases and sentences.

Theory   A general idea that attempts to explain and ultimately predict the interrelationships among phenomena in any scientific discipline.

Totem   A plant or animal considered to have an intimate relationship with a human group, sometimes as an ancestor.

Transformational generative grammar   A model of language that focuses on the relationship of deep structures of sentences to surface structures, and the rules that relate the two.

Transhumance   A pastoralist pattern in which herd animals are moved regularly throughout the year to different areas as pasture becomes available.

Tribe   A culturally distinct population, the members of which consider themselves to be descended from the same ancestor.

Unilineal descent rule   A rule that specifies that membership in a descent group is based on links through either the maternal or paternal line, but not both.

Vocabulary   The total stock of words in a language.

Voluntary association   A social group based on voluntary membership, typically found in complex and modernizing societies.

Wealth   The accumulation of material resources or access to the means of producing these resources.

Whorf-Sapir hypothesis   The hypothesis that perceptions and understandings of time, space, and matter are in part conditioned by the structure of a language.

Witchcraft   The attempt to harm people through supernatural means and powers, using only psychological processes and not any material objects.

BIBLIOGRAPHY

Aberle, David F., et al.
   1963 "The Incest Taboo and Mating Patterns of Animals." *American Anthropologist* 65:253–65.

Abrahams, Roger D.
   1970 *Deep Down in the Jungle.* Chicago: Aldine

Alland, Alexander, Jr.
   1973 *The Human Imperative.* New York: Columbia University Press.

Allen, J. P. B., and van Buren, Paul, eds.
   1971 *Chomsky: Selected Readings.* London: Oxford University Press.

Arens, W.
   1979 *The Man Eating Myth: Anthropology and Anthropophagy.* New York: Oxford University Press.
   1976 "Professional Football: An American Symbol and Ritual." In *The American Dimension.* W. Arens and Susan P. Montague, eds. Pp. 3–14. Port Washington, N.Y.: Alfred.

Baker, Randall
   1981 " 'Development' and the Pastoral People of Karamoja, Northeastern Uganda: An Example of Treatment of Symptoms." In *Contemporary Anthropology: An Anthology.* Daniel Bates and Susan Lees, eds. Pp. 66–78. New York: Alfred A. Knopf.

Balicki, Asen
   1963 "Shamanistic Behavior Among the Netsilik Eskimos." *Southwestern Journal of Anthropology* 19:380–96.

Basso, Keith
   1979 *Portraits of "the Whiteman."* New York: Cambridge University Press.

Barth, Frederik
   1964 *Nomads of South Persia.* New York: Humanities Press.
   1956 "Ecologic Relationships of Ethnic Groups in Swat, North Pakistan." *American Anthropologist* 58:1079–89.

Bascom, William
   1970 "Ponapean Prestige Economy." In *Cultures of the Pacific: Selected Readings.* Thomas G. Harding and Ben J. Wallace, eds. Pp. 85–93. New York: Free Press.

Beidelman, Thomas O.
   1971 *The Kaguru: A Matrilineal People of East Africa.* New York: Holt, Rinehart and Winston.
   1966 "The Ox and Nuer Sacrifice." *Man* (new series) I:453–67.

Benedict, Ruth
   1961 *Patterns of Culture.* Boston: Houghton Mifflin (first publ. 1934).
   1946 *The Chrysanthemum and the Sword.* Boston: Houghton Mifflin.
   1938 "Continuities and Discontinuities in Culture Conditioning." *Psychiatry* 1:161–67.
   1934 "Anthropology and the Abnormal." *Journal of General Psychology* 10:791–808.

Benet, Sula
1976   *How to Live to Be 100: The Life Style of the People of the Caucasus.* New York: Dial Press.

Berreman, Gerald D.
1959   "Caste in India and the United States." *American Journal of Sociology* LXVI:120–27.

Berry, J. W.
1974   "Ecological and Cultural Factors in Spatial Perceptual Development." In *Culture and Cognition: Readings in Cross-Cultural Psychology.* J. W. Berry and P. R. Dasen, eds. Pp. 129–40. London: Methuen (first publ. 1971).

Bettelheim, Bruno
1962   *Symbolic Wounds.* Rev. ed. New York: Collier.

Boas, Franz
1891   *Race, Language, and Culture.* New York: Macmillan.
1940   *Race, Language, and Culture.* New York: Free Press.

Bohannan, Paul
1971   "Artist and Critic in African Society." In *Anthropology and Art.* Charlotte M. Otten, ed. Pp. 172–81. Garden City, N.Y.: The Natural History Press.

Bott, Elizabeth
1957   *Family and Social Network: Roles, Norms and Extended Relationships in Ordinary Urban Families.* London: Tavistock Publications.

Brady, Ivan
1982   The Man Eating Myth. Review article. *American Anthropologist* 84:595–610.

Briggs, Jean
1974   "Eskimo Women: Makers of Men." In *Many Sisters.* Carolyn J. Matthiasson, ed. Pp. 261–304. New York: Free Press.

Bronfenbrenner, Urie
1974   "The Origins of Alienation." *Scientific American* 2:53–61.

Brown, Judith
1965   "A Cross Cultural Study of Female Initiation Rites." *American Anthropologist* 65:837–55.

Brown, P., and Podoloefsky, A.
1976   "Population Density, Agricultural Intensity, Land Tenure, and Group Size in the New Guinea Highlands." *Ethnology* 15:211–38.

Burkitt, D. P.
1977   "Relationships between Diseases and the Etiological Significance." *American Journal of Clinical Nutrition,* 30: 262–67.

Cage, John
1961   *Silence.* Middletown, Conn.: Wesleyan University Press.

Callimanopulos, Dominique
1982   "The Tourist Trap—Introduction." *Cultural Survival Quarterly* 6:3–5.

Cannon, Walter B.
1942   "The 'Voodoo' Death." *American Anthropologist* 44:169–80.

Carneiro, Robert
1970   "A Theory of the Origin of the State." *Science* 169:733–38.

Caudill, William
1973   "Psychiatry and Anthropology: The Individual and his Nexus." In *Cultural Illness and Health.* Laura Nader and Thomas W. Maretski, eds. Pp. 67–77. Washington, D.C.: American Anthropological Association.

Chagnon, Napoleon
1979   *Yanomamo: The Fierce People.* 2nd ed. New York: Holt, Rinehart and Winston.

Childe, V. Gordon
1951   *Man Makes Himself.* New York: Mentor.

Chodorow, Nancy
1974   "Family Structure and Female Personality." In *Women, Culture, and Society.* Michelle Rosaldo and Louise Lamphere, eds. Pp. 43–66. Stanford, Calif.: Stanford University Press.

Chomsky, Noam
1965   *Syntactic Structures.* London: Mouton.

Clark, Margaret
1973   "Contributions of Cultural Anthropology to the Study of the Aged." In *Cultural Illness and Health.* Laura Nader and Thomas W. Maretski, eds. Pp. 78–88. Washington, D.C.: American Anthropological Association.
1970   Health in the Mexican American Culture. Berkeley: University of California.

Cohen, Ronald, and Service, Elman, R., eds.
1978   *Origins of the State: The Anthropology of Political Evolution.* Philadelphia: ISHI.

Cohen, Yehudi, ed.
1971   *Man in Adaptation: The Institutional Framework.* Chicago: Aldine.

Cole, Michael, et al.
1971   *The Cultural Context of Learning and Thinking.* New York: Basic Books.

Cole, Michael, and Scribner, S.
1974   *Culture and Thought.* New York: Wiley.

Conklin, Harold C.
1969   "An Ethnoecological Approach to Shifting Agriculture." In *Environmental and Cultural Behavior.* Andrew P. Vayda, ed. Pp. 221–33. Garden City, N.Y.: The Natural History Press.

Cronin, Constance
1977   "Illusion and Reality in Sicily." In *Sexual Stratification.* Alice Schlegel, ed. Pp. 67–94. New York: Columbia University Press.

Dalton, George
1967   "Primitive Money." In *Tribal and Peasant Economies.* George Dalton, ed. Pp. 254–81. Garden City, N.Y.: The Natural History Press.

Damas, David
1972   "The Copper Eskimo." In *Hunters and Gatherers Today.* M. G. Bicchieri, ed. Pp. 3–50. New York: Holt, Rinehart and Winston.

Daniken, E. V.
1971   *Chariots of the Gods.* New York: Bantam.

D'Andrade, Roy G.
1974   "Sex Differences and Cultural Conditioning." In *Culture and Personality.* Robert A. LeVine, ed. Pp. 16–37. Chicago: Aldine.

Denich, Betty
1974   "Sex and Power in the Balkans." In *Women, Culture, and Society.* Michelle Rosaldo and Louise Lamphere, eds. Pp. 243–62. Stanford, Calif.: Stanford University Press.

Dentan, Robert
1968   *The Semai: A Nonviolent People of Malaya.* New York: Holt, Rinehart and Winston.

Divale, William Tulio, and Harris, Marvin
1976   "Population, Warfare and the Male Supremacist Complex." *American Anthropologist* 78:521–38.

Dobyns, Henry F.
1972   "The Cornell-Peru Project: Experimental Intervention in Vicos." In *Contemporary Societies and Cultures of Latin America.* Dwight Heath, ed. Pp. 201–10. New York: Random House.

Dobzhansky, T., et al., eds.
1972   *Evolutionary Biology*, Vol. 6.

Dobyns, Henry F., Carlos, Monee M., and Vazquez, Mario
1962   "Community and Regional Development: The Joint Cornell-Peru Experiment." *Human Organization*, vol. 21, no. 2, summer.

Dollard, John
1937   *Caste and Class in a Southern Town.* New Haven, Conn.: Yale University Press.

Douglas, Mary
1970   *Purity and Danger.* Baltimore: Penguin Books.

Draper, Patricia
1974   "Comparative Studies of Socialization." In *Annual Review of Anthropology.* Bernard J. Siegel, ed. Pp. 263–78. Palo Alto, Calif.: Annual Reviews.

Drucker, P., and Heizer, R. F.
1967   *To Make My Name Good.* Berkeley: University of California Press.

Dumont, Louis
1970   *Homo Hierarchicus: An Essay on the Caste System.* Chicago: University of Chicago Press.

Durkheim, Emile
1961   *The Elementary Forms of the Religious Life.* New York: Collier.

Edgerton, Robert
1971   *The Individual in Adaptation.* Berkeley: University of California Press.

Edgerton, Robert, and Dingman, H. F.
1964   "Good Reasons for Bad Supervision: 'Dating' in a Hospital for the Mentally Retarded." *Psychiatric Quarterly Supplement* 38:221–33.

Eggan, Fred
1950   *The Social Organization of Western Pueblos.* Chicago: University of Chicago Press.

Ekman, Paul
1977   "Biological and Cultural Contributions to Body and Facial Movement." In *Anthropology of the Body.* John Blacking, ed. Pp. 34–89. New York: Academic Press.

Elkin, A. P.
1967   "The Nature of Australian Totemism." In *Gods and Rituals.* John Middleton, ed. Pp. 159–76. Garden City, N.Y.: The Natural History Press.

Ember, Melvin, and Ember, Carol R.
1971   "The Conditions Favoring Matrilocal vs. Patrilocal Residence." *American Anthropologist* 73:571–94.

Evans-Pritchard, E. E.
1968   *The Nuer.* Oxford, England: Clarendon Press.
1967   "The Nuer Concept of Spirit in Its Relation to the Social Order." In *Myth and Cosmos.* John Middleton, ed. Pp. 109–26. Garden City, N.Y.: The Natural History Press.
1958   *Witchcraft, Oracles, and Magic among the Azande.* Oxford, England: Clarendon Press.

Fagan, B. M.
1980   *People of the Earth: An Introduction to World Prehistory.* Boston: Little, Brown.

Fallers, Lloyd
1955   "The Predicament of the Modern African Chief: An Instance from Uganda." *American Anthropologist* 57:290–305.

Ferguson, Brian, ed.
1983   *The Ecology and Political Economy of War: Anthropological Perspectives.* New York: Academic Press.

Fischer, John
1961   "Art Styles as Cognitive Maps." *American Anthropologist* 63:79–93.

Flannery, K.
1973   "The Origins of Agriculture." In *Annual Review of Anthropology.* Bernard J. Siegel, ed. Pp. 271–310. Palo Alto, Calif.: Annual Reviews.

Ford, Clellan S.
1938   "The Role of a Fijian Chief." *American Sociological Review* 3:542–50.

Forde, Daryll
1950   "Double Descent Among the Yako." In *African Systems of Kinship and Marriage.* A. R. Radcliffe-Brown and Daryll Forde, eds. Pp. 285–332. London: Oxford University Press.

Foulks, Edward F.
1974   *The Arctic Hysterias.* Washington, D.C.: American Anthropological Association.

Frake, Charles O.
1964   "The Diagnosis of Disease among the Subanum of Mindanao." In *Language in Culture and Society.* Dell Hymes, ed. Pp. 192–210. New York: Harper and Row.

Freed, Ruth S.
1977   *Space, Density, and Cultural Conditioning.* Annals of the New York Academy of Sciences 285:593–604.

Freed, Stanley A., and Freed, Ruth S.
1978   "Shanti Nagar: The Effects of Urbanization in a Village in North India. 2. Aspects of Economy, Technology and Economy." *Anthropological Papers of the American Museum of Natural History* Vol. 55, Part I. New York: American Museum of Natural History.

Freeman, Derek
1983   *Margaret Mead: The Making and Unmaking of an Anthropological Myth.* Cambridge, Mass.: Harvard University Press.

Fried, Morton
1967   *The Evolution of Political Society.* New York: Random House.

Friedl, Ernestine
1975   *Women and Men: An Anthropologist's View.* New York: Holt, Rinehart and Winston.
1974   "Kinship, Class and Selective Migration." In *Family in the Mediterranean.* J. Peristiany, ed. London: Cambridge University Press.

Frisancho, A. R.
1979   *Human Adaptation.* St. Louis: Mosby.

Gardner, B. T., and Gardner, R. A.
1967   "Teaching Sign Language to a Chimpanzee." *Science* 165:664–72.

Gardner, Peter
1966   "Symmetric Respect and Memorate Knowledge: The Structure and Ecology of Individualistic Culture." *Southwestern Journal of Anthropology* 22:389–413.

Garn S. M.
1969   *Human Races.* Springfield, Ill.: Charles C. Thomas.

Gay, John, and Cole, Michael
1967   *The New Mathematics and an Old Culture.* New York: Holt, Rinehart and Winston.

Geddes, William
1963   *Peasant Life in Communist China.* Society for Applied Anthropology, Monograph No. 6. Ithaca, N.Y.: Society for Applied Anthropology.

Geertz, Clifford
1973   *The Interpretation of Culture.* New York: Basic Books.

1963 *Agricultural Involution: The Process of Ecological Change in Indonesia.* Berkeley: University of California Press.

Goodall, J.
1968 "A Preliminary Report on Expressive Movements and Communication in the Gombe Stream Chimpanzees." In *Primates: Studies in Adaptation and Variability.* P. Jay, ed. New York: Holt, Rinehart & Winston.
1971 *Tiwi Wives.* Seattle: University of Washington Press.

Gorer, G., and Rickman, J.
1949 *The People of Great Russia.* London: Cresset.

Graves, Nancy B., and Graves, Theodore D.
1974 "Adaptive Strategies in Urban Migration." In *Annual Review of Anthropology.* Bernard J. Siegel, ed. Pp. 117–51. Palo Alto, Calif.: Annual Reviews.

Gross, Daniel
1973 "The Great Sisal Scheme." In *Man's Many Ways.* Richard Gould, ed. Pp. 371–79. New York: Harper and Row.

Hall, Edward
1959 *The Silent Language.* Greenwich, Conn.: Fawcett.

Hanna, Judith
1977 "To Dance Is Human." In *The Anthropology of the Body.* John Blacking, ed. Pp. 211–32. London: Academic Press.

Harlow, Harry
1962 "Social Deprivation in Monkeys." *Scientific American* 206:1–10.

Harner, Michael
1977 "The Ecological Basis for Aztec Sacrifice." *American Ethnologist* 4:117–33.

Harris, Marvin
1982 *America Now: The Anthropology of a Changing Culture.* New York: Simon and Schuster.
1975 *Cows, Pigs, Wars, and Witches: The Riddles of Culture.* New York: Random House (Vintage).
1968 *The Rise of Cultural Theory.* New York: Crowell.
1966 "The Cultural Ecology of India's Sacred Cattle." *Current Anthropology* 7:51–66.

Harrison, Robert
1973 *Warfare.* Minneapolis: Burgess.

Hart, C. W. M.
1967 "Contrasts Between Pre-pubertal and Post-pubertal Education." In *Personality and Social Life.* Robert Endelman, ed. Pp. 275–90. New York: Random House.

Hart, C. W. M., and Pilling, Arnold R.
1960 *The Tiwi of North Australia.* New York: Holt, Rinehart and Winston.

Heider, Karl
1970 *The Dugum Dani.* Chicago: Aldine.

Henry, Jules
1963 *Culture Against Man.* New York: Random House.

Herdt, Gilbert H.
1981 *Guardians of the Flutes: Idioms of Masculinity.* New York: McGraw-Hill.

Herskovitz, Melville
1965 *Economic Anthropology.* New York: Norton.

Hinshaw, Robert E.
1980 "Anthropology, Administration, and Public Policy." In *Annual Review of Anthropology.* Bernard J. Siegel, ed. Pp. 497–545. Palo Alto, Calif.: Annual Reviews.

Hockett, C. F., and Ascher, R.
1964 "The Human Revolution." *Current Anthropology* 5:135–68.

Hodge, William
1981 *The First Americans: Then and Now.* New York: Holt, Rinehart and Winston.

Hoebel, E. Adamson
1974 *The Law of Primitive Man.* New York: Atheneum (first publ. 1954).
1960 *The Cheyennes: Indians of the Great Plains.* New York: Holt, Rinehart and Winston.

Hoffer, Carol
1974 "Madam Yoko: Ruler of the Kpa Mende Confederacy." In *Women, Culture, and Society.* Michelle Zimbalist Rosaldo and Louise Lamphere, eds. Pp. 173–88. Stanford, Calif.: Stanford University Press.

Hoijer, Harry
1964 "Cultural Implications of Some Navajo Linguistic Categories." In *Language in Culture and Society.* D. Hymes, ed. Pp. 142–60. New York: Harper and Row.

Holmberg, Allan R.
1969 *Nomads of the Long Bow: The Siriono of Eastern Bolivia.* Garden City, N.Y.: The Natural History Press.

Holtzman, Wayne H., Diaz-Guerrero, Rogelio, and Swartz, Jon D.
1975   *Personality Development in Two Cultures.* Austin: University of Texas Press.

Horton, Robin
1973   *Modes of Thought: Essays on Thinking in Western and Non-Western Societies.* Robin Horton and Ruth Finnegan, eds. London: Faber.

Hunt, George T.
1944   *The Wars of the Iroquois.* Madison: The University of Wisconsin Press.

Hymes, Dell
1972   *Reinventing Anthropology.* New York: Random House (Vintage).

Itard, Jean-Marc-Gaspard
1962   *The Wild Boy of Aveyron.* Trans. George and Muriel Humphrey. Englewood Cliffs, N.J.: Prentice-Hall.

Jensen, A. R.
1969   "How Much Can We Boost I.Q. and Scholastic Achievement?" *Harvard Education Review.* Winter: 1–123.

Johnson, Allen
1978   "In Search of the Affluent Society." *Human Nature,* September, pp. 50–59.

Kardiner, Abram, et al.
1945   *The Psychological Frontiers of Society.* New York: Columbia University Press.

Kawamura, S.
1962   "The Process of Sub-Culture Propagation among Japanese Macaques." *Journal of Primatology* 2: 43–60.

Kinsey, Alfred C., Pomeroy, Wardell B., and Martin, Clyde E.
1948   *Sexual Behavior in the Human Male.* Philadelphia: W. B. Saunders.

Klass, M., and Hellman, H.
1971   *The Kinds of Mankind.* Philadelphia: Lippincott.

Komroff, Manuel, ed.
1965   *The History of Herodotus.* George Rawlinson, tr. New York: Tudor Publications.

Kroeber, Alfred L.
1939   "Cultural and Natural Areas of Native North America." *University of California Publications in American Archeology and Ethnology,* Vol. 38. Berkeley: University of California Press.

LaBarre, Weston
1969   *And They Shall Take Up Serpents.* New York: Schocken Books.

Labov, William
1972   "On the Mechanisms of Linguistic Change." In *Directions in Sociolinguistics.* John J. Gumperz and Dell Hymes, eds. New York: Holt, Rinehart and Winston.

Lancaster, J. B.
1975   *Primate Behavior and the Emergence of Human Culture.* New York: Holt, Rinehart & Winston.

Langness, L. L., and Gelya, Frank G.
1982   *Lives: An Anthropological Approach to Biography.* Novato, Calif.: Chandler and Sharp.

Leach, Edmund
1976   *Culture and Communication.* New York: Cambridge University Press.

Leacock, Eleanor Burke
1981   *Myths of Male Dominance.* New York: Monthly Review Press.

Lee, Dorothy
1959   *Freedom and Culture.* Englewood Cliffs, N.J.: Prentice-Hall.

Lee, Richard B.
1978   *The !Kung San: Men, Women and Work in a Foraging Society.* Cambridge, England: Cambridge University Press.
1974   "Eating Christmas in the Kalahari." In *Conformity and Conflict.* James Spradley and David W. McCurdy, eds. Pp. 14–21. Boston: Little, Brown.
1968   "What Hunters Do for a Living, or, How to Make Out on Scarce Resources." In *Man the Hunter.* Richard B. Lee and Irven DeVore, eds. Pp. 30–48. Chicago: Aldine.

Lehnert, Martin
1960   *Poetry and Prose of the Anglo-Saxons,* Vol. I: Texts. 2nd ed. rev. Verlag/Halle, Germany: Vebmax Niemeyer.

Lessinger, Hanna
1983   *The Guardian.* February 23, 1983, p. 7.

Levine, Morton
1957   "Prehistoric Art and Ideology." *American Anthropologist* 59:949–62.

Lévi-Strauss, Claude
1969   *The Elementary Structures of Kinship.* Boston: Beacon Press (first publ. 1949).
1967   *Structural Anthropology.* Garden City, N.Y.: Doubleday.

Lewis, Oscar
1966   *La Vida.* New York: Random House.

1960   *Tepoztlán, Village in Mexico.* New York: Holt, Rinehart and Winston.

Liebow, Elliot
1967   *Tally's Corner.* Boston: Little, Brown.

Lindenbaum, Shirley
1979   *Kuru Sorcery: Disease and Danger in the New Guinea Highlands.* Palo Alto, Calif.: Mayfield.

Linton, Ralph
1937   "One Hundred Per Cent American." *The American Mercury* 40:427–29.

Lomax, Alan
1968   *Folk Song Style and Culture.* American Association for the Advancement of Science Publication No. 88. Washington, D.C.

Lowie, Robert H.
1963   *Indians of the Plains.* Garden City, N.Y.: The Natural History Press (first publ. 1954).
1948   *Social Organization.* New York: Holt, Rinehart and Winston.

Lynch, Owen K.
1969   *The Politics of Untouchability.* New York: Columbia University Press.

Lynd, Robert, and Lynd, Helen
1937   *Middletown in Transition.* New York: Harcourt, Brace and World.

Malinowski, Bronislaw
1961   *Argonauts of the Western Pacific.* New York: E. P. Dutton (first publ. 1922).
1954   *Magic, Science, and Religion.* Garden City, N.Y.: Doubleday (first publ. 1926).
1953   *Sex and Repression in Primitive Society.* London: Routledge and Kegan Paul (first publ. 1927).
1944   *A Scientific Theory of Culture and Other Essays.* Chapel Hill: University of North Carolina Press.
1929   *The Sexual Life of Savages.* New York: Harcort, Brace and World.

Manning, Frank E.
1982   "The Caribbean Experience." *Cultural Survival Quarterly* 6:13–15.

Marshall, Donald
1971   "Sexual Behavior on Mangaia." In *Human Sexual Behavior: Variations in the Ethnographic Spectrum.* Donald S. Marshall and Robert C. Suggs, eds. Pp. 103–62. New York: Basic Books.

Marshall, Laura
1967   "!Kung Bushman Bands." In *Comparative Political Systems.* R. Cohen and J. Middleton, eds. Pp. 15–44. Garden City, N.Y.: The Natural History Press.

Martin, M. K., and Voorhies, Barbara
1975   *Female of the Species.* New York: Columbia University Press.

Mauss, Marcel
1954   *The Gift.* New York: Macmillan.

Mayer, Philip, and Mayer, Iona
1970   "Socialization by Peers: The Youth Organization of the Red Xhosa." In *Socialization: The Approach from Social Anthropology.* Philip Mayer, ed. Pp. 159–89. London: Tavistock Publications.

Maynard, Eileen
1974   "Guatemalan Women: Life Under Two Types of Patriarchy." In *Many Sisters.* Carolyn J. Matthiasson, ed. Pp. 77–98. New York: Free Press.

McKean, Philip
1982   "Tourists and Balinese." *Cultural Survival Quarterly* 6:32–34.

McNetting, Robert
1977   *Cultural Ecology.* Menlo Park, Calif.: Cummings.

Mead, Margaret
1975   "Discussion: The Role of Anthropology in International Relations." In *Anthropology and Society.* Bela C. Maday, ed. Washington, D.C.: The Anthropological Society of Washington.
1963   *Sex and Temperament in Three Primitive Societies.* New York: Dell (first publ. 1935).
1961   *Coming of Age in Samoa.* New York: Dell (first publ. 1928).
1942   *And Keep Your Powder Dry: An Anthropologist Looks at America.* New York: Morrow.

Mead, M., et al.
1968   *Science and the Concept of Race.* New York: Columbia University Press.

Meek, Charles K.
1972   "Ibo Law." In *Readings in Anthropology.* Jesse D. Jennings and E. Adamson Hoebel, eds. Pp. 247–58. New York: McGraw-Hill.

Mencher, Joan P.
1980   "On Being an Untouchable in India: A Materialist Perspective." In *Beyond the Myths of Culture, Essays in Cultural Materialism.* New York: Academic Press.
1974   "The Caste System Upside Down: Or the

Not-So-Mysterious East." *Current Anthropology* 15:469–94.

1965 "The Nayars of South Malabar." In *Comparative Family Systems.* M. F. Nimkoff, ed. Pp. 162–91. Boston: Houghton Mifflin.

Merriam, Alan P.
1967 "The Arts and Anthropology." In *Horizons of Anthropology.* Sol Tax, ed. Pp. 224–36. Chicago: Aldine.

1964 *The Anthropology of Music.* Evanston, Ill.: Northwestern University.

Messenger, John C.
1971 "Sex and Repression in an Irish Folk Community." In *Human Sexual Behavior: Variations in the Ethnographic Spectrum.* Donald S. Marshall and Robert C. Suggs, eds. Pp. 3–37. New York: Basic Books.

Montagu, M.F.A.
1975 "Comparative Aspects of Communication in New World Primates." In *Primate Ethology* by D. Morris. Chicago: Aldine.

Montague, Susan, and Morais, Robert
1976 "Football Games and Rock Concerts: The Ritual Enactment." In *The American Dimension.* W. Arens and Susan P. Montague, eds. Pp. 33–52. Port Washington, N.Y.: Alfred.

Moody, Edward J.
1974 "Urban Witches." In *Conformity and Conflict.* James P. Spradley and David W. McCurdy, eds. Pp. 326–36. Boston: Little, Brown.

Moran, Emilio F.
1979 *Human Adaptability: An Introduction to Ecological Anthropology.* Boulder, Colo.: Westview Press.

Moynihan, Daniel P.
1965 *The Negro Family: The Case for National Action.* Washington, D.C.: Department of Labor.

Munroe, Robert L., and Munroe, Ruth H.
1977 *Cross-Cultural Human Development.* New York: Aronson.

Murdock, George
1949 *Social Structure.* New York: Free Press.

Murphy, Robert
1964 "Social Distance and the Veil." *American Anthropologist* 66:1257–73.

Murphy, Yolanda, and Murphy, Robert
1974 *Women of the Forest.* New York: Columbia University Press.

Myerhoff, Barbara
1978 *Number Our Days.* New York: Simon and Schuster.

Nash, Dennison
1968 "The Role of the Composer." In *Readings in Anthropology.* Vol. II. *Cultural Anthropology.* Morton H. Fried, ed. Pp. 746–48. New York: Thomas Y. Crowell.

Nash, Manning
1967 "The Social Context of Economic Choice in a Small Society." In *Tribal and Peasant Economies.* George Dalton, ed. Pp. 524–38. Garden City, N.Y.: The Natural History Press.

Ogbu, John
1978 "African Bridewealth and Women's Status." *American Ethnologist* 5:241–60.

O'Kelly, Charlotte G.
1980 *Women and Men in Society.* Belmont, Calif.: Wadsworth.

Oliver, Symmes C.
1965 "Individuality, Freedom of Choice, and Cultural Flexibility of the Kamba." *American Anthropologist* 67:421–28.

Ortiz de Montellano, Bernard R.
1978 "Aztec Cannibalism: An Ecological Necessity?" *Science* 200:611–17.

Parenti, Michael J.
1967 "Black Nationalism and the Reconstruction of Identity." In *Personality and Social Life.* Robert Endelman, ed. Pp. 514–24. New York: Random House.

Partridge, William
1978 "Uses and Nonuses of Anthropological Data on Drug Abuse." In *Applied Anthropology.* W. L. Partridge and E. M. Eddy, eds. Pp. 350–72. New York: Columbia University Press.

Patterson, F., and Cohen, R.
1978 "Conversations with a Gorilla." *National Geographic* 154: 454–462.

Pelto, Pertti
1973 *The Snowmobile Revolution: Technology and Social Change in the Arctic.* Menlo Park, Calif.: Cummings.

Pettitt, George A.
1972 "The Vision Quest and the Guardian Spirit." In *Readings in Anthropology.* Jesse Jennings and E. Adamson Hoebel, eds. Pp. 265–71. New York: McGraw-Hill.

Pfeiffer, John
    1972   *The Emergence of Man.* New York: Harper and Row.

Phongpaichit, Pasuk
    1982   "Bangkok Masseuses." *Cultural Survival Quarterly* 6:34–37.

Pilbeam, David
    1972   *The Ascent of Man.* New York: Macmillan.

Polyani, Karl
    1944   *The Great Transformation.* New York: Holt, Rinehart.

Pospisil, Leopold
    1963   *The Kapauku Papuans of West New Guinea.* New York: Holt, Rinehart and Winston.

Potter, Jack M.
    1967   "From Peasants to Rural Proletarians: Social and Economic Change in Rural Communist China." In *Peasant Society: A Reader.* Jack M. Potter, May N. Diaz, and George M. Forster, eds. Pp. 407–18. Boston: Little, Brown.

Queen, Stuart, and Habenstein, Robert W.
    1974   *The Family in Various Cultures.* New York: J. B. Lippincott.

Radcliffe-Brown, A. R.
    1965   *Structure and Function in Primitive Society.* New York: Free Press.
    1964   *The Andaman Islanders.* New York: Free Press (first publ. 1922).

Rappaport, Roy A.
    1971   "The Flow of Energy in an Agricultural Society." *Scientific American* 225:116–32.
    1967   "Ritual Regulation of Environmental Relations among a New Guinea People." *Ethnology* 6:17–30.

Redfield, Robert
    1971   "Art and Icon." In *Anthropology and Art.* Charlotte M. Otten, ed. Pp. 39–65. Garden City, N.Y.: The Natural History Press.

Reynolds, Vernon
    1965   *Budongo: An African Forest and Its Chimpanzees.* Garden City, N.Y.: Doubleday.

Richards, Audrey I.
    1956   *Chisungu: A Girl's Initiation Ceremony among the Bemba of Northern Rhodesia.* New York: Grove Press.

Rohner, Ronald, and Rohner, Evelyn
    1970   *The Kwakiutl: Indians of British Columbia.* New York: Holt, Rinehart and Winston.

Rosaldo, Michelle Z., and Lamphere, Louise, eds.
    1974   *Women, Culture, and Society.* Stanford, Calif.: Stanford University Press.

Rosenfeld, Gerry
    1971   *Shut Those Thick Lips: A Study of Slum School Failure.* New York: Holt, Rinehart and Winston.

Rowell, T. E.
    1972   *Social Behavior of Monkeys.* Baltimore: Penguin.

Sahlins, Marshall
    1972   *Stone Age Economics.* Chicago: Aldine.
    1971   "Poor Man, Rich Man, Big Man, Chief." In *Conformity and Conflict.* James P. Spradley and David W. McCurdy, eds. Pp. 362–76. Boston: Little, Brown.
    1961   "The Segmentary Lineage: An Organization of Predatory Expansion." *American Anthropologist* 63:332–45.
    1957   "Land Use and the Extended Family in Moala, Fiji." *American Anthropologist* 59:449–62.

Salzman, Philip C.
    1972   "Multi-Resource Nomadism in Iranian Baluchistan." In *Perspectives on Nomadism.* William Irons and Neville Dyson-Hudson, eds. Pp. 61–69. Leiden, The Netherlands: E. J. Brill.

Sanday, Peggy Reeves
    1981   *Female Power and Male Dominance.* New York: Cambridge University Press.

Sapir, Edward
    1949a   "Culture, Genuine and Spurious." In *The Selected Writings of Edward Sapir in Language, Culture and Personality.* David Mandelbaum, ed. Pp. 308–331. Berkeley: University of California Press.
    1949b   "The Status of Linguistics as a Science." In *The Selected Writings of Edward Sapir in Language, Culture and Personality.* David Mandelbaum, ed. Pp. 160–66. Berkeley: University of California Press.

Schlegel, Alice, ed.
    1977   *Sexual Stratification: A Cross-Cultural View.* New York: Columbia University Press.

Schneider, Harold K.
    1973   "The Subsistence Role of Cattle Among the Pokot and in East Africa." In *Peoples*

and Cultures of Africa. Elliott P. Skinner, ed. Pp. 159–87. Garden City, N.Y.: The Natural History Press.

Schumacher, William
1975   Small Is Beautiful. New York: Harper and Row.

Schwartz, Gary
1972   Youth Culture: An Anthropological Approach. Reading, Pa.: Addison Wesley.

Schwartz, Norman
1978   "Community Development and Cultural Change in Latin America." In Annual Review of Anthropology. Bernard J. Siegel, ed. Pp. 235–62. Palo Alto, Calif.: Annual Reviews.

Schwartz, Theodore
1976   Socialization as Cultural Communication. Berkeley: University of California Press.

Service, Elman
1971   Profiles in Ethnology. New York: Harper and Row.

Sharma, Ursula
1979   "Segregation and Its Consequences in India." In Women United, Women Divided. Patricia Caplan and Janet M. Bujra, eds. Pp. 259–82. Bloomington: University of Indiana Press.

Sharp, Lauriston
1952   "Steel Axes for Stone Age Australians." In Human Problems in Technological Change. Edward H. Spicer, ed. Pp. 69–90. New York: Russell Sage Foundation.

Singer, Milton
1968   "The Indian Joint Family in Modern Industry." In Indian Society: Structure and Change. Milton Singer and Bernard Cohn, eds. Pp. 432–52. Chicago: Aldine.

Smith, M. Estelli
1982   "Tourism and Native Americans." Cultural Survival Quarterly 6:10–12.

Southworth, F. C., and Daswani, C. J.
1974   Foundations of Linguistics. New York: Free Press.

Spiro, Melford
1979   Gender and Culture: Kibbutz Women Revisited. Durham, N.C.: Duke University Press.
1974   "Is the Family Universal?—The Israeli Case." In The Sociological Perspective. Scott G. McNall, ed. 3rd. ed. Pp. 509–20. Boston: Little, Brown.

1958   Children of the Kibbutz. Cambridge, Mass.: Harvard University Press.

Spitz, Rene A.
1975   "Hospitalism: The Genesis of Psychiatric Conditions in Early Childhood." In The Human Life Cycle. William C. Sze, ed. Pp. 29–44. New York: Aronson.

Spradley, James
1970   You Owe Yourself a Drunk. Boston: Little, Brown.

Stack, Carol
1974   All Our Kin. New York: Harper and Row.

Steadman, Lyle B., and Merbs, Charles F.
1982   "Kuru and Cannibalism." American Anthropologist 84:611–27.

Steward, Julian
1972   The Theory of Culture Change: The Methodology of Multilinear Evolution. Urbana: University of Illinois Press.

Sturtevant, Edgar H.
1947   An Introduction to Linguistic Science. New Haven, Conn.: Yale University Press.

Talmon, Yohina
1964   "Mate Selection in Collective Settlements." American Sociological Review 29:491–508.

Terrace, H.
1979   Nim. New York: Knopf.

Tomasic, Roman, and Feeley, Malcolm M.
1982   Neighborhood Justice. New York: Longman.

Tonkinson, Robert
1974   The Jigalong Mob: Aboriginal Victors of the Desert Crusade. Menlo Park, Calif.: Cummings.

Turnbull, Colin
1972   The Mountain People. New York: Simon and Schuster.
1968   "The Importance of Flux in Two Hunting Societies." In Man the Hunter. Richard B. Lee and Irven DeVore, eds. Pp. 132–37. Chicago: Aldine.
1961   The Forest People. New York: Simon and Schuster.

Tylor, Edward
1920   Primitive Culture. 2 vols. New York: G. P. Putnam's Sons (first publ. 1871).

U.S. Department of Health, Education and Welfare
1975   Third National Cancer Survey. Washington, D.C.: U.S. Government Printing Office.

Valentine, Charles
  1971 "The 'Culture of Poverty': Its Scientific
        Significance and Its Implications for
        Action." In *The Culture of Poverty: A Cri-
        tique.* Eleanor Burke Leacock, ed. Pp.
        193–225. New York: Simon and Schuster.

Valentine, Charles A., and Valentine, Betty Lou
  1970 "Making the Scene, Digging the Action
        and Telling It Like It Is: Anthropologists
        at Work in a Dark Ghetto." In *Afro-Amer-
        ican Anthropology.* Norman E. Whitten,
        Jr., and John F. Szwed, eds. Pp. 403–18.
        New York: Free Press.

Vayda, Andrew P.
  1976 *War in Ecological Perspective.* New York:
        Plenum.

Wagner, Roy
  1975 *The Invention of Culture.* Englewood
        Cliffs, N.J.: Prentice-Hall.

Wallace, Anthony
  1970 *Death and Rebirth of the Seneca.* New
        York: Knopf.
  1966 *Religion: An Anthropological View.* New
        York: Random House.

Warner, Lloyd
  1963 *Yankee City.* Abridged ed. New Haven,
        Conn.: Yale University Press.

White, Leslie A.
  1949 "Energy and the Evolution of Culture."
        In *The Science of Culture.* Leslie A.
        White, ed. Pp. 363–93. New York: Farrar,
        Straus and Cudahy.

Whitehead, Harriet, ed.
  1981 *Sexual Meanings: The Cultural Construc-
        tion of Gender and Sexuality.* New York:
        Cambridge University Press.

Whiting, Beatrice, ed.
  1963 *Six Cultures: Studies of Child Rearing.*
        New York: Wiley.

Whiting, John, and Child, Irvin L.
  1953 *Child Training and Personality: A Cross-
        Cultural Study.* New Haven, Conn.: Yale
        University Press.

**Whiting, John, Kluckhohn, Richard, and
Anthony, Albert**
  1967 "The Function of Male Initiation Cere-
        monies at Puberty." In *Personality and
        Social Life.* Robert Endelman, ed. Pp.
        294–308. New York: Random House.

Whiting, John, and Whiting, Beatrice
  1973 "Altruistic and Egoistic Behavior in Six
        Cultures." In *Cultural Illness and Health.*

Laura Nader and Thomas W. Maretski,
eds. Pp. 56–66. Washington, D.C.: American Anthropological Association.

Whorf, B. L.
  1956 *Language, Thought and Reality.* Boston:
        M.I.T. Press.

Whyte, William F.
  1955 *Street Corner Society.* Chicago: Univer-
        sity of Chicago Press.

Wilson, Edward
  1970 *Sociobiology: The New Synthesis.* Cam-
        bridge, Mass.: Harvard University Press.

Wilson, Monica
  1963 *Good Company.* London: Oxford Univer-
        sity Press.

Wissler, Clark
  1926 *The Relation of Man to Nature in Aborig-
        inal North America.* New York: Appleton.

Witkin, H. A.
  1974 "Cognitive Styles Across Cultures." In
        *Culture and Cognition: Readings in Cross-
        Cultural Psychology.* J. W. Berry and P. R.
        Dasen, eds. Pp. 99–118. London:
        Methuen.

Wolf, Arthur
  1968 "Adopt a Daughter-in-Law, Marry a Sis-
        ter: A Chinese Solution to the Incest
        Taboo." *American Anthropologist*
        70:864–74.

Wolf, Eric B.
  1966 *Peasants.* Englewood Cliffs, N.J.: Pren-
        tice-Hall.

Woodburn, James
  1968 "An Introduction to Hadza Ecology." In
        Man the Hunter. Richard B. Lee and
        Irven DeVore, eds. Pp. 49–55. Chicago:
        Aldine.

Worsley, Peter M.
  1959 "Cargo Cults." *Scientific American*
        200:117–28.

Zito, Laura
  1982 "Settling Down: Bedouin in the Sinai."
        Cultural Survival Quarterly 6:22–24.

Page references in italic type refer to illustrations and photographs; page references in bold type refer to Suggested Readings at the end of chapters.